THE RED DUSTER AT WAR

THE RED DUSTER AT WAR

A History of the Merchant Navy during the Second World War

JOHN SLADER

WILLIAM KIMBER · LONDON

First published in 1988 by
WILLIAM KIMBER & CO. LIMITED
100 Jermyn Street, London, SW1Y 6EE

© John Slader, 1988

ISBN 0-7183-0679-1

Typeset by Ann Buchan (Typesetters), Middlesex
Printed and bound by
Adlard and Son Limited,
Dorking, Surrey, and Letchworth, Hertfordshire

This book is dedicated
to all Officers and Men
of the British Merchant Navy
who served during the Second World War
and particularly to those
who gave their lives
that Britain might live.

Contents

List of Illustrations

Preface

To include every event relating to the 'Red Duster' would mean many volumes. The most dramatic and the most interesting records have therefore been selected. It is not forgotten however, that some of the finest service was rendered by men who, exposed to all the dangers, in ships both large and small, came through the war unscathed and without spectacular adventure.

Inevitably more attention has been paid to the 'liner' shipping companies and some of the famous ships which they owned. The brunt of the attack, however, was often borne by that workhorse of the seas, now virtually extinct, the tramp steamer. Their personnel, unsung heroes of many races and creeds, are not forgotten.

Although this volume pays scant regard to ships and crews of other nations, both Allied and foreign, their contribution to the British nation, and to the war effort in all theatres, was both considerable and commendable. This is by no means overlooked.

There are a few points I should like to make for the reader's guidance:

Unless stated otherwise, times quoted are local ship's time.

Ships which changed ownership during 1939–45 were not allowed to change their names. Hence there are instances where owners were operating vessels not of their nomenclature.

Ships built to the order of HM Government during 1939–45 bore the following prefixes. They were managed by shipowners on behalf of either the Ministry of Supply or the Ministry of War Transport.

Ocean and *Sam* – United States built.

Fort – Canadian built. (Vessels bearing the suffix *Park* were also Canadian built).

Empire – Built in UK shipyards though some pre-war vessels, both those taken in prize and ex American were given *Empire* prefixes.

The work of the Ministry of Supply (Import Executive) was combined with the Ministry of Transport. The latter was combined with that of the Ministry of Shipping to form the Ministry of War Transport as from 1 May 1941.

Acknowledgements

Acknowledgements and thanks are due for the use of copyright material to The Society of Authors as the literary representative of the Estate of John Masefield for extracts from certain of his poems; to the Bodley Head Ltd for an extract from 'Convoy Job' from *Dispersal Point* by John Pudney; to Jane's Publishing Co Ltd for two paragraphs from page 107 of *War under the Red Ensign* by Doddy Hay; to Ellerman Lines plc for extracts of masters' reports etc deposited in the Archives, University of Glasgow; to the Controller of Her Majesty's Stationery Office for permission to reproduce certain material appearing in HMSO books (as listed in the bibliography); and to the Public Record Office for allowing me to reproduce material stored in their records. Every effort has been made to trace the owners of copyright material; where it has unfortunately proved in vain, I offer my apologies.

A full list of printed sources is given on page 319. In addition many people have contributed valuable information following my appeals in newspapers and in the magazines *Sea Breezes* and *Ships Monthly*. It would not be fair to mention individual names without mentioning all. I am particularly indebted to Professor Dr J. Rohwer and his classic *Axis Submarine Successes 1939–1945*; to Charles Hocking and his *Dictionary of Disasters at Sea during the Age of Steam 1824–1962*, a work of immense value to all students of our maritime heritage; the Ministry of Defence, Naval Historical Branch; the Public Record Office and Lloyds Register of Shipping. My thanks to them all.

I am also grateful to Bruce Quarrie who gave me early encouragement, and to my wife whom as a young deck apprentice I courted during those difficult days a half century ago. Without her this book would remain unwritten.

J.S.

Introduction

Prior to the blitz of September 1940 when German bombers destroyed much of the city and Port of London, there remained in the boardroom of one of its shipowners, a reference to ships and their value to an island race such as the British. Cut in stone it had been there since the seventeenth century: 'It is that which everyone knoweth and can say, they are our armaments, they are our weapons, they are our strength, they are our pleasures, they are our defence, they are our profits.'

In the days of Charles II there was no great difference between a King's ship and a merchant ship. Today merchant seamen are classed as civilians. But the sea has showed a peculiar harshness to men of the Merchant Navy requiring of them a continuously active courage never ordinarily asked of civilians in war. Those who sailed merchantmen during two world wars were never fighting men and never had fighting men's weapons.

It has been estimated that during the Second World War a quarter of the men who were in the Merchant Navy at the declaration of war, and perhaps an even higher proportion, did not survive until the end, or, if they survived, lived permanently damaged lives.

Just over 7,000 were killed by enemy action in 1941, nearly 8,000 were killed in 1942. All told, the deaths due directly or indirectly to the war were estimated by the Registrar-General of Shipping and Seamen on 30 June 1952 as 31,908. It is known, however, that this total, which does not include DEMS gunners and those of the Maritime Royal Artillery, is far from complete. If a man died ashore of disease due to his service at sea, and if he had no dependent relatives to claim a pension, his death would not figure in the Registrar-General's lists. The Merchant Navy also contained throughout the war many young men without dependants, and a number of these men died leaving no trace.

Never a large force in comparison with the fighting services –

about 185,000 with an estimated 144,000 at sea at any given date – casualties at times were so grievous as to be much greater than the contemporary losses in the armed services. Additionally, some 4,200 seamen were seriously injured and, whilst merchant seamen taken prisoner were covered by the Geneva Convention, they were not strictly classed as prisoners of war. Nevertheless 2,985 from 211 British ships were held at the Milag Nord Camp, Westertimkie, near Bremen.

Never in its long history had the merchant service to contend with so many devices aimed at its destruction. To the Axis powers every merchant ship was a defensive 'stockade' towards their inspired domination of the world. Every Allied ship that made port was to aid the war efficiency of their enemies. Yet it was a war waged upon those who disliked war, who were largely unprepared for war and who had, of necessity, to wage war incessantly against the elements every time they put to sea.

The story of the Merchant Service 1939–45 is as glorious as any in the annals of the sea. It is one of duty, of heroism and endurance, of gallantry in the face of danger, of loyalty to employers and intense devotion to King and Country although seafarers, a brave and hardy breed of men, have always followed a calling rich in the records of adventure and courage. Largely an untold story, it has been gathered from a great variety of sources. The task has not been an easy one for those at sea have always had a marked reluctance to talk of their achievements. It is not in their nature to boast of their exploits.

This is not only a story of British seamen, albeit that the majority of officers were British born, for fifty years ago the merchant fleet was crewed by those of many races and creeds; amongst them were Lascars, Arabs and Chinese from the far-flung outposts of the British Empire. In 1939 some 26 per cent were in the category of men known as Lascars, meaning a native of Asia or East Africa, employed on special types of articles which opened and terminated in Asia.

Despite all the difference of colour and race, upbringing and character, even the most cosmopolitan crews usually worked in harmony and behaved nobly when disaster threatened. There was a common bond of purpose from the youngest cabin boy to the most weatherbeaten old skipper. It was this one great 'democracy' which kept men at sea during the darkest hours: from cabin boys straight from the slums of Glasgow and Bootle, from ordinary seamen, some of no fixed abode, to wartime 'Sparks' brought up in the 'corner shop' or on the family farm, cadets and apprentices with sheltered lives and public school backgrounds.

In the engine room of *Sampep* (Houlder Bros & Co Ltd) a wartime Liberty ship at the Normandy invasion, there served the 45-year-old vicar of the Scilly Isles as fourth engineer. He had spent seven years in the Royal Navy as an engineer, retiring as lieutenant-commander and entering the Church. The call of the sea proved too great. He returned to serve in the Merchant Navy and sailed in Atlantic convoys. He was just one of an amazing bunch of characters, many of whom paid the supreme sacrifice and helped in saving a nation.

'The merchant seaman never faltered. To him we owe our preservation and our very lives,' said the Right Honourable Alfred Barnes, Minister of War Transport, after the war had been won in Europe and in the Far East. On 30 October 1945 the Houses of Parliament unanimously carried a resolution expressing gratitude to the armed services and the Merchant Navy on the victorious end of the war. That part of the motion having reference to the Merchant Navy was as follows:

> That the thanks of this House be accorded to the officers and men of the Merchant Navy for the steadfastness with which they maintained our stocks of food and materials; for their services in transporting men and munitions to all the battles over all the seas, and for the gallantry with which, though a civilian service, they met and fought the constant attacks of the enemy.

One of the greatest tragedies to befall the British Merchant Navy since that famous resolution is the virtual demise of its fleet. In this year of 1988 we have less than ten million tons of shipping against the fifty million tons we had only twelve years ago. In terms of shipping this means we have lost over 1,200 vessels of British registry since 1975. In terms of manpower, qualified seafarers have declined from 90,000 to some 30,000. The British merchant fleet used to be the biggest single provider of 'invisible earnings'. Now Britain has a shipping deficit as foreign fleets seize more of the business.

In January 1945 the First Lord of the Admiralty, Mr A.V. Alexander, reminded Parliament and the British nation that, even at that late stage, the Germans still considered U-boat warfare the best hope of averting defeat against a power that lived by seaborne supplies. 'I trust', he said, 'this highly important fact will never be forgotten by future First Lords, future Boards of Admiralty, or future Governments, or by the people of this country.'

The possibility of nuclear war has changed little. Comment is perhaps best left to one of our greatest army generals, the late Field Marshal Lord Montgomery. It was he who predicted that in the nuclear age, the passage of men and supplies over the sea will be more and not less important, than ever before. Nuclear propulsion of submarines and long range jet aircraft will contribute only to make the life of the merchant seamen a more difficult one.

NUMAST (The National Union of Marine Aviation and Shipping Transport Officers) believes that the consequences of the fleet's decline are disastrous. Moreover, as they quite rightly point out, unless action is taken to arrest that decline the situation may become irreversible.

The strategic implications of the demise of the fleet relate essentially to Britain's ability to maintain its independence, and its vulnerability would arise because it would not have the means to ensure this independence. Current defence policy envisages a role for the merchant fleet but doubt remains about whether the fleet could fulfil this role. The use of British-owned but foreign-registered ships under the command of and crewed by foreign nationals would bring many legal and practical difficulties in requisitioning such vessels. It is acknowledged too that to-day's fleet, much of it consisting of large container ships, very large tankers and ro-ro ferries incorporating car decks without transverse bulkheads, are very vulnerable when faced by the destructive power of the submarines and long range bombers of the 1990s.

The threat of war in the sea lanes remains and our island nation would do well to heed these warnings.

JOHN SLADER
Abergavenny
January 1988

CHAPTER ONE

The Calm before the Storm
(September 1939–May 1940)

The ports of both Britain and Germany were hives of activity during the last two weeks of August. Both powers realised that the conduct of the war at sea, particularly during the first few months, would be crucial. Britain above all realised that her power lay not only with fighting ships but with ships of the Red Duster, her lifeline both in peace and in war.

Sixteen of Germany's crack U-boats of the large 740-ton long range class captained by peacetime naval professionals, set sail from their bases. Sailing during the hours of darkness for exercises and destinations unknown, they kept submerged for long periods. By 3 September they had positioned themselves off the south-western approaches, keeping watch on British sea lanes, only surfacing to recharge batteries. U-boat *U-38* moved as far south as the coast of Portugal, being joined by three others by 6 September. There followed twelve of the 250-ton coastal attacker and six of the 500-ton ocean-going class who dispersed between the Orkneys and Shetlands. Among the last to leave was *U-23* bound for the mouth of the Humber with the future ace Kretschmer as commander. Some twenty other U-boats were armed and made ready to sail, *U-13*, *U-15*, *U-17* and *U-26* being loaded with mines. Fifty-four out of Germany's total of 57 operational U-boats all of modern design, had therefore sailed or were preparing to sail.

The German pocket battleship *Admiral Graf Spee* had sailed from Wilhelmshaven on 21 August; her supply ship *Altmark* had been sent ahead to the USA on 5 August to take on supplies of diesel oil. On 25 August, *Deutschland* sailed together with her supply ship *Westerwald*. The *Graf Spee* passed between the Faeroe Islands and Iceland on 24 August and at the time Prime Minister Neville Chamberlain was preparing Britain for a state of war, was approaching the Equator, far from the German advance into Poland. *Deutschland* took the northern route between Iceland and Greenland, then turning south she made for Bermudan waters. Neither warship had been spotted by British naval forces.

During the same period, ships of the Royal Navy were moving, or were preparing to move, to their war stations. The British merchant fleet, scattered across the trade routes of the world, was summoned to duty; to be re-routed, to be armed defensively, on the poop deck aft; to be marshalled into convoys, to obey orders issued by the British Admiralty. The sailings of many passenger liners and cargo-passenger liners were cancelled.

Requisitioning actually began on 26 August. On that day *Antenor* (11,174 grt, Alfred Holt & Co Ltd), which was one of the 50 merchant ships earmarked for conversion to armed merchant cruisers, was ordered to Calcutta. On the same day the British Admiralty issued instructions to shipyards, both in Britain and overseas, to prepare for already agreed conversions. Many ships were at sea and knew little of events. Unprepared and unprotected they steamed full ahead, some homeward, some outward-bound for other shores.

There were others: coasters, tankers and tramps, lying at anchor in harbours and estuaries, some rusting, many out of date, all without work with just a watchman aboard, often a master or mate unable to find a berth during the long years of the 'Slump'. Suddenly dawn awakened – gangs of workmen boarded, crews were summoned. They were called to duty.

On 2 September, the first British convoy, of eight ships, left Gibraltar for Capetown. On the same day *Athenia* (13,581 grt, of the Donaldson Atlantic Line) commanded by Captain Cook was allowed to sail from the Clyde. She was earmarked, together with her sister ship *Letitia*, for conversion in a Canadian shipyard to an armed merchant cruiser. After calling at Belfast and Liverpool to pick up remaining passengers, many of them Jewish refugees from Nazi Germany and American tourists anxious to escape the threatening war clouds of Europe, she was en route to Montreal upon the declaration of war. She carried a total of 1,418 persons.

At 1945 hours on 3 September, (position 56. 44N 14.05W) less than nine hours after Chamberlain had told the nation a state of war existed between Britain and Germany, she suddenly found herself the first victim. There was no warning. The torpedo was fired at close range and opened up the port side abaft the engine room. From the very first day the Merchant Navy found itself in the front line.

That afternoon Lieutenant Fritz Julius Lemp, the 26-year-old commander of *U-30*, had received the expected signal from Grand-Admiral Dönitz.

> To Commanders in Chief and Commanders afloat. Great Britain and France have declared war on Germany. Battle-stations immediate in accordance with instructions already promulgated for the Navy.

In the fading light of dusk the lights failed and panic struck. Passengers were trapped in the tourist and third class dining rooms. With the ship listing six degrees to port, it was difficult for those trying to reach the lifeboats on the upper deck. Members of the crew who went below in an effort to release those trapped were met by the screams of women and children. Bulkheads collapsed and the rush of water threatened even those who had got out of their cabins.

U-30 surfaced some 800 yards from the stricken ship. As Lemp watched, he realised he had sunk a passenger ship in violation of both international law and his strict instructions. He fired two shells in an effort to shoot away her radio aerials to prevent the transmission of distress signals. *U-30* then submerged, without attempting to offer the assistance demanded by the submarine protocol.

One lifeboat crowded with people fell from the davits, throwing the occupants into the sea. Another capsized sometime later. In the heavy swell and in the dark of the night, a third boat, crewed by three seamen and containing 52 women passengers, ran foul of the propeller of the Norwegian *Knute Nelson*, the first rescue vessel to arrive on the scene. The bottom was ripped out of the boat and only eight or nine of the occupants survived.

Two destroyers, the American *City of Flint* and the Swedish motor yacht *Southern Cross*, joined in rescuing the survivors before *Athenia* finally sank stern first on the following morning. 118 persons were lost including 69 women and sixteen children (of whom 22 were American citizens) and nineteen crew. News of the torpedoing sent a wave of horror around the world and Lemp, concerned lest he should be reprimanded upon his return to base, allowed *Duchess of Bedford* to pass unharmed the following day.

On 5 September the homeward-bound unarmed *Royal Sceptre* (4,853 grt, owned by Hall Bros, of Newcastle-upon-Tyne) was signalled to stop by the surfaced *U-48* in position 46. 23N 14.59W. Ignoring the instructions of Lieutenant Herbert Schultze, she steamed full ahead radioing SSS signal (attacked by submarine).

U-48 replied with a salvo of shells accurately placed sending her to the ocean floor with a torpedo as soon as the crew had abandoned ship. Later the same day Schultze attacked the 1919-built *Browning* (5,332 grt), but seeing her crew already abandoning ship, he relented on condition she did not use her radio and directed her to rescue the crew of the *Royal Sceptre*. *Browning* was subsequently torpedoed and sunk in the Mediterranean in November 1942.

Two days after war was declared convoys were being assembled. On 5 September the first British troop convoy comprising eleven ships left the Clyde for Gibraltar bound for the eastern Mediterranean. The following day the first east coast convoy (designated FN) sailed from the Thames (Southend) to the Firth of Forth (Methil); it was a route vulnerable to attack, by E-boats, U-boats, aircraft and to mines laid in the shallow off-shore waters. On 7 September OA1 sailed from the Thames estuary to the south-west of Ireland via the English Channel and OB1 from the Bristol Channel and Liverpool on the same day. 200 miles west of Ireland, the ships dispersed for their destinations.

Manaar (7,242 grt, owned by T. & J. Brocklebank Ltd) had sailed from Liverpool the day prior to the declaration of war bound for Calcutta. At daybreak on 6 September she was steaming alone and without navigation lights; her speed was 12 knots and it was not thought necessary to zig zag. Then suddenly she was torpedoed. It was the first kill of Lieutenant Heinrich Liebe, commander of *U-38* who had sailed from Wilhelmshaven on 19 August. He quickly surfaced his boat and began shelling in an effort to complete the destruction hitting the bridge and radio on the starboard side.

Although the crew attempted to launch the four port lifeboats, the vessel swung around and seven were killed and a further seven seriously injured. A further torpedo then hit the engine room and she broke in two quickly disappearing beneath the choppy waters. Eighty-five survivors and the body of one seaman were landed in Lisbon 48 hours later. On 7 September and 8 September six British merchant ships were sunk in the western approaches, two of them, *Regent Tiger* and *Kennebec*, being tankers carrying precious oil for the refineries.

On 10 September the mines laid by *U-13* and *U-15* claimed their first victims, *Goodwood* (2,796 grt) and *Magdapur* (8,641 grt), the latter being Brocklebank's second loss in four days. She had been requisitioned by the Government to transport equipment to France and was en route from South Shields to Southampton to load. Between Sizewell Buoy and Aldeburgh Napes she was struck and the bridge and four lifeboats were shattered, the ship breaking in two from the keel upwards. Six crew members were killed and the captain seriously injured. Later in the month *City of Paris* (10,902 grt) and the French *Phryne* (2,660 grt) were also mine victims, though the former was taken in tow and eventually repaired.

From ports in the Bristol Channel and from Southampton the first troop transport convoys arrived without loss at Cherbourg, Nantes and St Nazaire, with the British Expeditionary Force. Many fine ships of the Alfred Holt fleet were employed including *Bellerophon*, *Rhesus*, *Maron*, *Achilles**, *Eurymedon*, *Lycaon*, and the heavy lift vessels *Glenstrae* and *Glenearn*. By 7 October 161,000 men, 24,000 vehicles and approximately 140,000 tons of stores had been carried, an enormous achievement by ships and crews which passed without mention.

Six small ships were specially adapted to carry ammunition to France. The veteran North Atlantic trader *Gloucester City* (3,071 grt, owned by the Bristol City Line of Steamships Ltd) was loading tobacco at Norfolk Virginia upon the outbreak of war. Upon her discharge at Bristol Docks she was sent to Falmouth where she was fitted out as an ammunition ship.

Before returning to Wilhelmshaven on 26 September, necessary due to damage sustained by a near miss during an aerial attack, *U-30* sank a further two ships: *Blairlogie* (4,425 grt owned by the Clydesdale Navigation Company) and the *Fanad Head* (5,200 grt, Ulster Steamship Co., Belfast).

After the attack on *Athenia*, *U-30* took a southerly course and came across *Blairlogie* during the early hours of 11 September in position 54.58N 15.14W. This time Lieutenant Lemp was careful to observe international law, even supplying a bottle of Schnapps and cigarettes to those in the lifeboats. Further he stayed with the boats and fired red stars into the air at intervals until dawn came and with it a neutral American ship, the *American Skipper*.

The Fanad Head, homeward-bound from Montreal for Belfast, was sunk south of Rockhall in position 56.43N 15.21W during the afternoon of 14 September. Lemp started to tow the lifeboats out of the danger area with the intention of putting them on the right course for the Irish coast. However he was attacked by two Blackburn Skuas from HMS *Ark Royal* and crash-dived, only later to discover the conning tower had been damaged. Unfortunately both Skuas crashed from their low approach and were hit by the explosion of

---

* Later taken over by the Admiralty and renamed HMS *Blenheim*.

their bombs. *Firby* and *Inverliffey* were sunk the same week bringing the total to 25 British merchant vessels sunk during the first fourteen days; the tonnage was 131,187. It was a disastrous start to the war at sea but the U-boats had been able to take full advantage of the fact that they were already at battle stations upon the declaration of war and many vessels were caught unprepared and without escort.

Firby (4,869 grt, owned by the West Hartlepool Steam Navigation Company) was torpedoed in position 59.40N 13.50W by *U-48* whose commander, Lieutenant Herbert Schultze, again closely adhered to instructions, even boldly radioing the position of the lifeboats to Churchill at the Admiralty. Later in 1941 when Schultze was captured and he became a prisoner of war, Churchill sought him out and wished him well. *Inverliffey* (9,456 grt) was one of five sister tankers built in Germany for Inver Tankers only twelve months previously by Deutsche Werft AG. All five were lost by enemy action and were engaged in transporting aviation spirit and gasoline from the Trinidad refinery. *Inverliffey* had sailed from the Thames on 26 August with 13,000 tons of gasoline and was torpedoed by *U-38* in position 48.14N 11.48W and finally sunk by gunfire 270 miles west-south-west of Land's End.

On 16 September the first homeward convoy of eighteen ships (HXI) sailed from Halifax Nova Scotia followed a day later by fast convoy HXFI under the protection of an armed merchant cruiser. During 1939 and 1940 there was a crippling lack of escort vessels; for ocean escort a converted passenger vessel with a very limited armament was the only protection. By the end of the month fourteen large ocean-going convoys were at sea; fast ships, those able to make over fifteen knots, continued to sail independently.

Although by the end of the month losses began to fall, air cover during those early days was negligible – Coastal Command was a mere embryo of the great force it was eventually to become. Airborne radar did not exist and weapons were inadequate, a limited number of bombs were available but they were only lethal in the case of a direct hit. Many U-boat commanders, without the threat of aerial attack, would first strike by torpedo, then seek to complete their task by the use of gunfire. Amongst other things, this led to economy in the use of torpedoes.

The first convoy loss on 16 September was *Aviemore* (6,060 grt) sailing from Liverpool for North America with OB4. Owned by Johnston Warren Lines of Liverpool, she was struck by two torpedoes from *U-31* (Lieutenant Johannes Habekost) in position

49.11N 13.38W and she started to sink immediately. Twenty-three lives were lost.

Kafiristan (5,193 grt), which was sunk in position 50.16N 16.55W on 17 September, was owned by the Hindustan Steamship Co. She was the second kill of Lieutenant Harald Grosse during the maiden voyage of *U-53*; two days previously he had sunk the motor tanker *Cheyenne*, carrying Benzine from Aruba for Swansea. At 1540 hours the torpedo ripped open the ship for'ard of the bridge and she started to settle immediately. Captain Busby at once gave the order to abandon ship but six of the crew were drowned when the first lifeboat, launched whilst the vessel was still making headway, capsized. The remaining boats got away and Grosse offered to send an SOS and also offered a tow towards the Irish coast but when a British aircraft appeared, spraying the submarine with machine gun bullets and dropping two bombs, he crash-dived, leaving the survivors who were later picked up by the *American Farmer* and landed in New York.

Captain Langsdorf in *Graf Spee* was meantime wandering aimlessly in the South Atlantic, his crew somewhat bored with their naval life and lack of action. He therefore set a north-westerly course which brought him to the shipping lanes off the Brazilian coast where on 30 September he sighted the steamer *Clement* (5,051 grt, owned by the Booth Steamship Company of Liverpool) in position 09.05S 34.05W. She was homeward-bound steaming at fifteen knots through a calm blue tropical sea when she sighted a seaplane which suddenly flew towards her spraying the bridge with machine gun bullets. *Graf Spee* was still hull down on the horizon but as she approached, Captain Harris realised that to resist would mean great loss of life.

In spite of the machine gunning by Langsdorf's spotter plane, *Clement*'s radio operator had managed to transmit a RRR warning (attacked by raider) so revealing for the first time the presence of the enemy in these waters. As the pocket battleship approached, Captain Harris gave the order to abandon ship and he, together with his chief engineer, was taken aboard *Graf Spee*, the remainder of the crew being left to their boats, which subsequently they beached upon the coast of Brazil.

Langsdorf was both friendly and polite even though his position had been revealed. As if to bring Harris up to date, he informed him that Germany and Great Britain were at war. Speaking as one sea captain to another, he said, 'I am sorry but I have got to sink your ship.' He then launched two torpedoes followed by 30 rounds from both his 6-inch and 11-inch guns, and as *Clement* broke up and sank he sped away to the eastward.

October saw only a small number of U-boats in the Atlantic as the German naval command directed their main effort towards minelaying in our inshore convoy routes. *Marwarri* (8,063 grt, T. & J. Brocklebank Ltd) was the first magnetic mine casualty; she had sailed from Belfast for Newport on 4 October and was brought to an abrupt halt by a devastating explosion at 3.5 miles – 190 degrees from Scarweather lightvessel. *Lochgoil* was mined the same day in close proximity, but both vessels were towed to port for repair and both survived the war.

Although *Deutschland* had sighted a few ships in Bermudan waters they were all flying foreign flags and were allowed to proceed. On 5 October, however, when in position 31.10N 54.00W, she intercepted the tramp steamer *Stonegate* (5,044 grt), belonging to the Turnbull Scott Shipping Company. She was laden with nitrate which she had loaded at Antofagasta and was en route for Alexandria well away from the principal sea lanes where she assumed the enemy would gather. The end came swiftly for no distress signals were sent and a further two weeks were to pass before it was realised that a second raider was loose.

In the South Atlantic *Admiral Graf Spee* continued her successful onslaught, sending four British vessels to the ocean floor during October: *Newton Beech*, *Ashlea*, *Huntsman* and *Trevanion*. Although ships sailing from Cape Town and Freetown were advised that a raider was loose upon the high seas, such information, as was the custom, was held by the master alone and was not passed by him to his officers and crew. As a result there were very few who imagined they were in any danger being so far distant from home waters.

Ocean convoys were now more organised. KJ3 (45 ships), the largest convoy yet, left Kingston Jamaica for the English Channel on 4 October with the cruiser *Berwick* and the Australian *Perth* as escort, which halfway were relieved by the cruiser *Effingham*. KJF3 was a fast convoy which followed a day later but without naval escort until some 200 miles south-west of Land's End. Acting upon intelligence Dönitz directed nine U-boats, led by *U-37*, to the attack but in the early light of dawn on 14 October only three were on station. *U-45*, commanded by Lieutenant Alexander Gelhaar, was quickly on the attack, sinking three ships within the hour: *Lochavon*, *Karamea* and the French *Bretagne*. Just after noon *U-48* torpedoed the 1925-built

Sneaton of Whitby, her fourth success of the month. This was the first attempt at a co-ordinated U-boat attack, a method which was to reap such dividends for the enemy in the years to come.

Three days later some 350 miles to the south, *U-48* and *U-37* were joined by *U-46* for the attack on convoy HG3 which had sailed from Gibraltar for the English Channel on the morning of 13 October. Dönitz again directed the operation by radio from his headquarters in Wilhelmshaven on information received from agents. Unfortunately the two destroyers acting as escort were called away the following day. Acting as commodore ship was *Yorkshire* (10,184 grt, owned by the Bibby Line of Liverpool), a well known vessel on the Far East sailings for nearly twenty years.

The classic lines of the heavily laden *Yorkshire* were suddenly obscured from the rest of the convoy as the torpedo fired from *U-37* struck at 0835 hours. The port side amidships was ripped open and many crew and passengers were trapped, many of whom were unable to be extracted from the devastation. Although efforts were made to save the stricken vessel, a second torpedo from *U-37* sent her to the bottom very quickly. Of the 160 crew, 35 were lost; of the 118 passengers, 33 were lost.

An hour later *City of Mandalay* was torpedoed by *U-46* in position 44.57N 13.36W. Owned by Ellerman Lines, tonnage 7,028, she was homeward-bound from Singapore and India via Port Said, her crew consisting of 79 persons (British officers and Lascar seamen) and one passenger. The force of the explosion opened up number three hatchway and very shortly afterwards she broke her back, disappearing beneath the waves in about 30 minutes. The survivors were picked up by the American *Independence Hall* by which time it was quite dark. The chief engineer and the ship's carpenter were both lost.

Later the same evening, at 2025 hours, *Clan Chisholm* (7,256 grt, owned by the Clan Line) was torpedoed by *U-48* in position 45.00N 15.00W. She was fully laden with tea and other foodstuffs from Calcutta for Liverpool and before sailing her master had protested about his ship, a modern two-year-old vessel, capable of 15 knots, being included in Convoy HG3 whose maximum speed was set at 9½ knots. It was one of the problems of convoy organisation. *Clan Chisholm* sank in seven minutes and whilst four lifeboats were launched, one boat was never seen again, the survivors being rescued after 36 hours.

An example of the heroic defence and fortitude shown by the Red Duster during these early days was the action of *Stonepool* (4,803 grt,

Ropner Steamship Company Ltd) on 13 October when convoy
OB17 (Liverpool outward North America) had just dispersed. *U-42*,
captained by Lieutenant Rolf Dau, surfaced on the starboard beam
at daybreak and immediately her gun crew opened fire – five rounds
in quick succession. *The Stonepool*, under Captain Harland, brought
her gun to bear and opened fire, forcing the submarine to submerge.
Later she surfaced again and the battle between guns that ensued
lasted 80 minutes. However the U-boat was damaged and could not
lie submerged for long.

In answer to Captain Harland's signal, a destroyer soon arrived
which subsequently sank *U-42* and captured her survivors. It was
the submarine's first and only action. The damaged *Stonepool* limped
into port some days later, and her master was awarded the OBE. A
year later he was to lose his life in the destruction of *Empire Bison*.

During the last days of the month, HX5 from Halifax Nova Scotia
which was sailing south of Ireland for Liverpool, was sighted by *U-34*
commanded by Lieutenant Wilhelm Rollman. Late on the evening
of the 27th, he torpedoed *Bronte* (5,317 grt belonging to Lamport and
Holt Ltd) and two days later, 50 miles off the Scilly Isles, in the early
hours with a bright moon illuminating his target, he torpedoed
Malabar (7,976 grt, T. & J. Brocklebank Ltd). Both were stout ships
as the wreck of the *Bronte* had to be sunk on 30 October by gunfire
from HMS *Walpole* and HMS *Whirlwind*, whilst the crew of *Malabar*
steadfastly stood by their ship for twelve hours before she broke in
two and sank. Five had been killed in the explosion.

The *Cairnmona* (4,666 grt, owned by the Cairn Line of Steamships)
was destined for her home port of Newcastle and proceeded with the
North Sea part of the convoy by way of the north of Scotland. She
was torpedoed and sunk off Rattray Head by *U-13*, one of the small
coastal attack submarines.

During November and December enemy mining of the
approaches to British ports was accelerated with several U-boats
and fast destroyers being employed. Mines were also parachuted
from Naval seaplanes. Shipping and convoys in the North Sea were
disrupted and for several days the Port of London was virtually shut
down.

The magnetic mines, triggered by the magnetic effect when a
ship passed over them, had a devastating impact upon the war in the
river estuaries and coastwise sea lanes. Churchill accused the Germans of committing 'an outrage upon the accepted international
law. Driven from the gun to the torpedo and from the torpedo
to the mine, U-boats have now reached the acme of villainy.' A

stock of 22,000 magnetic mines was held ready in German ports at this time. On the night of 12/13 November an enemy destroyer flotilla laid some 300 mines in the Thames estuary and was completely undetected.

Now it was the small coasters taking the brunt of the attack, the east coast colliers, the ships plying to and from the Channel ports with supplies for the British forces in France, the *Blackhill, Carmarthen Coast, Corea, Hookwood, Lowland, Ponzano, Rubislaw, Torchbearer* and *Woodtown*. The loss of life was heavy such as when the *Merel* (1,088 grt) was mined off Ramsgate; Captain Wastall and fifteen of his crew were killed and two brought ashore seriously wounded.

The port of London and the Thames estuary were a virtual graveyard: *Matra* (8,003 grt) and *Mangalore* (8,886 grt), both owned by T. & J. Brocklebank Ltd, *Ionian* (3,114 grt), *Sheaf Crest* (2,730 grt), *Dalryan* (4,558 grt) and the tanker *San Calisto* (8,010 grt). The refrigerated vessel *Sussex* (11,063 grt, Federal Steam Navigation Co. Ltd) was badly damaged and although she suffered further damage after being bombed by a Focke-Wulf Condor in the Atlantic ten months later, she survived the war.

The German offensive suffered a major setback when a Navy pilot dropped two magnetic mines on the mudflats of Shoeburyness during 23 November. They were immediately spotted, one of them being recovered and defused by Lieutenant-Commander J.G.D. Ouvry from the mining school HMS Vernon at Portsmouth, enabling counter measures to be taken. For several months however the only certain way of establishing the presence of a magnetic minefield was to wait until the first victim had been claimed.

The courageous effort of Lieutenant-Commander Ouvry led to the development of the 'LL' electrical sweep and a system of 'degaussing' a ship's magnetism by passing a current through cables wrapped around its hull. However it took many months to equip the merchant fleet, some ships being degaussed as late as 1941.

November 1939 is also notable for the sinking of the armed merchant cruiser *Rawalpindi* (16,697 grt), the ex-P & O liner which was built in 1925 and had been converted at some considerable cost only three weeks previously. On 23 November she was in action with the newly completed fast battleships *Scharnhorst* and *Gneisenau* between the Faeroes and Iceland. Crewed by Merchant Navy personnel with Royal Naval gunners and technicians, she was commanded by Captain E.C. Kennedy and made a heroic stand before sinking. Captain Kennedy died at his post and only 37 of her crew were rescued.

The action illustrated how vulnerable the AMC was to enemy attack and was a foretaste of what was to come in the short history of this type of ocean escort. The arming of passenger liners was a short-sighted policy as was proved during the following eighteen months when fifteen were lost during a period when troopships were becoming such a valuable asset to the Allied forces.

The sinking of the *Arlington Court* (4,915 grt, owned by the Court Line Ltd) by *U-43* (Lieutenant Wilhelm Ambrosius) on 16 November gives an early example of the fortitude and bravery of the many deck apprentices who at such a young age showed the qualities of leadership, calmness and discipline which, later in the war equipped them to become officers and leaders of men 'nursing' their ships, often out of date and ill-equipped, not only through convoy battles and through attacks of surface raiders and dive bombers, but through the savagery of the elements; the storms, the fogs, the snow and the pack-ice of the northern latitudes.

Two torpedoes ripped open the side of *Arlington Court* as she was steaming in the homeward-bound convoy SL7 from Freetown, 320 miles 248 degrees from Start Point. The radio room and bridge were wrecked, three being killed in the explosion and Captain Hurst, who had been sunk three times in the First World War and shipwrecked in the Indian Ocean in peacetime, immediately gave the order to abandon ship. One lifeboat of 22 survivors (though the chief engineer died from exposure) was rescued by the Dutch *Alengib* but the second boat with six survivors became separated, wallowing in the turbulent bitterly cold Bay of Biscay for six whole days during which time eighteen-year-old Malcolm Morrison took charge, and worked out his course, steering the boat himself with the aid of a small pocket compass, giving advice and encouragement to his shipmates, though severely suffering from frostbite himself.

The sinking of the *San Clisto*, belonging to the Eagle Oil & Shipping Co Ltd, in the Thames estuary was typical of the havoc wrought by the new menace of the magnetic mine in coastal waters. Sailing from Hull on 30 November in ballast for Southend where she was due to join an OA convoy, *San Clisto* detonated two mines within a few minutes of each other some two and a half miles from the Tongue light vessel. Two officers and four ABs were killed instantly by the explosions and six other members of the ship's company, including two radio officers, were wounded. Captain Hicks was obliged to abandon ship within five minutes of being struck, leaving the twisted wreck of the tanker sitting on the bottom to add to the dangers experienced by mariners entering the port of London.

Seven days later a second tanker belongong to the Eagle Oil and Shipping Co Ltd was destroyed. The *San Alberto* (7,397 grt) en route to Trinidad in convoy OB48 was torpedoed by *U-48* south of Fastnet Rock, in position 49.20N 09.45W. In command was Captain Waite who later was to command the renowned *San Demetrio* and the equally ill-fated *San Ernesto*. Launching the boats in the darkness and wintry gale was no mean feat with December witnessing some of the worst North Atlantic weather for forty years. The after end of the *San Alberto* remained afloat for three days until finally sunk by HMS *Mackay*. During this time Captain Waite and his crew reboarded in an effort to bring her to port; the main engines were re-started and for some ten hours the half ship was kept stern-on to the seas. Unfortunately the weather continued to worsen and she was abandoned a second time.

The first loss of the Royal Mail Line was the cargo vessel *Navasota* (8,705 grt, convoy OB46) torpedoed in position 50.43N 10.16W on 5 December by *U-47*, commanded by Lieutenant-Commander Günter Prien, Knight's Cross with oak leaves, who on 14 October had sunk the battleship *Royal Oak* at her anchorage in Scapa Flow. Within eight minutes *Navasota* had gone. The force of the explosion either unseated some of the davits or caused the ropes to jump the falls so that only two boats got away. Captain Goble went down with his ship, together with all his navigating officers, the chief and three other engineers and 24 crew. Out of a total complement of 81 men, 37 were lost including two who died from exposure after some 30 hours in one of the lifeboats.

The first of the Commonwealth troops arrived in the Clyde on Christmas Eve, crossing a stormy Atlantic in thirteen days. The first troop convoy, TC1, with 7,400 men of the 1st Canadian Division sailed from Halifax, Nova Scotia in the transports *Andes*, *Aquitania*, *Empress of Australia*, *Empress of Britain*, *Duchess of Bedford* and *Monarch of Bermuda*. The 'tail of the bank' in the Clyde estuary became the world's largest passenger port, an honour it held all during the war years. Upriver lay the uncompleted *Queen Elizabeth*, beset by controversy over what should be done with her.

In the South Atlantic *Graf Spee* was still creating havoc in the shipping lanes, three further merchant ships being destroyed by her guns. *Doric Star* of 10,086 grt, built in 1921 and the first of the Blue Star fleet to be sunk (there were to be 27 of them) was caught on 2 December as she steamed homeward bound at twelve knots from New Zealand and Australia by way of the Indian Ocean and the Cape of Good Hope. Commanded by Captain Stubbs she was fully laden with a refrigerated cargo of mutton, lamb, cheese and butter, with a quantity of wool in the 'tween decks.

So accurate were the guns of the *Graf Spee* that, although the first shells were fired with only the control tower showing above the horizon, they found the range immediately as a heavy shell exploded within 100 yards of the bow. Four bombs were planted by the German boarding party which were detonated after the passengers and crew had been taken off and this was then followed up by seven 5.9-inch shells. Finally a torpedo crippled the *Doric Star* and she quickly settled in the calm tropical sea, 660 miles east by south of St Helena. It was her distress call, transmitted in defiance of German orders, that enabled Commodore Harwood to bring his cruisers *Ajax*, *Exeter* and *Achilles* to bear upon the raider.

The very next morning it was the turn of the Shaw Savill and Albion's 7,983 grt steamer *Tairoa*. En route from Brisbane for London via Cape Town she was sunk by six rounds from *Graf Spee*'s 5.9 inch guns followed by a torpedo fired at close range. Five of her crew were wounded. Four days later, the tramp ship *Streonshalk* of 3,895 grt, owned by Rowland & Marwood, was sunk in position 25.00S 27.05W whilst on her voyage from Rosario to Falmouth for orders with a full cargo of wheat. Her crew of 30 were taken off to join 61 still held captive on the battleship, 167 survivors having been transferred to the supply ship *Altmark* the previous day.

The battle of the River Plate followed when the damaged German warship put into neutral Montevideo while the British cruisers waited outside. On 17 December, the *Admiral Graf Spee* with a toll of nine merchant ships sunk, was scuttled. By the year end, the total sunk by the enemy was 96, all of British registration, taking the lives of 237 seamen with them.

As the year 1940 opened the German High Command was paying special attention to the west coast of Norway and the port of Narvik. Not only was this an important route into the Atlantic for its navy but, like Britain, the German steel industry was dependent upon the Norwegian port for supplies of Swedish iron ore during the winter months when the Baltic was ice bound. Some sordid tales are told of how, at this time, British and German seamen drank together and entertained young Norwegian girls in the bars of Narvik. As was so often the case, many only lived for the day and as many at sea realised, the carriage of iron ore was the most dangerous of cargoes. All through the war, merchant navy crews of ore carriers lived with the knowledge that if their ship was struck, they literally had seconds between the time of the explosion and the moment when their ship

WE'RE O.K., BOYS— HERE'S THE R.A.F.

Forgetting their own danger, survivors of the torpedoed British freighter, Fanad He
stand up in their rolling lifeboat to cheer one of the aeroplanes whch bombed the s
marine that sank their ship.

Diving low over the boats, an R.A.F. plane flashed the signal, "Help is coming," to
them rescue ships were on the way.

(*Above*) Survivors from the SS *Fanad Head*. There was little censorship early in the war. Here a Northern Ireland newspaper gives space to the sinking of the Belfast registered *Fanad Head*, 14 September 1939. The Swordfish aircraft is from HMS *Ark Royal*; the Fleet Air Arm, not the RAF as headlined.

(*Below*) A dangerous deck cargo. Alfred Holt's 1911 built *Atreus*, 6,645 grt, carrying mines as deck cargo. Haifa, October 1939.

SS *Otranto* December 1939. A boxing match on the Orient liner *Otranto* as she crosses the Equator, December 1939, on passage to Australia. Captain Arthur Baxter, RD, RNR, centre front row facing camera. On his right is the ship's nursing sister, the only woman on board. The range finder for the 6-inch gun is visible on the poop deck.

An HG convoy. December 1939. Homeward bound convoy from the Mediterranean, December 1939. In the foreground is Alfred Holt's 6,490 ton *Laomedon*, built in 1912.

plunged to the bottom.

Two British iron ore ships were lost without trace at the beginning of the year, the *Polzella* (4,751 grt, Eclipse Shipping and Trading Co.) was torpedoed by *U-25* on 17 January whilst steaming between Narvik and Middlesbrough and the *Leo Dawson* (of 4,330 grt, owned by the Edwardian Steamship Company of Newcastle) sunk about 4 February by *U-37* between Narvik and Immingham. Crews of 37 and 35 were lost, their families waiting several weeks before being given confirmation by their employers.

En route from Australasia at this time were the Commonwealth troops who were subsequently to be engaged in protecting the Mediterranean trade route to the Far East and the North African territories. Twelve luxury liners hastily converted to troop transports: the *Empress of Canada, Orion, Rangitata* and *Strathaird* from New Zealand and the *Dunera, Empress of Japan, Orcades, Orford, Otranto* and *Strathnaver* together with the Polish *Sobieski* and the French *Suffren* from Australia. Convoy USI arrived safely in Suez on 12 February.

Magnetic mines were still effecting a great toll, in both ships and personnel. On 8 January the *Dunbar Castle* (10,002 grt) was yet another casualty. One of the Union Castle Mail boats operating out of London, she had sailed only a few hours previously for Beira with a crew of 158 and 48 passengers. In convoy at the time the foremast crashed down on the bridge, fatally wounding Captain Causton and killing the storekeeper and one seaman. She listed heavily and fierce fires started in the galley before she finally broke her back at the point of impact. The lifeboats got safely away, one passenger was listed as missing and she rested on the bottom of the channel (position 51.23N 01.34E) her superstructure plainly visible at low tide. Wreckage littered the beach at Deal for many weeks and the wreck remained until blown up in 1949.

Following the minelaying activities of *U-30* in the Irish Sea with Lemp of *Athenia* fame in command, the entrance to the Mersey became particularly dangerous. On 11 January *El Oso* foundered, a tanker of 7,267 grt newly arrived from Halifax, N.S. with convoy HX14. Six days later the *Cairnross* (5,494 grt, Convoy OB74) outward-bound for North America sank. There was considerable loss of life and both wrecks became a hazard in the busy shipping channel.

In the North Sea *Granta* (2,719 grt, owned by Witherington & Everett Ltd) was mined off Cromer on 12 January. Coastwise convoys were becoming particularly hazardous; with the fogs and gales of winter, with the narrow shipping channels, sandbanks and treacherous tides, ships leaving and joining at the various ports en route, with ships of many tonnages, some slow, some fast, but all obliged to keep station and steam at the pace of the slowest. The end came suddenly to the *Granta* leaving twelve crew members lost and one wounded.

At the end of the month (28 January) came the sad tale of *Eston* (1,487 grt, P & O Steam Navigation Co. Ltd). She had sailed from Hull coastwise for Blyth on a bitterly cold night. Nothing more was heard of her or her crew of seventeen until one of the lifeboats and the body of one of the crew were washed ashore some days later. She had struck a mine laid by *U-22* on 20 December 1939.

In the approaches to the Bristol Channel ports, the situation was little different. On 16 January the *Inverdargle* (9,456 grt and owned by Inver Tankers) was inward bound from Trinidad for Avonmouth with a cargo of aviation spirit when she suddenly disappeared in a sheet of flame shortly before she was due to pick up her pilot in Barry Roads. With a crew of 49, none of whom survived, the cause of the loss was unknown. It is now assumed she detonated one of several mines laid by *U-33* in these waters on 5 November 1939.

Five days later, the *Protesilaus* (9,577 grt, of the Blue Funnel Line, Alfred Holt & Co. Ltd), having unloaded in Liverpool, was approaching Swansea to load outwards for the Far East. She was virtually in sight of her destination, at position 51.31N 04.04W, when the mine, detonated as she approached the pilot boat, split her down the middle abaft the engine room. She listed to port and quickly began to settle by the stern and although her master, Captain Shand, after abandoning ship, subsequently reboarded with the chief mate and a nucleus crew, she grounded off the Mumbles lighthouse and became a total loss. The mine had been laid by *U-28* on 13 November 1939.

January 1940 brought a new menace to Britain's coastal shipping as the Luftwaffe extended their activities and sought out North Sea and English Channel convoys. The *Kenyes* of 1,706 grt was bombed twice on 11 January and on the second attack her engine room was ripped out and she quickly sank by the stern; there was the *Bancrest* of 4,450 grt, the *Highwave* (1,178 grt), *Oakgrove* (1,985 grt), *Upminster* (1,013 grt) and *Voreda*, a tanker of 7,216 grt. The *Stanburn* (2,881 grt), the third of fifteen vessels belonging to the Stanhope Steamship Company which were lost, was struck off Flamborough Head, by three bombs from an enemy Stuka dive bomber which came suddenly out of cloud cover. Captain Lewis and 25 of her crew were killed in the attack, and there were only three survivors. *Giralda* (2,178 grt), bombed off the Orkney Islands in below zero temperature, was one of several vessels requisitioned as a supply ship by the Admiralty from the South Georgia Company. Captain Rasmussen and her crew of 22 were all lost.

Between 17 December and 17 February a total of eleven fishing vessels were bombed and sunk and a further 31 vessels of all types were damaged, some making port under their own steam, others being towed but all withdrawn from service for repairs. Often attacks were accompanied by machine gun fire in addition to bombs and casualties were high. New efforts were made to defend merchant ships against aerial attack and the Admiralty had ordered five hundred 20mm Oerlikon guns from Switzerland which had been paid for in gold though few had been delivered. Later in the war the 20mm Oerlikon was manufactured in Britain and also in the USA.

Canadian Pacific's *Beaverburn* of 9,874 grt was one of the fastest cargo liners on the North Atlantic, yet on 1 February, sailing from London in convoy OA84, she was obliged to keep station at nine knots, the speed of the slowest ship. Lying in wait five days later in position 49.20N 10.07W was *U-41*, commanded by Lieutenant Gustav-Adolf Mugler, who earlier in the day had attacked and damaged the new Dutch motor tanker *Ceronia*.

The torpedo struck beneath the bridge and she broke in two amidships, the water being halfway up the engine room as the boats were being lowered. Sinking by the head with her propellers out of the water she was gone within nine minutes, Captain 'Farmer' Jones, the last to leave, jumping from the stern to join the other 75 survivors, who were later rescued by the US tanker *Narraganset* – one crew member was lost. HMS *Antelope*, the sole convoy escort, later pursued and sank *U-41*.

On 7 February *Munster* (4,305 grt, Coast Lines Ltd), under the command of Captain Paisley and carrying over 200 passengers, was mined in position 53.36N 03.24W on her usual nightly passage between Belfast and Liverpool; fortunately there were no fatal casualties. Less than two years old, *Munster* was the pride of the Irish Sea and the largest vessel owned by Coast Lines. Her destruction can be credited to the minelaying activities of *U-30* in early January, which two days later led to the sinking of the 5,406 ton *Chagres*, five and a half miles from Liverpool Bar light vessel.

The *Imperial Transport* of 8,022 grt was an outward tanker in ballast belonging to the Empire Transport Co. Ltd when on 11 February 1940 she was torpedoed by *U-53* (Lieutenant-Commander Harald

Grosse) approximately in position 59N 12W. So great was the explosion that she was blown into two pieces being severed just abaft the bridge. Eleven crew were killed but the others jumped onto the after end just before the final break occurred and the forepart disappeared beneath the waves. The rear half was sailed at 3½ knots by use of the jury steering gear on the poopdeck and as the bridge with all instruments had been lost, Captain Smail navigated by atlas and ruler. An escort was later provided and course was set for the Scottish coast. The weather worsened, the steering gear developed a fault but eventually a tug took her in tow. She was later beached on the Isle of Bute and much later brought into the Clyde and a new forepart built on to her. Twelve days after the attack *U-53* was sunk whilst returning to base by HMS *Gurkha*.

There is a postscript to the saga of the *Imperial Transport*. She was again torpedoed, then abandoned in the North Atlantic on 25 March 1942 yet she remained afloat and was reboarded, later to be towed into St John's Newfoundland for repair – a stout ship indeed.

The stormy waters of the North Sea, south of the Pentland Firth and the Orkneys were always a dangerous area. Here the small coastal U-boats would lurk beneath the surface, periscope up, or from out of the sky would come a bomber, heralded by a scream and a hiss as it pulled out of its dive, both seeking the convoy straggler, those ships which couldn't keep headway, which had to reduce speed because of engine trouble, those that in bad weather, in fog or snowfall, in spite of feats of seamanship, lost their way and sought the tell-tale sign of their friends, often no more than a marker buoy towed from the stern of the ship ahead. *Greatafield*, a tanker of 10,191 grt belonging to the Northern Petroleum Tank Steamship Company, was just such a straggler. On 14 February, heavily laden with aviation spirit, she was within 24 hours of her destination, having crossed the 5,000 miles from the Caribbean via Halifax (Convoy HX18) when she was torpedoed by *U-57* (Lieutenant Claus Korth). Catching fire she was beached and remained blazing for several days after which she was declared a total loss. Of the 41 crew eleven perished.

Some 600 miles to the north-east a further iron ore carrier was lost without trace. No signal whatever was received from *Tiberton* (5,225 grt owned by R. Chapman & Son) after she sailed from Narvik for Middlesbrough. She carried a crew of 32 and two gunners and, as no U-boat claimed responsibility, it is assumed she was mined a few hours after sailing. The vulnerability of the ore carriers was of great concern to the British Government as with the shortage of escort vessels, and with Narvik being north of the Arctic Circle, it was not possible to give them convoy protection; already greater attention was being given to African and Canadian sources.

On the same day, some 200 miles west of the Scilly Isles, the 16½ knot steamship *Sultan Star* (12,306 grt), commanded by Captain Bevan, was approaching the United Kingdom having sailed from Buenos Aires on 27 January with 8,000 tons of frozen meat and 1,000 tons of butter. Suddenly, at 1655 hours she was torpedoed on the starboard side aft by *U-48* (position 48.54N 10.03W), one seaman being killed by the explosion. She went down very fast with a heavy list but the radio operator Mr P. Winsor stuck to his post to the very last moment making sure that his SOS signal had been received. As he slid down a rope over the side, the ship was standing on her stern with bows in the air and water going down the funnel. For his service he was awarded the MBE and Lloyds War Medal for Bravery at Sea, though sadly, he was lost when serving in *Empire Lakeland*, torpedoed 11 March 1943.

Josenfjord near Kristiansand was the snowladen backdrop which heralded HMS *Cossack* (Captain Vian) on 16 February and the famous cry, 'The Navy's here' when she woke the peaceful fjord from its slumber as she drew alongside the supply ship *Altmark* taking refuge from the British Navy. It was over ten weeks since she had embarked 299 British merchant seamen in the South Atlantic, crews from ships sunk by the *Graf Spee*, for the voyage back to Germany. Between 23 December and 21 January she lay secretly at anchor in the lonely Kergulen Islands lorded over by the arrogant and harsh Captain Dau. Really a modern fast tanker, her homeward course took her to Dakar to refuel, then close inshore off Newfoundland and Greenland before sailing north of Iceland to Norway. All the British seamen were rescued, and five Germans killed in the daring raid.

The Alfred Holt cargo liner *Pyrrhus* of 7,418 grt, built in 1914 was one of 44 merchantmen which sailed from Liverpool with convoy OG18 for Gibraltar; a French destroyer and an auxiliary French naval vessel were the only escorts. Bound for the Far East with general cargo she was Vice-Commodore ship and was commanded by Captain Spencer. Although the *Pyrrhus* was capable of fourteen knots it was considered too dangerous for her to proceed independently as it was known that several U-boats were operating off the coast of Portugal. However the instructed speed of convoy OG18 was only eight knots and this led to many difficulties when a south-westerly gale was encountered on the third day and ships became scattered; many were 'missing' altogether. It was typical of the situation which faced a slow convoy of this type.

As Vice-Commodore ship, *Pyrrhus* had to leave the main body of ships to collect fourteen ships which had romped ahead and at 1600 hours in position 44.02N 10.18W she was torpedoed by *U-37*, a large type IX Atlantic class boat built 1938–39 and commanded by Captain Werner Hartmann. The whole stern disappeared within a few seconds of the explosion in No 5 hold which brought down the mainmast, main and emergency radio aerials at the same time. Seventy-seven crew were picked up by the *Uskside* and *Sinnington Court*, but eight Chinese engine room staff were missing.

At the end of February Vice-Admiral Dönitz issued new orders to his U-boat commanders – which heralded a new frightening era for the men of the Red Duster.

> Do not rescue any men, do not take them along and do not take care of any boats from the ship. Weather conditions and the proximity of land are of no consequence. Concern yourself only with the safety of your own boat and with the efforts to achieve additional success as soon as possible. We must be hard in this war. The enemy started the war in order to destroy us and thus nothing else matters.

With the delivery of new boats from the shipyards, Dönitz was now firmly in control. He planned co-ordinated ocean convoy attacks further to the west using the new magnetically triggered electric powered torpedoes with which his fleet was now being equipped, though these were later considered a failure. The offensive, however, was postponed due to plans being prepared by the German High Command for the invasion of Denmark and Norway and the fact that some submarines were being held in home waters against the threat of a British occupation of Norway which appeared likely at the time. March was a relatively quiet month.

The first passenger-carrying vessel to be bombed by the German Air Force was British India's diesel engined *Domala* (8,441 grt). At the break of dawn on 2 March 1940 she was heading into a strong wind and heavy sea down channel from Antwerp and was due to call at Southampton outwards for Bombay. On board were many Indian seamen travelling as passengers; most of them had been serving on board the German merchant ships *Birkenfels*, *Falkenfels*, *Lautenfels* and *Truenfels* and had been released so that they could return to their homeland.

Domala was steaming thirty miles east of the Isle of Wight when a lone Heinkel came from astern, flying low, and dropped a stick of bombs amidships leaving the superstructure and cabins above the engine room a mass of flame. In the blast many were killed outright and the fourth mate was thrown overboard. The fire was immediately out of control and the order was given to abandon ship but the weather made it difficult to lower the boats. Meantime the aircraft returned to make a second run, this time screeching low over the bow and hitting the bridge with further bombs killing Captain Fitt and the second mate outright.

Whilst the survivors were trying to get away from the ship's side and the heat of the flames, the enemy began raking the ship and the boats with machine-gun fire causing further casualties. Of the total complement of 291 there were 108 souls lost, including sixteen British crew, two stewardesses and 130 Indian crew; the remainder, which included many wounded, were picked up by a destroyer and the Dutch *Jonge Willem*. Later in the day the *Domala*, still on fire, was brought into Portsmouth where she was subsequently reconstructed and taken over by the Ministry of War Transport.

On the same day, after trials in the Clyde the previous week, the new Cunarder *Queen Elizabeth*, destined to become with the *Queen Mary* the greatest troopship of all time, sailed secretly for New York. On 7 March she tied up at Cunard's pier on the Hudson river, only a few yards from her sister. Later in the month, the *Queen Mary*, together with the *Mauretania* sailed for an unknown destination, eventually arriving on 17 April at the Australian port of Sydney, having voyaged over 14,000 miles and averaging a speed of 27.2 knots.

Two weeks later she sailed in company with *Andes*, *Aquitania*, the three Empress liners *Empress of Britain*, *Empress of Canada* and *Empress of Japan*, together with the *Mauretania* carrying a total of 14,000 Australian and New Zealand troops for Cape Town and the Clyde. Convoy US3 arrived without incident and dropped anchor at 'the tail of the bank' on 16 June, the *Empress of Japan* having been left behind in Cape Town. The preceding troop convoy, US2, which left Australia on 13 April for the Middle East was comprised of the *Dunera*, *Ettrick*, *Neuralia*, *Nevasa* and *Straithaird*.

During the first week of March Lieutenant Otto Schuhart, commander of *U-29*, brought his boat to the approaches of the Bristol Channel; he had recently been awarded the Knight's Cross for sinking the Fleet Carrier *Courageous* on 17 September 1939. The trampship *Thurston* of 3,072 grt, carrying manganese ore from Takoradi for Workington, and owned by the Murrell Steamship Company of West Hartlepool, was torpedoed 32 miles west by north of Trevose Head just before dawn on 4 March and sank within three minutes taking 34 crew with her.

Six hours later the 6,717-ton *Pacific Reliance* belonging to Furness Withy (Norfolk and North American Steam Shipping Co. Ltd) was struck amidships in position 50.23N 05.49W and shortly afterwards she broke her back sliding beneath the waves within ten minutes. *U-29* claimed to have hit the *San Florentino* at about the same time but it would appear the two torpedoes fired failed to detonate. (*San Florentino* was later sunk on 1 October 1941.)

The small shipping company of George Gibson lost two vessels during March. Reported missing in the North Sea on 9 March the 1,585 ton *Abbotsford* became a victim of *U-14* sinking with all hands, 24 officers and men. (The same dark night *U-14* claimed the *Akeld* of which there was no trace other than wreckage). Six days later the 34-year-old *Melrose*, her tonnage identical to *Abbotsford*, was mined approaching Ostend in position 51.21N 02.13E; only Captain Johnson and five seamen were saved from a crew of 23.

At the end of the month the enemy was ready to put into operation its plan for nine converted merchantmen to sail the ocean routes of the world as surface raiders. The *Atlantis* (7,862 grt) sailed on 31 March commanded by the brilliant and honourable Captain Rogge followed by the *Kormoran* twelve days later, the *Orion* on 6 April and the *Widder* a month later.

During April the majority of action took place off the coast and in the fjords of Norway following the invasion by German forces on 9 April. Landings were made simultaneously at Oslo, Kristiansand, Stavanger, Bergen, Trondheim and Narvik. Many British merchant ships were trapped, the greatest loss being at Narvik. Lying at anchor waiting to load and taken completely by surprise were the *Blythmoor* (6,582 grt, Moor Line/Runciman), *Mersington Court* (5,141 grt, Court Line Ltd), *North Cornwall* (4,304 grt, North Shipping Co. Ltd), and the *Riverton* (5,378 grt, R. Chapman and Son). Lying alongside the ore jetty, partly loaded, and subsequently sunk by a German destroyer, was *Romanby* (4,887 grt owned by the Ropner Shipping Co. Ltd). Prize crews took over the ships at anchor but in the following action by Norwegian, French and British forces, all were sunk.

Probably the first person on the ships at anchor to see the enemy entering the harbour was Captain Evans of the *North Cornwall* when at 0445 hours he was awoken by gunfire from the direction of the iron ore quay. Upon going up on the bridge he suddenly saw a destroyer appear from behind the *Blythmoor* and in the growing light, as it was passing, he saw the swastika flying from the stern – he quickly ordered all confidential papers to be destroyed.

The officers and men of the five ships were confined on board the *Jan Wellem*, a German supply tanker, a converted whale factory ship, carrying fuel oil for the destroyers and diesel oil for the U-boats, but as the battle of Narvik Harbour drew to its close, 47 seamen, led by Captain Evans of the *North Cornwall*, gave their German guard the slip and mingled with the crowd. He then led them through Ankenes and Emmenes to Skjomnes, crossing by the ferry where they were given a free ride. They then caught up with the survivors of HMS *Hardy* and were later rescued by the minelaying destroyer HMS *Ivanhoe*.

As indicated earlier, U-boat Command was ordered to support the Norwegian operation with every available boat and cruising off the coast were *U-25*, *U-48*, *U-51*, *U-64* and *U-26*. The latter trapped the motorship *Cedarbank* (5,159 grt, Andrew Weir & Co., Bank Line) off Alesund on 21 March as she was making for Namos with supplies for the British infantry brigade which had landed there four days earlier (only to be withdrawn on the night of 2 May). Two torpedoes hit the *Cedarbank* killing fifteen of her crew of 42. Between 13 and 15 April troop convoy NP1 left the Clyde and Scapa Flow, the *Chrobry* and *Empress of Australia* for Namsos, the *Monarch of Bermuda*, *Reina del Pacifico* and the Polish *Batory* for Harsted. The 11,442 ton Polish passenger ship *Chrobry* was lost the following month (14 May) when she was bombed and set on fire at Bodo.

Other merchantmen lost in Norway and seized by the Germans were the Allan Black Thistle Line vessel *Thistlebrae* (4,747 grt) at Trondheim, the *Salerno* and *Salmonpool* at Saudafjord and the *Thorland* (5,208 grt), belonging to Thor Dahl (London Whaling Company) at Sandefjord, one of the earliest fish factory ships; she was found damaged at Tonsberg in May 1945. After service as Norddeutcher Lloyd's *Putzig*, Messrs Ropner's *Salmonpool* was recaptured on the reoccupation of Norway in 1945. Several British trawlers were also seized, all of which were later worked by the Germans protecting convoys along the coast of Northern Norway. As with all Red Duster ships seized or taken in prize, many crews were captured to spend the rest of the war in prison camps.

In their occupation of Denmark, the Germans took over two new ships being completed for British shipowners, Alfred Holt's *Glengarry* (9,838 grt) and Blue Star's *Adelaide Star* (12,636 grt), both lying in Burmeister & Wain's fitting out basin at Copenhagen. *The Glengarry* converted as a surface raider and renamed *Hansa*, was recovered at

Hamburg at the end of the war whilst the Blue Star vessel, mined off Danzig, was later salvaged by Poland and renamed *Jastarnia* in 1954.

On 16 April a battered lifeboat was washed ashore in the north of Scotland containing sixteen seamen in an exhausted condition; lying huddled in the bow were six dead bodies. It was later learned that their ship, the 4,511 ton *Stancliffe* had been torpedoed by *U-37* four days earlier in rough seas 45 miles north-east of the Shetland Isles. A second lifeboat with fifteen on board was wrecked just after the vessel was abandoned making a total loss of 21 men including the master.

The steamer *Haxby* (5,207 grt, owned by Ropner Shipping) was the first vessel to be sunk in the Second World War by a German surface raider originally built as a merchantman. Sailing on 8 April in convoy from the Clyde for Corpus Christi in ballast, she left the convoy in the latitude of the Cape Verde Islands nine days later and on 24 April when in position 31.30N 51.30W she was taken completely by surprise as the 7,021 grt *Orion* with swastika flying in the stiff breeze bore down upon her. Captain Arundel refused to stop when asked to do so and instructed his radio officer to signal his plight whereupon the raider opened up with her guns; the action lasted only six minutes, leaving two officers and fourteen other members of the crew dead. Captain Arundel and 23 of his crew were taken prisoner; fortunately they were later rescued (3 September 1940) from the supply ship *Tropic Sea* which was scuttled by her prize crew after being stopped by the British submarine *Truant*.

May 1940 was destined to be a momentous month. It opened with further action from an enemy surface raider, the first kill of *Atlantis* now cruising in the South Atlantic and closed with the holocaust of Dunkirk. *Atlantis*, now disguised as a Japanese merchantman, shelled and finally torpedoed the Harrison vessel *Scientist* (6,199 grt, Charente Steamship Company) south of St Helena in position 20.00S 04.30E. She was homeward bound with copper and grain from Beira and Lourenço Marques. Five seamen were killed and after abandoning ship, the remainder of the crew, together with Captain Windsor, 78 in all, were taken on board the raider. Later some were transferred to the Norwegian *Tirrana* (taken as prize on 10 June) with the intention of taking them, together with others captured, to a prison camp in Europe but when she was torpedoed and sunk by a British submarine in the Bay of Biscay several were lost. Fifteen of the crew of *Scientist* were transferred to the *Durmitor* in the Indian Ocean and subsequently, together with some 200 Merchant navy officers and seamen, were put ashore on a deserted beach in Somaliland there to be held in an Italian prison camp near

Mogadishu. There they remained some four months until rescued by Brigadier-General Fowkes and his East African Corps.

On 10 May the Germans invaded the Netherlands, Belgium and Luxembourg which was followed by the appointment of Winston Churchill as Prime Minister of Great Britain. The war in Europe exploded and by 19 May, Dieppe, Le Havre and Rouen were threatened. The British and French forces, after the capitulation of the Belgians, fell back to Dunkirk and there began on the 26th the virtual impossibility of evacuating nearly 500,000 troops. Operation Dynamo called for an armada of small ships and whilst they were successful in extracting 338,226 of them it was at considerable cost, both in ships and seamen. In addition to 230 trawlers and the fleet of small craft, 216 ships of the British merchant fleet were involved. The remarkable fact is that losses were not greater.

On 21/22 May enemy bombers had launched particularly savage attacks on the port area of Dieppe and in the vicinity of Boulogne and Calais. Two Southern Railway cross channel ferries were sunk at Dieppe, the 2,391 ton *Brighton* alongside the quay and the 2,693 ton *Maid of Kent* in the harbour. Both were acting as hospital ships bringing out wounded troops and the loss of life was heavy. During the days that followed the bombers carried their fury to the beaches, to the water's edge, and beyond to the Straits of Dover. The week that commenced on 27 May, 'Bloody Monday' as it became known, was one of the longest weeks in the history of Britain's merchant navy. The names of the ships which fought and died are still written in the sands of Dunkirk.

Lying in the main basin at Dunkirk was the twisted hulk of the *Spinel*, a motor-coaster of 650 grt. She was struck repeatedly in the early stages of the evacuation and burned furiously for many hours. Later she was salved by the Germans and taken in prize being reconstructed and placed in service in the Channel Islands where she was found at the end of the war. The motor-cruiser *Sequacity* (870 grt) was approaching the harbour from Calais on 27 May when she was smashed by gunfire from shore batteries and quickly sank. *Worthtown* (868 grt) was dive-bombed in the harbour channel and smashed beyond recognition. There were no survivors.

The following day the *Queen of the Channel* (1,162 grt, General Steam Navigation Company) was lost. She was one of 45 troop transports employed of which eight were sunk and a further eight were so badly damaged they had to be withdrawn. She had stopped off Dunkirk waiting for a suitable moment to approach the harbour when she was bombed but fortunately there was no loss of life and the crew and 950 soldiers were rescued by the *Dorrien Rose*. The small coaster *Marjory H*, of only 84 grt was also lost (later salved and taken in prize), as was the *Abukir* (694 grt), an ex-Egyptian vessel being operated by the General Steam Navigation Company. She was acting as a personnel carrier and was the first accredited loss to an E-boat attack, a method of naval warfare which was to prove so costly in the months to come.

On 29 May *Mona's Queen* (2,765 grt), one of several vessels employed belonging to the Isle of Man Steam Packet Co. Ltd, struck a mine in the approach channel and sank within two minutes, taking 26 of her crew with her. *Lorina* of 1,578 grt (Southern Railway) was bombed amidships and broke her back, eight being killed and four seriously wounded. The *Fenella* (2,376 grt), a paddle-steamer belonging to the Isle of Man Steam Packet Co. Ltd commanded by Captain Cubbon, was loading stretcher cases from the eastern arm of the harbour and had almost 700 men on board when she received a direct hit from a Stuka dive bomber killing many soldiers both above and below deck. A second bomb hit the mole and blew pieces of concrete through her side below the waterline and flooded her engine-room. *Crested Eagle* moored close by, had just slipped her lines and was also hit and being an oil burner, she burned furiously, her decks covered with the dead and the dying. Happily she was beached and later refloated. *Fenella* became a total loss, leaving fifteen of her crew dead.

The *Clan MacAlister* (6,787 grt, Clan Line Ltd), the largest ship used in the evacuation and commanded by Captain Mackie, was laden with landing craft sent to assist the evacuation and whilst unloading these with her own lifting gear and embarking troops at the same time, she was bombed by a Ju88 aircraft and sunk at her anchorage. A third of her crew and many soldiers were either killed by the explosion or burned to death in the fire that followed. The survivors were rescued by HMS *Malcolm*.

There were many instances of heroism on this momentous day. The *Pangbourne*, a coal burning minesweeper ran aground but managed to refloat herself after more than 1,000 soldiers had clambered aboard. *Brighton Belle*, the oldest paddle minesweeper afloat, ripped her bottom on the wreck of a ship sunk a few hours earlier. The *Gracie Fields*, *Waverley*, *Devonia*, *Brighton Queen* and *Skipjack*, requistioned by the Admiralty and serving as minesweepers, although crewed by merchant seamen, were all lost. Numerous trawlers and drifters, sailing barges such as *Lark*, *Royalty*, *Duchess*,

Lady Roseberry, Doris, Barbara Jean, Aidie, Ethel Everard, and the tug *Fossa*, all found their grave on the beaches of Dunkirk.

Shelled and damaged were the *Biarritz* (2,388 grt), *Fulham IV* (1,584 grt) and *Princess Maud* (2,883 grt) and the hospital ship *Worthing* (2,294 grt). The small coaster *Yewdale* with a crew of eleven and 900 troops aboard, limped to Deal after being bombed by Stukas. With her wheelhouse completely destroyed, her sides holed in several places and steam pipes fractured, she was steered from the poopdeck, her master plotting his course by coastal objects.

Mona's Isle was cast off from the harbour mole amidst a whole cascade of bombs; 23 men were killed and 60 wounded by shrapnel. The coaster *Bullfinch* ran herself up the beach so that troops could climb ladders to board her. When floated off on the rising tide she had 1,500 men on board. Outstanding were the efforts of *St Seirol* and her crew. Whilst escaping damage, she made seven trips to Dunkirk carrying an average of 900 troops each time. At the end, having had little rest and under constant strain, the whole crew were in an advanced state of physical and nervous exhaustion.

One of the last tragedies of Dunkirk was the loss of the *Scotia* on 1 June. Of 3,454 grt and owned by the London Midland and Scottish Railway, she was under the command of Captain Hughes and was carrying some 2,000 French soldiers en route for Dover when she was attacked by twelve dive bombers; she was hit by three bombs one of which went down the funnel exploding the boilers with devastating effect destroying her superstructure and smashing almost all the lifeboats. She sank by the stern, and survivors clambered over the bow on to the deck of HMS *Esk*. Thirty crew and some 300 French troops were lost.

As a lasting tribute to those left behind, some captured, others dead, the *Normannia* of 1,567 grt (Southern Railway) although bombed and resting on the bottom in shallow water, lay on an even keel with her signal flags still flying from the masts which stuck out above the surface.

> You seamen I have eaten your hard bread
> And drunken from your tin, and known your ways;
> I understand the qualities I praise
> Though lacking all, with only words instead.
>
> I tell you this, that in the future time
> When landsmen mention sailors, such, or such,
> Someone will say 'Those fellows were sublime!
> Who brought the Armies from the Germans' clutch.

Through the long time the story will be told
Long centuries of praise on English lips,
Of courage godlike and of hearts of gold
Off Dunquerque beaches in the little ships.

And ships will dip their colours in salute
To you, henceforth when passing Zuydecoote.
                    John Masefield, Poet Laureate 1940

After nine months of calm the storm raged – from the far north of
Norway to the west coast of France, across the 'Western' ocean and
south of the equator; already there were signs of what was to come.
During eleven days at the end of May, *U-37* sank nine merchantmen, three of them British, along the shipping routes off Cape
Finisterre. Although the convoy system had been proved, the
toll was mounting: over nine months, 204 British registered ships,
827,825 grt.

CHAPTER TWO

Atlantic Holocausts
(June–October 1940)

June was a month of defeat, of evacuation and disasters, from the air, from the sea and from the depths of the ocean – losses included the Cunarder *Lancastria* and the Orient liners *Orford* and *Orama*. There were few other occasions during the whole six years when the call upon the merchant fleet and its personnel was so demanding. Owing to the deteriorating situation in Europe with the German dash for the Channel and Biscay ports, the British and French forces in Norway were quickly brought out; almost immediately many of the same ships were engaged in Operations 'Cycle' and 'Ariel', the evacuations from Northern and Western France respectively, about which little has been written, yet in some respects, with so many of Britain's finest ships involved, the situation was far more desperate than at Dunkirk.

With the Germans firmly entrenched from North Cape to Ushant they dominated communication in the North Sea and the English Channel. The Biscay ports gave them uninterrupted access to the whole 'western' ocean – 250,000 tons of Allied shipping were sunk by submarine warfare in four weeks with only six operational boats. Further, the threat of invasion and the need to hold the Mediterranean, which suddenly with the advent of Italy (and its 116 submarines) into the conflict had become another front line, meant that valuable escort vessels were withdrawn from ocean work. Once again the merchant ships and those who manned them bore the brunt of the attack.

The evacuation of Norway, principally from Narvik and Harsted, took place during 4 – 10 June and included several large transports which had been hastily marshalled from various ports, some only recently converted. They included the *Atlantis, Arandora Star, Duchess of York, Franconia, Georgic, Lancastria, Monarch of Bermuda, Orama, Ormonde, Oronsay, Royal Ulsterman, Ulster Prince*, the Polish *Batory* and *Sobieski* together with a fleet auxiliary, the armed boarding vessel *Van Dyck*. Supply ships and tankers included the *Acrity, Blackheath,*

Cotswold, Couch, Cromarty Firth, Glenaffaric, Glengarry, Harmattan, Oil Pioneer, Oligarch and *Theseus*. Over five nights some 25,000 men and equipment were evacuated.

On 8 June, the 19,840 grt Orient liner *Orama* together with the requisitioned tanker *Oil Pioneer* (5,666 grt, owned by British Oil Shipping Co. Ltd) were sunk in the far north off Narvik (position 67.44N 03.52E) by an enemy naval force which included the German battleships *Scharnhorst* and *Gneisenau*, and the cruiser *Admiral Hipper*, and which completely overwhelmed the British operation; the aircraft carrier *Glorious* and the destroyers *Acasta* and *Ardent* were also sunk. The *Orama*, under the command of Captain Sherburne, was sunk by gunfire from *Hipper* which also torpedoed her. Although not carrying troops at the time, nineteen men were killed and 280 crew including Captain Sherburne were taken prisoner. The boarding vessel *Van Dyck* in convoy at the time was also lost.

The 'Narrow Sea', that thin line of resistance between Britain and the coast of Europe, became a bulwark in the defence of freedom; along this tightrope men of the Merchant Navy faced all the might that Hitler could muster. The destruction of the *Paris* during the afternoon of 2 June was just one holocaust in a long series between the withdrawal from Dunkirk and the landing upon the beaches of Normandy some four years hence.

The *Paris* of 1,790 grt, owned by the Southern Railway, sank in position 51.11N 02.07E close to where the *Scotia* had found her grave. Coming from out of the sun, the Stuka dive bomber, machine-guns firing, dropped two bombs in quick succession, the first opening up her port side amidships, the second went down the after cross bunker trunkway and exploded deep down, blowing out the ship's side to starboard, killing those in the engine room.

The whole ship shivered and trembled violently, taking a list to starboard of fifteen degrees. The forestay and foretopmast stay carried away and the foremast shook and swung aft. Two more bombs followed falling into the sea close by, blasting away the propeller which by now was high out of the water with the bow churning beneath the water, the ship still making headway. The attack, from sighting the aircraft until those remaining jumped over the side, lasted less than one minute – then, she heeled over and was gone.

The evacuation which commenced at Le Havre on 9 June (11,050 British troops rescued) was to be repeated at numerous ports along the French coast right down to the Spanish frontier, the last remnants being ferried out to P & O's newest ship, the trooper

(*Right*) The Orient Line
steamships *Otranto* and
Orcades embarking Australian
troops. The *Otranto* and
Orcades, lying astern,
embarking Australian troops
at Sydney, Australia, in
January 1940. They were just
two of the liners which made
up troop convoy USI. *Orcades*
was subsequently sunk in
October 1942.

(*Below*) The Anzac convoy
(USI) in the Indian Ocean. In
the foreground, one of the
escorts, the battleship
Ramillies. Behind, from left to
right, the Orient steamship
Orford and Canadian Pacific's
Empress of Japan and
Empress of Canada.

SS *Otranto* at Diego Suarez. The Orient liner *Otranto* after embarking French Colonial troops at Diego Suarez, 5 May 1940. They were put ashore at Djibouti and Marseilles. Two years later when Vichy French Madagascar was invaded to forestall a danger threatening the route to Suez, the troopships returned.

Aboard the *Otranto* 1940. Assistant Pursers; (*from left to right*) Tony Mitchell and John Jukes SS *Otranto*, showing the daytime 'rig' of white shirts and shorts. Even in 1940 pre-war tunics and trousers were obligatory in passenger liners of the P&O Group.

Ettrick, at St Jean du Luz on 22 June. Ship losses were considerable and in addition to several small coasters seized, the *Baron Saltoun*, *Bruges*, *Dulwich*, *Lancastria*, *Teiresias* and *Train Ferry No 2* were lost. After Le Havre, withdrawals were made from Cherbourg (30,630 troops) and St Malo (21,474 troops) which took place between 15 and 18 June whilst a large scale operation was mounted at Brest, to which port a considerable number of ships were sent.

Departing fully loaded from Brest on 18 June were the *Arandora Star*, *Franconia* and *Ormonde* which had all achieved a quick turn around in the Clyde after arriving from Norway; *Otranto* and *Strathaird* and the Alfred Holt vessels *Bellerophon*, *Euryades* and *Lycaon*. *Lancastria* arrived in the same convoy but was then directed to Quiberon Bay. 32,584 troops were embarked at Brest including 6,000 on board the P & O liner *Strathaird*. She also carried many civilians, 200 cadets from the military school at Brest, gold from British banks in Paris, some de Gaullist leaders and even some pet dogs.

At St Nazaire, to where some 60,000 Allied troops were retreating, about 13,000 non-combatant men with stores and transport got away on 15 June without interference on the transports *Batory*, *Duchess of York*, *Georgic* and *Sobieski*. The next day *Oronsay* arrived to be followed in the early hours of the 17th by a great assortment of vessels called up from the South of England and South Wales. *Lancastria* lay approximately three miles from the port itself owing to the comparatively shallow water at the mouth of the Loire. She was to be joined by the *Ulster Prince*, *Ulster Monarch*, *Royal Scotsman* and *Royal Ulsterman*. The *Dundrum Castle*, diverted from Dunkirk, was waiting to discharge a military cargo from South Africa (with wool in the 'tween decks). The hospital ship *Somersetshire* also lay at anchor.

Arriving in convoy from the Bristol Channel was the *Robert L. Holt* with her master Captain Fuller acting as commodore – she was accompanied by the *City of Lancaster*, *David Livingstone*, *Fabian* and *Glenlea*. Also in the Loire river anchorage was the *Clan Ferguson*, the tanker *Cymbula*, *Braharistan*, *Floristan*, *Glenaffaric*, *John Holt* and *Teiresias*. In the whole port there were only three destroyers to protect such a vulnerable array of shipping. Alfred Holt's *Teiresias* (7,404 grt) loaded with military vehicles and stores, was later lost in an enemy air attack outside the port limits. Captain Davies made many attempts to save his ship but later, together with his crew, he was taken off by *Holmside* and landed in Falmouth. One member of the crew, the bosun, lost his life.

At St Nazaire on 17 June few imagined that they were about to witness one of the greatest British maritime disasters of all time. The

16,243 ton *Lancastria* became a target for German bombers from an early hour and suffered damage from a near miss at about 1300 hours when the first airmen and infantrymen were boarding. *Oronsay* some half a mile distant, which had completed embarkation, was also damaged by this attack but remained seaworthy. The destroyers *Havelock* and *Highlander* served as ferry boats to the anchorage but some begged lifts on trawlers, others on pleasure boats; in fact anything that possessed an outboard motor was pressed into service.

Some two hours later after a period of frantic activity *Lancastria* with some 6,000 on board but with lifeboats and rafts for only a fraction of that number, was ready to sail. Believing that U-boats were outside waiting to attack the evacuation force, Captain Sharp, knowing that he was unlikely to be escorted if he went it alone, delayed sailing in the hope that a convoy would be organised.

At about 1600 hours came the scream of Dornier Do17 aircraft releasing a hail of bombs, one of which scored a direct hit in the hold where a large RAF contingent had been billeted. Shortly afterwards the ship took a strong list to starboard, then, a minute later, she rolled back on her port side exposing a gaping hole in her side. Steam was hissing everywhere, crashes and thuds resounded as bulkheads collapsed. There were shouts, moans, and the cry of thousands as they fought for their lives. All the time the planes were returning, bursts of machine gun fire adding to the chaos and panic. By 1705 hours she was well down by the head surrounded by 1,600 tons of fuel oil which freely flowed from her shattered tanks. Twenty minutes later she was gone.

Rescue work was difficult because of the oil, because of renewed enemy attacks. HMS *Highlander*, the trawler *Cambridgeshire, Cymbula, Fabian, Glenaffaric, John Holt, Oronsay, Robert L. Holt* and *Ulster Prince* were all engaged in the rescue. Little is recorded about the loss of *Lancastria*; its loss was not advised to the public until 26 July, 39 days after the event when the war cabinet admitted a loss of 3,000 lives. The real figure has never been known but was very probably higher – a veil of silence was drawn over the event. Many of the crew of 300 were lost, Captain Sharp swimming for some four hours before being picked up.

During the same evening 23,000 other troops sailed for Plymouth in a convoy of ten ships, two of the last to leave being *Glenaffaric* and *Robert L. Holt*. During 18 and 19 June the evacuation continued. The Royal Mail steamship *Nalon* from Bordeaux took 129 refugees, men, women and children including 40 members of the Polish Government; diverted from Brest, she had been due to discharge her cargo of meat from Buenos Aires. In Le Verdon Roads lay *Nariva*, also with meat from Buenos Aires, destined for the French Army. On the night of 18 June 263 refugees embarked during an enemy air attack. The *Madura* owned by British India Steam Navigation Company was also diverted to the Gironde estuary. A passenger ship with accommodation for 190, she took on board 1,300 refugees in addition to her normal complement before sailing for Falmouth. At the port of Rochefort two British vessels, the 1,199 ton *Hester* and the 1,766 ton *Ronwyn* were damaged and abandoned, their crews being taken prisoner.

The *Ettrick* had been originally ordered to St Nazaire but as she arrived off the Loire estuary it was learnt that the town was already in enemy hands. She then steamed south to Bayonne, and on 22 June, the day France fell, to St Jean du Luz where she embarked 2,000 – Polish, French and British together with King Zog of Albania. *Glenaffaric*, after landing some 4,000 soldiers at Plymouth, sailed together with *Cyclops* and *Clan Ross* for Bordeaux, Bayonne and St Jean du Luz to assist *Ettrick*. The *Clan Ross* was bombed by the Luftwaffe off Bayonne and suffered damage on 24 June. The overworked *Arandora Star*, with an exhausted crew, also returned after disembarking her Brest refugees at Falmouth. 19,000 were evacuated from these ports during 19–25 June. From the Channel and Biscay ports, 191, 870 troops in total, several thousand civilians, 2,292 military vehicles, 310 guns and 1,800 tons of stores. It was no mean achievement.

Meanwhile in other theatres the war at sea was increasing with all the ferocity which the enemy could muster. The 20,043 ton Orient liner *Orford*, under the command of Captain Savage, engaged in evacuating Free French forces from the south of France, was bombed and set on fire on 1 June off the coast between Marseilles and Toulon. She became a total loss; fourteen were killed and 25 wounded. On the following day to the north of Scotland *Astronomer* (8,401 grt), one of the Harrison fleet taken over as a fleet auxiliary, was torpedoed by *U-58* just before midnight. She was on special duties as a boom carrier, the submarine commander, Lieutenant Herbert Kuppisch, mistaking *Astronomer* for an armed merchant cruiser – four crew and a number of naval ratings were lost together with eleven injured.

AMC *Carinthia* of 20,277 grt, converted January 1940, was sunk off the west coast of Ireland on 7 June by *U-46*, sailing under Lieutenant Engelbert Endrass who had served his apprenticeship with Günter Prien. One of the up and coming aces, it was his first command; during the same week he sank the 4,223 ton *Barbara Marie* and the

5,041 ton *Willowbank* in addition to severely damaging the 8,782 ton tanker *Athelprince*. In the middle of the month *U-25* torpedoed AMC *Scotstoun* (17,046 grt) west of the Hebrides and UA, an ex-Turkish Navy submarine taken over by the Germans, sank AMC *Andania* (13,950 grt) some 250 miles south of Iceland. In an attack on convoy HX48 in the North Atlantic three ships were torpedoed including the British-owned 5,834 ton *Balmoralwood* which had straggled due to engine trouble and was sunk by Prien (*U-47*) in position 50.19N 10.28W. Although it was the first ocean convoy attack for twelve weeks the next seven Halifax convoys were attacked five of which led to losses. Although Hitler thought he was about to sever the lifeline without which the island fortress of Britain could not hope to survive, he had just directed the German construction industry to build the new U-boat base at Lorient; he reckoned, however, without the British merchant seamen. Nevertheless six U-boats between them sank 31 Allied ships totalling 156,420 grt between 9 June and 2 July. Lemp in *U-30* was the first ace to bring his boat into Dönitz's new base of Lorient on 5 July – it was operational in twenty days from the lowering of the first concrete casson.

The following week, on 19–22 June, two important heavily laden convoys were attacked. HGF34 a fast convoy from Gibraltar which was the last homeward convoy from the Mediterranean before it was closed to Suez Canal traffic due to the combined German Italian threat, and Trans Atlantic convoy HX49 from Halifax, Nova Scotia. In the HGF34 action, *U-48* sank Hogarth's *Baron Loudon* (3,164 grt, Bône for Barrow) in the early hours of the 19th followed 50 minutes later by Raeburn & Verel's *British Monarch* (5,661 grt), whose master, Captain Scott, together with 39 of his crew, was killed. *U-48* then sped westward joining *U-30*, *U-32* and *U-47* for the attack on HX49 which lost four ships including Eagle Tanker's *San Fernando* (13,056 grt), two Norwegian tankers and a Dutch tanker.

Quite unexpectedly at 0330 hours on 20 June the war at sea erupted on the other side of the world when Canadian Pacific's *Niagara* (13,415 grt, Captain Martin) was mined after she left the port of Auckland for Suva, Honolulu and Vancouver. She was carrying gold ingots valued at £2,500,000 consigned to the USA by the Bank of England in payment for war supplies plus a large consignment of small arms ammunition – all was salvaged in due course, in great secrecy, but it was not until eighteen months later that the operation was complete and even then a balance of 30 gold bars lay on the ocean floor until brought up in the summer of 1953. The *Niagara* remained upright after the explosion and all the 136 passengers and 200 crew got away in the ship's lifeboats. The minefield (162 mines) had been laid seven days previously by the surface raider *Orion*.

In mid Atlantic the cruel and ruthless Hellmuth Von Ruckteschell was now on the rampage in the German raider *Widder*; he was the only enemy naval captain brought to trial and convicted as a war criminal in 1947. Coming across British Tanker's *British Petrol* (6,891 grt), which had been requisitioned by the Admiralty as a Royal Fleet Auxiliary and was sailing independently, he quickly brought his guns to bear and sent her to the bottom in position 20N 50W approx.

Within seventeen days at this period in the war the Blue Star Line lost three ships, totalling 42,089 grt; two refrigerated cargo ships, one of which was fitting out at Harland & Wolff's yard in Belfast at the outbreak of war, together with the cruise liner *Arandora Star*, one of the best known ships in the world whose usual waters were those of the Scandinavian capitals, the Mediterranean and the West Indies.

The new 16 knot 13,212 ton *Wellington Star* was 300 miles west of Cape Finisterre on her homeward voyage from Melbourne on 16 June with a cargo of wool and refrigerated foodstuffs when, although zig-zagging and at full speed, she was torpedoed by *U-101* commanded by Lieutenant Fritz Frauenheim. She was quickly down by the head and after Captain Williams and the ship's company had abandoned ship, *U-101* fired a second torpedo, then surfaced and shelled the Blue Star vessel setting her afire. Three of the lifeboats were picked up by a French vessel and landed at Casablanca whilst a fourth boat was adrift for eight days before reaching Oporto.

The cargo ship *Avelona Star* (13,376 grt) homeward-bound from South America with a refrigerated cargo which included 8,800 tons of frozen meat was commodore ship of SL38 from Freetown when at 2130 hours on 30 June she was torpedoed by *U-43*, just twelve hours after *Clan Ogilvy* had been torpedoed by *U-65*. (Although the crew took to the boats they later returned and brought her into Falmouth.) *Avelona Star* was only 100 miles from where *Wellington Star* had been sunk and as the ship lifted forward with the explosion, killing four members of the crew, a huge column of water was sent skyward and she took a twenty degree list to starboard, following which one of the boilers blew up enveloping her in a large cloud of steam. Captain Hopper quickly gave the order to abandon ship, the survivors being picked up by the tramp *Beignon*, a 1939-built motor vessel owned by Morels of Cardiff, which was herself torpedoed, together with Chapman's *Clearton* by *U-30* in the early hours of the following morning. A total of 110 were on board *Beignon*, a vessel equipped for a crew of 30, and many found themselves hanging on to pieces of wood and overladen rafts. Fortunately the survivors of the three ships were rescued by the destroyers *Vesper* and *Windsor* which eventually landed them in Plymouth.

It was the day after *Arandora Star* (15,501 grt) returned from St Jean de Luz that she embarked 1,213 German and Italian internees plus 86 German prisoners of war at Liverpool for St John's Newfoundland. In addition there was a military guard of 200 together with 174 officers and crew. Unescorted and zig-zagging (unnotified, as the enemy complained after the event) she was steaming at 15 knots when she was torpedoed just before dawn on 2 July by Prien's *U-47* in position 55.20N 10.33W. The after engine room flooded at once to sea level, the ship was plunged into complete darkness, two lifeboats were smashed, she took on a twenty degree list and panic reigned as many of the Germans and Italians refused to jump to the liferafts which had been thrown from the upper deck, at the same time they overcrowded the ten lifeboats which were lowered. At 0720 hours the *Arandora Star* with bows raised rolled over on her side and then went under carrying many with her – the death roll was 805 including Captain Moulton, twelve of his officers and 42 crew.

The latter part of June heralded the start of the German E-boat campaign – powerful torpedo boats with a speed of 40 knots carrying a heavy punch in the way of armament. They were to harass coastal shipping even to the end of the war. On 19 June E-boats based at Boulogne made repeated attacks on *Roseburn* (3,103 grt) owned by Smith Hogg & Co. Ltd, three miles east of Dungeness when one of four torpedoes fired struck the stern, an attack followed up by machine gunning which eventually led to the crew abandoning ship. Arriving from New Zealand for the Tyne with timber, she was eventually beached off Denge Mash west of Dungeness. Four days later in the same area the steamer *Albuera* (3,477 grt), belonging to Ch. Salvesen & Co., en route from Halifax, Nova Scotia to the Tyne with pit props, was torpedoed; the 29 survivors were rescued by a Dutch ship.

During the first week of July two outward bound ocean convoys (OA177 and OA178) were subjected to combined air and E-boat attacks in the English Channel. During the month of July a total of 40 Allied ships (75,698 grt) were sunk in the Channel by air attacks. During the passage of OA177, comprising 22 ships, Alfred Holt's 10,058 ton *Aeneas*, the commodore ship and the largest ship in the convoy, received the lion's share of the attention from the attacking Ju87's. Approaching Start Point, the *Aeneas*, commanded by Captain Evans and with a crew of 120 officers and men, was hit by two bombs, one of which hit amidships in the cross bunker trunkway causing great devastation in the engine room and blowing out the starboard side. Eighteen crew were killed, the survivors being rescued by the destroyer *Witherington*. A further member of the crew died in hospital.

Two days later on 4 July, OA178 comprising fourteen heavily laden ships, was badly hit; there was no air cover off Portland and the Ju87's were coming in waves of six at a time. Bombed and sunk was Reardon Smith's motor vessel *Dallas City* of 4,952 grt; damaged were the *Antonio*, *Argus Hill*, *Briarwood*, *Eastmoor*, and *Lifland*. Later the same day the enemy returned to Portland Harbour where several ships were taking shelter. Ignoring the shore-based AA defences, they sank the naval anti-aircraft ship *Foylebank* and a small tug damaging three large merchant ships, the *City of Melbourne*, *East Wales* and the motor vessel *William Wilberforce*. At dusk OA178 lost the 4,343 grt *Elmcrest* thirteen miles south of Portland from an E-boat attack, and the *Hartlepool* (5,500 grt) was damaged. The *Elmcrest*, owned by the Crest Shipping Company, outward bound for Newfoundland to load iron ore, lost sixteen of her crew of 38.

The result of these attacks was that OA convoys were cancelled and ships from the Thames and East Coast ports were routed around the north of Scotland to Loch Ewe on the west coast. Further, Churchill ordered English Channel coastal convoys to be provided with a six plane escort though rarely were six aircraft available. Inward ships were re-routed to the Clyde, the Mersey and the Bristol Channel ports, the latter playing a far greater part in the import of essential foodstuffs and munitions for defence. The ports of Great Britain and Northern Ireland were now also under attack – there were many vicious raids. The first phase was in July 1940 when Dover, Weymouth, Portland, Plymouth, Falmouth and Cardiff were bombed in daylight.

There was a series of air-raids on Portland, serving as a haven of refuge from E-boats. On 11 July the *Peru* (6,961 grt) and the *Eleanor Brooke* (1,037 grt), both at anchor, were severely damaged, and the *City of Melbourne* was damaged a second time. At Cardiff, the 5,919 ton tanker *San Felipe* was damaged on 9 July; eleven days later the 2,290 ton *Stesso* was sunk alongside the quay. At Falmouth on 10 July the enemy sank the 6,499 ton fleet auxiliary tanker *Tascalusa* and damaged the *British Chancellor* (7,085 grt). To men of the Merchant

Navy it meant they were now hunted even in port. To drop anchor, to tie up fore and aft, was no longer a time to relax.

Coastal convoys CW6, CS7 and CW8, heavily attacked by Ju87 and Ju88 aircraft, all suffered losses. The shattering of CW8 came on 'Black Thursday' during the last week of July when 90 aircraft were followed up by a flotilla of E-boats. Of the 21 colliers and coasters which sailed westward around 'Hellfire Corner' from the Thames estuary, only eleven passed Dungeness, and of these, only two reached their destination.

The enemy surface raiders secured notable successes during July 1940, sinking eight British vessels totalling 49,444 tons, six in the Atlantic and two in the Indian Ocean. The raider *Thor* (3,862 grt) had sailed from Germany on 6 June and a month later was cruising in the Atlantic south of the Equator, sinking *Delambre* on 7 July, *Gracefield* on 14 July and *Wendover* two days later. Lamport and Holt's *Delambre* of 7,032 grt was on passage from Rio Grande for Liverpool when she was shelled and sunk in position 04.00S 26.00W approximately. All the crew were taken aboard the raider.

Widder, meanwhile, was in the North Atlantic north of the Leeward Islands. *Davisian* (6,433 grt, owned by T. & J. Harrison Ltd) was shelled without justification on 10 July, as the captain, under threat of being blasted out of the water, instructed that the radio should not be used nor were preparations to be made to fire the 4-inch gun. Nevertheless Von Ruckteschell ordered his men to fire, later claiming that men he had observed running aft were in fact making their way to the gun on the poopdeck. Three of *Davisian*'s crew were killed.

Three days later the motorship *King John* (5,228 grt belonging to the King Line) was sunk by *Widder* after Captain Smith instructed his radio officer to send a distress call resulting in three being killed and six injured. The 59 survivors (which included 21 rescued by the *King John* after their ship had been torpedoed by a U-boat) were led by Captain Smith in an attempt to escape by pointing their boat away from the raider, but reluctantly they had to surrender and were taken prisoner.

Atlantis sank two vessels in the Indian Ocean during July, the *City of Bagdad* on 11 July and *Kemmendine* two days later. Ellerman's *City of Bagdad* (7,506 grt) sailed from Lourenço Marques for Penang on 28 June with a full cargo loaded in the UK. Her instructed route took her between Madagascar and Mauritius and at 0730 hours on 11 July, as she was about to cross the Equator, longitude 90.00E, a vessel came into sight before the starboard beam; her appearance and behaviour were such as to indicate a modern British cargo vessel; already she had changed her Japanese disguise. After passing astern, however, she suddenly rounded up to a parallel course, increasing her speed as she came up on the port quarter.

When about one and a half miles off, *Atlantis*, flying a signal not understood at the time either by Captain White or his chief mate, opened fire as *City of Bagdad* was transmitting her distress signal. The signal being flown by the raider instructed that no radio was to be used nor was the order to abandon ship to be given. Rogge, the commander of *Atlantis*, pounded her with 42 rounds before he sent his boarding party on board to place bombs in the engine room. Considerable damage was done to the foredeck and hatches by the shells. The chief radio officer who stuck at his post until the radio room itself was struck suffered a smashed knee, the same salvo bringing down the foretopmast and the aerial with it. Two seamen were killed and a quartermaster seriously injured. He later died aboard the raider.

It was surprising that the casualties were so small in view of the almost point blank range at which *City of Bagdad* was under fire but this was probably because Captain Rogge directed his fire at the foredeck rather than the amidships accommodation and the engine room. As he had expected to make a capture on the previous day and *City of Bagdad* was some 24 hours late because of bad weather, it would appear an agent in Lourenço Marques had communicated the route and date of sailing.

The time bombs exploded at about 1400 hours, the vessel finally disappearing about eight minutes later. The survivors, with the exception of the chief engineer and those injured, spent 108 days on *Atlantis*, 28 days on the Yugoslav prize ship *Durmitor* and 96 days in the Italian prison camp in Somaliland. Here the fourth and fifth engineers died of dysentery in appalling conditions.

The chief engineer (because of his age) and the injured were transferred to the prize ship *Tirrana* for the voyage back to Europe. However the Chief was drowned when the *Tirrana* was intercepted and sunk; a quartermaster and the radio officer survived to spend the rest of the war in prison camps in Germany.

On 15 June the sixth enemy raider sailed from Germany. The 7,766 ton *Pinguin* was undetected as she entered the Denmark Strait and set her course for Ascension Island. It was in these latitudes (05.26S 18.06W) on 31 July that she sighted *Domingo de Larrinaga*, belonging to the Larrinaga Steamship Co. Ltd, one of many famous British tramp shipping companies no longer in existence.

Larrinaga's was founded in Liverpool in 1864 by the redoubtable
Captain Ramon de Larrinaga, a Basque from Bilbao. On voyage
from Bahia Blanca to Belfast with grain, *Domingo de Larrinaga* was
making for Freetown to join an SL convoy when she challenged
Pinguin to a fight but Captain Chalmers had to admit defeat after his
bridge and amidships accommodation had been wrecked and eight
of his crew had been killed by repeated shelling. Thirty survivors
were taken on board *Pinguin* which then set course for a rendezvous
with her supply ship in the Indian Ocean.

U-boats and long range bombers working from bases in Western
France were now able to reach much farther out into the Atlantic.
Many were now operating from Lorient and with the threat of
Italian submarines entering the arena the outlook for the merchant
fleet was grim indeed. From the middle of July until October was a
period when the U-boats literally pounced on the lifeline of Britain,
whether sailing independently or in convoy the merchant vessel was
at a great risk, it was called 'the happy time' by the ace U-boat
commanders but to the Merchant Navy it was the commencement of
the Battle of the Atlantic, a campaign that lasted three long years.
The Atlantic holocausts were many, the cream of Britain's merchant
fleet was destroyed and many of her gallant seamen perished.

When *U-57* sailed, it was Lieutenant-Commander Erich Topp's
first command – his orders took him to the North-Western
Approaches where on 17 July he intercepted convoy HX55 from
Halifax Nova Scotia – *U-61* had already sunk *Scottish Minstrel* six of
her crew being killed in the explosion; Brocklebank's *Manipur* (8,652
grt) the second vessel to be hit, had loaded valuable war material at
ports along the US east coast. She was struck by two torpedoes fired
by *U-57* off Cape Wrath. There were only five minutes for Captain
Mallett and 64 survivors to lower the lifeboats and stand off before
she plunged beneath the swell taking fifteen of her crew to their
grave; five others were wounded.

The following week, on 26 July, Elder Dempster Ltd lost their first
vessel, the 15 knot twin-screw motorship *Accra* of 9,337 grt. Outward
bound in a convoy of 30 ships for the west coast of Africa, serving as
Vice Commodore ship, she was torpedoed by *U-34* (Lieutenant-
Commander Wilhelm Rollmann) south-west of Rockhall in position
55.40N 16.28W. Her complement was 496 including a crew of 163.
Struck on the starboard side amidships at 1447 hours the engine
room was wrecked, two lifeboats were destroyed and two damaged,
there being considerable destruction on the promenade deck.
Although she developed a list to starboard the remaining lifeboats

were lowered and passengers and crew abandoned ship by the use of rope ladders under the close supervision of Captain Smith and his officers. *Accra* sank some twenty minutes after she had been struck, with the loss of nineteen lives who were drowned when the motor lifeboat capsized in the choppy sea. The survivors were picked up by the *Hollinside* (herself torpedoed 3 September 1942) the Norwegian *Loke*, who rescued 137 at considerable risk to herself, the sloop *Enchantress* and the corvette *Clarkia*. *U-34* continued her trail of destruction by sinking *Vinemoor*, *Sambre* and *Thiara*, all in the space of twelve hours.

U-99, with Otto Kretschmer in command, sailed from Lorient on 24 July, sinking four British ships between 28 and 31 July. His first kill was Blue Star's *Auckland Star* (13,212 grt), only twelve months old and commanded by Captain MacFarlane. She was homeward-bound from Australia via the Cape of Good Hope heavily laden with a cargo which included 10,700 tons of refrigerated meat. Steaming at 16½ knots and zig-zagging on the morning of the 28th, she was suddenly torpedoed just before dawn (position 57.17N 12.32W) the explosion ripping out the port side of number 5 and 6 holds. She started to settle at once and 30 minutes later the captain gave orders for the ship to be abandoned. A little later a second torpedo pierced the engine room, sending debris flying high into the sky. Kretschmer, in an effort to finish the job quickly, fired yet another torpedo before the *Auckland Star* rolled over to port, flung her bows into the air and sank by the stern. The crew got away in the four lifeboats and landed safely on the Irish coast three days later.

U-99 went on to sink the *Clan Menzies* the following night and *Jamaica Progress* and *Jersey City* on 31 July. The 7,336 ton *Clan Menzies* under the command of Captain Hughes, homeward-bound from Melbourne, was steaming independently at 17 knots when she was mortally wounded by a torpedo which struck the starboard side of the engine room killing two engineers and four Lascar seamen. *Jamaica Progress* (Captain McColm), the 5,475 grt banana boat owned by Jamaica Banana Producers Steamship Company, was also proceeding independently. Fifty miles north-west by west of Skerryvore she was caught; seven were killed and one wounded in the explosion. Kretschmer then caught up with an outward-bound convoy in approximately 9 West, making his attack together with *U-59*. *Gloucester City*, the BEF ammunition ship, had now returned to familiar territory carrying china clay from Fowey to Trenton, New Jersey, and steaming in the fourth position in the middle column was designated rescue ship. This was a recent innovation in order that the hard-pressed escorts could be saved the responsibility of rescuing survivors so that they could concentrate on the job of sinking the enemy. It was the *Gloucester City* that rescued survivors from Reardon Smith's *Jersey City* (6,322 grt) in position 55.47N 09.18W. Two members of the crew were killed in the explosion.

Thirty-three British merchant vessels were sunk by U-boats in the North Atlantic during August 1940. A further two converted passenger ships were also lost, the armed merchant cruiser *Transylvania* on 10 August and *Dunvegan Castle* on 28 August. Both were on ocean convoy escort, depleting still further the number of escorts that could work with the HX convoys in mid Atlantic; HX60, HX61 and HX62, sailing at weekly intervals, were all attacked.

The larger type submarines (such as *U-99*) were now coming into service, the most successful operational submarines of all time and of any navy. Of about 700 tons and a crew of 44, five torpedo tubes, a surface speed of 18 knots, an underwater speed of 10 knots, they had a range of some 9,000 miles. On 4 August Winston Churchill minuted his concern to the First Lord of the Admiralty, Mr A.V. Alexander, and the First Sea Lord: 'The repeated severe losses in the North Western Approaches are most grievous and I wish to feel assured that they are being grappled with the same intense energy that marked the Admiralty treatment of the magnetic mine.'

Three Red Duster ships from convoy HX60 were lost during six hours of battle, some 400 miles west of the Hebrides on the morning of 4 August. *U-52* (Lieutenant Otto Salman) had shadowed the convoy for two days clinging to the wake of the sole escort waiting for cloud to obscure the moon. He was rewarded when he sank *Gogovale* and *King Alfred* simultaneously and the *Geraldine Mary* some six hours later. The 5,272 ton *King Alfred* was en route from St John's Newfoundland to Methil and lost five of her crew in the torpedo explosion.

On the same day a short distance to the north-east the outward bound 8 knot convoy OB193 of 53 ships was attacked by *U-56* with Lieutenant Otto Harms in command. Elder Dempster's *Boma* (5,408 grt, Captain Anders) had loaded coal at Cardiff. She was in third line astern and sixth from the port side so that she virtually occupied a central position, considered probably to be the safest, yet at 2048 hours she was struck without warning, ripping open the deck by way of number 3 hatch; the beams were blown sky high and much of the engine room destroyed together with one of the four lifeboats on the boat deck above. Three engine room crew were killed outright. The survivors were picked up by the Norwegian *Vilja* which had been appointed rescue ship and although the escorting destroyer and an aircraft from Coastal Command endeavoured to detect the enemy, *U-56* escaped. It is possible that Lieutenant Harms had surfaced to periscope level within the columns of the convoy, crash diving immediately after the explosion, a tactic successfully employed during the battles to come.

The 7,257 ton *Mohamed Ali el-Kebir*, an Egyptian vessel owned by the Pharaonic Mail Line but registered in London, was the only casualty of HX61, being torpedoed by *U-38* at dusk on 7 August in position 55.22N 13.18W. She was carrying troops and military stores, 110 lives being lost out of a total complement of 860.

Two degrees west on the following day Houlder's *Upwey Grange* (9,130 grt), commanded by Captain Williams, was struck by two torpedoes, the first entering the engine room on the port side and the second at number 6 hatch, both explosions being of great violence; the ship immediately settled by the stern. Fifteen minutes later, after *U-37*, the attacking submarine, had surfaced, and with the crew at close quarters in the lifeboats, she went down absolutely vertical and quite slowly. The following evening the lifeboats became separated owing to heavy weather and nothing further was heard of Captain Williams and the 30 other survivors in his boat although sometime later the bodies of Chief Engineer Mackrow and Apprentice Butcher were washed ashore on the Irish coast. The remainder of the crew were picked up by the steam trawler *Naniwa* on the evening of 10 August. The *Upwey Grange* was one of fifteen vessels and Captain Williams was one of three masters, lost by Houlder Bros during the Second World War.

On 12 August British Tankers' 8,406 ton motorship *British Fame* in convoy OB193, had the distinction of becoming the first vessel sunk by an Italian submarine during the Second World War. *Malaspina* (Commander Mario Leoni) was now based at Bordeaux and under the command of Admiral Dönitz operating from Lorient. She had just taken up her cruising position between Madeira and the Azores.

The motorship *Empire Merchant* (ex *Pomona*) of 4,864 grt, owned by the Ministry of Shipping and managed by Kaye Son & Co., was the first vessel sunk by *U-100*, one of the new class V11A boats. *U-100* was captained by Lieutenant Schepke, previously commander of *U-3* and *U-19*, who went on to become one of Germany's most successful aces. On 28 August during an attack on convoy OA204 he torpedoed five ships within three hours. *Empire Merchant* was on voyage from Avonmouth to Kingston Jamaica when she was torpedoed on 16 August 1940 in position 55.23N 13.24W.

On the same day the Clan Line lost the sixth vessel of their fine fleet. Built in 1911, the *Clan MacPhee* (6,628 grt) had survived the First World War but she was caught by *U-30* waiting for the dispersal of convoy OB197 from Liverpool and the Bristol Channel. Setting course for Freetown en route for East Africa and Bombay she had already lost sight of the American-bound ships when the torpedo struck amidships sinking her in eight minutes and taking her master, Captain Granwell down with her. Only three members of the crew were injured in the explosion but more than 30 lost their lives when one of the lifeboats fell from the davit during launching. The survivors were rescued by the Hungarian *Kelet* the following morning but she too was sunk two days later after being torpedoed and shelled by the submarine *UA*. The survivors of *Clan Macphee* spent five days adrift in the Atlantic before they were finally rescued.

The Battle of the Atlantic continued in all its fury. Twenty-two out of the 33 ships lost between 19 and 31 August were British; it was the most successful two week period the German U-boat Command achieved throughout the whole war. The German strength was now increased to 57 operational boats, assisted by the 27 boats of Mussolini's Italian Atlantic Flotilla, a force nevertheless which proved largely to be ineffective.

The first convoy from Sydney, Cape Breton, to the UK sailed at the middle of the month. These were slow convoys designated SC and were designed to speed up the HX convoys and relieve the congestion at Halifax. Up until the assembly port was moved to New York in September 1942 there were considerable losses, both in ships and in personnel. SC1 was attacked by *U-37* on 24 August losing the escort sloop *Penzance*, the 4,141 ton *Blairmore* and the Norwegian *Eva* by *U-28* two days later. The other successful convoy attacks were mounted against OB202, HX65, OA204 and OB205.

Convoy OB202 lost the *Cumberland* and the *Saint Dunstan*, and the *Havildar* was damaged, in a U-boat attack 25 miles north by east off Malin Head, Co Donegal, just before midnight on 24 August. In all three incidents the torpedoes were fired by *U-57* with Lieutenant-Commander Erich Topp in command. The death toll in Federal's *Cumberland* (10,939 grt) was four and in the Saint Line's *Saint Dunstan* (5,681 grt) fourteen. Though the latter vessel was still afloat and taken in tow on the 26th, she sank during the next day between Pladda Point and Holy Island.

Losses in Merchant Navy personnel were mounting alarmingly. Of the five British ships lost from submarine attacks against convoy HX65 on 25 August, a total of 162 lives were lost, all trained officers and seamen. Homeward-bound, approaching the north of Scotland at the time, they were the *Athelcrest* (6,825 grt), *Empire Merlin* (5,763 grt), *Fircrest* (5,394 grt), *Harpalyce* (5,169 grt) and *Pectern* (7,648 grt). For *U-124* which sank four of these vessels it was her maiden voyage – it was a particularly dark night as she sped up on the surface from astern, her 18 knots catching the slender escort unawares. For over 30 months, until she was sunk in April 1943, *U-124* was responsible for the slaughter of many of our finest young seafarers sinking 47 ships with four damaged. Even the lightships came under attack. Without the men of Trinity House the coastal convoys were at risk from the tides and treacherous currents, the sandbanks and the submerged wrecks.

The following day off Kinnaird's Head HX65 was attacked by four Heinkel 115 torpedo bombers and eight Ju88 aircraft based at Stavanger. The 1911-built *Remuera* (11,445 grt), owned by the New Zealand Shipping Company (Captain Robinson) sustained a direct hit from an aerial torpedo causing her to sink and the 5,027 ton motorship *Cape York* (Lyle Shipping Co. Ltd) was so badly damaged by bombs that she had to be abandoned the following day. This was a repetition of the Luftwaffe's success on 23 August when the Heinkel torpedo bombers from Stavanger sank the *Llanishen* and *Makalla* and badly damaged the *Beacon Grange*.

The *Makalla* (6,677 grt, Captain Bain), owned by T. & J. Brocklebank Ltd, received direct hits in the after hold and engine room and was ablaze from stem to stern within a very short while. Twelve were killed, and seventeen injured; the survivors were picked up by HMS *Leith*. During the month of August a total of nine British merchant ships were sunk by bombing and 26 damaged off the coasts of Britain and in the North Western Approaches.

The next convoy from Nova Scotia, HX66, was also badly mauled. Four ships were lost in the North Western Approaches, three of them British, the 4,804 ton *Chelsea*, the *Kyno* of 3,946 grt, and *Mill Hill* 4,318 grt. The latter, on voyage from Boston for the Tees with steel scrap, lost all her crew of 34 together with her one gunner when she sank like a stone after being torpedoed by *U-32* in the darkness of the early hours.

Enemy raiders continued to harass the world's more distant shipping routes. New Zealand Shipping Company's *Turakinia* (9,691 grt) was on passage from Sydney to Wellington where she was to complete loading with frozen meat before proceeding on her way to the United Kingdom. On 20 August in the Tasman Sea she was intercepted by *Orion*. When her radio officer sent out the distress signal the raider opened up with all her armament but Captain Laird, instructing his gunners to return the fire, brought his 4.7 inch gun to bear upon the enemy. The fight lasted some twenty minutes during which time half the crew of 56 were either killed or wounded, the ship heavily on fire and badly battered. *Orion* then approached to within one mile and fired two torpedoes both of which were on target, the second causing such serious damage that *Turakinia* sank within two minutes, Captain Laird and 34 of his officers and men going down with her. Twenty-one survivors, one of whom died later from his injuries, were picked up by the raider.

On the following day in the North Atlantic, position 26.10N 34.09W, the notorious Von Ruckteschell fought the coal carrier *Anglo Saxon* (5,596 grt), owned by Nitrate Producers Steamship Co. Ltd, in similar circumstances though with more horrific results. Having dispersed from her outward convoy she was en route from Newport for Bahia Blanca with a crew of 40 when she sank within a few minutes of heavy shelling from the raider *Widder*. Two lifeboats got away carrying about half the crew, many of them wounded but were ignored by Von Ruckteschell who set his ship on a southerly course to get away from the area as quickly as he could. By radioing the distress signal he claimed *Anglo Saxon* was resisting capture and he was quite justified in blasting her out of the sea and in his treatment of the captain and crew.

By 10 September Wilbert Widdicombe and Robert Tapscott, both seamen, were the only survivors and were reduced to drinking their own urine and alcohol from the boat's compass, eating seaweed and tiny shrimps. They were to survive in their boat for a total of seventy days after which they were cast ashore in an exhausted condition on Eleuthera Island. They were found on 30 October and taken to Nassau's Bahamas Hospital.

Atlantis sank her fourth British merchantman on 24 August when she intercepted Reardon Smith's *King City* 4,744 grt, in the Indian Ocean, position approximately 17.00S 66.00E. Requisitioned by the Admiralty as a collier, she was commanded by Captain Marshall and after being shelled and then torpedoed she rolled over and sank leaving six of her crew killed, four of whom were young cadets trapped in their burning cabin. The 38 survivors, which included Captain Marshall, were transferred to the raider to join comrades from *Scientist*, *Kemmendine* and *City of Bagdad*.

September and October 1940 proved to be two of the most costly months in respect of vessels lost. Atlantic convoys were particularly at risk, the situation being aggravated by the need to give protection to the troop convoys destined for the Middle East which were now being given priority in the light of the Italian invasion of Egypt on 14 September. Naval vessels too were being diverted from the North Atlantic to the Mediterranean which already was becoming a new theatre of war. Of the 59 merchant vessels (of 295,000 tons) sunk by U-boats in September, 40 were in convoy. By far the greatest danger lay in the U-boat packs, lying in wait for convoys, shadowing at extreme range during daylight, closing in at dusk. Flooded down with little more than their conning-towers visible, they were extremely difficult to spot, particularly as their attacks usually came from the side of the darkest horizon.

Three-quarters of the attacks were at night when the chance of rescuing survivors was slender indeed, particularly as instructions had been issued for other ships in convoy and even escorts not to stop to pick up mariners (instructions sometimes ignored) as the risk of themselves being struck was too great. There were of course those vessels designated as convoy rescue ships but they were really only an asset to vessels in the same column – often a convoy was spread over many square miles. Invariably too they were heavily laden with valuable war cargoes, the speed and manouvreability required of such ships left a lot to be desired.

Often the weather contributed to disaster, boats would be launched only to be smashed against the side of the stricken ship, they would be drawn down when she sank, or overturned later in turbulent seas. Officers and men were at their loneliest. As the days shortened so apprehension and fear grew. Even masters, that breed of men not easily drawn into controversy, were ill at ease. Captain Percival of the *City of Simla*, a master of eighteen years in command and a Royal Naval Reserve Officer, protested to his employers after his ship was sunk:

> When the *Guinean* (detailed to act as rescue vessel) had embarked about 320 persons from the *City of Simla* she had with her own crew between 360 and 370 persons in the ship, with boat accommodation for about 100 only and a torpedo into such a ship could have ended in tragedy yet she was allowed to steam the 110 miles to Gourock without an escort of any kind. The adequacy of the Naval escort is a matter for Naval Authorities only but a Shipmaster in command of a valuable ship with a valuable cargo and 167 passengers of whom 103 are women, children and infants cannot but have his own opinion. Considering the locality the inadequacy of our escort was only too sadly borne out.

The aces concentrated their attacks between 50/60 North and 5/25 West – the all important homeward-convoys; from Halifax HX71 and HX72 and from Sydney SC2 and SC3. The outward-bound convoys OA207, OB213, OB216, OB217 and OB218 also witnessed many holocausts. Stragglers and dispersed ships came in for particular attention; *Luimneach*, *St Agnes* and *Kenordoc* were even sunk by gunfire.

The first successful wolf-pack operation was against SC2, comprising 53 ships which sailed from Nova Scotia on 25 August. Manned by some 2,000 men, these ships, many old and slow, the majority dirty coalburners, virtually set out for the unknown. Three out of the five lost were British. Making contact between 7 and 9 September were Kuhnke, Kretschmer and Prien; the first to be hit was *Neptunian* (5,155 grt), owned by W.A. Souter and Co. She had left Santiago loaded with sugar on 30 July and waited several days at Sydney for all the ships to assemble. She literally disappeared during the night in position 58.27N 17.17W taking 35 of her crew and one naval gunner with her. Prien in *U-47* logged her tonnage as 10,000 which would appear to indicate that his torpedo was fired at a much larger ship but which missed and hit *Neptunian* in the adjoining column.

Seventy-five minutes later, in spite of emergency zig-zags in an effort to shake off the attacker, it was the turn of the 5,303 ton *Jose de Larrinaga* as *U-47*, from the centre of the convoy, struck again. Loaded with steel and linseed from New York for Newport, her crew of 39 and her one gunner were lost. Ellerman's *Mardinian* (2,434 grt, Methil for orders), had loaded in Trinidad and after the long haul north from the Caribbean and eastward to within 150 miles of the Hebrides, so near to her destination, she was struck by a torpedo from *U-28* killing six in the engine room. Lieutenant Gunter Kuhnke, Knight's Cross, had commanded *U-28* since the commencement of war.

Convoy SC3 followed only a week later with Bleichrodt *U-48*) sinking five ships including *Empire Volunteer*, *Kenordoc* (already mentioned) and the escort sloop *Dundee*. *Empire Volunteer* (5,319 grt, owned by the Ministry of Shipping and managed by J. Cory & Sons) was loaded with iron ore, Wabana Newfoundland for Glasgow. Whilst six of her crew were killed in the torpedo explosion, the others managed to escape before the ship plunged to the bottom.

HX72 from Halifax was subjected to a devastating attack. Prien (*U-47*) acting as weatherman sighted the 41 ships shortly after the ocean escort AMC *Jervis Bay* had left for other duties. Having only one torpedo left himself he immediately called up *U-32*, *U-43*, *U-48* and *U-65* although it was *U-99* which was first upon the scene having been in the vicinity. In a seven-hour action eleven ships carrying over 100,000 tons of American supplies and some 45,000 tons of fuel oil were slaughtered. Later, when nearing the west of Scotland, convoy HX72 experienced heavy weather and bombing by the Luftwaffe. The total loss was twelve ships of 77,863 grt.

The battle commenced at 0312 hours on 21 September when Kretschmer (*U-99*) torpedoed the motor tanker *Invershannon* (9,154 grt, Inver Tankers Ltd) in position 55.40N 22.05W. Suddenly there was a tremendous flash from the bows and she quickly began to settle by the nose. Sixteen of her crew perished in the explosion. The ship was abandoned without delay but *Invershannon* stayed afloat several hours until *U-99* fired a second torpedo which broke her in half, the stern being the last to go amid black smoke and flames.

Kretschmer then headed away to the dark side of the convoy to escape the starshells sent aloft by the escorts. From a range of some 800 yds, he then placed a torpedo amidships on *Baron Blythswood* (3,668 grt, H. Hogarth & Sons). Carrying iron ore she sank like a stone amid a huge sheet of flame taking Captain Davies and 34 crew down with her. According to recollections of the submarine crew later in the war, she sank in 40 seconds. No ship in their experience had sunk that fast. Thirty minutes later it was the turn of the 5,156 ton *Elmbank*, owned by Andrew Weir & Co. Ltd. Again the enemy was *U-99* which scored a direct hit amidships at a range of just over half a mile. Laden with timber she stayed afloat long after the crew had taken to their boats and later she was sunk by gunfire from both *U-99* and *U-47*.

During the day Kretschmer sighted a survivor on a raft like out of a Punch cartoon; he wrote in his diary: 'A tiny raft was wallowing in the swell with an oar erected as a mast with a white shirt flying from it stiffly in the wind. Balancing himself by holding on to the makeshift mast was a lone man in his underwear.' Truly this was one of the unsung heroes of the western ocean.

The crew of *U-99* were so taken up with the lone man that they later went back to search for him, took him on board, gave him dry clothes and a warm drink. They then wrapped him in blankets and put him to bed for a couple of hours with a tumbler full of brandy. Kretschmer subsequently transferred him to a lifeboat from *Invershannon* together with food and water, giving the officer in charge of the boat the course to steer for Ireland and shouting 'Good luck' as they parted their ways. The lone seaman on the raft was the only survivor from *Baron Blythswood*.

During daylight on 21 September *U-48* (Bleichrodt) torpedoed the

4,409 ton *Blairangus* (George Nisbet & Co) and the following night the slaughter continued, Schepke in *U-100* claiming seven: *Canonesa, Torinia, Dalcairn, Empire Airman, Scholar, Frederick S. Fales* and the Norwegian *Simla*. Both *Broompark* and *Collegian* were damaged.

Houlder Bros' *Canonesa* of 8,286 grt, under the command of Captain Stephenson, was sunk in position 54.55N 18.25W. She was hit by one of two torpedoes fired simultaneously; the second sank the tanker *Torinia*. The starboard side amidships was completely wrecked, the fourth engineer being killed instantly with water rapidly flooding the engine room and stokehold. Number 4 hatches were blown up and the decks abreast were buckled, one of the lifeboats was destroyed and the topmast broken. As the crew got away, they were taken aboard HMS *La Malouine*; *Canonesa* was awash from the stern to the mainmast.

Convoy OB213 of nineteen ships which sailed from the Mersey on Friday 13 September is remembered for the horrific sinking of the commodore ship *City of Benares* (11,081 grt), when 121 members of the crew were lost, together with 134 passengers of whom 77 were children being evacuated to Canada. Only thirteen children survived.

Under the Children's Overseas Resettlement Scheme young children aged from five to fifteen years were offered homes in the Dominions for the duration of the war. The scheme prospered at first and 1,530 had been sent to Canada, 577 to Australia and 202 to New Zealand in the Polish *Batory* during August together with 353 to South Africa in *Llanstephan Castle* during the same month. But on 31 August the Dutch *Volendam* (convoy OB205) had been torpedoed and seriously damaged off the west coast of Ireland whilst conveying 321 children though all on board were saved.

Built for Ellermans in 1936, *City of Benares* had a maximum speed of 16 knots but as she set out for Canada on that fateful Friday she was required to head the convoy in the centre column at the convoy speed of 8½ knots. During the early hours of 17 September the escort, consisting of a destroyer and two sloops, left, being at the limits of their range. Proceeding without ocean escort, it was necessary later that day to discontinue zig-zagging owing to adverse weather conditions and at 2205 hours, when some were already asleep, and most had retired to their cabins there was a violent explosion, almost immediately followed by the ringing of the alarms. With a confused sea, wind force 6, with squalls of gale intensity accompanied by hail and rain, *City of Benares* had been torpedoed by *U-48* (Lieutenant Heinrich Bleichrodt) in position 56.43N 21.15W.

The torpedo had hit the port side abreast No 5 hold throwing off the beams and hatches. Within minutes water began to fill the hold and Captain Nicoll ordered the lifeboats to be lowered to the embarkation deck and gave orders to abandon ship, the boats being lowered in an orderly manner some fifteen minutes from the time of the explosion. It was then that the sea claimed the lives of those who, in spite of the heavy weather, were anxious to get clear of the ship which was already beginning to break up. On reaching the sea, however, several boats were swamped; in two instances (boats Nos 5 and 7) some passengers returned to the ship, afraid to venture into the unknown. Extra buckets were lowered in an effort to bale the boats out and they were ultimately induced by the crew to re-embark in them. Some of the children in lifeboat No 8 were injured by the explosion, some seriously, and as the boat cast off, shipping water badly, they were laid flat in the bottom, the blood-tinted sea water giving indication of their plight.

Difficulty was experienced in getting the boats away from the weather side owing to the adverse conditions; two were swamped by the commotion caused in the water when the ship sank; their occupants were thrown into the water and not seen again. With the ship virtually deserted, the master and his chief mate stood together on the bridge with the senior radio officer as *City of Benares* listed heavily to port; she was rapidly sinking by the stern. With the sea coming over the after end of the promenade deck, the ship's bows rising vertically, they jumped together though Captain Nicoll and his senior radio officer were never seen again. The convoy commodore, Rear Admiral Mackinnon DSO, also went over the side at the same time and was not seen again. The time was 2245 hours, 17 September.

After the vessel sank a quantity of wreckage broke surface, several of the passengers and crew could be seen clinging to whatever they could find. The crew of the 5,088 ton *Marina*, sunk by *U-48* close by only six minutes after *City of Benares*, had yet to abandon ship. From across the dark gale-lashed sea could be heard the screams and cries of helpless children. Nothing could be done to save them. Others died from exposure in the lifeboats; twenty hours later 105 survivors were rescued by the destroyer *Hurricane*, which also had on board the survivors from *Marina*. Three children died from injuries in the ship's sick bay. One boat with 46 survivors including six children under the leadership of the fourth mate, helped by two of the escorts sent along to look after the children, was adrift for eight days until sighted by a patrolling Sunderland aircraft which directed the destroyer *Anthony* to the rescue. There were no more Children's Overseas Resettlement ships; the sailing of *Llandaff Castle* scheduled for Capetown on 20 September was cancelled.

To confuse the enemy, the number of ships sailing in OB convoys was reduced and they were despatched at more frequent intervals though of course this again aggravated the escort situation; OB216 comprising eighteen vessels sailed during the early hours of 20 September following close on the heels of the three earlier convoys. Yet again tragedy was to strike at Ellerman's City Line as another of their intermediate steamers, the 1921 built *City of Simla* (10,138 grt), bound for South Africa, was sunk only 23 hours after weighing anchor in Rothersay Bay.

After loading general cargo in London at the end of August *City of Simla* had a narrow escape from incendiary bombs in the Royal Albert Docks and again as she was proceeding under pilot's orders down Thameshaven Reach on 6 September. Later she had to avoid E-boat attacks on the East Coast convoy to Methil; later still, after rounding the north of Scotland she was attacked by a single enemy aircraft as she approached the Clyde at dawn on 17 September. During a machine gun and bombing action two violent explosions occurred which seemed to lift *City of Simla* out of the water; the bombs had missed the port side abreast the funnel by only 20 feet. It was a typical coastal voyage for a vessel still loading in the port of London.

Other vessels were less fortunate. In this Battle of Britain month it became increasingly difficult for the Royal Air Force to defend coastal shipping. Amongst those sunk by dive bombers off the Scottish coast were *Dalveen*, *Nailsea River* and Port Line's 8,043 ton *Port Denison* which was hit by an aerial torpedo six miles north-east of Peterhead. In the second run, flying from stem to stern, with the ship listing badly, the aircraft sprayed her with machine gun bullets, seriously injuring the signalman and causing many of the crew to jump overboard to seek the safety of the North Sea.

To return to convoy OB216, *City of Simla* was the leading ship of the sixth column and was carrying a total complement of 345, of which 165 were crew, the passengers having boarded at anchor in Rothesay Bay. Adjacent was *Trefusis* (sunk in the Atlantic 5 March 1943) acting as commodore ship, speed 7 knots. The convoy was being closely trailed by *U-138* on her maiden voyage and captained by the experienced Commander Wolfgang Luth, previously in command of *U-9*. Shortly after 2100 hours, *U-138* torpedoed three ships within the space of five minutes: the tanker *New Sevilla* (13,801 grt);

the *Empire Adventure* (5,145 grt, 22 of her crew of 29 perished) and the Panamanian *Boka*.

The night of 21 September, lit by a bright harvest moon and with the convoy steering a north-westerly course, was suddenly rocked by a deafening explosion as at 0227 hours the torpedo struck the starboard side of *City of Simla* abreast the mainmast. She immediately took a heavy list to starboard but after a few minutes righted herself and began to settle by the stern. The starboard engine had been smashed and the hatches on Nos 5 and 6 holds had been blown off; the water was rising fast. Cargo from No 6 hold and the No 7 lifeboat was thrown as far as the gun platform on the poopdeck. By the time Captain Percival had given the order to abandon ship, the *City of Simla* had settled so fast that it was possible to put passengers into the boats direct from the after deck. By 0300 hours all boats were standing off well clear of the ship with two passengers and one of the native crew dead in their cabins from the explosion.

As indicated earlier, rescue was made by the *Guinean* (United Africa Company) which was in ballast making it particularly difficult to haul the passengers and crew aboard – coal bags were used as slings in hauling infants and small children up the ship's side. *City of Simla* was still afloat at 0600 hours but was awash from the stern to forward of the mainmast and foundered very soon afterwards.

Convoy OB217 of 25 ships following three days later was also attacked, this time by a pack of five submarines, *U-29*, *U-32*, *U-37*, *U-43* and *U-46*. At midday on 25 September when the convoy was in position 53.00N 20.00W approximately, the escort instructed the ships to disperse for their many destinations. Within a period of 36 hours five vessels were sunk: *Corrientes*, *Darcoila*, *Eurymedon*, *Sulairia* and the Norwegian *Tancred*.

Eurymedon (6,223 grt, Alfred Holt & Co. Ltd) was caught by *U-29* which left Wilhelmshaven on her sixth war cruise on 2 September. *Sulairia* (5,820 grt) had been torpedoed 30 minutes earlier. All the engine room crew were killed instantly and two lifeboats were destroyed as the torpedo struck the port side – the topmast and radio aerials completely collapsed. After 45 minutes a second torpedo devastated the starboard side destroying the two starboard lifeboats which were about to be lowered from the davits. The passengers and crew who were in them were killed. The total death roll was twenty crew and nine passengers. Captain Webster and his chief mate remained aboard after the rest of the crew had abandoned ship in the hope that she could be towed to port but with *Eurymedon* sinking lower in the water, and a westerly gale forecast, the attempt had to be abandoned. They were taken off by the Canadian destroyer *Ottawa* and *Eurymedon* sank at 2000 hours on 27 September.

Darcoila (4,084 grt, belonging to Douglas & Ramsey), sailing in ballast from the British Channel for Philadelphia, was lost without trace. She was torpedoed by *U-32* on the afternoon of 26 September in approximately 26.00W, the final loss from OB217; it is probable that the westerly gale in the area gave the crew no opportunity to save themselves.

Convoy OB218 was following only two days behind. On 25 September, in position 54.50N 10.00W, it was sighted by *U-137*, another new boat pressed into service. She was commanded by peacetime professional Herbert Wohlfarth, previously commander of *U-14*. Manchester Liners' *Manchester Brigade* of 6,042 grt was the first to be torpedoed; the time was 50 minutes past midnight. Acting as commodore ship, Captain Clough together with 51 of his men perished, as did the commodore, Vice-Admiral H.H. Smith. *Ashanian*, 4,917 grt (damaged), followed a few minutes later and the tanker *Stratford* went up in a sheet of flame 45 minutes after. Then the waters were peaceful for 38 hours. However *U-32* had been called up after sinking *Darcoila* and steering an easterly course she made contact with *Empire Ocelot* (5,759 grt) just three hours after the convoy dispersed on 28 September. Soon after the torpedo was fired she surfaced to finish *Empire Ocelot* off by gunfire. The protection of Atlantic convoys had become a nightmare, both to the Admiralty and to those who sailed in them.

Fast independently routed ships were no longer safe from aerial attack. The *Aska*, of 8,323 grt, owned by the British India Steam Navigation Company, sailed for Britain from Bathurst on 7 September carrying 350 French troops, some of whom wished to return to France and others to join General de Gaulle. At 0230 hours during a bright moonlit night nine days later she was steaming at 19 knots off Rathlin Island in the North Channel when an aircraft suddenly appeared over the bow dropping two heavy calibre bombs. They passed through the engineers' quarters exploding in the engine room; a further bomb hit the fo'c'sle and the master gave instructions to abandon ship. Six engineers and six Indian crew were killed, the survivors being rescued by the armed trawler *Jason* which, because of lack of space, had to tow some of the lifeboats behind her. The burnt out hulk of the *Aska* later drifted ashore.

During this second September of the war the Ben Line lost two of its fleet, both to surface raiders in the Indian Ocean and within 48 hours of each other. The *Benarty* (5,800 grt) was sunk by *Atlantis* on 10 September, in position 18.40S 70.54E, followed by *Benavon*, caught by *Pinguin* disguised as a Norwegian trader, in position 26.00S 51.00E approximately, a brutal action which resulted in 24 of her crew losing their lives.

The *Benavon* was one of the few Allied vessels that dared to stand up to raiders. Homeward-bound from Penang via the Cape she engaged in a gun battle although outclassed in every department. The shelling went on for about an hour inflicting great structural damage with *Benavon* becoming a blazing inferno and with all but one of her lifeboats destroyed; the one remaining was badly damaged. *Pinguin* fired some 60 shells from her 5.9 inch guns, one of the last killing Captain Thomson who was directing the survivors to abandon ship and who, never leaving the bridge, fought with his ship to the last.

On the home front the war at sea was overshadowed by the blitz on both London and Liverpool with the brunt of the attack being borne by merchant seamen, dockers and the fire fighting services. In the three nights of raids on London commencing on 7 September, the 5,049 ton *Minnie de Larrinaga* was a total loss and eighteen vessels of 84,336 tons were damaged.

Of the five steamers in Victoria Dock only one, the *Duquesa* (8,651 grt), was afloat when dawn broke on 9 September. Owned by Houlder Bros, she was sunk three months later on the Equator by *Admiral Scheer*. Her sister ship *Baronesa* was seriously damaged in the Royal Albert Dock when a bomb fell between the ship's side and the quay. The explosion split many plates abreast the engine room which soon began to fill with water together with Nos 4 and 5 holds. The ballast pumps and general pumps kept the vessel afloat until Admiralty pumps finally pumped her dry twelve days later. Glen Line's *Glenstrae* (9,460 grt), commanded by Captain Coulton, was passing through locks to her berth in the King George V Dock as the raid started. Whilst one bomb burst six feet from the port side, another passed through her decks and through No 4 deep tank which was full of copra. An hour later the bomb exploded causing considerable damage.

Another Glen Line vessel, the 9,809 grt *Glenroy*, was seriously damaged in Liverpool on 12 September. In the Canada Dock, Royal Mail's *Highland Princess* was struck on the starboard side by a large bomb. She quickly took fire, five of her crew were injured and it was some hours before the flames were brought under control. On 26

September the *Diplomat, Peterton* and *West Kedron* were all damaged in Brunswick Dock, the tanker *Henry Dundas* was bombed and damaged whilst at anchor in the Mersey four days later. Liverpool was again the target on 11 October when the *Clan Cumming, Clan MacTaggart, Highland Chieftain* and *Virgilia* were all seriously damaged, a total tonnage of 34,744.

For the enemy October 1940 was the happiest of the Atlantic happy time. In just one week the U-boats sank 27 British merchant ships. During the period of the full moon, two convoys were cut to pieces with the loss of 31 ships; everything was overshadowed by the disasters which beset convoys SC7 and HX79. Altogether it was a cruel month: HX77, OB227, OB228 and OB229, *Highland Patriot, Benlawers, Natia, Empress of Britain* and many more. Were the Germans on the brink of victory on the high seas?

Convoy SC7 it has been said, sailed into the history books as the victim of one of the biggest and most painful surprises sprung by the Germans in the war at sea. Thirty-five ships sailed, half of them British. Only fifteen arrived safely. It was a massacre. At noon on 16 October, eleven days out of Sydney, they reached the furthest north, 59.31N; as they passed the 21st meridian they entered the danger zone but already one straggler had been sunk, a Canadian 'laker', the *Trevisa*. As the day wore on, a total of nine U-boats converged.

U-48 was the first to make contact during the night that followed; the ex-French tanker *Languedoc* (9,512 grt), vice-commodore ship, was sunk just as the middle watch came on duty. *Haspenden* (4,678 grt) followed, though she remained afloat and subsequently made port. Simultaneously Ropner's *Scoresby* (3,843 grt) was torpedoed in No 3 hold abaft the engine room; the water began filling the hold immediately and she began to settle by the stern. She had loaded 1,586 fathoms of pitprops at Francis Harbour on the coast of Labrador both below and above deck. As *Scoresby* began to sink the pitprops on deck moved dangerously imperilling the crew as they launched the lifeboats. In less than five minutes she slid stern first and near vertical. At daybreak the survivors, from both *Languedoc* and *Scoresby*, were rescued from a sea of pitprops by the corvette *Bluebell*.

During daylight on the seventeenth, *U-38* torpedoed the Greek straggler *Aenos* and although throughout the day the escorts made the long search for the enemy, no trace of them could be found. Led by the commodore ship *Assyrian*, the convoy forged ahead by nightfall passing 15 West. But the U-boats lay in ambush, *U-38, U-46, U-99, U-100, U-101* and *U-123*, the battle really commencing at

0204 hours the following morning. During the next 27 hours sixteen of the convoy were sunk and two were damaged. The first to attack was *U-38*; the *Carsbreck* (3,670 grt) shuddered violently as the torpedo struck and then listed to port. Although she started to settle by the head, her cargo of timber kept her afloat; by midday she was limping along at 5 knots leaving a trail of timber in her wake. The *Carsbreck* was torpedoed and sunk in the North Atlantic the following year (24 October 1941). On the night of the eighteenth, the destruction continued – *Beatus*, *Creekirk*, *Empire Miniver*, *Blairspey* (damaged), *Shekatika*, *Fiscus*, *Assyrian*, *Empire Brigade*, *Sedgepool*, and *Clintonia* together with six Allied and two Swedish vessels.

Beatus (4,885 grt) and *Fiscus* (4,815 grt), Cardiff tramp steamers belonging to the Tempus Steamship Company, had both loaded steel ingots, timber and crated aircraft on deck at Three Rivers on the St Lawrence river. *U-46* dealt *Beatus* a deadly blow with the sea rushing in following the violent explosion; there was a gaping hole in her side, she shuddered to a stop and began to settle. Only the starboard lifeboat and jolly boat got away, Captain Brett and the gunner jumped overboard. The Dutch *Boekolo* following behind, slowed down to rescue survivors and as the first were climbing a rope ladder flung over the ship's side, she too was torpedoed; this time *U-123* was responsible. Eventually the survivors of both ships were picked up by HMS *Fowey*. Six months later Captain Brett was master of Tempus Steamships' *Salvus* when she was bombed and sunk during a raid upon a convoy off the east coast of England.

Captain Williams of *Fiscus* (4,815 grt) had a premonition that SC7 was doomed long before the convoy sailed. Kretschmer's torpedo (*U-99*) exploded with the most violent explosion of the night. She broke in two near the stern, the larger section keeled over and vanished, the stern section following suit a few minutes later in a sheet of flame. The log of *U-99* reads:

> Fires bow torpedo at large freighter of 6,000 grt at 750 metre range. Hits abreast mainmast. Immediately after the torpedo explosion there is another explosion with a high column of flame from bow to bridge. Smoke rises 200 metres. Ship continues to burn with green flame.

There was only one survivor. Captain Williams and 37 of his crew, which included two brothers aged fifteen and sixteen years, perished in the sea.

Empire Miniver (6,055 grt), heavily laden with iron and steel, was struck by *U-99*. The torpedo struck amidships blowing part of the port side away and shattering the lifeboats above. The oil fuel tank was blown apart, the pigs of iron in No 3 'tween deck shot into the air. The engine room was torn apart, killing the chief and fourth engineers together with the firemen on watch; the grating on the boat deck was blown away allowing anyone to fall the entire depth of the ship. The whole of the midships section was enveloped in a cloud of steam. Within ten minutes Captain Smith had abandoned ship.

The oldest ship in the convoy, the 1912-built *Creekirk* (3,971 grt) owned by Muir Young, was loaded with iron ore for Workington. Torpedoed by *U-101* she sank immediately; the entire crew of 34 including Jersey-born Captain Robilliard were lost.

The 2,962 ton *Assyrian* (Ellerman & Papayanni Lines) loaded with grain from New Orleans was torpedoed by *U-101* on the starboard side just forward of the engine room. A few minutes earlier she had tried to ram a U-boat which had crossed her bow. With her engines stopped, without light and power, starboard lifeboat smashed, steam escaping everywhere, she was a doomed vessel. In the confusion her stern crashed against the stern of the torpedoed Dutch *Soesterberg* which then, with her bow rising almost vertical before she foundered, released thousands of pitprops which shattered many of the liferafts thrown from *Assyrian*. With the Ellerman ship low in the water, her bow submerged, those left on board had neither boats nor rafts.

On the bridge of *Assyrian* were Captain Kearon, the commodore, Vice-Admiral Mackinnon, and ten others who were obliged to jump as she went under – fortunately the weather was now kind. With confusion everywhere, the sea full of people and wreckage, it was a spectacle rarely seen. Vice-Admiral Mackinnon was hauled aboard HMS *Leith* in a net after hanging on to a plank of wood for several hours; the death toll on *Assyrian* was seventeen. Captain Kearon was awarded the OBE and Lloyds War Medal for Bravery at Sea. The latter was bestowed upon officers and men of the Merchant Navy in cases of exceptional gallantry at sea. (See Appendix XV)

The *Empire Brigade* (5,154 grt) formerly the *Elios* of the Italian Lauro Line and managed by Cairns Noble & Company was torpedoed by *U-99* blowing a great hole in No 2 hold. She immediately caught fire and in near panic the lifeboats were launched without instructions and whilst she was still under way. She was quickly down by the head, the stern suddenly rising high out of the water as Captain Parkes and his officers jumped from the bridge. Still ploughing ahead, the propellers racing, she drove down into the sea with a deafening roar as water flooded the boiler room and cargo holds. According to Kretschmer's report there was a huge spout of yellow and red flame as the torpedo hit and the ship simply ripped apart. The smoke-cloud mushroomed up in a large billowing column and the ship vanished in the calm almost undisturbed sea in less than 50 seconds.

On Ropner's *Sedgepool* (5,556 grt), loaded with grain for Manchester, the torpedo from *U-123* (Lieutenant Karl-Heinz Moehle) ripped open the foredeck blowing away one side of the bridge. The captain and second mate were never seen again. The *Blairspey* (4,155 grt) of Glasgow, survived two torpedoes and later was towed into the Clyde by the tug *Salvonia*. The *Shekatika* (5,458 grt) of Leith, loaded with steel and pitprops on deck, took four torpedoes at different times during the night from two different U-boats, *U-100* and *U-123*. Wood was spewing from the holes in her sides as she began to settle, the final torpedo from *U-123* sending her under.

The 3,106 ton *Clintonia* owned by the Stag Line had loaded woodpulp at Francis Harbour. Commanded by Captain Irwin she fought a gun battle in the half moon with *U-99* only to be torpedoed thirty minutes later, the last victim of the wolf pack. The explosion blew the mainmast from the deck which came crashing down on the bridge demolishing the radio room. With the water rising rapidly in the engine room the crew abandoned ship – not before time as a second torpedo struck shortly afterwards blowing up the boiler. She sank by the stern amidst a cloud of steam as *U-123* surfaced and fired shells into her. It was the climax to a night of terror. The search for survivors continued for many hours; several taken from the water collapsed from exposure, others were found floating dead amidst the wreckage.

On the morning after the rout of SC7 (19 October) Prien's look-out sighted another convoy. This was the fast 9-knot inward convoy HX79 comprising 49 ships loaded with valuable American military supplies and petrol. Because of its importance it was given greater protection – one destroyer, two sloops, two corvettes, four armed trawlers and the Dutch submarine *O-14*. However, old type naval escort vessels and inexperienced naval seamen, again failed to sink the enemy. Thirteen ships including five tankers were wiped out in a battle spread over nine hours of darkness. Again it was a massacre.

The Red Duster vessels in the order in which they were sunk were: *Matheran, Uganda, Shirak, Wanby, Ruperra, Caprella, Sitala, La Estancia, Whitford Point* and *Loch Lomond*. The *Athelmonarch* was damaged and reached port. The 7,653 ton *Matheran* (T. & J. Brocklebank Ltd) was torpedoed on the port side No 3 hold and plunged to the bottom within seven minutes. Nine crew, including Captain Greenall, lost their lives. The eager Heinrich Liebe (*U-38*) had been the first to attack and following the pattern of the two previous nights he surfaced his boat darting between the columns. Only six minutes later he struck at Mackay & McIntyre's *Uganda* (4,966 grt). All but one of her lifeboats were destroyed when the torpedo exploded. For Ropner's *Wanby* (4,947 grt), it was only her second voyage; she had loaded in Vancouver with pig iron and timber which was stacked high on deck. Two torpedoes fired simultaneously by *U-46* and *U-47* hit forward of the engine room causing a tremendous explosion which shattered the port lifeboat and wounded Captain Kenny standing on the bridge. All 35 crew got away in the remaining lifeboat and were rescued by HMS *Angle*.

The 5,026 ton *Whitford Point* owned by the Gowan Shipping Company and sunk by Prien in *U-47* had loaded 7,840 tons of steel in Baltimore. As she broke up only three got away, 36 crew and one gunner being lost. The last ship of convoy HX79 to be torpedoed, by Schepke in *U-100* was *Loch Lomond* (5,452 grt, Royal Mail Lines) which was the designated rescue ship and had been pulling people out of the sea all night. Fortunately they were all rescued later by one of the escort vessels. It was at this time that the War Cabinet considered the introduction of small specially equipped rescue ships whose sole purpose was to accompany convoys and rescue seamen, a service that came into operation during 1941.

What of the other convoy losses during this month? HX77 was attacked by *U-37*, *U-48* and *U-101*, again in the area between 12 and 19 West. Of the six ships torpedoed and lost, three were British, the motorship *Port Gisborne*, the motorship *Pacific Ranger* and the tramp steamer *Stangrant*. The 10,144 ton *Port Gisborne* (Port Line Ltd) homeward-bound from New Zealand was under the command of Captain Kippins (later in the war he was awarded the OBE and DSC). It was dusk on 11 October, position 56.38N 16.40W as *U-48*, firing from her bow tube, struck her target amidships. Twenty-six were killed being half of the ship's company, the survivors being rescued by the tug *Salvonia*.

Convoy OB228 was attacked by *U-93* and *U-138* on 15 September and 17 September. Four vessels were sunk including the *Uskbridge* (2,715 grt) and Lamport & Holt's *Bonheur* (5,337 grt) outward-bound for Rosario. On 20 October, Elders and Fyffes' *Sulaca* (5,389 grt) was torpedoed by *U-124* whilst outward-bound, convoy OB229.

Captain Bower and 66 others were killed. This followed quickly on the tragedy of Elders & Fyffes *Samala* (5,390 grt) lost without trace on 30 September when independently routed from Kingston, Jamaica for Garston. She was torpedoed in position 46.00N 33.00W approximately by *U-37*. Her crew of 65, one gunner and two passengers all perished.

The Royal Mail 14,172 grt motorship *Highland Patriot* was torpedoed by *U-38* on the first of the month in position 52.20N 19.04W. Commanded by Captain Robinson she had left St Vincent, Cape Verde Islands, eight days earlier with 40 passengers and a full cargo of meat from Buenos Aires. She was sighted by Lieutenant Liebe of *U-38* who mistook her for an armed merchant cruiser but as the sun rose over a calm sea he fired his torpedo striking her just as the passengers were sitting down to breakfast. The order to abandon ship was given immediately as the engine room and Nos 5 and 7 lifeboats were destroyed and fire was spreading rapidly. Three of the crew were killed and five injured. As the lifeboats stood off, a second torpedo struck *Highland Patriot* sending her to the bottom, the largest vessel lost by the Royal Mail Line. The 169 survivors were picked up later in the day by the sloop *Wellington*.

The following week on 8 October Royal Mail lost the 8,715 ton *Natia* on the Equator near the Brazilian island of St Paul (00.50N 32.24W). The raider *Thor* came up from astern at 17 knots and fired a warning shot on the port quarter followed by several salvoes from her 5.9 inch guns. *Natia*'s steering gear was smashed preventing her from altering course and although she raced at full speed and dropped smoke floats over the stern, in an effort to lose the enemy, she was repeatedly hit during fifty minutes of action. With one of the lifeboats smashed, the radio room and part of the bridge wrecked, and with the engine room telegraph out of action, Captain Carr had no alternative but to stop and hoist the signal to signify he was abandoning ship.

No sooner were the lifeboats clear than *Natia* was torpedoed; she reeled drunkenly and listed to port. A second torpedo sank her and with the survivors on board, *Thor* set off at full speed. There were officers and crews of many ships aboard, some, such as those from *Delambre*, *Gracefield* and *Wendover*, had been there since the second week of July. Conditions were not good in the 'tween decks where they were quartered: there was a lack of fresh air, water for drinking was in short supply and the food barely edible.

For five weeks they cruised in the South Atlantic. On 15 November, with the exception of ships' masters, the crews transferred to the German *Rio Grande* for the voyage back to France and eventually to a prisoner of war camp in Germany. It was March 1941 before Captain Carr arrived at the camp having been held prisoner in *Thor* for sixteen weeks, then transferred to the *Nordmark* (ex-*Westerland*). Not until the survivors reached Germany were next of kin informed of their whereabouts – in many homes they were mourned as lost.

The fourth engineer of *Natia* (Mr P. Harwood), escaped from a hospital near Paris in October 1941, eventually reaching Spain where he was imprisoned. Fortunately the British Ambassador in Madrid secured Harwood's release after five months and he arrived in Glasgow in June 1942 by way of Gibraltar. Donald Beverly, the steward's boy, escaped from the train whilst crossing France and made his way to Spain where he virtually lived as a slave working for many months as a farmer's boy on a mere pittance. He eventually reached Lisbon where he secured a passage to London only to be promptly arrested on arrival as having no identity papers. It was only due to the intervention of his employers that he was at last reunited with his family.

Ben Line's *Benlawers* (5,943 grt) had performed valiant service carrying troops and equipment back from Calais in June 1940. As the Germans were within one mile of the docks, and whilst under heavy fire, she took on board 700 wounded soldiers, most of them stretcher cases, from the last train to get through. Twelve weeks later (6 October) she was sunk by *U-123* in the North Atlantic, in position 53.20N 26.10W. The convoy had dispersed two days previously and she was on passage to Port Said via Durban carrying a general cargo. Although there was a rough sea with a heavy swell at the time, Captain Campbell and his crew managed to take to the boats, with the exception of a Chinese fireman who was killed in the explosion. Some of the survivors were rescued after seven hours by the *Bengore Head* of Belfast, others after twelve hours by the Cardiff tramp steamer *Forest*. Unfortunately, as one of the lifeboats came alongside the *Forest*, she was swamped by the heavy swell and 23 lost their lives.

In the closing days of October, *Empress of Britain* (42,348 grt, Canadian Pacific Steamships Ltd) was approaching the end of her voyage from Suez via Cape Town. In addition to her crew of 419 she was carrying 224 military personnel and their families, eagerly awaiting disembarkation the following day in Liverpool. At dawn (26 October) off the north-west coast of Ireland, her fighter escort from RAF Coastal Command failed to appear as had been promised and at 0920 hours, an enemy Focke-Wulf 200 aircraft appeared from

(*Left*) Food from America arrives in Britain. Without the food ships Britain would have starved. Here a crane load of cheeses is taken from the hold of a British ship. She also carried dried milk, flour, wheat and lard. (*Right*) A merchantman being armed, 1940. Merchant ships were defensively armed. Here a 4-inch gun (background) and an anti-aircraft gun go aboard.

(*Left*) The 1923 built P&O *Maloja*, 20,914 grt. The icebound foredeck of AMC *Maloja* (converted 1939) on Northern Patrol between the Faeroes and Iceland gives a little idea of the conditions. (*Right*) The ship's pet was always a favourite. Here the pet bull terrier of P&O's *Maloja* is ensconced in a hammock. North Atlantic 1940.

(*Left*) Narvik. 9 April 1940.
During the German invasion
of Norway in April 1940, the
port of Narvik bore the brunt
of the attack. Five British
vessels were sunk in the
fjord.

(*Below*) The evacuation from
Boulogne. RAF personnel on
deck of an Isle of Man
steamer at Boulogne during
the evacuation from France,
May 1940.

the north releasing a bomb which directly hit the boat deck creating damage on four decks below. Fire spread immediately, the ship filled with black smoke and shortly afterwards the whole of the midship section was ablaze. As the aircraft was making its third run, machine gunning the bridge and scoring a further direct bomb hit, Captain Sapsworth gave the order to abandon ship. Six hours later HMS *Echo* arrived and took the survivors on board; 45 were missing.

Later in the day the fire subsided and two Admiralty tugs arrived to tow *Empress of Britain* to the Clyde. However, following communication between the Luftwaffe and U-boat headquarters at Lorient, *U-38* (Jenisch), who had sailed from his base on 24 October, was called up. By midday on 27 October she sighted the *Empress* on the horizon. Trailing the liner and evading the protecting screen of the escorting destroyers, Jenisch fired three torpedoes during the early hours of the following day, two of which found their target. *Empress of Britain* heeled over to port and quickly disappeared in position 55.16N 09.50W, the largest merchant ship to be sunk during the Second World War. Requisitioned as a troopship in November 1939 she had travelled 61,000 miles during her eleven months of service and carried 9,231 military personnel, 925 civilian passengers and 2,850 tons of cargo.

The continuous loss of merchant vessels was a mounting danger. U-boats had now sunk 471 vessels (mines and aircraft very nearly as many). The situation was of great concern both to Prime Minister Winston Churchill and his War Cabinet. Britain needed 43,000,000 tons of imports to keep up her resistance. By October 1940 this had been whittled down to an insufficient 38,000,000 ton rate. Churchill warned Roosevelt:

'The decision for 1941 lies upon the seas – unless we can establish our ability to feed this island, to import the munitions of all kinds which we need, unless we can move our armies to the various theatres – we may fall by the way.'

What did the future hold for the men at sea? Already the enemy was planning an ambitious confrontation. On 27 October the pocket battleship *Admiral Scheer* entered the Kiel Canal on passage for the west coast of Norway. By 2 November she had broken through undetected into the North Atlantic. Some 3,000 miles away in Halifax, Nova Scotia, convoy HX84 weighed anchor and set a north-easterly course. The sailing date was 28 October.

The feeling of desperation felt by those at sea at this time is perhaps best exemplified by a young Radio Officer (J.G. Smith) who before sailing, penned these lines:

I have heard the call, my love, seen the sign,
From this trip I will not return,
My fate was sealed in the mists of time,
Without me, my love, let the home fires burn.

Do not be sad, my love, that I must go,
My spirit will soar high and free,
For yourself let the tears flow,
But not for me, my love, not for me.

Farewell, my love, ours is paradise lost,
Be happy for me as I take my leave,
Keep me forever in your secret thoughts,
But do not grieve, my love, no, do not grieve.

Do not weep for me, my love,
For where I go all things start anew,
My heart leaps at what is to come, my love,
I have been to paradise before – with you.

CHAPTER THREE

Neptune's Fury
(November 1940–February 1941)

As dawn broke on 5 November 1940 the 37 ships of convoy HX84 were steaming at 8 knots in nine columns, course ENE, some 1,000 miles east of Newfoundland. They were under the protection of the armed merchant cruiser *Jervis Bay* (14,164 grt, Aberdeen and Commonwealth Line) commanded by Captain Fogarty Fegen RN She was in the centre of the convoy between the fourth and fifth columns and close to Reardon Smith's *Cornish City* (Captain Isaac) in which the Commodore Rear-Admiral Maltby had raised his standard. The Canadian escort had left the previous night and there was now a day's steaming before the escort vessels from an outward convoy would rendezvous. One ship, the Polish *Morsha Wola*, had straggled four days previously.

The largest ship in the convoy was the 16,698 ton *Rangitiki* owned by the New Zealand Shipping Co. Ltd carrying a crew of 223 together with 75 passengers, and a cargo of butter, cheese, meat and wool. There were eleven tankers carrying precious oil fuel and aviation spirit: *Athelprincess, Atheltemplar, Cordelia, Delphinula, Erodona, James J. Maguire, Oil Reliance, San Demetrio, St Gobain, Solfona* and *Sovac*. Astern of the *Cornish City* in the fifth column were Canadian Pacific's *Beaverford* and Brocklebank's *Maidan*. The remainder were a motley collection, British and foreign: *Andalusian, Anna Bulgari, Briarwood, Castilian, Cerus, Danae II, Dan-y-bryn, Delhi, Emile Franqui, Empire Penquin, Fresno City, Hjalmar Wessel, Kenbane Head, Lancaster Castle, Pacific Enterprise, Persier, Puck, Stureholm, Trefusis, Trewellard, Varcy* and *Vingaland*.

At noon HX84 was passed by Elders and Fyffes' 14 knot *Mopan*, (5,389 grt), carrying about 70,000 stems of bananas, Kingston Jamaica for Garston. She passed close abeam, Captain Sapsworth rejecting the invitation of Rear-Admiral Maltby to join the convoy.

One hundred miles to the north steamed the 10,000 ton pocket battleship *Admiral Scheer*. She had been despatched 'to relieve pressure on German operations in the North Sea and English

Channel by rapid action which would tend to upset normal
dispositions of the British escort forces'. Guided by intelligence
reports she was on course to intercept 'a large convoy ETD Halifax
Nova Scotia, 28 October'. She had broken through the Denmark
Strait, between Iceland and Greenland, undetected in weather so
violent that she had lost two men overboard despite all preparations.

Admiral Scheer, commanded by Captain Theodor Krancke, had
been designed to 'raid and run', her draft of 23 feet allowing her to
enter shallow harbours and rivers, ideal for hiding from her enemy or
refuelling and victualling from her supply tanker. With a speed of 15
knots she could sail 10,000 miles without refuelling. Equipped with
two spotter planes her six 11 inch guns could throw a shell weighing
670 lbs nearly twelve miles. Additionally she was equipped with
eight 5.9 inch and six 4.1 inch high-angle guns, eight torpedo tubes,
radar, range-finding equipment and gun-control systems.

At 1240 hours *Admiral Scheer*'s Arada reconnaissance seaplane
sighted HX84 at 88 miles distant. Flying at 10,000 feet she was too
high to be spotted and because of this she did not notice the
independent *Mopan*. Captain Krancke set full speed and altered
course at 1300 hours so as to engage the convoy at 1600 hours.
However, shortly after 1400 hours he came upon *Mopan* which was
taken completely by surprise, her DEMS gunner even believing they
had met up with a *Royal Oak* class vessel. Speed was essential to
Krancke whose aim was to destroy the convoy and steam 150 miles
during the hours of darkness. He despatched a warning shell at close
range destroying one of *Mopan*'s four lifeboats following which,
without making any distress signal, Captain Sapsworth abandoned
ship. Krancke quickly set about finishing her off, taking the
survivors on board amidst a veritable sea of bananas.

The lookout on *Rangitiki* was the first to alert the commodore after
smoke (from the burning *Mopan*) was seen on the horizon at 1545
hours and a few minutes later *Empire Penguin* confirmed the sighting.
Jervis Bay was informed. At 1635 hours Captain Fegen himself
sighted the battleship's hamper and within ten minutes he identified
her as an enemy. He immediately hauled his ship out of line towards
her, trailing a smoke screen and when he was well ahead, sent up red
rockets, a signal for other ships to set off smoke flares following which
Rear-Admiral Maltby signalled an emergency turn 40 degrees
starboard. At 1710 hours, range 10 miles, Krancke turned to bring
all six 11 inch turret guns on target and opened fire. As *Jervis Bay*
turned to port to engage with her 6 inch guns, the commodore gave

the scatter signal by which time the first salvoes were falling in the centre of the convoy.

It was then that Captain Theodor Krancke turned his full attention to the *Jervis Bay*. She was hit with the first salvo directed at her, smashing her bridge and radio room, severely wounding Captain Fegen – one of his legs was torn off and the other was smashed. Amazingly he only momentarily lost consciousness calling for the ship's surgeon to bandage the stump of his leg. He remained in command of his ship and, although outgunned and outranged, he fought back despite the fact that his midship guns were destroyed, the steering gear jammed and the superstructure burning furiously. A whole gun, its mounting and its entire crew were blown to pieces with one shell burst. Although *Jervis Bay* was a doomed ship, Captain Fegen dragged himself to the stern gun to direct its fire; for 22 minutes he stood between the might of the German Navy and the ships he was protecting.

The ship's steelwork now mangled and twisted, great holes were torn in the hull, watertight doors buckled and jammed; the dead and the dying littered the decks. Two hours after the action ceased she rolled over and sank, her colours still flying. Captain Fegen and 186 of his men were dead; 68 survivors were miraculously plucked from the water by the Swedish *Stureholm* (Captain Olander) who had turned back and lowered his boats.

Darkness was now falling and the ships were making their escape. But the *Admiral Scheer* was already amongst them, her 5.9 inch guns concentrating on the tanker *San Demetrio* (8,073 grt, Eagle Oil & Shipping Co. Ltd). She was blazing furiously and Captain Waite lost no time in abandoning ship. *Scheer* then tried to gun *Rangitiki* (Captain Barnett) which Krancke believed to be a troopship; the nearest shell, however, was fifty yards away and she escaped under cover of the smokescreen on a northwesterly course. *Andalusian* (3,082 grt, Ellerman & Pappayanni Ltd) was also attacked and although she sustained some damage to the accommodation amidships, she too escaped.

The 10,042 ton *Beaverford* then opened up with her two guns in an effort to assist *Kenbane Head* (5,225 grt), brilliantly illuminated against the night sky by a star shell which had exploded overhead. The time was 1815 hours. Firing her own gun (Japanese 1914 vintage) in an effort to defend herself, *Kenbane Head* took the full force of a salvo from *Scheer* which blew gaping holes in the sides of Nos 1 and 4 holds. She was repeatedly hit in the engine room, her funnel casing was smashed, her starboard lifeboat reduced to matchwood and the main and emergency radio aerials were carried away. With the poop hatch afire and her gun blown away, with the magazine ablaze and her steering gear damaged she listed to port and began to disintegrate, her master having no alternative but to abandon ship. The courageous 1919-built *Kenbane Head*, Ulster Steamship's third loss, sank at 1930 hours.

Meanwhile *Beaverford*, under Captain Pettigrew, continued her task of taking some of the fire well knowing that her cargo of munitions loaded in Montreal, topped up with foodstuffs and timber, could explode at any moment. *Maidan* (7,908 grt), commanded by Captain Miller, had loaded in Baltimore. She too was carrying munitions together with a variety of other cargo – iron, steel, brass, timber, tobacco and trucks. Escaping on a southerly course she was unlucky in being struck by a salvo of shells which suddenly ripped the ship apart; she became an intense ball of fire, then heeled over and sank. All hands, 90 officers and men, were lost.

Trewellard of 5,201 grt, owned by the Hain Steamship Company, (Captain Daniel) was the next to succumb to the enemy. *Scheer* used her whole armament in destroying her and she sank within minutes, her cargo of steel and pig iron taking her to the very depths of the Atlantic sea-bed. Seventeen of her crew were killed although three of her lifeboats got away. At 2245 hours the inevitable happened. Amid a tremendous roar, *Beaverford* exploded and sank with all hands, 77 officers and men. She had taken twelve rounds from the main armament of the *Admiral Scheer* and 71 rounds from her secondary armament. Three direct hits by main and sixteen by secondary armament were recorded but to sink her, Krancke had to finish her off with a torpedo.

Reardon Smith's *Fresno City* (4,955 grt), steaming at full speed on a westerly course was the final victim. As *Admiral Scheer* overtook her on a parallel course only 3,000 yards away she illuminated the whole ship by her searchlights and then shelled at very close range. One member of the crew was lost; fortunately 34 including Captain Lawson survived. The battle, officially recorded as having taken place in position 52.26N 32.34W, was at a close.

As the *Admiral Scheer* sped off at midnight to continue her cruise her commander knew full well how costly the operation had been. Whilst she had sunk the *Jervis Bay* and six merchant ships plus two ships damaged, one third of her 11 inch shells had been used together with half of her secondary armament. However, the convoy system in the North Atlantic was disorganised for twelve days; there was panic and confusion at Halifax NS as two convoys were recalled, traffic only being resumed on 17 November when HX89 sailed. Furthermore, loss of life had been heavy and alarm bells rang in Whitehall. As a direct result, major convoys forthwith received battleship escort, a measure which the British Admiralty could ill afford.

Captain Edward Stephen Fogarty Fegen of *Jervis Bay* was awarded the posthumous VC 'for valour in challenging hopeless odds and giving his life to save the many ships it was his duty to protect'. Masters of HX84 were full of admiration for the way *Jervis Bay* had drawn fire away from their ships. AMC's, in spite of their shortcomings, were admirable watchdogs against enemy surface ships and could do valiant work, particularly when commanded by such gallant seamen.

Andalusian and *San Demetrio* limped to port in spite of their 'wounds'. The second mate and chief engineer of the *San Demetrio*, and thirteen of their comrades, found their ship two days later still afloat with the fire subsided. After many attempts they reboarded her, taking ten hours to restart the engines; having no compass they steered to the Clyde by the fashion known to seamen and aviators as 'by guess and by God', covering 1,000 miles in eight days. Alas *San Demetrio** did not survive the war; she was torpedoed and lost on 17 March 1942 in position 37.03N 73.50W. Her voyage in November 1940 was officially recorded by F. Tennyson Jesse (*The Saga of San Demetrio*, HM Stationery Office 1942) and a film was subsequently made of it under the title *San Demetrio, London*.

At 1700 hours on 5 November Bristol City Line's *Gloucester City*, under the command of Captain Smith, had just dispersed from an OB convoy 290 miles to the north-east when her radio officer picked up the 'attacked by raider' message from *Rangitiki*. Captain Smith, in the finest tradition of his service, altered course, heading his vessel towards the stricken convoy. The following night he had to heave to because of southerly storm force 10 winds but as daylight broke the storm petered out and 37 hours after responding to the distress call he came upon the scene of the battle, and seven boatloads of survivors spread over a fifteen mile radius. Twenty-five were rescued from *Trewellard*, 23 from *San Demetrio*, 20 from *Kenbane Head* and 24 from *Fresno City*. A total of 92 survivors were landed at St John's Newfoundland on 13 November.

What of *Mopan*, the unannounced Fyffes' banana boat who

* Her Red Ensign is held by the Imperial War Museum, presented by the Eagle Oil & Shipping Co. Ltd in December 1959.

surprised even Theodor Krancke? During seven hours of battle Captain Sapsworth and his crew of 67 huddled together below deck beneath the battleship's forward guns, terrified of what fate held for them. Would the situation have been different if *Mopan* had radioed a distress signal or had attempted to contact Commodore Maltby in *Cornish City*? Probably the superiority of the *Admiral Scheer* was so overwhelming that little difference would have been made; on the other hand, a signal might have enabled the convoy to scatter an hour earlier. Several weeks later Captain Sapsworth and his crew arrived in Germany as POWs.

It was a disastrous month for Elders & Fyffes. Just 48 hours previously they had lost *Casanare* (5,376 grt, Captain Moore), torpedoed by Kretschmer in *U-99*, 200 miles west of Ireland with the loss of eight lives, then on 30 November, the 1911 built *Aracataca* (5,378 grt, Captain Browne) sank after being torpedoed by Mengersen in *U-101*, in position 57.08N 20.50W, also with the loss of eight crewmen. The survivors were rescued three days later in stormy seas by Royal Mail's *Potaro* outward-bound on her maiden voyage.

Although the future looked bleak in November 1940, the appearance of Germany's newest 'war machine', the pocket battleship, in the shipping lanes was just another extension of the war at sea, the month was in fact a milestone, possibly a turning point, yet it was to take 28 months to overcome the enemy and before anyone could assume the tide was running against the naval might of the Axis powers.

The Battle of Britain pilots had already shown they could defeat the enemy in the skies – due to their heroic actions Hitler had postponed his plans to invade. Yet during the winter that followed, and for many months thereafter, the masters and their crews, freighters and tankers alike, were as much a part of the defence as were the Spitfire pilots – without them Britain faced disaster. There were some masters still serving in their sixties, many of them with square-rigged 'tickets', most had served throughout the First World War; there were others in their thirties, even as young as 27 years, yet for the first time in their seafaring lives they were pessimistic. They were afraid of what the future held.

The German U-boats now sailed further west, to between 15° and 25° West, a stretch of water which became known as 'the graveyard'. To try to ward them off, convoys were routed as far north as 60°, dangerous from storms, fogs and icebergs. Yet masters who had hated these waters were now glad to go there even though the enemy followed them. During the 92 days of November, December and January, gales of force 7 or more were reported on 52 days. The weather was atrocious – Neptune would roar with all his fury; 40-foot waves, fogs, ice floes and snowstorms. War conditions had increased the risks of navigation by five times, to keep station was often a nightmare, collisions in fog were all too frequent and on more than one occasion vessels were wrecked by icebergs. Marine hazards accounted for 1,600 Allied ships totalling over 3,000,000 tons between 1939 and 1945. The northern latitudes meant a great increase in the casualty list. Of the 23,922 merchant seamen obliged to abandon ship in 1940, 5,622 perished, the majority due to the temperature of the water and exposure.

There were other major worries. The fall of France had given the enemy the secret of our Asdic apparatus for detecting submarines, the 'long haul' route, around South Africa to Port Said, although now developed, was one of the most difficult to protect and the most frightening development of all, that of mine warfare. The enemy was now laying mines that worked on the acoustic principle and fired by the sound waves caused by the movement of ships through the water. Then there was the magnetic mine with a delay-action device; this would lie on the sea-bed without reacting to sweepers or convoys passing over it. Days later the tremendous explosion and resultant destruction would reveal its position.

The British Admiralty however was not sitting back, prodded as it was by Prime Minister Winston Churchill who saw all the dangers of a broken lifeline; the protection of merchant vessels was now given every priority as was the fitting of radar to escort vessels. As a defence against the enemy's long range aircraft, certain ships were being fitted out to carry a single seater fighter aircraft, usually a Hurricane which was catapulted off the foredeck. Escort carriers which could fly fighter aircraft on and off, were being fitted out. Mine barrages were being laid off the east coasts of England and Scotland, and further north between Orkney, Shetland, the Faeroes and Iceland, to catch U-boats and surface raiders. More frigates, larger faster and more seaworthy than the corvettes, together with more corvettes and sloops, were being built in the United Kingdom whilst 50 American destroyers, built during the First World War, were being delivered. They were soon on service as a welcome reinforcement to the sorely tried escort force. Canadian escort services were now being expanded and the responsibility of escorting HX and SC convoys as far east as longitude 40° had passed to them.

In Coastal Command of the Royal Air Force, radar was really

coming into its own. In August 1940 Number 502 Squadron was rearming with Whitleys and these aircraft of greater range were equipped with a new type of radar which enabled ships of less than 1,000 tons to be located at ranges of up to 27 miles. The use of anti-submarine bombs too had been abandoned and was now replaced by depth charges of naval design. This enabled air crews to attack from very low altitudes and consequently to obtain much greater accuracy in their attacks. In October the first RAF squadron was moved to Iceland which had been occupied by British forces and by the end of 1940 an anti-submarine squadron under the orders of the Commander-in-Chief Coastal Command, was stationed there also. As proof that progress was being made a Sunderland Flying boat fitted with ASV-1 radar equipment located *U-47* on 18/19 November, the first radar locating of a U-boat by an aircraft.

There was progress in other spheres. The Admiralty's Defensively Equipped Merchant Ship (DEMS) organisation was being extensively enlarged; later, the Maritime AA Regiment of the Royal Artillery was formed. The U-boat base at Lorient was now being bombed by the Royal Air Force and British submarines were having considerable success in action against U-boats in the Bay of Biscay where they were keeping watch on the sea lanes in the vicinity of Lorient. Though merchant ships were now being sunk faster than they could be built, much thought was being given as to how their number could be increased, how to use them with the greatest skill, how to economise in their use and how to avoid waste of shipping space.

In the skies the Luftwaffe was showing mastery, not only against coastal shipping and convoy stragglers but against fast independent ships far out into the Atlantic. During November they accounted for eighteen ships, totalling 66,438 tons. The troopers *Windsor Castle* (19,141 grt) and *Empress of Japan* (26,032 grt) were both damaged in attacks by Focke-Wulf long-range Condors, the former in longitude 13.18 West and the *Empress* in 14.28 West. Royal Mail's *Nalon* (7,222 grt) was lost in longitude 15.02 West after being bombed and machine-gunned though all her crew were rescued. On 6 November the Clan Line lost their 6,365 ton *Clan MacKinlay* off Noss Head, Captain Masters in command. She was struck by two bombs which killed five of her crew including the chief engineer. After about 90 minutes she was abandoned and quickly broke up. The 1,925 ton *Balmore* owned by John Bruce & Co. was bombed and sunk with all hands on the morning 11 November 300 miles south-west of Ireland.

The twin-screw motorship *Apapa* (9,333 grt), owned by Elder

Dempster Lines and commanded by Captain Davies, was bombed by a lone Focke-Wulf aircraft on 15 November, 200 miles west of Achill Head, Co Mayo. She had sailed from Freetown with 23 other vessels, convoy SL53, and was acting as commodore ship with Rear Admiral Knowles aboard. Proceeding at 8 knots with a westerly wind force 6, a heavy swell and thick low cloud, the enemy suddenly dived to 150 feet dropping delayed action bombs, one of which penetrated the engine room, another which pierced No 3 hatchway. The engines were completely wrecked, fire broke out in the passenger cabins either side of the engine room and No 3 cargo hold. Black smoke was pouring from the engine room skylight and funnel. A gaping hole had been left in the port side and as she was being abandoned, she took a heavy list to port and fire took hold of all the passenger accommodation between No 3 hold and the funnel. The survivors were picked up by other ships in the convoy including Elder Dempster's *Mary Kingsley* and *New Columbia*. Out of a total complement of 261, eighteen crew and six passengers were lost.

The waters off Aberdeen were particularly vulnerable to the Junkers aircraft based at Stavanger. On 11 November Hain Steamships *Trebartha* (4,597 grt) was bombed and machine gunned; the 3,997 ton *Creemuir*, owned by Muir Young, was sunk by an aerial torpedo when 26 of her crew and one gunner were lost. The *St Catherine* (1,216 grt, owned by the Orkney & Shetland Steam Navigation Company) had just sailed from Aberdeen for Kirkwall on 14 November when an aircraft swept in low from the east releasing a torpedo which struck amidshhips. Fourteen of her crew and one passenger were killed.

Losses from U-boats continued to be heavy. Thirty-eight ships during November of which 26 were British including the armed merchant cruisers *Laurentic* (18,724 grt) and *Patroclus* (11,314 grt). During the third week of the month two convoys were subjected to several days of harassment which led to the loss of fourteen vessels, half of this total being sunk by Schepke in *U-100*; the long hours of darkness contributed to the loss of valuable personnel.

Lieutenant Joachim Schepke was responsible for the sinking of *Justitia*, *Bradfyne* and *Leise Maersk* on 23 November, convoy SC11 from Cape Breton. Within a space of eight hours he destroyed six tramps with their valuable war cargoes, a total tonnage of 20,965. The *Justitia* of 4,562 grt, owned by Chellew Steamship Management Co. and commanded by Captain Davies, was sunk in position 55.00N 13.10W with the loss of thirteen of her crew. Forty-five minutes later the 'woodbine' funnel *Bradfyne* of 4,740 grt, which cost

Reardon Smith's £85,237, new from the builders' yard in 1928, exploded and disappeared taking her master, Captain Vanner, and 38 crew with her. Miraculously there were four survivors. *Leise Maersk*, ex-*Svendborg*, a motorship of 3,136 grt, managed by the Burnett Steamship Co. on behalf of the Ministry of Shipping, had loaded at Three Rivers for Sharpness. Her master and sixteen of her crew were lost.

Convoy OB244 was attacked by *U-103* and *U-123*, losing seven vessels over a period of 48 hours. The largest loss of life was on board *Tymeric* (5,228 grt), owned by the Bank Line and outward bound for Buenos Aires. She lost 72 of her complement there being only three survivors. Twelve perished when the King Line's *King Idwal* (5,115 grt) was torpedoed. She was commanded by Captain Storm who had been master of the *King Alfred*, torpedoed and sunk only three months before. *Oakcrest* (5,047 grt, Crest Shipping Co.), en route for New York in ballast, lost 35 of her 44 crew. There were many unrecorded acts of heroism.

On 1 November *Empire Bison* (5,612 grt, managed by the Ropner Shipping Co.), a straggler from convoy HX82 because of heavy weather, was torpedoed by *U-124* in position 59.30N. 17.40W. The previous night, *U-124*, commanded by Wilhelm Schulz, had sunk the 1,437 ton *Rutland*, also a straggler. Captain Harland of *Empire Bison* and 37 of his crew were killed, the second mate and three of his comrades were adrift nine days before being rescued. Sixteen men were lost on the *Scottish Maiden* (6,993 grt) commanded by Captain Gibson and owned by Tankers Limited. Carrying crude oil she was torpedoed by Kretschmer (*U-99*) while occupying a protected position near the centre of convoy HX83 in the early hours of 5 November, in position 54.36N 14.23W. 'A tremendous roar split the night and the stern of the ship was blown to pieces,' Kretschmer wrote in his log. It was a day of double celebration for Lieutenant Otto Kretschmer whose base at Lorient radioed that the Führer had awarded him the Oak Leaves to the Knight's Cross, the highest decoration Germany could award for valour in the face of the enemy.

On 15 November *U-65* (Lieutenant-Commander Hans-Gerrit von Stockhausen) torpedoed *Kohinur* and the Norwegian *Havbor* on the 'long haul' between Freetown and the Middle East only 250 miles north of the Equator. On the following day she sank *Fabian* and then rendezvoused with the supply ship *Nordmark*. During the six weeks of her tropical cruise she sank eight ships of 47,785 tons and damaged the tanker *British Zeal* of 8,532 grt. During the Christmas Day sinking of *British Premier*, (5,872 grt) two hundred miles off Freetown,

Captain Dalziel and 31 of his crew were killed. There was much concern at the Admiralty whose facilities at Freetown were already overstretched. Bad weather had compelled the *Kohinur* (5,168 grt, owned by the Asiatic Steam Navigation Co. Ltd), to heave to, head to wind, her engines barely turning over. She sank before a single boat could be launched and many were lost; only 30 hours previously she had left the protection of the Royal Navy and King Tom anchorage in the Sierra Leone river. The chief mate was swept off the bridge though by lashing two rafts together, which had floated off as *Kohinur* went under, he dragged some 40 exhausted members of the crew aboard with him. Three hours later they raised a great cheer as they sighted the Norwegian motor tanker *Havbor* which slowed to rescue them. Suddenly there was a tremendous explosion as she too was torpedoed and a sheet of flame, fed by the force 9 gale, shot in all directions as the oil from her tanks flowed from the gaping hole in her side – a sea of fire crept closer and closer to the men on the rafts.

Seeing an upturned lifeboat amidst the wreckage, the chief mate led his frightened men, and many brave men become frightened in such circumstances, whatever the official citations may say, in righting the boat and cutting loose some oars still lashed in place. They then transferred to the boat and rowed away from the blazing tanker. There was no food, no water, no mast or sail but by taking one of the oars and a piece of canvas, they rigged a make-do sail. For three days and nights they suffered agonies of thirst. Eventually rain fell and later they were picked up by a British vessel.

Although the U-boat war was now spreading to tropical waters, a far greater worry towards the close of 1940 in these warmer climes, even eastward to Australasia and beyond, was the surface raider disguised as a peaceful merchantman. The Red Duster was at their mercy in all waters. In the Indian Ocean there was *Atlantis* and *Pinguin*, in the Pacific, *Komet* and *Orion* and in the South Atlantic *Kormoran* and *Thor*. (The raider *Widder* had returned to Brest on 31 October.) It was all a long way from the land war, still confined to Europe. Several naval vessels, which could have been better employed in the North Atlantic and the Mediterranean were now held in the southern hemisphere in an effort to curtail their activities and hunt them down.

In the space of two weeks, *Pinguin* sank four British vessels totalling 35,083 tons: *Nowshera*, *Maimoa*, *Port Brisbane* and *Port Wellington*. Together with *Atlantis* she ruled the waves that were bordered by the heart of the British Empire – South and East Africa,

India and Ceylon, Burma and Malaya, New Guinea and Australia.

Alfred Holt's 7,528 ton *Automedon*, Liverpool for Penang via
Freetown and Durban, was about halfway between Colombo and
the northernmost tip of Sumatra (04.18N 89.20E) when she was
attacked on 11 November. *Atlantis*, in skilful disguise, hoisted her
swastika when steaming a parallel course little more than half a mile
distant. Her master, Captain Ewan, and the third mate were both
killed in the first engagement; there was appalling destruction on the
bridge and throughout the officers' accommodation, though
fortunately the RRR message had already been transmitted. The
chief mate, knowing that she carried many secret documents in the
strong room was badly wounded in his attempt to find and destroy
them. The report, made by the German commander, Captain
Rogge, after his officers had planted bombs to send her to the bottom,
gives an interesting, and probably accurate, account of the
devastation that was wrought and the secret papers that were
carried.

> Hits had riddled all the superstructures, wrecked the davits and boats,
> penetrated the funnel and turned the masters' and mates' cabins into a
> shambles. A number of dead and wounded were lying about the deck.
> The master, mangled by a direct hit, had fallen on the bridge and the
> extra second mate had been killed outside the chart house . . . The death
> of the officers and the heavy damage had hindered the destruction of
> secret material. We found all the Admiralty's instructions, course
> directions and secret log books and after breaking into the master's safe
> we found the merchant navy code, conversion tables etc. In the Mail
> Room we found a number of bags marked 'Safe hand. By British Master
> only'. This contained material surpassing our expectations – the whole
> of the top secret mail for the High Command Far East: new code tables
> for the fleet: secret notices to mariners: information about minefields and
> swept areas, plans and maps; a War Cabinet report giving a summary on
> the defence of the Far East: Intelligence Service material and many other
> documents.

After *Automedon* had been sunk, the remainder of the crew plus a few
passengers which she carried, were taken on board the raider,
subsequently, on 9 December to be transferred to the captured
Norwegian tanker *Storstadt* which, after meetings with *Admiral Scheer*,
Nordmark, *Thor* and *Pinguin*, landed them in Bordeaux on 5 February
1941. Following this catastrophe all merchant vessels were provided
with an electrically detonated destruction device to prevent secret
documents falling into enemy hands – in the case of *Automedon* it

would appear that Captain Rogge had been tipped off that secret material was aboard.

Seven days later, some 25° to the south, British India's *Nowshera*, (7,920 grt), with Captain Collins in command, was sunk by Krüder's *Pinguin*; it was his eighth victim. After the action, in which the second engineer, who was on watch, lost his life, the officers and crew were given fifteen minutes to abandon ship after which they were taken on board the raider; Captain Collins was allowed on the bridge to witness the destruction. Fourteen time bombs had been planted by the boarding party. Subsequently the survivors landed in Bordeaux from the *Storstadt* from where the fifth engineer escaped and made his way south to Gibraltar and eventually by ship to Greenock.

Shortly afterwards (20 November) it was the turn of Shaw Savill's *Maimoa* (10,123 grt), sunk in position 31.50S 100.21E. Homeward-bound from Australia averaging 13 knots, a biplane with British markings suddenly flew across her path trailing a plummet on the end of a line and with it attempted to tear away the radio aerial. She succeeded at the second attempt, machine-gunning the deck and dropping a message calling upon Captain Cox to surrender and instructing that the ship's radio was not to be used – however the distress signal had already been sent. *Maimoa* then rigged an emergency aerial and attempted to make a run for it but with *Pinguin*'s 20 knots the distance between them closed and after about three hours, and at a range of one mile, *Pinguin* opened fire. Captain Cox had no alternative but to abandon ship.

There were no casualties and after being put ashore from the *Storstadt* at Bordeaux the crew spent five weeks in a transit camp outside the city before being sent by train to Germany. Two Australian born engineers jumped from the only unlocked door of their carriage as the train slowed near Tours and crossing into unoccupied France they immediately received great kindness and hospitality. They were put on a train for Marseilles whence they trekked to the Spanish frontier where they parted company to ensure they had the best possible chance of gaining their freedom. One of them spent a month in a labour camp under the most unpleasant conditions, finally reaching Gibraltar and arriving home on 14 June 1941. His comrade was also caught by the Spanish authorities who regarded him as a spy. He had many adventures and some very harsh treatment before he was released. He finally arrived home in March 1942.

Port Line's homeward-bound *Port Wellington* (8,301 grt) was caught by *Pinguin* halfway between Adelaide and Durban, (32.10S 75.00E) during the night of 30 November. The raider approached unseen and unsuspected to within 500 yards on a dark night and near to midnight, without previous signal, firing nine rounds from her 5.9 inch guns which virtually destroyed the bridge and radio room together with the steering gear aft. The master, Captain Thomas, was severely wounded and died later on board *Pinguin*; the first radio officer on duty was killed outright. When the *Port Wellington* was abandoned 25 minutes after she was struck by the first salvo, she was on fire from the funnel to the stern. Time bombs placed by the enemy saw her to her grave at 0130 hours. It was later known that Commander Kruder of *Pinguin* knew the exact hour at which *Port Wellington* had dropped her pilot off Adelaide.

When *Rangitane* was blasted from the high seas on 26 November 1940, the Second World War had reached the Pacific, yet over twelve months were yet to pass before the momentous events at Pearl Harbour. Owned by the New Zealand Shipping Co. Ltd, *Rangitane*, of 16,712 grt, had left Auckland two days previously on her regular run (Voyage 31) to the United Kingdom via the Panama Canal. Commanded by Captain Upton on this her seventh wartime voyage, she carried a full cargo of dairy produce, meat and wool. Her complement comprised 200 crew and 111 passengers, including 36 women.

The raider *Komet* had arrived in the Pacific via the icebound northern route (with the assistance of Russian icebreakers) and the Bering Sea, sinking the 546 ton island steamer *Holmwood* off Chatham Island the day previously. She met *Orion* by pre-arrangement only hours before *Rangitane* was sighted hull down in the fading light of dusk, with radioed knowledge that the liner was due to pass. In 36.58S 175.22E during the darkness of the night, they confronted their prey from ahead, one on the port bow, the other to starboard. As the suspicious vessels were sighted about ¾ mile ahead, it was clear with good visibility, *Rangitane* radioed a 'suspicious ship' message and immediately the enemy opened fire, the 'raider' message.

Captain Upton then brought his ship about; at full speed he put the raiders astern using his 4 inch gun on the poop deck in defence but *Komet* and *Orion*, the sea illuminated by their powerful searchlights, opened a deliberate and accurate fire, the first shells blew away the bridge, putting the radio room out of action and destroying all communication with the engine room. The attack was savage and ruthless and at 0300 hours Captain Upton surrendered

Elder Dempster's mv *Apapa*. Sunk by a Focke-Wulf Condor, 15 November 1940, the motorship *Apapa* was the first vessel sunk in convoy by the four-engined bombers.

Tanker survivors. The survivors from the tanker *W. B. Walker*, Captain 'Bill' Simpson, sunk 29 January 1941. They are seen on board HM Armed Trawler *Arab* after transfer at sea from HMS *Antelope*.

SS *Ranee*. Mined in Suez Canal, 5 February 1941. The 5,060 ton *Ranee*, Asiatic Steam Navigation Co Ltd, w one of several vessels mine in the Suez Canal. She was declared a total loss.

FW200's attack convoy HG On 9 February 1941 five sh were bombed and sunk wh six FW200 aircraft from 1/KG40 based at Merignac near Bordeaux attacked convoy HG53 homeward bound from Gibraltar.

The FW 200 attacks. From under 300 feet in the half li of dawn on 25 March 1941 FW200 attacks Canadian Pacific's lone *Beaverbrae*, 9,956 grt. Flames overcame her and she had to be abandoned. (From a paintin by Charles Bloomfield who was her second radio office at the time.)

amidst great devastation with flames and smoke adding to the horror of the scene. Sixteen were killed, of whom six were passengers; many others were wounded.

Rangitane was badly damaged and the superstructure was torn about. In spite of the desperate situation the chief radio officer had rigged the emergency radio and continued to send out the distress message. As the lifeboats got away, the wounded in agony, launches from the raiders cruised about with machine guns ready trained. One of the boats capsized, many were thrown into the sea and there were many unrecorded acts of bravery. Four hours after the attack, *Rangitane* was sent to the bottom, by torpedoes and shells; 295 souls drifting helplessly amidst the wreckage were distributed among *Komet*, *Orion* and the supply ship *Kulmerland*.

After much hardship, and many adventures, including the sinking of four phosphate ships by the raiders in the vicinity of Nauru, some of the survivors were put ashore on Emirau Island on 20 December, others being transferred to *Ermland* at Lemotrek in the Caroline Islands on 5 January 1941 (she was also carrying survivors from the *Turakina*) which then crossed the Pacific and rounded Cape Horn to rendezvous with *Nordmark*. By the time they reached Bordeaux, the survivors from *Turakina* had been prisoners at sea for eight months, those from *Rangitane*, for six months.

The first week of December saw the *Admiral Scheer* in tropical waters. On 24 November the crew of the *Mopan* were joined by that of Port Line's *Port Hobart* (7,448 grt) sunk off Bermuda and then on the first of the month, *Tribesman* (6,242 grt), T. & J. Harrison's third loss in sixteen days, shelled and sunk in position 15.00N 35.00W approximately. She was outward-bound from Liverpool for Durban and Calcutta and was intercepted at 2100 hours, the crew and passengers taking to the boats, two of which reached the raider. The remaining two boats however, containing the master, Captain Philpot, eight officers, five European ratings and 45 Lascar seamen escaped in the darkness and were never seen or heard of again.

At midday on 18 December, *Scheer* sighted Houlder's coal burning refrigerator ship *Duquesa*, of 8,651 grt, homeward-bound from the River Plate under Captain Bearpark and carrying 3,500 tons of meat and 15 million eggs. Coming up fast from astern she allowed her to send a radio signal reporting a raider – a deliberate attempt to divert attention away from the North Atlantic where the *Admiral Hipper* had broken out through the Denmark Straits on 6/7 December followed by the 8,736 grt merchant surface raider *Kormoran* six days later. She then placed a warning shot across her bows at nine miles distant to prevent further communication and later, in position 00.57N 22.42W, put on board an armed prize crew. Captain Bearpark was taken on board the German battleship along with the first and second radio officers, the gunner and an apprentice; the rest of the crew remained on board.

Duquesa was sent to a secret supply anchorage, off the Brazilian coast near Paranagua, called South Wilhelmshaven by the Germans. Here she furnished supplies for a long list of grateful ships; at one time there was *Admiral Scheer*, four other surface vessels and two U-boats at anchor all victualling from *Duquesa*. Later, when her coal was exhausted, she was towed by *Nordmark* whilst her prize crew burned her woodwork to keep the refrigeration plant running. She was kept afloat until 18 February 1941 when she was sunk by explosives placed in the engine room, stokehold and bunkers, her British crew members being transferred to a prison ship for the eventual voyage to Bordeaux.

The *Admiral Scheer* remained in the South Seas until March when she started the long voyage to her homeland arriving in Kiel to great jubilation on 1 April 1941. During her 161 day cruise she had sunk a total of seventeen ships of 113,233 tonnage, the most successful pocket battleship sortie of the war.

Convoy HX90, which sailed from Halifax, NS on 21 November, was another homeward-bound convoy where losses of both ships and men were heavy. In the absence of a battleship escort off Newfoundland, protection was afforded by two armed merchant cruisers *Laconia* and *Forfar*, the former leaving on 1 December at the time the convoy was sighted by Mengersen in *U-101*. U-boats *47, 52, 94,* and *99* were then called up and in the 30-hour interval before the destroyer escort arrived, nine merchant ships of 52,819 grt with their valuable war cargoes had been sunk and a further two, *Loch Ranza* and *Dunsley*, damaged. Included in the death roll were both the convoy commodore and vice-commodore, lost in the mountainous seas that raged.

First to be torpedoed was the 8,826 ton motor tanker *Appalachee*, Anglo American Oil Company, 32 of whose crew were saved. She was struck during the darkness of the late evening on 1 December, (position 54 30N 20 00W) by Mengersen who a few minutes later torpedoed *Loch Ranza* (Royal Mail 4,958 grt) then Moss Hutchison's *Kavat* (2,782 grt) in the early hours – Captain Napier and 24 of his crew were killed in the explosion. Just before dawn *U-101* torpedoed her fourth victim; *Lady Glanely*, the 1938-built motorship owned by the Tatem Steam Navigation Company, of 5,497 tons, Vancouver for London, sank with all hands lost. Tatem's *Goodleigh*, a sister ship, built in the same year, followed her to the bottom a little over two hours later – her assailant was Lieutenant Otto Salman in *U-52*.

As dawn broke over a stormy North Atlantic on 2 December, the 'black pit', as this part of the western ocean became known, claimed a further five victims, one of them the AMC escort *Forfar*. She was about to leave the convoy to escort OB251 in close proximity to the north and being shadowed by *U-43* (which subsequently sank *Pacific President* and *Victor Ross*). She was the third converted passenger liner to be sent to her watery grave since HX84 and *Jervis Bay* – all three were sunk by ace Kretschmer in *U-99*. The tanker *Concho*, (8,376 grt, owned by Anglo Saxon Petroleum Co. Ltd) was a stout ship needing three submarines (*U-47*, *U-95*, *U-99*) to sink her; five torpedoes in total were fired into her. Bibby Line's 6,022 ton *Stirlingshire*, commanded by Captain O'Byrne, and carrying frozen meat and generals from Sydney, Australia, was sunk by *U-94* (Lieutenant Herbert Kuppisch). The survivors were rescued by *Empire Puma* whose master, Captain Ramsay, turned his ship about to make the rescue when not detailed by convoy instructions to do this duty.

Reardon Smith's *Victoria City* (4,739 grt) the vice-commodore ship, became separated from the convoy owing to the weather and neither she nor her crew of 43 was ever seen again. Carrying steel, New York for London, she sent no distress signal but according to German sources was torpedoed by *U-140* (Lieutenant-Commander Hans-Peter Hinsch) who reported that she sank in twelve minutes. Some wreckage identified with her was later found off Portstewart.

HX92, sailing from Halifax on 29 November, lost four ships in the North Western Approaches during 11/12 December when, due to bad weather, contact had been lost with the escort ships. The first to be torpedoed was the commodore ship, the veteran *Rotorua*, (10,890 grt), owned by the New Zealand Shipping Company and commanded by Captain Kemp when she was 100 miles west of St Kilda. She had sailed from Lyttleton on her 43rd voyage on 16 October carrying a cargo of meat and dairy produce for Avonmouth via Panama. The torpedo struck abreast the engine room; a heavy sea was running and she quickly began to settle. About twenty minutes later, as the survivors in the lifeboats stood off, *Rotorua* sank taking all those on the bridge down with her; Captain Kemp, the commodore, Rear-Admiral Fitzgerald, the chief, second and third mates, two New Zealand naval gunners and thirteen others perished. Over 100 survivors were landed at Stornaway two days later.

On 18 December *Napier Star* (10,116 grt), Blue Star Line Ltd, commanded by Captain Walsh was steaming westward independently at 13 knots in latitude 59 North. She had sailed from Liverpool three days earlier for New Zealand with a general cargo, 82 officers and men, and seventeen passengers. With a full south-westerly gale on the port bow she was pitching and straining, with green seas breaking over the forecastle; heavy spray was flying overall. She had been shadowed for some time by *U-100* which had been keeping watch in these waters for over a week and had torpedoed *Euphorba* and *Kyleglen*, both lost with all hands, on 14 December. Suddenly at dusk, in longitude 23.13 West, *Napier Star* lurched violently to port as the torpedo struck, a great column of water shot skywards, all the lights failed and she quickly began to settle by the stern.

Launching the four remaining boats (one had been destroyed in the explosion) proved extremely difficult and as the survivors pulled away, the fierce seas breaking over them, a second torpedo found her target with a deafening roar – *Napier Star* was a doomed ship and she sank shortly afterwards. Many died from exposure during the severe weather and sub-zero temperatures and although those that remained were rescued by the Swedish *Vaalarem*, only fifteen people, including three women, stepped ashore in Liverpool three days later. In all 84 had perished.

Waiotira (12,823 grt, Shaw Savill & Albion Co Ltd), homeward-bound from New Zealand and commanded by Captain Richardson, was sunk in the same waters, 58.05N 17.10W, at dusk on Boxing Day, eight days later. A motor refrigerated cargo ship delivered from the builders only in November 1939, she was also sailing alone on a pre-arranged course, her maximum speed was 17 knots, when she was brought to a standstill by a torpedo fired by *U-95*, Lieutenant Gerd Schreiber. The boats were manned but as they were getting away, two more torpedoes ripped into her, fragments from one of them killing the engineers' storekeeper and wounding several others. The survivors were picked up by the destroyer *Mashona* and, although Captain Richardson later led a party on board to investigate the possibilities of salvage, there was no hope for her and she foundered the following morning.

A worrying feature of the war at sea at the close of 1940 was where would the enemy strike next? Would there be an extension of the war against our merchant fleet and our whole plan for survival? Could Britain last out until our new defences and new escort vessels were in operation? The situation was particularly worrying to Prime

Minister Churchill and his War Cabinet. Between 12 and 19 December the Luftwaffe undertook an extensive mining operation in the Thames estuary. During the week prior to Christmas there were damaging air-raids aimed at the whole operation of the port of Liverpool and on Christmas Day itself, an encounter between the German cruiser *Admiral Hipper* and a well defended troop convoy.

The Thames mining operation, coupled with a similar operation on the Mersey and the continuing E-boat menace, 22 ships of 45,685 tons had been sunk by E-boats in the six months following Dunkirk, reminded all those of the seriousness of the situation. At least 300 mines, of which fifty were magnetic, were laid between Southend and the Isle of Sheppey; many were fitted with a 4½ day delayed action fuse and became live simultaneously. Great havoc was produced – on 17 December five ships were sunk. Twelve were sunk on these barrages up to the close of the year. Queueing to get through the 'gate' into the Port of London on Boxing Day were the *Tamworth*, led by the coaster *Kinnaird Head*, the Royal Mail motorship *Araby* bringing up the rear. The *Araby* (4,936 grt, Captain Whittle) set off an acoustic mine with an exploding roar, a few seconds later the coaster detonated a mine but *Tamworth* in the centre sailed through safely. Six men were killed aboard *Araby*, whose bottom was burst open almost along its entire length.

The night bombing of Liverpool on 20, 21 and 22 December sank the 1,293 ton *Silvio* and seriously damaged nineteen ships totalling 121,678 tons. Included were such well known vessels as the *Almeda Star*, *Eastern Prince*, *Highland Princess* and *Llangibby Castle*. Mines in the Mersey accounted for the 3,071 ton *Innisfallen* and five others were damaged. The port was virtually shut down for over two weeks; over the next three months there were air raids on many British ports: Avonmouth, Cardiff, Glasgow, London, Manchester, Plymouth, Southampton and Swansea.

Probably one of the most poorly documented actions involving Red Duster ships was the *Admiral Hipper* foray against the twenty ship 'Winston Special' convoy WS5A bound for India and the Middle East and carrying some 40,000 troops. WS convoys whose code letters are alleged to have stood for Winston's Specials, were important well defended and highly secret troop and supply convoys, which, from June 1940 until June 1943, sailed at monthly intervals for the Middle East via the Cape of Good Hope. During the second half of 1940 a total of 213,540 troops were sent from Britain to the Middle East in 150 Red Duster ships.

WS5A was escorted by three cruisers and two aircraft carriers; she was sighted by *Hipper*, 700 miles west of Cape Finisterre just after dawn on Christmas Day. Bringing her 8 inch guns to bear upon the convoy she quickly found range scoring hits upon P & O's *Empire Trooper* of 13,994 grt and the commodore ship *Jumna* (6,078 grt), owned by James Nourse Ltd, which was en route from Liverpool for Calcutta. *Jumna* took the brunt of the assault and within a few minutes the bridge and accommodation had been destroyed. All on board, including the commodore, Rear-Admiral H.B. Maltby, were killed; only six weeks previously he had led the *Jervis Bay* HX84 convoy. Forty-three of the 111 dead were Lascar merchant seamen being repatriated after being torpedoed in T. & J. Harrison's *Planter* on 16 November. As *Jumna* sank, the convoy scattered, *Empire Trooper* limping into Gibraltar several days later.

In typical hit and run fashion, *Admiral Hipper* then broke off the engagement chased by the cruisers *Berwick* and *Bonaventure*. They lost sight of her just before 1100 hours owing to bad visibility but not before *Berwick* had been damaged. Less than half an hour later the chase was abandoned and two days later *Hipper* returned to the port of Brest. Strangely, on the last day of the year and on New Year's Day 1941, no British ship was lost by enemy action but the toll was alarming and mounting – since Dunkirk 440 British merchant ships had been lost, a tonnage of 2,026,857 had been destroyed.

The New Year saw the Focke-Wulf 200 Konder aircraft based at Merignac near Bordeaux under the command of the Commander U-boats and successfully co-operating with U-boats in the North Atlantic, both long range reconnaissance and bombing sorties. In January, enemy aircraft accounted for the loss of eleven British merchant ships with a tonnage of 46,395; losses from U-boats, due to the atrocious winter, were considerably reduced, the tonnage being the lowest since October 1939. Fogs, however, added to the hazards of the mariner, Elder Dempster's *Bodnant* and Ellerman's *City of Bedford* both sank after collision south of Ireland when outward-bound convoy OB264 and inward-bound SL58 suddenly discovered they were proceeding on almost directly opposite courses. The *Bedford* was carrying seven and a half million cartridges, and her loss was a grievous blow.

Of the eight vessels sunk in January by FW200 Kondor aircraft in the Western Approaches, two were lost with all hands; the total casualties were 150. The 36 crew and one gunner were lost when *Langleegorse* (4,524 grt), owned by the Medomsley Steamship Co., was attacked in position 53.19N 13.11W on 23 January when homeward-bound from Durban, convoy SL61. The 5,159 ton

Rowanbank (Bank Line Ltd) was bombed and sunk in 57.00N 16.30W on the last day of the month some 1,100 miles from Merignac. En route from Lourenço Marques to Oban for orders, (convoy SL62 ex Freetown) all her crew of 68 were lost. The homeward-bound convoys from Freetown were particularly at risk, as sailing from the south, they were not routed to the north of Scotland, as were the OB, HX and SC convoys (North America).

Alfred Holt's *Clytoneus* (6,273 grt, Captain Goffey) was bombed 280 miles north-west of Bloody Foreland on the last leg of her voyage from the Dutch East Indies via Freetown carrying general cargo including tea, sugar and flour. At about 0800 hours on 6 January the four-engined aircraft came from astern dropping two bombs which exploded in the sea close amidships. She was shaken from stem to stern, the foremast and radio aerial crashed onto the deck and the engines stopped due to the propeller shaft being fractured. *Clytoneus* quickly dropped back, the convoy proceeding on course protected by her screen of escorts. Captain Goffey and his crew were now alone and at the mercy of the lone bomber which this time crossed from starboard to port at 250 feet releasing two more bombs which struck the foredeck abreast No 2 hatch. *Clytoneus* struck back with her 12-pounder AA gun but she was heavily damaged for'ard of the bridge; fire broke out in the hold and within minutes, with the engine room rapidly filling with water, the ship was blazing furiously. During a third run the enemy released several more bombs, all of which were near misses, machine gunning from fore to aft as she was attacked.

The whole assault lasted only eight minutes and as the Focke Wulf climbed to cloud cover, Captain Goffey had no alternative but to abandon ship. Miraculously there were no casualties, though one member of the crew was wounded when he was hit by machine gun bullets, and rescue was made the following afternoon by the destroyer *Wild Swan* and AMC *Esperance Bay*.

The first casualty of 1941 was British India's *Nalgora* (6,579 grt, Captain Davies), which was making for Freetown on her voyage from Bombay. Close to midnight (2 January) she was struck by two torpedoes in position 22.24N 21.11W from *U-65* still on patrol after eight weeks operating off West Africa. *Nalgora* immediately took on a pronounced list, lurching suddenly to port from which she did not recover and because of this, great difficulty was experienced in getting the lifeboats away. The submarine now surfaced, shelling her and setting her on fire, raking her at the same time with bursts of machine gun fire so that those in the boats, which lay alongside, had to keep their heads down to avoid being hit. The purser's boat was picked up two days later but the captain's boat was not so fortunate having to endure the shark infested waters for eight days before reaching the Cape Verde Islands.

Cadet Cockcroft, who was in Captain Davies' boat (together with the ship's cat), had been taking a bath when the ship was struck; he spent the whole time in his pyjamas and a fine new bridge coat belonging to someone else and suffered no ill effects.

The second week saw the arrival in the Mediterranean of the important 'Excess' convoy (MC4) destined for Malta and Piraeus. Included were the *Essex*, carrying 4,000 tons of ammunition, 3,000 tons of seed potatoes and twelve Hurricane fighters on deck, the *Clan Cumming*, *Clan MacDonald* and *Empire Song*. In the opposite direction from Alexandria there sailed the heavily laden *Breconshire* and *Clan MacAuley*. Both convoys were heavily escorted, the forerunners of many that were to sail in the defence of Malta and in reinforcing British and Allied forces in North Africa.

Whilst the 11,063 ton *Essex*, owned by the Federal Steam Navigation Co. Ltd, was discharging in Malta on 16/17 January, she was severely damaged in an air raid and two days later *Clan Cumming* (7,264 grt) was damaged in a torpedo attack made by the Italian submarine *Neghelli* (Lieutenant-Commander Carlo Ferracuti) off Piraeus. It was the first submarine attack on a British merchant ship in the Mediterranean, though the first and last by *Neghelli* which was sunk by a British naval force shortly afterwards.

During 1941 Italian submarines were engaged in the conflict in many areas though in many cases against the will of their commanders. The *Shakespear* action of 5 January was perhaps typical. Owned by Glover Bros, the 5,029 ton *Shakespear* (dispersed from convoy OB262), fought a protracted duel off Senegal with *Cappellini* (Lieutenant-Commander Salvatore Todaro). Armed with a standard 4 inch gun, the British vessel kept the submarine at bay for over two hours though taking a heavy battering herself. She refused to surrender until her own gun had been knocked out and eighteen of her crew including two DEMS gunners had been killed. On board the submarine lay two gunmen dead and several wounded. As the survivors from *Shakespear*, including the master, took to the two lifeboats remaining, further gunfire sank the ship and Todaro brought his submarine alongside the boats remarking upon the dogged resistance of the mariners. He then took the lifeboats in tow until they came in sight of land and treated the survivors in a most humane manner.

Just over a week later (14 January), Todaro sank *Eumaeus* (7,472 grt, Alfred Holt & Co. Ltd), under the command of Captain Watson, some 150 miles west of Freetown; the submarine *Cappellini* was sighted on the surface by the chief mate. When the range closed to 4,000 yards *Eumaeus* opened fire; during the subsequent duel the bridge was hit and she was shelled amidships on the starboard side. After about fifteen minutes, with her gun damaged and gun-crew wounded, and with her lifeboats smashed, Lieutenant-Commander Todaro began machine-gunning the bridge and upper works; altogether *Eumaeus* received some 40 shell hits. With her engines stopped and listing to starboard Captain Watson gave the order to abandon ship, and the survivors jumped overboard where they found wreckage to keep themselves afloat.

Ninety minutes after the Italian submarine was sighted she fired a torpedo at close range and *Eumaeus* sank beneath the waves. Eight of her crew of 91, including the chief officer, the chief and fourth mates, and fifteen naval ratings travelling as passengers, lost their lives. Those that survived were picked up by naval vessels a few hours after having been sighted by a Walrus amphibian from HMS *Albatross* based at Freetown.

The Blue Star liner *Almeda Star* (14,936 grt) bound for South America was lost with all hands in heavy seas on 17 January, position 58.16N 13.40W, just 35 miles north of Rockhall. A mystery surrounds her sinking as *U-96* reported she first attacked at 0745 hrs followed by two more attacks, but each time the 16 knot *Almeda Star* took evasive action. She finally sank six hours later but only after three more torpedoes had been fired. Although destroyers and other vessels searched the area following receipt of her distress call, no wreckage, no trace of anything was found; neither was anything recognisable as belonging to her washed ashore. Captain Howard, commodore of the Blue Star Line, his crew of 166 officers and men, and 194 passengers, perished in the disaster.

As T. & J. Brocklebank's *Mandasor* was being shelled by the raider *Atlantis* in the Indian Ocean on 24 January, two of the most powerful raiders in the German fleet, *Gneisenau* and *Scharnhorst*, crept undetected through the Skagerrak – the enemy was again determined to harass the North Atlantic shipping lanes with the big guns of its navy.

Mandasor, loaded with tea, hessian and pig iron, was caught by the raider *Atlantis* as she proceeded from Calcutta to Durban for bunkers on her homeward voyage; she had sighted 'the stranger' the previous day in excellent visibility as she crossed the Equator. Changing course she noticed 'the stranger' followed and taking no chances she altered course through 130 degrees and lost her only to find that she was being buzzed by a seaplane at 0845 hours the next morning. The plane then crossed from port to starboard, dragging a wire which tore down the radio aerial and emergency aerial, opening up with her cannon and machine gun as she did so.

The independently-routed *Mandasor* had been especially armed to defend herself; although she carried two machine guns and a 12 pounder in addition to a 4 inch gun, the intruder was not deterred. Making two further runs the seaplane dropped bombs which fell close to the port bow – one man was killed and several wounded. *Atlantis* was now closing fast and, although a distress signal had been sent, the WT aerial having been repaired, the first salvo destroyed the radio room and the second salvo caused immense damage. Now a fire raged in Nos 1 and 3 holds, the bridge, saloon and pantry were smashed and there were more casualties. Not until the ship had stopped did the firing cease and even when she was abandoned the survivors were not safe – three members of the crew each lost a leg, one dying of his wounds in the lifeboat, as a salvo of shrapnel hit them. The enemy had apparently fired at sharks in an effort to avoid further lives being lost.

Time bombs which had been laid on *Mandasor* by the German boarding party sent her slowly to the bottom stern first. The red duster still flying as she went under, Captain Hill and his depleted crew (the second mate died as he was hauled aboard the raider) stood and saluted. Another fine British ship had been lost in the cause of war.

A week later *Atlantis* captured Bank Line's *Speybank* (5,154 grt) without a shot being fired, 230 miles north of Seychelles during her voyage from Cochin to Port Elizabeth. Subsequently she sailed under various names (*Levernbank, Inverbank, Doggerbank*) under the command of a German merchant navy officer, Captain Paul Schneidewind, during which time she created great havoc by laying mines at the approaches to Cape Town. Later she was sent to Yokohama to bring home a valuable cargo to Bordeaux. Sailing as *Doggerbank*, she left in December 1942, the German naval headquarters setting a detailed course for her and warning all U-boats to give her a clear passage. Unfortunately Captain Schneidewind raced home ahead of his timetable and on 3 March 1943 when 2,000 miles from Bordeaux she was torpedoed by *U-43* who mistook her for a steamer of the *Dunedin Star* type. Nearly 150 went down with her; fifteen managed to clamber aboard a small flat-bottomed boat but only one was still alive when sighted by the Spanish tanker *Campoamor* on 19 March.

The Blue Star Line lost a further vessel during January 1941; in a little over seven months they had lost seven ships, a total tonnage of 92,253. *Afric Star* (11,900 grt) sailed from Rio de Janeiro at the middle of the month bound for Avonmouth with a cargo of meat. Commanded by Captain Cooper, she carried a crew of 72, two DEMS gunners and two women passengers. On the morning of 29 January, position 8.44N 24.38W, she sighted a large ship flying the Russian flag which shadowed her most of the day and then, as light was failing, bore down upon her at 18 knots, hoisting the swastika and opening fire at close range. *Afric Star* was set on fire immediately and, as the shelling continued, Captain Cooper felt it was necessary to take to the boats and row towards the raider. It turned out to be *Kormoran*, her third victim now sinking quickly in the calm tropical sea.

Setting a north-westerly course, *Kormoran* almost immediately sighted Alfred Holt's 5,722 ton *Eurolochus* which ten days previously had left the protection of outward convoy WS5B. She was bound for Takoradi carrying bombers on deck from whence such planes were flown across the desert to Egypt. As the night closed in a star shell suddenly illuminated a surprised *Eurolochus* whose master, Captain Caird, immediately ordered a raider attack signal to be sent. *Kormoran* then opened fire with one of her six 5.9 inch guns, blasting 67 rounds into her in a murderous attack in which, although only lasting nine minutes, with four or five rounds being sent in reply, the odds were hopeless. With her steering gear wrecked, she was crippled and the order was given to abandon ship.

The raider then raked her fore and aft with machine guns, firing a torpedo to finish her aft, the blast from which shattered one of the lifeboats still standing close by. Some of the occupants were killed outright. Three Europeans and 39 Chinese were captured by the Germans but Captain Caird and 27 others escaped being rescued from the shark infested waters the following day by the Spanish *Monte Teide*. A total of eleven were killed and the chief mate seriously wounded. The chief radio officer owed his life to one of the cadets who, after swimming to a raft himself, jumped in again to rescue his colleague, exhausted at some distance away. At the very moment he was about to clamber back aboard, a shark jumped from the sea, so close that his deadly teeth ripped his clothing – an heroic effort for which he was awarded the Albert Medal as well as Lloyd's War Medal. Some days later, the prisoners aboard *Kormoran* were transferred to the *Nordmark*, subsequently to be put aboard the German-owned *Portland* on passage from Chile to Bordeaux where they landed on 14 March.

At the end of the month three U-boats trailed convoy SC19 sinking six vessels of 33,724 tons, three of which were stragglers. During the night of 28/29 January, *U-93* (Claus Korth), last active when she attacked OB227 and OB228 in October 1940, sank two cargo ships and a tanker, all within fifteen minutes in position 56.00N 15.23W. First it was the *King Robert* (5,886 grt, King Line Ltd), followed by the tanker *W.B. Walker* (10,468 grt) and, thirdly, the Greek *Aikaterini*.

The 1935-built *W.B. Walker* (Captain Simpson), owned by Oriental Tankers, was carrying 13,000 tons of aviation spirit on the long haul from Aruba for Avonmouth via Nova Scotia when, at midnight 150 miles south-west of Rockhall and nearly home, she was ripped open on the starboard side, the torpedo passing right through No 5 tank. She split into two, both parts remaining afloat, her cargo floating atop the calm sea. The 43 survivors, four had been killed, lowered the lifeboats on the port side only to become unconscious from the effects of the aviation spirit on the water. There they remained until pulled aboard by their rescuers on HMS *Antelope* and HMS *Anthony*. The men of the *W.B. Walker*, in view of the fact that they were carrying such a highly inflammable cargo, were extremely fortunate to be alive.

The tramp steamer *West Wales* (4,354 grt, owned by the West Wales Steamship Co), New York for Newport, had great difficulty in maintaining headway due to engine trouble and fell some miles behind the convoy. As dawn broke she was sighted by Kuppisch in *U-94*, the torpedo exploding in the engine room, killing all those on watch. Sixteen of her crew of 37 perished.

Amongst other tragedies in the North Atlantic in January was that of the Pacific Steam Navigation Company's *Oropesa* (14,118 grt). Torpedoed by *U-96* she was serving as an auxiliary transport and Captain Croft and 112 men lost their lives. Shaw Savill and Albion's motorship *Zealandic* (10,578 grt, Captain Ogilvie) outwards for Australia was lost with all hands three days after sailing from Liverpool – 65 crew, two DEMS gunners and six passengers. *U-106*, commanded by Lieutenant-Commander Jurgen Oesten (previously in command of *U-61*), claimed responsibility. Ellerman's *Florian* (3,174 grt), in ballast from Hull to New York, was also lost with all hands, sunk by *U-94*. On 20 January a naval trawler sighted wreckage and a lifeboat in 61.14N 12.05W but no trace of her crew of 44 was ever found.

During February, with improved weather and, with the longer days, the added menace of the Kondor attacks, the convoy battles resumed – HX106 and 107, HG53, SC20 and 21, and four successive outward convoys, OB287, 288 289, and 290. It was a menacing time; the German siege of Britain began to bite deep. Britain's monthly imports were now less than the early months of 1940 and the German Naval High Command were in jubilant mood. They had every reason to be optimistic for in addition to the successes being achieved by the new surface raiders, the Luftwaffe expected that it would soon be capable of sinking 300,000 tons of shipping per month and they estimated, with some justification, that an average of 750,000 tons would force Britain out of the war if maintained for twelve months. Already total sinkings and vessels seriously damaged (i.e. vessels unable to carry on their trade for a minimum of six months) were estimated at 400,000 tons per month. With new British shipbuilding estimated at only 200,000 tons, the German optimism could well have been borne out had they not invaded Russia in June 1941.

On 9 February in one of his famous wartime speeches Prime Minister Winston Churchill gave a hint of the menacing situation, 'We must therefore expect that Herr Hitler will do his utmost to prey upon our shipping and to reduce the volume of American supplies entering these islands. Having conquered France and Norway, his clutching fingers reach out on both sides of us into the ocean.'

In North Africa the capture of Tobruk by the Australians on 22 January saw the White Ensign fluttering over the harbour and the wrecks of Italian transports and supply vessels. And in the wake of the Royal Navy came the old Red Duster of the Merchant Navy. It was the start of three long years of war in the Mediterranean when Britain's merchant fleet, later aided by the resources of the United States merchant marine, served the Allied forces from El Alamein to Oran, Greece, Crete and Malta, through Sicily and Italy and on to the beaches of the south of France.

The convoy battles entered a new phase. The sight of the four engined Focke-Wulf often indicated that a U-boat attack was imminent. On the other hand, the U-boat which located the convoy would call up the bombers such as happened with deadly effect when *U-37*, commanded by Lieutenant-Commander Nicolai Clausen, first sighted the homeward-bound convoy HG53, 160 miles south-west of Cape St Vincent. After sinking *Courland* and *Estrellano* Clausen homed six FW Kondors, which bombed and sank a further five, of which four were British: *Britannic, Dagmar I, Jura* and *Varna*.

The sixteen ships of HG53 sailed from Gibraltar on 6 February making a wide detour into mid-Atlantic to avoid the dangers off the coast of Portugal and in the Bay of Biscay. Three days later at 0430 hours, in position 35.53N 13.13W, Clausen fired two torpedoes simultaneously, the first struck the 1,324 ton *Courland* (James Currie and Company) the second destroying Ellerman's *Estrellano* (1,983 grt), Leixoes (Oporto) for Liverpool. Falling astern, James Currie's *Brandenberg*, at considerable risk to herself, rescued survivors from the water, three had been killed on *Courland*, six on the Ellerman vessel. Then at midday came the big four-engined bombers, at masthead height, from port to starboard, from fore to aft. The little *Jura*, of 1,759 tons, owned by the Admiral Shipping Company, loaded with iron ore, Huelva for Aberdeen, sank like a stone, a mass of tangled ironwork. Fifteen of her crew and two DEMS gunners were killed.

Here perhaps is an opportune time to praise the DEMS gunners. Little has been written about them; neglected and often forgotten by the Senior Service of which they were part, their heroic efforts would fill a volume in themselves, efforts protecting our merchant fleet and the men of the Red Duster who sailed in them.

The following morning at daybreak, 10 February, in position 36.10N 16.38W, Clausen resumed his attack. *Brandenberg* (1,473 grt) was struck by two torpedoes which had missed a large tanker in the next column. Built in 1910, *Brandenberg* was a stout old ship but the iron ore she was carrying quickly took her to the depths of the ocean, taking with her, Captain Henderson, all her crew of 23, together with Captain Smith and his crew of 29 rescued from *Courland* the previous day. James Currie and Company had lost two of their ships, two of their masters and 52 crew members. The sole survivor of this calamity was a passenger later landed at Gibraltar.

Out of the 47 vessels sunk by U-boats in February 1941, 33 were independently routed or were convoy stragglers. The stragglers suffered dearly in casualties. Out of twelve sunk by U-boats in the North Atlantic (tonnage 76,574) eight of British registry were sunk with all hands; 479 persons lost plus two taken prisoner of war. Anyone who suffered as a straggler during those days and has lived to tell the tale will know the suspense which prevailed on board whilst tumultuous seas strained every rivet, those in ballast just as much as those deeply laden, and those who were stopped altogether, wallowed and were tossed like corks, at the mercy of King Neptune and the enemy alike, whilst engineers strove deep down in the ship's belly to right some breakdown. Gallant ships all, a few are now remembered:

Alnmoor	Runciman Shipping Company. All hands, 55 persons. Sunk by *U-123*.
Arthur F. Corwin	Oriental Tankers. All hands, 35 persons. *U123*. Two torpedoes. *U-96*. Two torpedoes.
Black Osprey	Cairn Line of Steamships (MOS) 25 lost, 11 saved. *U-96*.
Canford Chine	Chine Shipping Company. All hands, 35 persons. *U-52*.
Clea	Anglo Saxon Petroleum Company. All hands, 59 persons. *U-96*.
Edwin R. Brown	Oriental Trade & Transport Co. All hands, 49 persons. *U-103*.
Empire Blanda	Larrinaga Steamship Co. (MOWT). All hands, 40 persons. *U-69*.
Empire Engineer	Weidner Hopkins & Co. (MOS). All hands, 40 persons. *U-123*.
Gairsoppa	British India S.N. Co. 85 lost (one saved). *U-101*.
Nailsea Lass	Nailsea Steamship Co. Ltd. 5 died in boats. Captain Bradford and chief mate POW. *U-48*.
Scottish Standard	Tankers Ltd. 5 killed. Damaged by bombs from FW 200 attack day previous. *U-96*.
Temple Moat	Temple Steamship Co. All hands, 42 persons. *U-69*.

British India's 1919 built coal burning *Gairsoppa* (5,237 grt), mentioned above was sunk by *U-101* (Mengersen) 300 miles south-west of Galway. She was commanded by Captain Hyland, loaded with pig iron and sailed from Freetown in the 8 knot SL64 convoy.

By 14 February bad weather had made her run short of bunkers and she was obliged to leave the convoy at dusk to make for the nearest port. By breakfast time two days later her speed was reduced to 5 knots to conserve fuel. Wallowing in the rising seas she was spotted by a reconnaissance FW 200 which circled the ship for an hour before disappearing and calling up *U-101* which happened to be in the vicinity (the day previously *U-101* had torpedoed and sunk the independent *Holystone*, lost with all hands). At 2030 hours local time the torpedo struck without warning on the starboard side, throwing up a great column of water by No 2 hold, and causing much damage including the foremast which came crashing down on deck, bringing with it the main and emergency radio aerials. Clouds of smoke and fire began to pour from the hold as she settled by the head; as the fo'c'sle went under Captain Hyland gave orders to abandon ship.

The lowering of the lifeboats, due to the high seas and heavy swell, was extremely difficult, more so because *U-101* had now surfaced and was firing her machine gun at the crippled *Gairsoppa*, now on fire from end to end, her stern so high out of the water that the propeller was racing at full speed. Rising upright as she slid under, only one lifeboat cleared the ship, narrowly avoiding being sucked under.

The time was 2050 hours as the occupants of the boat, nine Europeans and 25 Lascar seamen, led by the second mate, hoisted sail amidst tumultuous seas. For nine days the gale raged as they drifted with a makeshift rudder – the original had been smashed against the ship's side upon launching the boat. The supply of fresh water was exhausted after the first couple of days and it was bitterly cold as the seas washed into the boat continuously; all but three European and four Indians died through thirst and exposure; the feet of the second mate were badly frostbitten. By the twelfth day those that survived were in a semi-conscious state, and then, 24 hours later, the Lizard was sighted. The boat was driven upon the rocks, the weakened men unable to beach her; all on board were flung into the water. As they struggled to get ashore one by one they were drowned, the second mate, the only survivor, being flung back upon the rocks unconscious. Captain Hyland, 82 crew and two gunners were lost.

The OB convoys which assembled at Loch Ewe on the west coast of Scotland were the most heavily attacked at this time, probably due to the presence of aces Kretschmer and Prien in the region. A successful reconnaissance by a FW200 aircraft led *U-96* to convoy OB288 which sailed on 20 February, 48 hours ahead of OB289. *U-96* then called up other submarines, *U-95*, *U-103*, *U-107* and *U-108* amongst them. Including those torpedoed and sunk after the escort departed and the convoy dispersed on the 21° West meridian, together with one straggler (*Temple Moat*); a total of eight British vessels were lost.

Huntingdon (10,946 grt, owned by the Federal Steam Navigation Co.) was the first to be struck. She was loaded with 'generals' for Brisbane and commanded by Captain Styrin who just seven weeks before had been master of the *Middlesex* when she was mined in the Bristol Channel. It was a bitterly cold night with frequent snow squalls as the convoy steamed north by west in latitude 58.25N, a magnificent display of the aurora borealis could be seen in the clear intervals. First one torpedo, then, 37 minutes later, a second. A large section of the port side forward of the bridge virtually disappeared. She settled rapidly by the head, the crew abandoning ship as the seas were pounding over the foredeck. Miraculously they were all rescued by the Greek *Papalemos* of the same convoy.

The following night on 24 February, in position 59.30N 21.00W, *Cape Nelson* (3,807 grt, Lyle Shipping Co. Ltd) was torpedoed by *U-95* which was on the surface between the columns, seas shipping overall and brilliantly illuminated by a multitude of 'snowflakes'. These were rockets firing a high-powered illuminant which had parachute attachments for long continued suspension in the night sky. The glare was steely and intense. Minutes later it was *Anglo Peruvian* (5,457 grt, Nitrate Producers Steamship Company), the River Tyne for Boston in ballast – there were only seventeen survivors. In the early hours, as the convoy was dispersing, it was *U-95* again 'up front'; the 4,542 ton *Marslew* (Walmar Steamship Company) disappeared within six minutes, Captain Watkins and twelve of his crew perished. Then came *Sirikishna* (5,458 grt, South Georgia Company) Stag Line's *Linaria* (3,385 grt) and finally, at 0220 hours, the 4,260 grt *Waynegate*, sunk by the Italian submarine *Bianchi*. The death roll was again heavy, with *Sirikishna* and *Linaria* losing all hands.

Convoy OB289 fared little better losing three British vessels and one Norwegian tanker damaged on the same night – 24 February. For a personal recollection of this battle refer to Chapter 10. OB290 which was not far behind, though taking a more southerly course, was located by Prien (*U-47*). Ordered to await Kretschmer in *U-99* before attacking, his accurate reports enabled six FW 200 aircraft to sink three vessels (*Mahanada*, *Swimburne* and *Llanwern*) and damaged two more (*Melmore Head* and *Leeds City*) while the submarines sank four vessels and damaged one. It is worth noting that 24 ships were damaged by air attacks during February necessitating extensive repairs.

A fifth vessel of OB290, the *Holmlea*, was sunk by Prien, already credited with *Kasongo*, the Swedish *Rydboholm* and the Norwegian *Borgland* (plus the damaged *Diala*). *Holmlea* was sunk by gunfire after the convoy dispersed and the escorts left on the seventeenth meridian. Captain Potts and 27 of his crew were killed in the shelling. According to German sources she had already been attacked by *U-99* but the torpedo missed, a rare occurrence for Kretschmer.

Fresh from their successes on the afternoon of the 26th, the four-engined Condors returned to the west of Scotland the following day. 120 miles north-west of Bloody Foreland a single aircraft, flying low into a force 8 wind, came in at masthead height. The 10,000 ton *Anchises* (Alread Holt and Co) homeward-bound from Australia via Cape Town and Freetown was following her prearranged course towards the North Channel as two bombs near missed and shook her severely. On the second run another two bombs exploded amidst the rattle of machine gun fire. *Anchises* shuddered and rolled violently in the high seas, the port side split from the gunwale amidships, the engine room and stokehold quickly flooded.

Returning for a third attack, the aircraft released a further two bombs which so increased the devastation that the master, Captain James, ordered the ship to be abandoned save for 33 of the crew with which to try to save her. Six lifeboats were launched with a total of 134 people on board, including five women and two children.

On 28 February Captain James and his skeleton crew, because of the full gale which was now blowing, abandoned *Anchises* for the safety of the corvette *Kingcup* but in the attempted transfer the boat was virtually wrecked, rudderless and without oars. About twenty men were thrown into the water, two of them, Captain James and one of the quartermasters, were never seen again. 120 survivors were later landed at Greenock, fourteen crew including the master were posted as missing, presumed drowned at sea. In view of the damage caused by the bombs and the atrocious weather, the loss of life could have been far heavier. During the afternoon of the 28th the Blue Funnel *Anchises*, again bombed by the enemy, turned over and sank.

The German heavy cruiser *Admiral Hipper* and the battle-cruisers *Scharnhorst* and *Gneisenau* sank eleven British merchant ships, tonnage 50,730, in the North Atlantic during February and whilst they could no doubt have sunk many more with their great firepower and speed it must be remembered that they were acting upon instructions to hit and run and to avoid contact with the Royal Navy. Their nuisance value, however, in tying down many vessels of the British naval fleet cannot be underestimated in the conduct of the U-boat campaign.

Admiral Hipper sailed from Brest on 1 February, returning thirteen days later during which time she intercepted the 7 knot convoy SLS64, homeward from Freetown. Out of the ten vessels which left the security of the Sierra Leone river, only one, Chapman's *Lornaston*, reached the United Kingdom and that was after she spent three months under repair in the Azores. Within 24 hours of sailing *Nailsea*

Lass fell behind with engine trouble and, as already noted, she was one of the stragglers lost – for fourteen days she struggled to reach her home port unaided, only to be sunk within 60 miles of Fastnet Rock.

At first light on 12 February, 200 miles south-east of the Azores, the little band of ships, eight British and one foreign, unprotected without escort, were taken completely by surprise as a lone 'battleship' came up fast from astern. As she sailed 'peacefully' in between the centre columns many assumed her to be HMS *Renown* which they had left behind at anchor in Freetown and which was now to escort them. Suddenly *Admiral Hipper* declared her identity, the swastika was hoisted aloft, the first salvo of shells crippling the commodore vessel, Ropner's *Warlaby* (4,876 grt), loaded with cotton seed from Alexandria. She reeled over and sank within minutes, taking her master, Captain Murray, eight officers and 27 men with her. For a few minutes there was pandemonium as ships 'broke ranks', turning, twisting, and zig-zagging in an effort to escape the salvos fired at such short range. When the dust settled and *Hipper* made off in case distress signals had alerted naval ships in the area, a further six ships were sinking and two, the *Lornaston* and *Ainderby*, were seriously damaged.

The 4,684 ton *Oswestry Grange* (Houlder Bros & Co. Ltd), under the command of Captain Stone (Rosairie for Liverpool) sighted the warship at 0610 hours. Forty minutes later she was struck on the portside aft, amidships, the shelter deck and the lower bridge structure. The shelling continued after the ship had been abandoned; Captain Stone, the fourth engineer and three seamen were drowned after their lifeboat was damaged and capsized. The remaining occupants were picked up by the second lifeboat, the survivors being landed in Funchal on 14 February by the damaged *Lornaston*. The crippled *Oswestry Grange* turned turtle and sank after the enemy put twelve rounds into her side.

The Alexander Shipping Company lost two of their fleet: the *Shrewsbury* of 4,542 grt and the *Westbury* of 4,712 grt. As the *Shrewsbury* sank, twenty of her crew were killed; eighteen of them were in a boat that was hit by a shell as they attempted to pull away. Her master, Captain Armstrong survived. As the *Westbury* sank, five of her crew including Captain Embleton were missing and were not seen again. The other British vessels lost were the 4,896 ton *Derryname* and the 1,236 ton *Iceland*.

Lornaston and *Ainderby* sailed from Funchal in early June after repairs had been completed but only *Lornaston* had a trouble free voyage. Ropner's *Ainderby* (4,860 grt) was sunk on 10 June by *U-552*, position 53.30N 12.10W. Twenty-one of her crew lost their lives. Even the 4,934 ton *Lornaston* did not survive the war for she was torpedoed and sunk off the west coast of Ireland on 8 March 1945, two months before peace was declared in Europe.

Scharnhorst and *Gneisenau* sighted HX106 on 8 February east of Newfoundland but did not attack when it was established that the convoy was escorted by the battleship *Ramillies*. Rather than risk one of his ships, Admiral Lutjens avoided them setting a southerly course for the quieter latitudes of the Tropic of Cancer. Fourteen days later, however, they returned to the north and in position 47.12N 40.13W came across the remnants of convoy OB283 which had dispersed twenty-four hours before.

Harlesden (5,483 grt,), owned by J. & C. Harrison, had been sighted the previous afternoon by a spotter plane from one of the battlecruisers. She was the first to be sunk by the subsequent shelling, and seven of her crew were killed. The enemy then caught up with the tanker *Lustrous* (6,156 grt), Hain Steamship's *Trelawney* (4,689 grt), *Kantara* (3,237 grt) and *A.D. Huff* (6,219 grt). All put up a tremendous fight with the battle raging over several hours and many square miles of ocean, the Germans were continually astounded at the refusal of British merchant ships to obey their orders to surrender and not use their radio. The heroic action of the *A.D. Huff* in actually returning the fire of the powerful *Gneisenau*, even though she was a broken vessel, low in the water, convinced the captain of the battle-cruiser of the 'madness of the British'.

As *Scharnhorst* and *Gneisenau* sped away to the south-west they were to evade detection for three weeks, creating much concern and confusion at the Admiralty. As we shall see in Chapter 5, it was not until 15 March that they again reappeared in the Atlantic 'black hole'.

The four months of winter had ended. King Neptune had taken his toll but the greatest toll of all, 250 British vessels of 1,092,867 tonnage, had been created by man himself.

> There is no danger seamen have not run
> Tempests have drowned them since the world began
> They have dared shipwreck, frostbite and the sun
> But they have dared a greater danger, Man.
>
> *John Masefield*

CHAPTER FOUR

The Tempest Rages
(March–June 1941)

Through efforts made by Prime Minister Churchill during the spring of 1941, the British War Cabinet, the heads of Government in the USA and Canada, together with the Military Commanders in the field were made aware of the importance of the merchant fleet. 'It is in shipping and the power to transport across the oceans that in 1941 the crunch of the whole war will be felt,' wrote Churchill to President Roosevelt. On 18 March, in a radio broadcast to the British people he added, 'Therefore we must regard the Battle of the Atlantic as one of the most momentous ever fought in all the annals of war.'

The Lend-Lease Act was passed on 11 March. The urgent need was to persuade the Americans to build ships as soon as possible to replace the British losses and also to hand over ships to Britain at once, for a building programme is slow to yield returns and even the most optimistic forecasts did not assume that the rate of new building would overtake the loss rate before the middle of 1942. Within three weeks of the signing, Sir Arthur Salter arrived in Washington as head of the British Merchant Shipping Mission in the United States to press Britain's claims for ships.

In addition to the ships lost, 2,800,000 tons of shipping were damaged and under repair, 1,800,000 tons of which were immobilised awaiting repair, the remaining 1,000,000 tons undergoing repair whilst being loaded or unloaded with much consequent delay in port.

Spring 1941 saw the first great troop movements. With the Axis onslaught through Egypt bringing them virtually to the gates of Alexandria, with the push through Greece and on to the island of Crete, the enemy threatened not only the valuable oil supplies of the Persian Gulf but democracy over the whole region. The Mediterranean became the principal theatre of war and during the months of March, April and May, a total of 134,320 troops were carried in 88 merchant ships in sixteen convoys from the United Kingdom to Suez via the Cape. The largest convoy of all sailed from Liverpool and the Clyde on 24 March; it was the largest troop convoy ever to sail from British shores. There were 23 troopers in all, Union Castle, Royal Mail, Cunard, Canadian Pacific, Orient and six P & O vessels, the five Straiths and *Viceroy of India*. Total tonnage was 500,000; 132,000 tons of it, more than a quarter of the total were P & O who carried some 80,000 troops to Egypt at this time.

On arrival at Suez there was great congestion. In the Red Sea the 'armada' met up with the two *Queens*, carrying 10,000 troops between them. They had sailed from Australia in company with *Mauretania*, *Nieu Amsterdam* and *Ile de France* (convoy US10) which disembarked their troops in Colombo. There was room for only one *Queen* at a time to disembark at Suez so when, on 3 May 1941 *Queen Mary* moved into the harbour, *Queen Elizabeth* lay off in the Red Sea awaiting her turn.

In spite of the new offensive launched by Dönitz, the German High Command were disappointed by results. In March a total of 41 merchant ships were sunk by U-boats, 26 of them British but at a cost of four leading aces – Günter Prien together with all hands on *U-47*. Otto Kretschmer captured from the sinking of *U-99*; the destruction of *U-70* cost Commander Joachim Matz his life and Joachim Schepke was crushed to death when *U-100* was sunk.

A serious situation had developed however with the action of *Scharnhorst* and *Gneisenau*. Within a space of two days they sank or captured sixteen ships, twelve of them of British registry; the total result of mercantile warfare operation 'Berlin' was 22 ships of 115,622 tons sunk. Brought up in pursuit were *Rodney* (from convoy HX114), *King George V* (from convoy HX115) and *Nelson*, the cruiser *Nigeria* and two destroyers. From Gibraltar came *Renown*, *Ark Royal*, *Sheffield* and further destroyers. Yet the two German battle-cruisers arrived at Brest on 28 March avoiding all contact with their searchers.

On 7 March the raiders suddenly appeared 350 miles north-east of the Cape Verde Islands bearing down on Convoy SL67 of 56 ships. Then, having sighted the battleship *Malaya*, sitting in the centre column like a mother hen protecting her brood, they veered away and were lost on the misty horizon. Not willing to risk themselves against the fire power of *Malaya* and her escort destroyers *Faulknor* and *Forester* they called up *U-124* and *U-105* which then sank five British ships, totalling 28,488 grt between them. The submarines had just refuelled in Las Palmas from the German tanker *Charlotte Schliemann*.

Harmodius, Nardana, Hindpool, Tielbank and *Lahore* were all heavily laden with foodstuffs from the Far East and South Africa and were sunk within 2½ hours of each other during the hours of darkness on the morning of 8 March. The first attack came in position 20.35N 20.40W, the last torpedoes were fired in 21.03N 20.38W, Wilhelm Schulz of *U-124* claiming hits on a sixth vessel, unidentified, which was left in a damaged condition.

Meanwhile *Scharnhorst* and *Gneisenau* headed north towards the Halifax route and on 15 March came upon seven unescorted ships, all of British registry, from dispersed westbound convoy OB295. Next day they sighted eight more, this time from OB296 and *Chilean Reefer*, an independent en route to Halifax. It was a happy hunting ground with *Gneisenau* credited with seven ships sunk (26,693 grt) and three tankers captured (20,139 grt); her accomplice six ships of 35,080 grt sunk.

At first light on 15 March, the 8,046 ton tanker *San Casimiro* (Eagle Oil and Shipping Co Ltd) sighted the control tower of *Gneisenau* hull-down. Pursuing normal practice Captain Shotton turned his ship away to put the stranger astern but immediately a yellow flash on the horizon denoted the firing of a gun. The raider closed fast and although the distress signal was sent the second shell burst on the tanker's starboard quarter, holing the engine room above the waterline, smashing a lifeboat and carrying away the main aerial. With the enemy fast overhauling, Captain Shotton decided that resistance was impracticable and escape impossible.

An hour later as fourteen well-armed Germans boarded as prize crew Captain Shotton and two gunners were taken prisoner. Though damaged the vessel got under way heading in a north-westerly direction for 24 hours, then turned east for the coast of France. Early on the fifth day she was sighted by RAF Coastal Command and in the late afternoon her course was plotted by several planes who directed HMS *Renown* and the carrier *Ark Royal* to the scene.

Knowing that he could not make the safety of the Norwegian coastline, the German commander of *San Casimiro* gave the order to scuttle and abandon ship. Salvage was out of the question and *Renown* (position 45.12N 19.42W) gave the coup de grâce with her six inch batteries, the survivors being landed in Gibraltar and repatriated to the United Kingdom by the transport *Empire Trooper*. A further captured tanker, the Norwegian *Bianca*, was also scuttled when she came in sight of Allied warships.

Another Shell Group tanker was directly in the path of *Gneisenau* after her capture of *San Casimiro*. This was the Anglo-Saxon 6,197 ton motor vessel *Simnia*, commanded by Captain Anderson, in ballast for Curaçao. Two salvos burst across her bows during a rain squall at about 1530 hours local time. As the German battle-cruiser hove in sight salvo after salvo thundered over the sea; then, four direct hits, one in the aft crew accommodation killing two Chinese cooks and wounding the chief engineer and a messroom boy; another carried away the telemotor gear that operated the rudder, making the ship unsteerable – she shortly began to go round in circles.

As *Simnia* was being abandoned several more high explosive shells burst near the stricken tanker. With her crew prisoners of war, below decks aboard *Gneisenau* the enemy opened fire with her secondary armament, firing over a hundred rounds until the vessel, now a raging inferno, sank beneath the waves.

Many other fine vessels were sunk. They all found their watery grave within a fifty mile radius of 43 North, 43 West – British Tanker's 7,139 ton *British Strength*, the ex-French 4,564 ton *Myson*, managed by Reardon Smith's, the 6,554 ton tanker *Athelfoam*, United Molasses Co. Ltd. There was Prince Line's Mediterranean trader *Sardinian Prince* (3,491 grt), Silver Line's *Silverfir* (4,347 grt), *Demeterton* (5,251 grt, owned by R. Chapman & Son) and *Empire Industry* (3,721 grt).

Captain Potts and his crew of 38 were taken prisoner from the 4,388 grt *Royal Crown* (Hall Bros Steamship Co.). The destruction of *Rio Dorado* (4,507 grt, owned by the Thompson Steamshipping Co.) cost Captain Clare and his crew of 39 their lives – she blew up amidst a sheet of flame.

The refrigerated motorship *Chilean Reefer* (1,739 grt), originally Danish and owned by J. Lauritzen, was handed over to Alfred Holt's when her country of origin had been overrun by the enemy. Commanded by Captain Bell, she had sailed from Loch Ewe on 9 March in ballast for Halifax, Nova Scotia to load bacon for London; her crew consisted of eighteen British, twelve Danes and six Chinese. Hearing the various distress calls, one from *Demeterton*, in the immediate vicinity, she increased speed to her maximum, corkscrewing dangerously, pitching heavily in her 'light' condition, engines racing as her propeller rose high out of the water. During the late afternoon of 16 March she came under fire from the heavy armament of *Gneisenau*.

For a brief period there developed a real David and Goliath action, probably one of the most gallant single ship actions ever fought by a British merchant ship against such a vastly superior adversary. Captain Bell brought his sole 4 inch gun, of 1914

Japanese vintage, to bear upon the enemy, replying round for round, losing twelve officers and men, three of whom died aboard the raider. As *Chilean Reefer* turned to flee to avoid further loss of life, the Germans were astonished and puzzled. Even though they closed to within half a cable, pounding round after round into her quarry, 82 rounds in all according to the official German report, Captain Bell, calmly in command, tried to zig-zag his way out of trouble, releasing smoke floats in a desperate attempt to confuse his attacker and save his proud ship. Alas! she became a burning hulk, her brave master and his men only abandoning her when it became impossible to stay aboard.

Because of the presence of British warships in the area, *Gneisenau*, after meeting up with *Scharnhorst*, raced away in a northern direction taking with her the second mate and the three crewmen who were later to die from their wounds. Second Mate Collett, after being landed in Brest spent five days in cattle trucks before reaching the prisoner of war camp near Bremen. Captain Bell and his survivors were picked up by the battleship *Rodney* later the same night.

The death and destruction could have been far greater but valuable ships and men had been lost and Whitehall was anxious lest further convoys were at risk from such powerful forces.

Kretschmer in *U-99* opened the attack against convoy OB293 on 7 March. His accurately placed torpedo amidships sent United Whalers' *Terge Viken*, the 20,638 grt whale oil refining tanker, at that time the largest ship of its kind in the world, reeling like a drunken sailor, her boiler room split asunder. Yet she rode the ocean like a *Marie Celeste*, eventually turning turtle and only sinking when fired upon by two British destroyers and a corvette on 14 March. Next in line ahead was *Athelbeach*, the 6,568 grt United Molasses tanker. *U-99* blew her stern away at 500 yards' range rendering her unmanageable, surfacing immediately to finish off her prey with her 6 inch gun, killing Captain McIntyre and six of his crew.

Weaving in and out of the centre column Kretschmer was joined by Eckermann in *UA* and Matz in *U-70* who subsequently torpedoed and damaged *Delilian* before being depth-charged and sunk by the escort. In these latitudes north of 60° Prien was sunk the same night when surprised in a heavy squall by the destroyer *Wolverine*.

Kretschmer was captured following his daring attack on the heavily escorted (five destroyers and two corvettes) 41 ship 8 knot convoy HX112 nine days later when, accompanied by *U-37*, *U-74*, *U-100* and *U-110*, he sank five vessels and damaged the ex-French 9,314 ton motor tanker *Franche Comte* managed by J.I. Jacobs &

Co. Ltd. *U-100* (Schepke), sunk the same night, was the first submarine to be lost as a direct result of radar contact.

In the attack on *Franche Comte*, in position 61.15N 12.30W, *U-99* raced in on the surface, twisting and turning between escorts. She was so close to the tanker that she was rocked by the torpedo blast and illuminated by the flames. The whole forepart of the stricken vessel was ablaze, the bridge and lower bridge fiooded with oil. There was a gaping hole in the hull some 65 feet long, plates were twisted and torn and flung outwards by the force of the explosion; the deck was torn away and the mast buckled. Later black smoke lay upon the sea like a thick fog.

After some ten hours of bad weather and at the third attempt, Captain Church, accompanied by his officers and chief steward reboarded their ship. After 2½ hours *Franche Comte* was under way, propelled by her own engines. Although the fo'c'sle was awash with the propeller nearly out of the water she made port five days later with an open wound in her side and with 11,000 tons of oil still remaining in her tanks. She was repaired in 78 days by Barclay Curle of Glasgow.

The Ben Line lost two ships within 48 hours: *Benwyvis*, convoy SL68, and *Benvorlich*, laden with ammunition for the Far East, caught by a Focke Wulf Condor two days out of Oban (54.48N 13.10W, convoy OB298). The enemy surprised both convoy and escort as, on 19 March, the four-engined bomber, flew in through low clouds with her engines shut off. Before Captain Copeman could reach the bridge, a bomb had exploded in No 1 hatch; twenty of her crew died as she caught fire and blew up, raining large pieces of jagged metal over the sea. Twenty-four survivors, including Captain Copeman, were picked up by the rescue ship *Zamalek*.

Other well known vessels caught in the western approaches by the Luftwaffe during the spring of 1941 were Port Line's *Port Townsville* (8,661 grt), Canadian Pacific's *Beaverbrae* (9,956 grt), and Elder Dempster's *Swedru* (5,379 grt).

Convoy SL68 of 59 ships lost eight vessels with a total tonnage of 44,000. Additionally *Clan MacNab* was lost when, during a sharp alteration of course, she was in collision with *Glenshiel*, a wartime hazard that was always present.

Benwyvis (5,920 grt) homeward-bound with a full general cargo was torpedoed during the hours of darkness on 21 March, position 20.00N 26.00W, simultaneously with the sinking of Clan Line's 5,802 ton *Clan Ogilvy*. The forward holds quickly filled with water and after taking a heavy list she virtually stood upon her sternpost with the deck nearly vertical. As she sank, no more than ten minutes after the explosion, there was a tremendous hissing of steam and the sea bubbled furiously as the air escaped from her.

Two lifeboats were launched but only one survived the 30-foot wave caused by the sinking vessel, five of the crew losing their lives. Captain Small and 39 survivors managed to get away in the remaining boat, eight others were adrift on a raft.

As the enemy surfaced (*U-105*) some of the survivors from *Benwyvis* were transferred to one of the two lifeboats from *Clan Ogilvy* and the three boats then set sail for the Cape Verde Islands. They were still together on the eleventh day but as they had sighted no islands they agreed to separate. Next day the *Clan Ogilvy* boat in charge of Captain Gough was picked up by the Spanish *Cabo Villano* and the other Clan boat by the British *King Edgar*.

Unhappily those survivors headed by Captain Gough were subjected to a second ordeal within two months. They sailed from Santos for the United Kingdom on 6 May as passengers aboard *Rodney Star*. 5° north of the Equator she was torpedoed and sunk.

Of the 33 men who set out in the *Benwyvis* boat, only one, a young Scottish cadet not yet eighteen years old, survived. He had buried his captain, by crawling aft and throwing him overboard; he had witnessed his shipmates lose all grip on themselves; most of them jumped overboard. One by one they were overcome by exposure and thirst until on the 25th day, his only companion, a young ordinary seaman, deserted him saying that he would walk ashore.

On 17 April, his 27th day in the boat, the lone Scottish lad was rescued. During all this time not a drop of rain fell and for the last two weeks he existed on half a tin of condensed milk and sea water mixed with iodine to take the taste of the salt away. There were longer lifeboat voyages but possibly no one during all the months of the war was so pleased to see his rescuers – the Vichy French *Ville de Rouen* bound for Madagascar. It was nearly Christmas before he reached his home on the banks of the Forth.

The Blue Funnel 7,056 ton *Memnon* (Alfred Holt & Co. Ltd), sunk in position 20.41N 21.00W on 11 March was one of the first casualties of the new U-boat drive to the south, sought to avoid the recent heavily defended HX convoys and with the idea of forcing the Royal Navy to disperse their escort vessels. Lying in wait was *U-106*, a type IX Atlantic boat commanded by the experienced Lieutenant-Commander Jürgen Oesten.

Memnon was heavily laden, homeward-bound from Suez, zig-zagging at 15 knots when the torpedo struck aft; she quickly began to sink. Captain Williams ordered the ship to be abandoned at once leaving the two radio officers on board to send the distress call after which they found all the lifeboats had been launched. Together with the junior second engineer, they jumped overboard and were fortunate not to be caught by the propeller. In the words of the fourth mate, 'the end was violent and terrible'. A bulkhead collapsed, the bows lifted higher and higher and when the deck reached an angle of 45° she began to slide under. The rush of water forced oil and fumes from out of the funnel in a great red cloud. As the funnel was disappearing it collapsed at the base, reared in the air and fell.

It was eight days before the survivors sighted land. 100 miles north of Dakar they entered a small fishing port, weak and exhausted. A second boat sailed 600 miles over a period of thirteen days until she met up with the French *Kilissi*; with one man dead and 37 in good heart they were guided to Bathurst and taken to a military hospital. The crews of both boats displayed fine seamanship, pluck and endurance – well worthy of the best traditions.

The two radio officers who remained at their post to the bitter end were working their passage home in an ex-French ship when she broke down and was intercepted by a Vichy French warship. Thus they remained in French hands until the reconquest of North Africa in November 1942.

Another example of a brave radio officer was when the independent 3,767 ton *Umona* (Bullard King & Co.) was sunk 90 miles south-west of Freetown on 30 March by *U-124* which had victualled from the raider *Kormoran* shortly before. He stayed to the last moment sending out the distress signal then threw himself exhausted over the side. Together with a badly injured gunner he clung to a raft and other wreckage, worried by sharks who made every effort to get at them. For three days and nights they drifted on the ocean with the sun beating down on them.

On the fourth day they sighted a submarine, attracting its attention by using a tobacco tin reflecting in the sun. It turned out to be *U-124* which had sunk their ship; Lieutenant-Commander Wilhelm Schulz gave them food and water before moving off and submerging. The following day the weather grew worse, the radio officer grew weaker and before nightfall he died. Miraculously the gunner, sole occupant of the raft, was rescued on the twelfth day. There were only three survivors from *Umona*; Captain Peckham, 82 crew, two gunners and fifteen passengers were lost.

Lifeboat Number Seven of *Britannia* has taken its place in maritime history through the book bearing the same name and the epic voyage it undertook following the destruction of Anchor Line's 8,799 ton intermediate liner by the raider *Thor*. Eighty-two souls set out in a boat built and certified for 56. She travelled 1,535 miles in 23 days with an old compass 20° out of true casting 38 survivors, including thirteen British officers, on to the coast of Brazil. A diary kept by an officer of the Royal Navy who was a passenger for Bombay is now in the National Maritime Museum.

A comfortable 14-knot ship belonging to the days of the Indian Raj, *Britannia* suffered all the horrors of the war at sea. For over an hour, on 25 March 1941, she put up a stout fight with her single gun beneath the heat of the tropical sun (7.24N 09.00W). 122 crew and 127 passengers (service personnel bound for India) lost their lives. Even when the order had been given by Captain Collie to abandon ship, the way taken off her and steam blown, the raider came quite close, continuing her bombardment – 159 shells in all, causing considerable damage to the lifeboats. Her boat deck became a shambles, dead and wounded lay everywhere and as she sank, *Thor* turned and ran lest distress signals had alerted the Royal Navy at Freetown.

Fifty-five survivors were picked up by the Spanish *Bachi* after 36 hours. The *Cabo de Hornos*, also Spanish Flag, rescued 77 of whom 49 were service personnel, near Tenerife on 29 March. A third lifeboat was sighted by Shaw Savill's *Raranga* and 67 more survivors were plucked from the sea. From a total complement of 484 which set out from Liverpool, 235 were saved.

A sequel to this tragedy came eleven days later when *Ena de Larrinaga*, position 01.10N 26.00W, came across wreckage and an empty lifeboat bearing the Anchor liner's name. She slowed to search for survivors and was torpedoed and sunk by *U-105*, five men being lost in the engine room. The remainder of her crew, led by Captain Craston, got away in the two lifeboats, one was adrift for eleven days before being sighted by a Belgium steamer, the second reached the Brazilian coast in thirteen days.

On 9 April Winston Churchill uttered a further warning to his War Cabinet: '. . . after all everything turns upon the Battle of the Atlantic which is proceeding with growing intensity on both sides. Our losses in ships and tonnage are very heavy, and, vast as are our shipping resources which we control, the losses cannot continue indefinitely without seriously affecting our war effort and our means of subsistence.'

His notice was exemplified by the reports of the battle of SC26 which were just being received. For two days and two nights a pack of eight U-boats had attacked a convoy far distant from the Western Approaches (between 27 and 28 West) where hitherto ships had been considered comparatively safe. Ten ships out of 22 had been sunk and the armed merchant cruiser *Worcestershire* damaged.

The total U-boat fleet had risen in four months from 89 to 113 and new building was now in its stride. In spite of enemy submarine losses, the immediate outlook looked bleak; the war at sea was now moving to within 500 miles of the coast of Canada and at this time only a few of the destroyer escorts had endurance sufficient to make the Transatlantic passage and to hunt U-boats on the way – the new frigates, fast, well armed and of long range, had yet to come into operation.

Churchill again drew attention to the situation only three weeks later.

> When you think how easy it is to sink ships at sea and how hard it is to build them and when you realise that we have never less than 2,000 ships afloat and 300 to 400 in the danger zone, and of the great armies we are nurturing and reinforcing in the east and of the world wide traffic we have to carry on, when you think of all this can you wonder that it is the Battle of the Atlantic which holds the first place in the thoughts of those upon whom the responsibility for final victory rests.

April losses from U-boats were 42 ships of which 30 were British, more than a quarter of a million tons. The pack lying in wait for SC26 from Sydney Cape Breton were *U-46*, *U-69*, *U-73*, *U-74*, *U-76*, *U-97*, *U-98* and *U-101*. The 22 ships were sailing at 7 knots in five columns, the outside columns had five ships in the column, the others four. The distance between columns was three cables, between vessels in column, two cables. They were old ships, slow and out-dated, tramps and tankers, small ships of Baltic and Mediterranean trades, home trade vessels which rarely ventured 'foreign-going'. All were press-ganged into the Trans-atlantic lifeline. On the night of 2/3 April they were brilliantly lit, in latitudes north of 58 the Northern Lights shone brightly. Their only escort was Bibby's *Worcestershire*, converted to an armed merchant cruiser, occupying position 031, in the centre and up front.

Lieutenant Engelbert Endrass opened the battle when a sheet of flame shot skywards from British Tankers' 7,000 ton *British Reliance*. An hour later, in position 58.21N 27.59W, Endrass fired three torpedoes in succession; the first sank Ropner's *Alderpool* (4,313 grt), the second damaged *Thirlby* (4,887 grt), also owned by Ropner and the third struck Sir Walter H. Cockerline's 5,351 ton *Athenic*.

Although low in the water she held up remarkably well but in the early light of dawn, *U-73* (Lieutenant Helmut Rosenbaum) sent a second torpedo into her and she quickly broke up. With the sinking of *Westpool* (5,724 grt, operated for Ministry of Shipping by N. Campbell & Co.) – 35 of her crew of 43 perished – the convoy was in disarray. Involuntarily they scattered only to reform the following evening when a further four vessels were sunk and the 11,402 ton AMC *Worcestershire* damaged.

Of the four vessels that foundered on the second night three were British:

British Viscount	British Tankers Ltd, 6,895 grt. Captain Baikie and 27 crew lost.
Harbledown	National Steamship Co, 5,414 grt. Fourteen crew and two gunners lost.
Wellcombe	Stanhope Steamship Co Ltd, 5,122 grt. Fifteen crew lost.

Convoy SC26 had paid a heavy price in both ships and men.

Homewards from the Far East for Liverpool with 'generals' Alfred Holt's deeply laden *Calchas* (10,305 grt, Captain Holden) was torpedoed in the engine room on 21 April 1941 by *U-107*, in position 23.50N 27.00W, close to where *Memnon* had foundered 40 days before. *U-107*, a type IX 'Atlantic' boat, was commanded by Lieutenant-Commander Günter Hessler who was Dönitz's son-in-law. He subsequently went on to sink a total of 87,000 tons of Allied shipping.

Seven men in the engine room and boiler rooms were killed outright and No 7 lifeboat was destroyed. The passengers and some of the crew then got away leaving Captain Holden, his officers and the remainder of the crew aboard to see what could be done to save her. It was then that the tragedy occurred. A second torpedo ripped open the other side of the engine room killing many of those who had stayed, and Captain Holden, although he was seen to go to his quarters, was never seen again. *Calchas* then broke in two and within three minutes she had sunk. The motorboat was launched from the lower bridge but even those who could escape were lost when the boat was dragged under by the suction as she sank.

Six lifeboats containing the fortunate ones but without their experienced navigators then set sail for the nearest land. Apart from a second sighting of *U-107*, a merchant vessel – a neutral for she had white upper works which astonishingly 'sheered off and proceeded on her way' and the loss, due to weather, of the small lifeboats, nos 3 and 4 (personnel and provisions transferred to boat no 5), the first ten days were surmounted. Then, the first casualty. The second radio officer, unable to stand the strain any longer, jumped overboard from lifeboat No 5 and was not seen again. On 4 May a passenger died, and the next day, a Chinese fireman. On 7 May another passenger died and many were in very bad shape; thirst, hunger and exposure were beginning to have their effect.

The following day, 650 miles from where *Calchas* had sunk, they landed upon the coast of Senegal, two died in getting ashore. Between 5 and 8 May the three other boats landed on the Cape Verde Islands. A remarkable 14–16 days' sailing for four boats without instruments, other than compasses and under the leadership of the ship's bosun, the carpenter, an able seaman and the chief steward – skilled seamanship coupled with the instinctive acceptance by all the others of a self-imposed discipline.

In northern waters the enemy struck hard at the end of April. Valuable ships, many of them independent and without escort, were lost: *Empire Endurance, Beacon Grange, City of Nagpur, Lassell* and *Nevissa* were among them.

Empire Endurance (8,570 grt), operated by the Booth Steamship Company on behalf of the Ministry of War Transport (Captain Torkington), was outward bound from the Bristol Channel for the Middle East, in position 53.05N 23.14W when she was torpedoed and sunk by *U-73* during the early hours of 20 April. Carrying a crew of 89 and five passengers she was caught in bad weather and the explosion wrecked the whole of the vessel amidships including two naval motor launches *ML1003* and *ML1037* being carried as deck cargo. The bridge was a shambles and the bridge lifeboats were covered with debris.

The order was given to abandon ship and, in spite of the full gale which was now blowing, four lifeboats were launched. The falls of No 4 boat had to be cut however with axes to free her and as she dropped some 15 feet into the raging sea, the master and the second mate began climbing down a rope ladder to try to secure her. It was then that a second torpedo struck, blowing both of them into the sea and cutting *Empire Endurance* completely in half. In ten seconds she had gone leaving the sea covered in wreckage.

Captain Torkington was badly injured but he, together with eight men, held on to a raft and with the chief mate and seventeen others they managed to right lifeboat No 4, hoist the sail and set course for the distant Cornish coast. No 2 boat, on the starboard side, was blown to bits with all on board except one man who was found on a raft and who later transferred to the chief mate's boat. A third boat with twenty crew and four of the passengers was picked up the next day but the fourth was found empty on 10 May 250 miles WNW of the Orkney Islands.

It was also on 10 May that the survivors of the chief mate's boat were rescued – by *Highland Pride*, which bore down upon them in convoy. Alas! of the 28 men who started on that tragic voyage twenty days earlier only five were picked up and of the three taken to hospital one died. Captain Torkington died of his injuries the day prior to being sighted by the rescue ship. During these long days amid the Atlantic rollers they had to endure very rough weather with low temperatures at night and one by one they succumbed to the elements – on five occasions they had been sighted by aircraft only to be lost again each time. Of the total complement of 94 persons 66 perished.

The motor vessel *Beacon Grange* (10,160 grt, Captain Friend), built for Houlder Bros Ltd in 1938 for the carriage of meat between Argentina and the United Kingdom, was struck by three torpedoes, all within fifteen seconds, as she was outward-bound, zig-zagging independently, on course to Admiralty instructions, on the afternoon of 27 April. Because this was a battle of foodlines, the refrigerator vessel was, to the enemy, a valuable target to sink. Previously, on 22 August 1940, she had been bombed and set on fire in the North Sea off the Scottish coast.

Beacon Grange, in position 62.05N 16.20W, was badly crippled and the order was given to abandon her; two lifeboats on the port side were launched whilst the master and three remaining crew members jumped overboard to a raft as *U-552* broke surface only 500 yards away. Lieutenant-Commander Erich Topp, in command of the enemy submarine, circled his prey firing a further torpedo amidships – subsequently Topp, previously he had commanded *U-57*, was to become the third highest scoring submarine ace of the Second World War.

As the fourth torpedo struck, a cascade of water shot skywards and when this had cleared, the vessel was seen to have sagged heavily amidships, her bows were up and her propellers were showing. She sank within five minutes.

Four days later, on 1 May, the chief mate's lifeboat was sighted by a Catalina flying boat which dropped emergency rations indicating an early rescue for the 39 occupants – they included five young army ratings and four deck boys aged fifteen or sixteen. However it was 48 hours later that they were sighted by the Belgium steam trawler *Edward Anseele*. In six days they had covered a distance of only 60 miles.

Captain Friend, after transferring from the raft to the second lifeboat, sailed 94 miles in a little over 48 hours until he, together with 40 of his men, was sighted by a patrol plane and rescued by the corvette *Gladiolus* the following day.

The destruction of Ellerman's 10,146 ton *City of Nagpur* was marred by a naval enquiry set up under the chairmanship of Admiral Leggett on the conduct of her master, Captain Lloyd, who, it was alleged, might have saved his ship – she remained afloat for three hours and forty minutes. Further, it was claimed by 'a naval expert' that the submarine when she was sighted 'should have been attacked with the 4 inch and 12 pounder and the Lewis guns situated on the bridge and boat deck'. Both were serious accusations.

It transpired that the guns were put under the control of a naval officer who was in charge of a draft of ratings taking passage in the ship and the captain was in fact 'quite in order in giving charge of these guns to this Naval Officer'. It was agreed that use was not made of the after guns as they could not be deflected sufficiently to get a line on the submarine.

Admiral Leggett and his Enquiry Board, after questioning Captain Lloyd, the chief mate, the second mate and the chief engineer at separate interviews, were satisfied that the master acted properly in ordering the ship to be abandoned. It was one of the rare occasions when a British merchant ship's master was brought up before a Royal Naval Admiral as to his conduct.

Far from acting improperly Captain Lloyd had, by his prompt action in abandoning the ship within twenty minutes of the first torpedo and before *U-75* (Lieutenant Helmuth Ringelmann) extensively shelled the vessel and launched the second torpedo, saved the lives of his crew and 273 passengers who included women and children. One passenger was killed by shrapnel in the lifeboat and the third and seventh engineers along with thirteen Lascar engine room ratings were killed when the initial torpedo struck.

The 15 knot *City of Nagpur*, en route from Glasgow to Bombay was doomed with sea water in the engine room up to the cylinder tops. She was unable to transmit any distress signal owing to valves in the radio room being broken by the explosion in both the main and emergency sets. Under the circumstances it was very fortunate that within a few hours they were sighted by a Catalina flying boat and later in the day rescued by HMS *Hurricane*.

To the north-east on the same day (60.16N 16.10W) Lieutenant Topp in *U-552* led the attack on the 48 ship convoy HX121, the first daylight wolf-pack attack upon a fully escorted convoy since the summer of 1940. In a daring raid two motor tankers and the 8,897 ton *Port Hardy* were sunk and a further motor tanker damaged. The ship's bell from the *Port Hardy* was later salved from some wreckage and given to the Port Line Master (Captain Lewis) who in turn presented it to the Wolverhampton High School for Girls with which his ship was linked by the British Ship Adoption Society. A total of 57 British crew from HX121 died.

Eighty-three crew and 124 passengers were lost in the disaster that befell *Nevissa* (5,583 grt, Bermuda and West Indies Steamship Company). She was 35 miles west of St Kilda homeward-bound for Liverpool when, with a full gale blowing she was torpedoed by Lieutenant Topp. Lamport and Holt's *Lassell* (7,417 grt) was caught by Lieutenant-Commander Hessler (*U-107*) when outward-bound for South America. Two men were killed in the explosion and she sank within five minutes, Captain Bibby surviving five hours in the sea before being picked up by one of the lifeboats. This boat with 25 men was picked up by the *Benvrackie* after nine days adrift but fifteen of these were lost when *Benvrackie* herself was torpedoed on the Equator on 13 May and sank within three minutes. Her 58 survivors spent thirteen days under the tropical sun before being rescued by the hospital ship *Oxfordshire*.

The Mediterranean war which commenced at Tobruk in January suddenly erupted with the coming of spring. In the last week of February, the British Government decided to send troops to Greece to support an old ally, most were from Wavell's desert army and were transported from Port Said. Operation Lustre began on 5 March. At the end of March Rommel made a lightning strike in Cyrenaica and within two weeks, Wavell's depleted Army was driven back to the Egyptian frontier. Only the 'fortress' of Tobruk was held. On 16 April the German blitzkrieg on Greece opened and within two weeks Greece had collapsed with 58,000 British troops at risk. During 24–29 April 51,000, together with some equipment, were evacuated from eight harbours; 21,000 men were then landed as reinforcements for the British garrison in Crete which had been occupied in October 1940. On 20 May the Battle of Crete began and eleven days later the remnants of the garrison were evacuated and transported to Port Said.

Altogether over the 45 days commencing 2 April 25 British merchant ships, totalling 141,444 tons were sunk in the Mediterra-

nean theatre; all were bombed by aircraft with the exception of two
which were mined. In addition, over the same period, six ships
totalling 39,124 tons were damaged. Again, as elsewhere, many fully
trained and experienced seamen were killed, as difficult to replace as
ships and the war materials they carried.

Probably the men of the Merchant Navy in the Mediterranean
during the first half of 1941 faced difficulties as great as any
worldwide. Merchant seamen and their ships were closely linked
with every landing and every evacuation; along the coast of North
Africa they became the lifeline, supporting every move made by the
armed services.

Captain Johnson of the 3,553 ton *Destro* (Ellerman and Papayanni
Line), together with his officers and men probably withstood more
attacks than any. Working the Eastern Mediterranean for some
sixteen months from January 1941 she was attacked by enemy
bombers no fewer than 100 times, suffering twenty near misses and
sustaining damage on six occasions. On 27 March 1942 at Tobruk
she took fire, necessitating her withdrawal from service for extensive
repairs. In convoy she exchanged fire with a U-boat; in Salamis
Straits outside Piraeus harbour her guns brought down an enemy
bomber, at Tobruk she probably accounted for two more. On one
visit she endured 68 bombing raids. In Suda Bay (Crete) she was
continuously bombed for two weeks; on sailing she was inadver-
tently shelled by British shore batteries.

Vessels of the British India Steam Navigation Company were
particularly active in the region, *Bankara, Chakla, Dumana, Goalpara,
Homefield, Quiloa* and *Juna* among them. The latter was requisitioned
for naval service as a convoy service ship and renamed HMS *Fiona*.
She was bombed and sunk off Sidi Barrani.

Homefield (5,324 grt) with her master, Captain Kiely, manning
one of the Lewis guns, was blasted by two bombs from a Stuka, one of
nine dive bombers which attacked her convoy on 2 April. She was
one of fourteen ships returning to Alexandria after unloading troops
and equipment in Piraeus. After listing heavily to port she was abandoned, her crew being picked by HMAS *Voyager*. On 15 April
the 5,314 ton *Goalpara* and the 7,765 ton *Quiloa* were both beached
and abandoned after an air attack on Eleusis Bay near Piraeus. The
crews made their way to Nauplion, walking through Athens and
forty miles on foot. They then 'hitched' a lift on a ship which took
them to Suda Bay.

Bankara (3,185 grt) was lost at Tobruk after arriving with
ammunition and stores from Greece during the evacuation (21

April). During a short but resolute attack by a force of German dive bombers No 1 hold was blasted and she quickly filled with water to 'tween deck level. Run aground in shallow water she was again attacked the following day and became a total loss. Captain Radge and his crew later reached Alexandria in a small schooner captured from the Italians.

Disaster struck Piraeus harbour on the night of 6 April. A large force of dive bombers crippled the port area together with many of the ships discharging valuable military equipment. *Clan Fraser* (7,529 grt, Captain Giles), unloading ammunition and high explosive shells, was struck by three bombs, forward, amidships and aft, killing seven crew and wounding nine. She blazed furiously and then, four hours later, with the fire out of control, blew up with a roar so tremendous that it shook buildings twelve and fifteen miles inland. *City of Roubaix* (7,108 grt), *Cyprian Prince* (1,988 grt) and *Patris* (1,706 grt) sank at their moorings close by, a total loss. Severely damaged were the 8,474 ton *Cingalese Prince* and the 6,054 ton *Devis*.

Clan Cumming (7,264 grt, Captain Matthews) also discharging ammunition and with 50 tons of TNT in No 2 hold reeled heavily under the impact. Catching fire she was abandoned though later the captain and five of his crew returned and brought the blaze under control. Not one ship in the port escaped damage of one sort of another; the total of those sunk was thirteen of 41,942 tons plus 60 lighters and 25 motor sailing ships. Sadly, on leaving Piraeus eight days later, *Clan Cumming* ran into an uncharted minefield and was sunk.

Six days later in nearby Salamis Bay, the 8,271 ton motor tanker *Marie Maersk*, managed on behalf of the Ministry of War Transport by C.T. Bowring and Co., was bombed and set on fire killing eight of her crew. She blazed furiously for 24 hours before sinking. She had limped into port after being bombed and set on fire on 24 March off Crete when six of her crew were killed. Later raised by the Italians and towed to Trieste she was finally bombed and destroyed by Allied aircraft in February 1945.

After disembarking troops and discharging stores at the Greek port of Volos, Ellerman's *City of Karachi* (7,140 grt) was instructed to proceed to sea and obtain orders from a destroyer at Oreus where the boom defence was situated. The master, Captain Melville, could find no such destroyer and after dodging about in the vicinity all night, felt compelled to return to Volos. As he was about to anchor in the harbour the ship was attacked by some seventeen enemy bombers. With machine guns firing they came from all directions dropping about twenty bombs, all of which were near misses.

The near misses however fractured the main inlet in the engine room and started the side plating. *City of Karachi* began to take water and within an hour she had been abandoned. Later, under cover of darkness, the European members of the crew returned to beach her with the assistance of Ellerman's *Destro* which had just arrived in the port. However, a twisted rudder and a further attack by enemy aircraft made this virtually impossible and it was not until the following day, with the assistance of a Greek destroyer, that she was finally beached. She was then again bombed and hit and became a total loss.

By this time evacuation was taking place from Volos and the surrounding villages. For ten days Captain Melville and his men walked and thumbed lifts in lorries and small craft in their flight south along with thousands of refugees fleeing in the path of the enemy. They eventually reached Athens where they were directed to Argos but somewhere along the way the European officers became separated from their Indian shipmates.

On 1 May Captain Melville and his officers reached Alexandria from Suda Bay and a few days later 25 members of the Indian crew arrived but the remaining 35 did not arrive. They were never seen or heard of again.

In Crete the facilities for unloading ships at Suda Bay were limited and were subjected to ever-increasing bombing attacks by the Luftwaffe. Between 30 April and 20 May fifteen supply ships arrived of which eight were sunk or damaged whilst in the harbour. In the chaotic situation which existed many men of the Merchant Navy joined their armed service 'brothers' in the field.

The crew of *Logician* (5,993 grt, Charente Steamship Company) bombed and abandoned in Suda Bay on 16 May, led by their master, Captain Jones, sought out the enemy, forming themselves in parachute parties. Captain Jones and 21 of his officers and men were taken prisoner. *Logician* was again bombed on 25 May and two days later at the end of a series of attacks she sank. *Dalesman*, (6,343 grt) also owned by the Charente Steamship Co Ltd, was abandoned on 14 May, her crew trekking across country to the south of the island seeking a passage to safety.

Some members of *Dalesman*'s crew were caught by German parachutists but Cadet Dobson escaped and seizing a machine gun turned it on his captors. He then found his way to a New Zealand battery which he assisted for a few days eventually boarding a landing barge where he found a mixed company of marines and soldiers. He then undertook the navigation and after ten days brought his barge and his comrades into Alexandria harbour.

Meanwhile Operation Tiger was put into operation to reinforce the garrison of Malta. From the west, strongly escorted sailing at 15 knots, came *Clan Campbell, Clan Chattan, Clan Lamont, Empire Song* and *New Zealand Star*; from Alexandria, four transports and two tankers. Then, on 9 May the first casualties of the infamous 'Malta run'. The 9,228 ton motorship, *Empire Song*, barely twelve months from the builders' yard (managed for the Ministry of Supply by Cayzer Irvine & Co) deeply laden with munitions and army equipment blew up on two mines in spite of possessing paravanes for mine sweeping. Eighteen of her crew were killed, 57 tanks and ten Hurricane fighters plunged to the seabed. Out of 39 merchantmen sent to Malta from the West in three convoys during 1941 however, *Empire Song* was the only vessel lost.

It was not only in the Mediterranean that the Luftwaffe was throwing its might against the Merchant Marine. In the United Kingdom, the distribution of essential foodstuffs and raw materials together with the loading of military supplies was in danger of coming to a halt; port installations were devastated and ships destroyed and damaged as they lay alongside quays and wharfs.

In March when a force of 370 bombers attacked the port of London and the surrounding area it was the heaviest blitz since Christmas week 1940. Six nights previously Liverpool withstood a particularly heavy raid. There followed attacks on Belfast, Bristol, the Clyde, Plymouth, Swansea, Liverpool and Manchester. During the first week of May Liverpool was blitzed on seven successive nights, the most concentrated destruction of shipping taking place on the night of 3/4 May when twenty ships, including barges and tugs, of 36,145 tons, were destroyed, and 25 of 92,764 tons seriously damaged. Out of 144 berths in the port, 69 were disabled.

The London raid on the night of 19/20 March brought the east coast trade to a virtual standstill for over two weeks. The Royal Group of docks in the Pool of London, already crippled because of mines in the Thames estuary lay in ruins from which they never really recovered. Trapped in the docks seriously damaged, which necessitated their withdrawal from service for over six months, were *Nailsea Meadow* (4,962 grt), *Telesfora de Larrinaga* (5,780 grt) and *Lindenhall* (5,248 grt). In the March raid on Liverpool, parachute mines accounted for *Tacoma City* (4,738 grt) and *Ullapool* (4,891 grt); they both ended up lying on the bed of the Mersey, their masts and funnels showing at low tide. Alfred Holt's 6,278 ton *Myrmidon* sank

inside the docks but was later raised and repaired. Damaged were
ten vessels of 57,990 grt including Blue Star's 12,427 ton *Imperial Star*
and Alfred Holt's 8,991 ton *Glenartney*.

The Glen Line's *Glenartney*, which was built for Alfred Holt and
Company Ltd, at the declaration of war, was repaired whilst loading
military stores adjacent to Cammell Laird's yard in Birkenhead. She
sailed under Captain Evans for the Middle East on 4 April and two
days later, amid a very heavy sea and with a south-easterly gale
blowing, successfully rescued 109 crew of her escort, the former P &
O *Comorin*, (converted to an armed merchant cruiser) when she
caught fire in the North Atlantic. HMS *Broke* and the destroyer
Lincoln rescued a further 201 lives and only twenty perished, an
astonishingly low figure when one considers the conditions
prevailing at the time.

In Liverpool on the night of 3/4 May *Malakand* (T. & J.
Brocklebank Ltd, 7,649 grt), loading ammunition for the Middle
East with 350 tons of bombs on board, was badly hit. She caught fire
and burned for nine hours. At 0730 hours she blew up in a
devastating explosion reducing her to a mass of torn and twisted steel
and causing severe damage to the dock and nearby warehouses as
well as to nearby ships. Among those sunk were *Elstree Grange* (6,598
grt), *Domino* (1,453 grt), the former Danish liner *Europa* (10,224 grt,
managed by Canadian National Steamships) and the 7,924 ton
Tacoma Star, subsequently raised and repaired.

Houlder's *Elstree Grange* (Captain Ablett), completing discharge
in the Canada Dock was herself struck by a parachute mine causing
considerable damage amidships and setting fire to the bridge
accommodation. Later shells from a blazing ammunition locker on
the ship exploded leaving the vessel a tangled mass of battered and
twisted metal.

Amongst those damaged were the 4,772 ton *Brittany*, the 8,663 ton
Baronesa and the 7,921 ton *Mahout*. Later in the week those damaged
included *Clan MacInnes* (4,672 grt), *Roxburgh Castle* (7,801 grt),
Silversandal (6,770 grt) and *Talthybius* (10,254 grt).

On 8 May 1941 the German surface raider *Pinguin* was destroyed
in the Indian Ocean by the British heavy cruiser *Cornwall* and with
her some 200 merchant seamen, held below deck as prisoners of war,
were lost. Ninety-seven were from *Clan Buchanan*, all but one member
of the crew of *Empire Light* and most of the 45 crew of *British Emperor*.
Only 22 were saved by *Cornwall*. During her voyage the raider had
sunk or captured 22 vessels (inclusive mine successes) totalling

154,619 tons. The last three that fell to her savage shelling were lost over a period of thirteen days.

Little was heard of *Pinguin*'s loss in Germany yet William Joyce (Lord Haw Haw) announced on German radio the same week the triumphant return of the raider *Thor* to Hamburg (30 April). Just three weeks previously she had intercepted and sunk the Lamport and Holt Line's 13,301 ton *Voltaire*, working as an armed merchant cruiser. With the loss of another valuable passenger ship and 75 of her crew, the Admiralty decided finally to withdraw armed merchant cruisers from convoy work. By August 1941 thirteen had been lost and of those remaining, most were converted to trooping. The tally for *Thor* was eleven merchant ships plus *Voltaire* sunk (96,602 grt) and a further two armed merchant cruisers damaged.

U-boat attacks on northern latitude convoys during May were confined to OB318 during the second week and HX126 on 20/21 May. The 42 ships of OB318, a well defended outward convoy sailed from Liverpool on 2 May. Eight days later eight merchant ships (over 45,000 grt) had been sunk, six of them British with the Sunderland-registered *Empire Cloud* and the London-registered *Aelybryn* both severely damaged. Yet as OB318 dispersed, 400 miles south-west of Reykjavik on 9 May, just two weeks before *Bismarck* sailed on her last voyage, there ended the career of *U-110* and the life of her commander, Lieutenant Lemp, who had sunk *Athenia* on the first day of the conflict.

The event was one of the most significant of the Atlantic campaign. It was a major breakthrough. Commander Lemp, when he realised his U-boat was not sinking, made a desperate attempt to get back aboard and scuttle her. As the merchantmen passed to the westward, 34 bedraggled Germans were rescued. George VI, when decorating one of the naval officers who accomplished the capture called it 'perhaps the most important single event in the whole war at sea'.

With the capture of *U-110* by a boarding party from HMS *Bulldog* came the prize which gave the British cryptanalysts the first chance to penetrate the complicated U-boat codes – the capture of her code-books and Enigma machine was to remain a closely guarded secret for thirty years. This fact alone led to a drastic reduction in ship losses in July and August.

The commodore of convoy OB318, Rear Admiral (retd) Mackenzie flew his flag in *Colonial*, bound for Cape Town with the duties of vice-commodore being undertaken by Captain Rees, master of *British Prince* bound for Halifax. In the centre sailed the armed merchant cruiser *Ranpura* (ex-P & O). It was a typical convoy of the 1941 period yet thankfully only a minority faced the enemy against such overwhelming odds; at least twelve other convoys were crossing the western ocean at the same time.

OB318 was sighted in approximately 62 North 22 West by Herbert Kuppisch, commander of *U-94* on 7 May. He immediately torpedoed the Norwegian *Eastern Star* and Alfred Holt's 29-year-old *Ixion* (10,263 grt); both were loaded at Glasgow and were carrying large quantities of whisky which burst into flames. As *Ixion*'s engine room rapidly filled with water, her master, Captain Dark, threw his confidential books overboard, fired his distress rockets and ordered his crew (105 officers and men) to abandon ship. *Nailsea Moor* which had been detailed as rescue ship then at once turned back to assist her stricken comrades rescuing five boatloads with 86 survivors whilst Captain Dark and his chief mate with seventeen others in the ship's jolly boat were rescued by HMS *Marigold*. Not one man was lost.

U-110, *U-201* and *U-556* then joined in the attack following the convoy like a pack of vultures awaiting their opportunity. Two days later *Bengore Head* followed *Esmond*, then *Gregalia* and *Empire Cloud*. The sickening smell of cordite from the exploding torpedoes seemed to linger for many hours in the light breeze.

The 4,976 ton *Esmond* (Anglo Newfoundland Steamship Co. Ltd) and the 2,609 ton *Bengore Head* (Ulster Steamship Co.) were the last vessels to be sunk by *U-110* before her capture. The last moments of *Esmond* were spectacular as she rose steadily to the vertical sitting on her stern in the calm sea, her deck cargo of vehicles and cased goods cascading into the sea like 'a child pouring toys out of a box'. Slowly she slid beneath the surface, still maintaining her vertical stance until only bubbles remained to mark her grave. *Bengore Head* assumed a triangular posture, the torpedo explosion breaking her back and the bow and stern staying afloat with the two masts actually crossing.

The 52 survivors of *Gregalia* (5,802 grt) had the experience of being twice torpedoed in the same convoy as they were picked up by *Aelybryn*, herself torpedoed 26 hours later, with her rudder and propeller being blown away in the explosion. In spite of this damage, and with the water high in the engine room and boiler room, she was located four days later by the Dutch tug *Zwarte Zee* and towed to Reykjavik by HMS *Hollyhock*.

The convoy having reached 35.40 West now dispersed but the

same afternoon *U-556* (Lieutenant Herbert Wohlfarth) caught the ex-American *Empire Caribou* (4,861 grt). She was managed by Sir William Reardon Smith & Sons on behalf of the Ministry of War Transport and had set a westerly course for Portland, Maine. The explosion burst her cargo of china clay asunder and she plunged to the bottom in two minutes taking her master, Captain Duffield, and 28 men with her – not one deck officer survived. The remainder of her crew, eleven deck hands who clung to rafts, were rescued by the destroyer *Malcolm* 38 hours later.

The commodore ship *Colonial* (5,108 grt, Charente Steamship Company) was another vessel that failed to reach its destination. On 27 May, in position 09.13N 15.09W and within 100 miles of Freetown, her master, Captain Devereaux, suddenly caught sight of a U-boat quite close to him. It was Hessler in *U-107* and although *Colonial* turned to try to ram her attacker, the submarine's 18 knots got her out of trouble. Three torpedoes were pumped into her before she finally sank, leaving Commodore Mackenzie and his staff clinging to a raft and 83 crew crowded into the only two lifeboats which could be launched. Twenty hours later they were rescued by the battleship *Centurion*.

HX126 was another typical 1941 convoy. Laden with essential foodstuffs, raw materials, planes and military equipment it was routed far to the north, to the southern limits of the polar pack ice, virtually within sight of Cape Farewell. Here in 40 West the U-boats lay in wait, striking on 20 May. Nine cargo ships of 54,451 tons were sunk, seven of them British and a further vessel, the 13,037 ton Eagle Oil & Shipping motor tanker *San Felix* damaged. It was an unlucky convoy, being the first Halifax convoy to suffer losses since HX121 on 28 April. It did, however, meet up with the enemy further west than any previous homeward convoy and in an area where escort by surface vessels was not possible. It was HX129 which sailed from Halifax on 27 May which was the first eastbound convoy to enjoy surface escort the whole way.

Because of the break-out of *Bismarck* and *Prince Eugen*, HX126, along with HX127, SC31, OB323 and OB324, had to make long detours. The surviving vessels took twenty days between Halifax and Malin Head. *Norman Monarch* (4,718 grt, Monarch Steamship Company) was the first casualty. Carrying Canadian wheat she was torpedoed by *U-94*, in position 56.41N 40.52W. All her crew of 40 and eight gunners were taken off by *Harpagus* (5,173 grt, Gowland Steamship Company) which was lying astern but just 24 hours later on 21 May, 26 of these perished when *Harpagus* herself was torpedoed. This time the enemy was *U-98* (Lieutenant-Commander Robert Gysae).

In spite of the approaching Atlantic summer and calmer seas, the loss of life continued to grow. *British Security* (8,470 grt, British Tankers Ltd) 53 killed including Captain Akers. *Darlington Court* (4,794 grt, Court Line Ltd) 25 killed. *Marconi* (7,402 grt, Kaye Son & Co.) 22 lost. There were casualties, too, on *Cockaponset* and *Rothermere*.

It was the second occasion in eighteen months for Captain Hurst of *Darlington Court* to lose his ship for he was master of his company's *Arlington Court* when she was torpedoed and sunk in November 1939. *Marconi* carrying a crew of 80 was commanded by Captain Hailstone and it was thanks to the US Coastguard cutter *General Greene* on ice patrol that so many were saved. For six days they drifted near Cape Farewell eight dying through exhaustion and the cold of the Arctic night. On being rescued they were taken to St John's Newfoundland where a further three seamen died in hospital. Eleven had been killed on board when the torpedo exploded.

May and early June saw the climax of submarine operations off West Africa assisted by the enemy supply ships *Nordmark* and *Egerland*. *U-107*'s patrol during which she sank fourteen ships of 86,699 grt was the most successful single U-boat patrol of the whole war.

The 8,286 ton *Piako* fell to Hessler's *U-107* south-west of Freetown, 07.52N 14.57W on 18 May. Built in 1920 *Piako* was the last coal-burning steamer belonging to the New Zealand Shipping Company and on this occasion, her 34th voyage, was commanded by Captain Evans previously torpedoed in his company's *Hurunui* (15 October 1940).

Carrying refrigerated cargo and general foodstuffs from Australia she was lost at a time when the Ministry of Food were again reducing the meagre rations of the British public. Sailing independently she had only 130 miles to go to reach the comparative safety of Freetown when the first torpedo hit the engine room killing instantly all those on watch and destroying all the lifesaving equipment plus the two lifeboats on the starboard side. With the engine room and boiler room filling with sea water within two minutes she sank rapidly. Three minutes after she had been abandoned, the two port lifeboats were got away, a second torpedo blew her apart. Fortunately her distress call had been heard and the survivors were picked up the next morning by HMS *Bridgwater*.

SOS – SOS. Here four lifeboats of steamship *Benvenue*; position latitude 4.19N longitude 18.10W; we are sailing on direct line from this position towards Freetown, making 4 knots, please help us.

The distress call came from the survivors of Benn Line's 5,920 ton *Benvenue* (Captain Struth). Twenty-three days out of Newcastle she was carrying 'generals' for Bombay and Karachi when the torpedo from *U-105* struck. Her propeller shaft was broken and with her engines racing furiously she settled very quickly. With her stern under water her bow rose vertically and she slid under. Three boats were sighted by the *English Trader* but the fourth lifeboat was adrift eight days before a destroyer found her 60 miles south-west of Freetown. Many were suffering badly from sunburn and blisters.

U-105 was particularly active during 13/16 May. In addition to *Benvenue*, and *Benvrackie* referred to on Page 131, there was Blue Star's *Rodney Star* (11,803 grt) torpedoed about 420 miles south-west of Freetown (05.03N 19.02W) on her regular run homewards from South America with refrigerated cargo. She listed heavily to starboard but was successfully abandoned before a further two torpedoes struck home which broke her back. However she needed 78 rounds from the U-boat's 4.6 inch gun before finally sinking. Her master Captain Phillips made light of their boat voyages, though they suffered the usual hardships of overcrowding and discomfort. The survivors, which included survivors from *Clan Ogilvy*, who had boarded in Santos, spent six days adrift, three boats being picked up and landed in Dakar, those of the remaining boat being landed in Takoradi. No lives were lost.

By the end of May, Ellermans had lost fifteen of their 'City' fleet, *City of Winchester* (7,120 grt) and *City of Shanghai* (5,828 grt), being sunk in close proximity to one another during the month. *City of Shanghai* under the command of Captain Goring, was sunk by *U-103* at dawn on 11 May, her sixth victim since she arrived on station three weeks previously. The torpedo struck amidships killing six in the engine room and smashing No 3 lifeboat together with much of the new boom defence for Cape Town harbour which she was carrying as deck cargo.

Commander Schütze of *U-103* then brought his gun to bear upon the stricken vessel but the three remaining boats, now waterborne, managed to get clear. One under the command of the third mate containing five Europeans and 21 Lascars lost touch with the others and miraculously survived thirty days amid the tropical South Atlantic with sharks and storms, the scorching sun, thirst and dwindling rations. All 26, rescued by the Dutch *Stad Arnheim*, stepped ashore at Freetown to tell their tale. The other two boats were more fortunate, only five days elapsed before they were sighted.

Losses by U-boats in the 92 days of March, April and May 1941 amounted to no fewer than 142 ships of nearly 818,000 tons. Of these, 99 ships of about 600,000 tons were British. In the same three months enemy aircraft, surface vessels and mines had accounted respectively for another 179, 44 and 33 merchant ships. The total British, Allied and neutral loss through all causes in this period totalled 412 ships of 1,691,499 tons, up to date the worst three months of the war.

After learning of these losses President Roosevelt echoed the warnings of Prime Minister Churchill; 'The Battle of the Atlantic now extends from the icy waters of the North Pole to the frozen wastes of the Antarctic. . . The blunt truth is the present rate of Nazi sinkings of merchant ships is more than three times as high as the capacity of British shipyards to replace them; it is more than twice the combined British and American output of merchant ships to-day.'

During the first six months of 1941 there was a deficit of 7,000,000 tons of imports and 2,000,000 tons of food. Certain foodstuffs were already in short supply and certainly no new military operations utilizing sea passages could be contemplated. With no new ships due to arrive from the USA for eighteen months the outlook for 1942 appeared bleak.

Apart from a venture in late June when HX133 (see Chapter 10) and OB336 were intercepted, the submarine wolf packs did not return to the waters 'twixt Cape Farewell and Cape Race until September. Instead the attack was switched to home waters and the warmer climes of the convoy routes to and from Gibraltar and Freetown, where success, although not on the same scale, in spite of there being more U-boats at sea (25 operational), was none the less spectacular.

Freetown and its river estuary now assumed the importance of Liverpool and the River Mersey plus Devonport and Plymouth Sound rolled into one. The tremendous increase in traffic, brought about by being a convoy and bunkering port as well as a naval base brought all sorts of problems. Visiting troopships required huge quantities of water so valuable tanker space was utilized to convey fresh water from the United Kingdom; the demand was over 1,500 tons a day. There was water not far from the town, but, or so it was maintained for some time, it was impossible to tap it, and when, finally, it was decided that a pipe line could be constructed, the project took many months to complete. Not until January 1943 did it come into operation.

As there was practically no area of foreshore there was little space to store coal. The coal required for the cargo ships (which unlike the oil fired troopships were largely coal burning) had to be delivered to the ships in canvas bags by native labour. The steam coal of course had to be imported, mainly from South Wales and sometimes even that was in short supply. Only from early 1942 were mechanical coal hulks organised. Then there were the mechanical defects which often delayed departures with subsequent shortage of ship anchorages. There were then the shipwrecked victims to be provided for – at the beginning of June 1941 there were some 1,000 in Freetown awaiting repatriation.

The amount of military cargo for delivery to Freetown continually increased; the facilities for dealing with it proved increasingly inadequate. It became known as 'the most soul– and energy–destroying place in the world'; indeed it was known to the merchant seamen, from master to deck boy, as 'Hitler's secret weapon'.

One of the most important sources of raw materials in West Africa was the iron ore deposits shipped from Pepel up river from Freetown. Since the loss of Swedish ore and the difficulty of ensuring safe passage for the iron ore shipments from Newfoundland, the steelworks of South Wales and the North-East Coast relied more and more upon the ore from Sierra Leone. Yet six British vessels from Pepel were sunk during June: *Ainderby, Cathrine, Djurdjura, PLM22, Rio Azul* and *River Lugar*. Between them they were carrying some 50,000 tons of ore.

Another big loss during June was the new grain carrier *Michael E.* (7,628 grt), first of the CAM ships (Catapult Aircraft Merchant Ship). CAM ships sailed under the red ensign and continued to ply their normal trade as merchantmen. The catapult consisted of a steel runway 85 feet long and the trolley carrying the fighter was driven along the track by a bank of cordite rockets for some 60 feet. Whilst the pilots and aircraft of later CAM ships, they were 35 in total, were volunteers from the RAF, those of the *Michael E.* were from the Royal Navy – a Fleet Air Arm pilot and a Sea Hurricane.

Michael E, owned by the Bury Hill Shipping Co. Ltd, was torpedoed by *U-108*, Lieutenant-Commander Klaus Scholtz on 2 June, in position 48.50N 29.00W. Happening soon after convoy OB326 had dispersed, the explosion caused immense damage and numerous injuries amongst the crew. For one seaman it meant two broken legs and being drawn up through a hole in the deck by his comrades. In great pain and terribly injured he then pulled himself to a lifeboat without losing consciousness and later gave his advice to the officer in charge of the small storm-tossed boat. On board the rescue vessel he was treated by the ship's doctor yet he died before reaching Halifax. He was one of many who, whilst saved from the deep, failed in their bid to reach the safety of the shore.

With much of the sea war transferred to the West African coast, albeit temporarily, the fleet of traders Elder Dempster was particularly hard hit, both through ship losses and the general disruption of their traffic. During May *Dunkwa* (4,752 grt, Captain Andrew) had been sunk 216 miles west-north-west of Freetown outwards from Glasgow and *Sangara* (5,445 grt, Captain Themeus), abandoned after being torpedoed by *U-69* off the port of Accra (open roadstead anchorage). She was later salvaged and repaired though it was as late as April 1947 before she returned to service.

On Whit Sunday, 1 June, *Alfred Jones* (5,013 grt, Captain Harding) was torpedoed by Hessler (*U-107*) less than 24 hours from Freetown, in position 8 North 15 West. She had sailed from the Mersey as commodore ship of convoy OB320 on the last day of the Liverpool blitz with a crew of 46 and twelve passengers. The torpedo struck amidships in the engine room, destroying the starboard lifeboats and the deck cargo of planes consigned for Takoradi. She took a heavy list to starboard and whilst the remaining lifeboats were launched, many jumped overboard and swam to rafts which had been released.

After a second torpedo exploded, *Alfred Jones* literally nosedived to the bottom and the survivors, now in two boats, eyed carefully the submarine which cruised amongst them. However after questioning Captain Harding, Hessler set a southerly course and they were left alone amid the wide expanse of a calm torrid sea; the sun blazed down and clad only in singlets and shorts they rowed only at night.

The boats became separated; one was picked up the next day by a corvette, but the second boat under the command of the second mate was at sea five days and six nights before sighting the mountains of Sierra Leone. During the first four nights they had covered a distance of only 60 miles and though, during this period they had been sighted by a Walrus flying boat which landed on the water close by and promised assistance, tropical storms then blew up making a land-based rescue virtually impossible.

The loss of *Alfred Jones* was followed by that of the 7,816 ton *Adda*, an Elder Dempster twin-screw passenger motorship. She sailed from

(*Above*) A 1941 convoy with the auxiliary fighter catapult ship *Ariquana*. The twin screw 6,746 ton *Ariquana* was built in 1926 and owned by Elders & Fyffes Ltd. Converted as an auxiliary fighter catapult ship she carried a Fulmar fighter, one 6-inch gun, one 12-pounder HA gun, two pom-pom anti-aircraft guns, four rocket projectors and two Holman projectors.

(*Right*) MV *Beacon Grange*, sunk by *U-552*, 27 April 1941. *U-552*, with Lieutenant-Commander Erich Topp, preparing to depart from the scene after torpedoing Houlder Bros, motorship *Beacon Grange*, 10,160 grt.

Convoy HX143 as seen from HMS *Prince of Wales*. On the return journey from Churchill's historic Atlantic meeting with President Roosevelt, HMS *Prince of Wales* with the Prime Minister on board (15 August 1941) passed convoy HX143 of 73 ships. The battleship altered course so that Mr Churchill could get a closer view. Only commissioned seven months earlier, *Prince of Wales* was sunk by Japanese torpedo bombers the following December.

City of Kimberley preparing to tow HMS *Glenearn*. Alfred Holt's 9,869 ton *Glenearn* converted as an infantry assault ship was rammed in Suez Roads on 14 July 1941 by the burning liner *Georgic*. Eighteen days later she is shown preparing to be towed by Ellerman's *City of Kimberley*.

the Mersey on 17 May with a total complement of 490 passengers and crew and was commodore ship of convoy OB336. She was commanded by Captain Marshall with Commander Kelly RNR sailing as commodore; sailing to the west this convoy lost three vessels in the vicinity of 55 North 39 West.

After dispersal on 27 May *Adda* set a southerly course and sailed without escort on Admiralty instructions. Just before dawn on 8 June, as she was zig-zagging in bright moonlight with a heavy swell running, there was a tremendous explosion as a torpedo ripped open the starboard side. Again it was Günter Hessler. *U-107* was notching up her seventh merchantman in 23 days.

Lurching to starboard and then listing to port, *Adda* was crippled. Apart from emergency floodlights overside the rest of the ship wallowed in darkness, the explosion destroying much of the engine room yet eleven out of twelve lifeboats were manned and lowered without mishap. All apart from ten of her crew, two passengers and Commander Kelly got away; surely a tribute to the discipline of her master and officers.

Captain Marshall was the last man to leave *Adda* and the last seen of Commander Kelly was when he was climbing over the bulwarks of the well deck. Regrettably he was never seen again. The same evening the survivors were landed in Freetown having been rescued by HMS *Cyclamen* only to find the town was bursting at its seams with DBS (Distressed British Seamen). The majority were taken on board *Monarch of Bermuda* which happened to be lying at anchor until later housed ashore in commercial firms' buildings.

Twenty-six days later there was a sequel to the loss of the *Adda*. Twelve survivors together with four survivors from *Lassell* and one from *Colonial* were fortunate to secure an early passage home in Elder Dempster's ex-German 7,603 grt *Empire Ability*, Captain Flowerdew. She was under management from the Ministry of War Transport, en route, from Mauritius with sugar and rum for Liverpool. Sailing from Freetown on 19 June with a crew of 60 plus seventeen gunners, she joined the 7 knot SL76 convoy. All went well until the night of the 26th when, 200 miles south-east of the Azores, and without warning, the 24 vessels with their escort of four corvettes faced the familiar pattern of convoy warfare. *U-66*, *U-69* and *U-123* between them sank seven vessels of 34,787 tons over a period of 42 hours.

Empire Ability was the second vessel to be hit; she caught fire immediately with flames reaching some 200 feet above the main deck. The main engines were shut down and although No 1 lifeboat was destroyed when the torpedo struck, the remaining three were

successfully launched and the ship abandoned. Rescue was made by
Armeria and HMS *Burdock*, the survivors, including those DBS from
Adda, arriving back in Freetown on 3 July.

The other vessels lost from SL76 included three of the ore carriers
previously mentioned: *PLM22* (5,646 grt, ex-French, managed by
E.R. Management Co. Ltd), 32 crew lost; *River Lugar* (5,423 grt,
Ayrshire Navigation Co.), 39 crew and 2 passengers lost; *Rio Azul*
(4,088 grt, Thompson Steamshipping Co.), 33 lost including
Captain Sutherland.

The *Rio Azul* sank within 90 seconds taking 24 of her crew down
with her. Eighteen were fortunate to survive finding two rafts which
they lashed together, rafts which had a one gallon flask and one glass
jar of fresh water between them. They were adrift for fifteen days
during which time eight men were to die of thirst. The remainder
owed their lives to the bosun who, though in an exhausted condition
himself, instructed one of his shipmates to lash a tobacco tin to a long
handled scoop to form an improvised heliograph. The flashes from
this were seen by a distant steamer which altered course to save them
but the *Rio Azul*'s bosun unfortunately died soon after he was taken
aboard.

The Saint Line steamer *St Anselm* of 5,614 tons was another which
was sunk on her voyage homewards from Freetown. She was sailing
a few hours ahead of SL76 on the last day of June, south-west of
Madeira, 31.00N 26.00W when *U-66* (Commander Richard Zapp)
suddenly surfaced and fired a spread of four torpedoes. Due either to
bad aiming on the part of the submarine or good zig-zagging on the
part of *St Anselm*, they all missed their target. A further two torpedoes
were then fired but these appeared to have failed to detonate. It was
then that *U-66* started to shell the Liverpool steamer killing 34 of her
crew.

Amidst the confusion and fire which raged, those remaining got
away in the only lifeboat but it was eighteen days before they were
sighted by a Spanish ship which stopped and took them aboard. An
amusing tale is told of how, after the fresh water in the boat was
exhausted, a Lascar seaman appeared to be dying and so one of the
engineers, thinking to make the man's life a little easier and happier,
took some sea-water, mixed tooth-paste with it and gave it to the
man to drink. Within an hour he was able to sit up and after being
taken on board the Spanish ship, he recovered.

Since April the raider *Atlantis* had been active in the South
Atlantic raising the anxiety felt by the Royal Navy at Freetown who
thought she might sail north to create more difficulties off the West

African coast. The sinking of *Tottenham* (4,762 grt, Watts Watts & Co. Ltd) on 17 June 300 miles north-west of Ascension Island left 29 crew including her master, Captain Woodcock, prisoners of war. Seventeen of her crew managed to escape in the blackness of the night and were rescued on the eleventh day by *Mahronda*.

The Lamport & Holt cargo liner *Balzac* (5,372 grt) met *Atlantis* five days later, in position 12S 29W. She was another that fought so bravely; the fire power of the enemy was tested as never before. A total of 192 5.9 inch and 53 3 inch rounds were necessary to sink *Balzac*, the most the raider ever fired. Fifty-one were taken prisoner, three men were killed and three officers wounded, the third mate so badly that he later died on board *Atlantis*.

On account of the increased surface speed of the new Atlantic type U-boats, the minimum speed for independently routed cargo liners was increased from 13 to 15 knots after the loss of *Norfolk* and *Silverpalm* in June. Both were valuable vessels in the Indian and Australasian trades.

Silver Line's *Silverpalm* of 6,373 grt left Calcutta under the command of Captain Pallett on 17 April. She sailed from Freetown on 31 May for Glasgow and was sighted the following day by the outward-bound *Silverlaurel*. There was then silence and nothing more was seen or heard of her until 17 July when a ship's lifeboat was found about 500 miles west of the Hebrides containing the bodies of eight seamen. Papers on them identified them as members of the crew of *Silverpalm*. Captain Pallett, a crew of 53, eleven gunners and three passengers had perished. According to German sources she was torpedoed and sunk by *U-101* on the afternoon of 9 June in position 51.00N 36.00W approximately. As she was unable to send any distress signal the end must have been very sudden.

The 10,948 ton *Norfolk* built in 1918 (Federal Steam Navigation Co) was under the command of Captain Lougheed. She sailed from Newport on 15 June, her 37th voyage, and was routed to New Zealand via New York and the Panama Canal. 150 miles north-north-west of Malin Head she was torpedoed by *U-552*.

In spite of a fresh westerly gale blowing with rough sea and heavy swell, with a vessel that was fast settling by the head, with water rushing into No 3 hold and the deep tanks on the port side leaking badly, Captain Lougheed kept her 'full ahead' with instructions for the zig zag course to continue. This action brought *U-552* to the surface and in pursuit; however *Norfolk* put the enemy dead astern firing at the submarine at 1,000 yards' range and forcing her to crash dive.

Norfolk continued at 'full ahead' for a further 30 minutes when she started to sink much lower in the water. She then took a serious list to starboard which necessitated stopping the engines. Just after she was abandoned, *U-552* fired a second and then a third torpedo. An hour later with her back broken *Norfolk* turned over and then sank, the survivors being rescued by the destroyer *Skate*. Only one of her crew was lost – from shock and exposure after lying in a waterlogged boat thickly coated with fuel oil. For the seventh engineer it was the third occasion in 22 months that his ship had been torpedoed.

Few tramp shipping companies felt the cost of the Second World War as did the Hain Steamship Company. They lost their entire pre-war fleet of 24 vessels. In June 1941, in the space of twenty days, they lost five of their fleet (25,750 tons), four of them from U-boats whilst they plied westward in ballast in a stormy North Atlantic.

In the case of *Trecarrel* (4 June), *Tregarthen* (6 June) and *Trevarrack* (8 June) there was not one survivor. A total of 134 souls perished in waves up to 40 feet high between latitudes 46 and 49 North and longitudes 29 and 36 West. Captain Daniel, master of *Tregarthen* had commanded *Trewellard* at the time of her destruction by *Admiral Scheer* eight months before.

Tresillian which followed was sunk on 12 June by *U-77* in position 44.40N 45.30W, the furthest west yet recorded. Eleven days later *Trelissick* was bombed and sunk by aircraft in the North Sea off Cromer.

U-48, which torpedoed *Tregarthen*, was on her twelfth and last mission into enemy waters and on 22 June she returned to Kiel amidst much jubilation. Eight missions had been completed by Lieutenant-Commander Schultze, two missions by Commander Hans Rosing and two missions by Lieutenant-Commander Bleichrodt. She had sunk one sloop and 54 merchantmen of 322,292 tons and damaged two merchantmen of 11,024 tons – the most successful submarine of the Second World War.

The 22nd June was also the day on which Germany invaded the Soviet Union. It probably marked the second turning point in the war of Britain's lifeline for from this day forward priority was given to the Russian front – the enemy's U-boat offensive might have been decisive during 1942 had not Hitler taken this step. But for the Merchant Navy the tempest raged as before, for another 21 months before the tide was turned, and with every month which passed the war at sea spread further and further afield.

This is the midnight – let no star
Delude us – dawn is very far
This is the tempest long foretold –
Slow to make head but sure to hold.
Rudyard Kipling

CHAPTER FIVE

North Cape to the China Sea
(July–December 1941)

The Merchant Navy, with Allied comrades, night and day, in weather fair or foul, faces not only the ordinary perils on the sea but the sudden assaults of war from beneath the waters or from the sky. Your first task is to bring to port the cargoes vital for us at home or for our armies abroad, and we trust your tenacity and resolve to see this stern task through.

We are a seafaring race and we understand the call of the sea. We account you in these hard days worthy successors in a tradition of steadfast courage and high adventure, and we feel confident that that proud tradition of our island will be upheld to-day wherever the ensign of a British merchantman is flown.

Rt Hon Winston S. Churchill, MP
Prime Minister. July 1941

Those that have gone down to the sea in ships have always understood the call. How else can one explain the men who were proud to wear the simple Merchant Navy badge and serve under the ubiquitous Red Duster; like a comrade who still has vivid memories: 'We were civilians, all volunteers, had little or no enforced discipline, no uniform. We did our duty, and we were proud to have done it, not only for King and Country, but for personal pride.' Duty such as the seaman sighted on a raft in the summer of 1941, in the latitude of Cape Verde. He was sighted by *Clan Campbell* outward bound for the Middle East.

The lookout reported an object broad on the port bow which was identified as a raft with someone on it. We altered course to investigate and as we got closer it was seen that it was indeed a raft but with what appeared to be a black man lying on his back with a towel over his face. We blew the steam whistle which made an ear-shattering blast but failed to rouse the man. By this time we were very close to him and as the raft got into the bow wave (we were still steaming at full speed in case there was a submarine about), the towel flapped away from his face and we saw that it was white, but the eyes were just empty sockets and his limbs were blackened by oil and sun.

The ship's doctor had one look through the telescope and said there was nothing that could be done as he must have been dead for days. We tried to overturn the raft so that the horror would be lost to the sea but it had reached the centre of our turning circle. It was the most awful sight to behold. We couldn't erase it from our thoughts for many days.

The raft could have floated off one of several ships sunk in the neighbourhood, possibly *Auditor* or more probably *Robert L. Holt* sunk by gunfire from *U-69* in position 24.15N 20.00W approximately on 4 July. She was lost with all hands.

The West African trader *Robert L. Holt* (2,918 grt, John Holt Company) was the last ship sunk by Jost Metzler, commander of *U-69*, before he set course for his home base which probably accounts for the fact that he shelled his last victim having exhausted his supply of torpedoes. Under the command of Captain Kendall, *Robert L. Holt* was outward-bound from Liverpool for Warri in ballast and was last seen as she dispersed from convoy OB336 in mid-Atlantic. She then proceeded independently under Admiralty routing for Freetown.

The month of July opened with the loss of Bristol City Line's *Toronto City* (2,486 grt), commanded by Captain Garlick. From September 1940 this vessel was placed on special meteorological service and was stationed along the route that urgently needed American bombers took from Newfoundland to Iceland and then to airfields in the United Kingdom. Captain Garlick had reported himself east of Cape Race bound for St John's Newfoundland when all contact was lost. The submarine *U-108* reported *Toronto City* torpedoed in position 47.03N 30.00W approximately. There were no survivors.

Only ten days previously, on 23 June, *U-77* reported that she had torpedoed and sunk *Arakaka* (2,379 grt, Booker Bros, McConnell and Co.) ten degrees further west in the same latitude. She was also a meteorological vessel. Her master, Captain Walker, together with his crew of 45 which included Admiralty personnel, all perished. The loss of two vessels engaged upon such important work, was a big blow to those brave pilots ferrying aircraft to Britain.

The Burnett Steamship Company was one of many small north-east coast shipowners which operated out of Newcastle. On 19 July they lost their 3,433 ton *Holmside*, the last ship out of Bergen before the Germans arrived. They also lost 22 of their loyal north-east coast seamen. *Holmside* was torpedoed by *U-66* in position 19.00N 21.30W, the explosion tearing her apart, devastating the engine room, the accommodation amidships and the two lifeboats.

Sixteen survivors nearly all injured put off on three rafts and
drifted for five days without food or water. In some cases they had no
protection from the elements, their clothing being blown from their
bodies when *Holmside* was struck. They were picked up in bad shape
by the Portuguese *Sandades* and taken to Lisbon. Later Captain
Rainho of the *Sandades*, when offered payment by the British Consul
for clothing and other necessities which he had provided declined to
accept, stating that what he had done repaid in some measure the
kindness vouchsafed to himself when picked up by a British ship
after being torpedoed during the First World War.

July 1941 is principally remembered for an E-boat attack on the
12,696 ton *Sydney Star*, east of Pantellaria, and an air raid on Suez Bay
during which the 27,759 ton *Georgic* was bombed by a force of Ju88's
based in Crete.

Blue Star's 1936-built *Sydney Star* was one of six fast heavily laden
merchant ships totalling 58,114 grt which sailed from the west in
convoy with essential supplies for Malta. In addition to *Sydney Star*
there was *City of Pretoria*, *Deucalion*, *Durham*, *Port Chalmers* and
Melbourne Star. The commodore was Captain MacFarlane, the
master of *Melbourne Star*; he was master of his company's *Auckland Star*
when she was lost on 28 July 1940.

As the convoy moved east from Gibraltar they were heavily
escorted: the battle-cruiser *Renown*, the battleship *Nelson*, the aircraft
carrier *Ark Royal*, four cruisers, a cruiser-minelayer and seventeen
destroyers. During 23 July they were heavily attacked by aircraft
when a destroyer was sunk and a cruiser damaged and as dusk fell,
Renown, *Nelson*, *Ark Royal* and four destroyers turned and proceeded
back to their base.

In the early hours of the following day, as the convoy was
proceeding in the channel between Pantellaria and the Cape Bon
peninsula, the E-boat attack began. With all the fire power of the
escort being thrown at them the Italian boats *MAS532* and *533*
twisted and weaved between the merchantmen. As *Sydney Star*,
under the command of Captain Horn, was struck by a torpedo on
the port side of No 3 hold, she suddenly took a list to port and
began to take water forward. Within twenty minutes there was 33
feet of water in No 3 and, in view of the deteriorating situation, the
460 troops which she was carrying were transferred to one of the
escorting destroyers.

By daylight it appeared that *Sydney Star*, with her engine room still
dry, had a fifty-fifty chance of reaching the comparative safety of
Valetta Harbour. Attacks by small groups of torpedo aircraft and

high altitude bombers followed but with only 130 miles still to go she pressed ahead. Then, with the ship slowly sinking by the head and with the list gradually increasing she was guided by three tugs to her berth in the naval dockyard. She was 12 feet down by the bows, the hole caused by the torpedo was about 40 × 16 feet with extensive tearing. Repair which was carried out at Malta took nearly four months to complete.

On the return voyage Federal's 10,893 ton *Durham* met a succession of misfortunes. Hitting a mine whilst passing Cape Bon on 22 August she was damaged forward of the bridge although the leaking water was kept under control by the bilge pumps. Then on the following day it was discovered another mine had become entangled with the paravane and she had been towing it for some twenty hours. Although there was imminent risk of it exploding, the crew, at considerable risk, cut the towing wire of the paravane and it drifted clear with the mine still attached.

It was not the end of the *Durham* saga however. Whilst under repair at Gibraltar (20 September 1941) Italian 'human torpedoes' attacked her, together with other ships lying at anchor. She was badly damaged and beached and lay at Gibraltar a whole twelve months before she was made seaworthy and towed to the United Kingdom. Not until the latter part of 1943 did she resume her cargo-carrying duties.

A similar situation arose in the case of Cunard White Star Line's *Georgic*, burnt out at Port Tewfik on 14 July. She was under repair in Karachi for nine months and did not resume trooping until early 1943.

It was a clear night with a full moon at Suez Roads as the bombers flew low following the moonlit canal southwards. *Georgic* and her neighbour *Almanzora* stood alone and unprotected except for their own anti-aircraft armament. On the third attack *Georgic* was hit and took fire immediately and within twenty minutes her superstructure was a mass of flame from stem to stern and beyond control. She was moved, with some difficulty, inshore to shallow water with her crew and service personnel dropping overside to escape the inferno. *Georgic* burned fiercely all night and lit by the fearful glare, lifeboats from *Almanzora* continued rescuing survivors for several hours.

By daylight the two-funnelled Trans-Atlantic liner had gone aground and later in the day had burnt out. Royal Navy experts from Port Said considered she was a total loss yet within days there commenced the biggest salvage operation of the war. She was towed to Port Sudan by *Clan Campbell* and *City of Sydney*, a slow voyage which took twelve days. There *Georgic* developed a bad list and remained in Port Sudan for several weeks whilst experts were called in to right her. Then the merchantman *Recorder* and the tug *St Sampson* took her in tow but the *St Sampson* was lost in bad weather, her crew being rescued by the hospital ship *Dorsetshire*. *Georgic* was then taken in tow by British India's *Haresfield* and the tug *Pauline Moller* though the pace was slow and difficult. It was a further four weeks before she reached Karachi.

The summer of 1941 marked the end of the first phase of the U-boat war in the North Atlantic and as more escort vessels were now available, outward-bound Freetown convoys were introduced. They were designated OS and were escorted the whole way to the coast of Sierra Leone. This led to a further strain on the resources of Freetown as a victualling base. In addition to more Royal Navy presence it meant that outward vessels were now arriving in convoy instead of independently. During the second week of August as SL82 homeward was being formed, OS1 arrived being quickly followed by WS10 which was en route for the Middle East.

The twelve troopers of WS10 (eighteen ships in total) made an impressive sight as they filed in through the harbour boom to anchor: *Britannic*, *Indrapoera*, *Stirling Castle*, *Strathallan*, *Windsor Castle*, *Volendam*, *Cameronia*, *Highland Monarch*, *Nea Hellas*, *Orcades*, *Rangitiki* and *Reina del Pacifico*.

Also at this time OB convoys were discontinued. They were replaced by ON Slow (7 knots) and ON Fast (9 knots) each on a six-day cycle, the Fast sailing two days after the Slow. They terminated at Halifax, Nova Scotia though from August 1942 this was changed to New York. The middle of September witnessed a big step forward in co-operation between the British Navy and their American counterparts. From this date HX and ON convoys were escorted by US warships in the waters between Newfoundland and Iceland; thus an undeclared state of war existed between the USA and Germany. SC and ON Slow convoys in the same area became the responsibility of the Canadian Navy. British escorts took over east of 22 West.

The return in triumph of *Orion* to France on 23 August marked the end of the first phase of the surface raider war even though *Kormoran* and *Atlantis* continued on patrol until November when the former was sunk by HMAS *Sydney* and *Atlantis* by HMS *Devonshire*. When *Orion* sailed into the estuary of the Gironde on 23 August she had completed a mission of 510 days during which she had covered a distance of 127,337 miles, the longest voyage of all raiders and sunk ten ships of 62,915 tons plus two more of 21,125 tons in co-operation with *Komet*. From south of the Azores she had been escorted by *U-75* and *U-205*, passing ahead of convoy OG71 during the night of 21 August.

Orion's last victim was the South American Saint Line tramp steamer *Chaucer* of 5,792 tons commanded by Captain Bradley. She was outward bound in ballast and on 29 July was sighted by the raider some 800 miles west of the Cape Verde Islands. *Orion* followed in her wake for seven hours before steaming abreast of her and firing a spread of torpedoes. She then fired her two 5.9 inch guns at a range of less than four miles.

As darkness fell the crippled *Chaucer* radioed the distress signal and courageously fired her 4 inch and 40 mm Bofor guns. But although the shells burst above the raider's deck causing minor damage, *Orion* closed, her searchlight illuminating *Chaucer*, firing a further spread of torpedoes, one of which was seen to hit but did not detonate. Captain Bradley, sensing that all was lost and anxious to save life, gave instructions to his crew to abandon ship. All 48, including thirteen wounded, were made prisoners of war.

It was during August that the first Russian convoy sailed. Six British steamers carrying 64 fighter aircraft, 33 special vehicles and over 15,000 tons of mixed military cargo set forth from Loch Ewe on their voyage north and east. They were led by Union Castle's *Llanstephan Castle* which, in addition to cargo, carried 550 RAF officers and men.

On the day that Operation Barbarossa was launched Winston Churchill had given his word 'to give whatever help we can to Russia and the Russian people'. In the official agreement to furnish massive supplies of armaments and munitions to the USSR, Stalin undertook to load all supplies in Russian ships at British or American ports and transport them to Russia. But the Russian lack of shipping made this impossible and the planning of the whole gigantic operation was thrust upon the sorely-tried British Admiralty.

By the close of the year 750 tanks, 800 fighter aircraft, over 1,400 vehicles and more than 100,000 tons of other military cargo had been landed in Murmansk. A total of 41 British merchantmen including three tankers and a further seven Russian had been employed sailing in eight separate convoys – all without loss.

The heavy Russian convoy losses were to come in 1942 though masters and crews faced the Russian theatre with much foreboding. In addition to the enemy, ships and men had to contend with the worst natural conditions of anywhere in the world. Between

Greenland and Norway, the gales, rain, sleet and snowstorms sweep north-east with waves of tremendous height. Fogs are frequent and the temperature rarely exceeds 40°F. Temperatures are often so low that sea spray freezes immediately it strikes the ship's superstructure, making small ones unstable and in danger of capsizing. Man has little chance of survival unless rescued in a very short time.

Pack ice sweeping down from the Polar regions can also create problems and in the approaches to Archangel, steamers cannot proceed without the assistance of an icebreaker. To avoid enemy aircraft it was necessary to route convoys to the north of latitude 77. Here there is perpetual darkness for 115 days (use of navigational lights was often fatal) yet on long summer days the sun never sinks out of sight for the whole 24 hours allowing attack 'all around the clock'.

Many Merchant Navy masters were aware of and indeed familiar with climatic conditions but steaming in convoy with the threat of a combination of submarine, surface ship and aircraft attack brought severe strain. To all who served in this theatre it was a question of human endurance, discipline and seamanship.

The convoy losses in the south during July and August amounted to a total of 28 vessels and two damaged which made port, of which 23 and one damaged were British. It was OG71 outwards to Gibraltar and OS4 outwards to Freetown which bore the brunt of the attacks.

The Yeoward Line cargo passenger *Aquila* (3,255 grt, Commodore Ship) led convoy OG71 through the Mersey Bar in the middle of August crossing the Irish Sea and into the North Atlantic via the North Channel. The Norwegian destroyer *Bath* heralded the attack when she was torpedoed astern of the convoy in the early hours of 19 August. Within a minute there followed the small *Alva* of 1,584 tons (Glen & Co.) and two hours later, 600 miles west of Ushant, course sou-west by south, speed 8 knots, *Ciscar* and *Aquila*.

The MacAndrews' vessel *Ciscar* (1,809 grt) was following *Aquila* in the centre column when a four-torpedo salvo fired by *U-201* (Lieutenant Adalbert Schnee) hit both ships simultaneously. An hour later when the survivors came to be counted on one of the escorting corvettes the loss of life had been heavy; thirteen from *Ciscar* had been killed outright; from *Aquila*, 65 crew, five gunners, the commodore and four of his staff, together with 89 passengers including twenty Wrens, were missing presumed dead.

Three nights later, in warmer climes, in position 40.43N 11.39W, with *U-201* and *U-564* still in contact, the battle recommenced with four British ships sunk within two hours – the steam tug *Empire Oak*, the motorship *Stock* and the steamers *Clonlara* and *Aldergrove*. After torpedoing a Norwegian Mediterranean fruit trader, *U-564* (Lieutenant Commander Reinhard Suhren) sank the corvette *Zinnia* just as dawn was breaking. She blew up with an explosion which echoed all round the convoy. It was with much relief that the remnants of OG71 entered the neutral Tagus river on the morning of 24 August.

Convoy OS4, led by the commodore ship *Henry Stanley*, lost five vessels including Hall Bros Steamship's 4,954 ton *Embassage* and the 10,298 ton *Otaio*, the thirteenth vessel owned by the New Zealand Shipping Company to be lost in twelve months. Convoys for Freetown were sailing at weekly intervals, the East Coast vessels such as *Embassage*, which sailed from Leith, taking the long and often dangerous voyage around the north of Scotland to Loch Ewe, and from there linking up with the main convoy in the North Channel.

A typical Newcastle registered tramp steamer of the 1930's, *Embassage*, with Captain Kiddie in command was in ballast, destined for Pepel to bring home a cargo of iron ore. At dawn on 27 August, in position 54.00N 13.00W, a westerly gale blowing and with a rough sea and heavy swell, she was torpedoed by *U-557* (Lieutenant Ottokar Paulshen). Two torpedoes had been fired at the ship ahead but missed their target, one of them striking *Embassage* forward of the bridge. Captain Kiddie and 38 crew were already dead as she ploughed under, the bosun and two seamen jumping overboard to cling to an upturned boat. They were rescued after nearly four days adrift. They were the only survivors.

Just two hours before, as the convoy desperately tried to keep station, Hain Steamship's *Tremoda* of 4,736 tons was lost. She too was torpedoed by *U-557*, breaking up very fast in the atrocious weather. Her master, Captain Bastian, 25 of his crew and six gunners lost their lives; the remainder, twenty crew and one gunner, were picked up later.

The cargo liner *Otaio*, commanded by Captain Kinnell, was sunk 36 hours later on the afternoon of 28 August but according to the records of her owners, the weather had by no means improved. Carrying general cargo for Australia via Panama she had just dispersed from the main convoy, in position 52.16N 17.50W, together with other ships bound for the Caribbean and South America. Her attacker, *U-558*, commanded by Lieutenant Günther Krech, was commissioned in February 1941. It was Krech's third war patrol and his first kill.

Two torpedoes were fired simultaneously. The first exploded

abreast No 5 hatch on the port side and was followed eight seconds later by the other which struck the engine room amidships killing all on duty. The electric light and all power failed. Then, with the wind and the heavy pounding of the sea, she took a heavy list to port and settled rapidly by the stern. There were considerable problems in lowering the lifeboats; two got away safely but the falls of No 3 were unhooked by the heavy swell as it was being lowered and quickly drifted astern with only two men in it. No 4 lifeboat was caught by the steel gallows of the accommodation ladder which ripped the inboard side, the swell then unhooked one fall, several of the crew were thrown into the sea and the boat capsized.

Fifty-eight survivors from *Otaio* were later picked up by the destroyers *Vanoc* and *Walker*; thirteen of her crew were missing and five were injured.

In September the submarines returned to the offensive; 55 ships were sunk in the Atlantic, sixteen of them (65,000 grt) were from one convoy, the ill-fated SC42. Others which suffered heavy losses, both in ships and men, were OG74, SL87 and HG73.

SC42, a 7½ knot convoy, 64 ships sailing in twelve columns, carried some 500,000 tons of cargo. Departing from Sydney, Cape Breton, on 30 August, five more vessels then joined five days later from St John's Newfoundland to make up a thirteenth column. The weather was atrocious with an easterly gale and heavy seas and for two whole days the ships were hove to, barely keeping steerage way on them. Over a period of four days the average speed was only 3 knots. At sunset on 8 September, Commodore Mackenzie RNR, flying his standard in *Everleigh* (Atlantic Shipping and Trading Company) ordered a diversion due north. It was to take the convoy to within 60 miles of Cape Farewell on the coast of Greenland.

Later that night, lit by a brilliant full moon, the convoy was sighted by Lieutenant Eberhard Greger, commander of *U-58*. Thirteen other U-boats waiting for the signal were called up. By sunrise the alarm had been raised. *Jedmoor*, straggling because of engine trouble, had seen two torpedoes pass ahead of her. Her position, 61.38N 40.40W. Immediately there was a loud explosion.

The vessel torpedoed was *Empire Springbuck* (5,591 grt), operated on behalf of the Ministry of War Transport by W.A. Souter & Co., herself a straggler. As reported by her assailant, *U-81* (Lieutenant Friedrich Guggenberger), there were two loud explosions and she blew up in a sheet of flame. Bound for Leith and London with steel and explosives *Empire Springbuck* sank with all hands, 42 officers and men. Her master, Captain O'Connell, had been in command of the motor vessel *Hylton* when she was sunk on 29 March, a little over five months before.

The following night, 10 September, the enemy submarines closed in, four of them breaking through the escort screen. Eight vessels including the CAM ship *Empire Hudson* were torpedoed over a period of fourteen hours. The 5,229 ton *Muneric* owned by the Bright Navigation Company, loaded with iron ore from Rio de Janeiro and destined for Middlesbrough broke in two and within fifty seconds plunged to the seabed. Hit by two torpedoes from *U-432* (Lieutenant Heinz-Otto Schultze), all hands were lost which included five DEMS gunners and two stowaways.

As Commodore Mackenzie ordered emergency turns, one of them a 45 turn to port with a heavy sea running, there was much confusion as the escorts tried to hunt the enemy. With a convoy speed of only 5 knots, the heavily laden merchantmen, difficult to manoeuvre, miraculously avoided collision. Amidst all this, tracer bullets criss-crossed the waves as the ships turned and twisted and ships' gunners fired at the blurred images of surfaced U-boats. Skywards the 'snowflakes' illuminated the battle scene and from beneath the sea came the sound of exploding depth charges as the Canadians went in for the kill. *U-207* and *U-501*, both on their first wartime missions, were sunk.

During the early hours of 11 September, with the convoy back in formation, steering north-east at 6 knots, there was again the familiar routine of explosions, rockets, starshells and snowflakes. With Dönitz's men behaving with increasing boldness a further seven ships were lost including the 7,519 ton motor tanker *Bulysses*, the *Gypsum Queen* (3,915 grt), *Stonepool* (4,815 grt), *Brerury* (4,924 grt) and *Empire Crossbill* of 5,463 tons.

Again the toll was heavy. Ropner's *Stonepool*, loaded with grain from Canada, lost her master, Captain Nicholson, ten of her officers and twenty others. *Empire Crossbill*, managed by J. Morrison & Son on behalf of the Ministry of War Transport, and with Captain Townend in command had loaded explosives in Philadelphia for discharge at Hull. All on board, 37 crew, ten gunners and one passenger perished.

As SC42 moved eastwards, a stronger escort kept the Germans at bay and on 16 September a blanket of fog came down so protecting the convoy from further destruction though not before the 4,392 ton motorship *Jedmoor*, owned by Runciman's Moor Line, had been lost. Carrying manganese ore from Santos she was torpedoed by *U-98*, 300 miles west of the Orkney Islands. The vessel which raised the alarm on 9 September was the last to be sunk seven days later. Sinking in two minutes, 26 of her crew and five gunners died. Five survivors were picked up by *Campus* and one by *Knoll*.

Hogarth's *Baron Pentland*, of 3,410 tons, torpedoed by *U-652* on 10 September and then abandoned, remained afloat, drifting for nine days on her lumber cargo before finally being torpedoed and sunk by *U-372*.

In early September one of Germany's most successful submarines, *U-94*, sailed from Lorient under a new commander; Lieutenant Otto Ites had replaced Lieutenant Kuppisch. On the fifteenth of the month in mid-Atlantic, latitude 54.00N, *U-94* torpedoed three vessels which had just dispersed from convoy ON14 to sail independently to their respective destinations in the south. The two British ships were lost with all hands, a total of 71 crew and eleven DEMS gunners. They were the 5,102 ton *Newbury*, Alexander Shipping Company, Cardiff for Buenos Aires with coal and the 5,613 ton *Empire Eland*, Ministry of War Transport managed by Douglas & Ramsey. She was in ballast from the River Mersey for Mobile and Tampa.

Convoy OG74 comprising 27 merchantmen for Gibraltar sailed from the Mersey and the Clyde on 12 September. The escort included the ocean-boarding vessel *Corinthian*, one sloop and five corvettes together with the 5,537 ton *Audacity*, the ex-German *Hannover*, captured in February 1940 between Dominica and Puerto Rico. She had recently been converted as an auxiliary aircraft carrier to combat the increasing menace of the FW200 bombers based in Western France.

The captain, deck officers and key technicians of *Audacity* were from the Royal Navy but most of the seamen and all the engine room staff were Merchant Navy men serving under T 124X articles which allowed them to continue their normal seafaring life in auxiliary war vessels.

The convoy was sighted by *U-124* on 20 September, closely followed by *U-201*. As midnight approached, Lieutenant-Commander Johann Mohr brought his submarine, *U-124*, within range, position 48.07N 22.07W. He then fired a spread of three torpedoes, one of which struck *Baltallinn* (1,303 grt), United Baltic Corporation) on the port side abaft the bow exploding in No 1 hold. She sank immediately with the loss of eighteen lives. Two minutes later, the 2,922 ton *Empire Moat*, was torpedoed.

Dropping back from her position on the starboard side of the convoy was Union Castle Mail Steamship's 906 ton *Walmer Castle*

Hong Kong harbour 19 December 1941. The battle for Hong Kong rages in the background with Quarry Bay dockyard framed in smoke, the North Point power station to the right.

The battle for Hong Kong nears its climax. 23 December 1941. In Hong Kong harbour lie many scuttled ships. The struggle has now reached Central District and Japanese troops are on the high ground. To the left, the Hong Kong & Shanghai Bank Building. In the foreground, the Kowloon–Canton Railway Station. (From a painting by Tsim Sha Tsin, Marine Police HQ.)

The Clan Line's *Clan Chattan*, Mediterranean, February 1942. The steamship *Clan Chattan*, 7,262 grt, seen on fire after being bombed 175 miles north of Benghazi, 14 February 1942. Taken from the deck of HMS *Beaufort*.

The survivors from *Clan Chattan* are rescued. The *Clan Chattan* was carrying 200 troops in addition to her crew. Rescue was made by the anti-aircraft cruiser *Carlisle* and HMS *Beaufort*.

under the command of Captain Clarke. It was her first voyage after being converted as a fully equipped rescue ship; until 1940 she had been engaged on Union Castle's feedship service between Southampton and European ports. Now she possessed a sickbay and operating theatre, a full medical and nursing staff, special rescue gear and comfortable cabins for survivors.

Walmer Castle already had on board 23 survivors from the Irish *City of Waterford*, sunk after she collided with a Dutch rescue tug on 19 September. Now, during the early hours and into the dawn of another day she rescued the entire crew of 30 from *Empire Moat* and 28 from *Baltallinn*. In doing so, however, she lost touch with the convoy.

Later that same morning, although *Walmer Castle*, with her 15 knot speed was catching up with OG74, she was suddenly surprised by a Focke-Wulf bomber which dropped out of the sun to within 250 feet of the sea. Releasing a bomb which was wide of its mark and fell into the sea, the aircraft circled, then flew from stem to stern firing all her cannon and killing the gunner on the bridge. On the second run a bomb again missed although this time both Captain Clarke and his chief mate were badly wounded by cannonfire. Then, as the FW200 came in for the third time, it was a direct hit. *Walmer Castle* was ablaze.

The fire was uncontrollable, the bridge was destroyed and the radio room wrecked. Captain Clarke, eleven officers and twenty crew were killed; 29 of those she had rescued from sunken ships also perished, the survivors being picked up by HMS *Deptford* and the corvette *Marigold*. The derelict was then sunk by gunfire being deemed a danger to other vessels. Thus the stout little rescue ship blasted by friend and foe alike was no more. It was a sad ending to a gallant ship.

During the evening of 21 September there were further losses. *U-201*, commanded by Lieutenant Adalbert Schnee, breached the defence sinking three small vessels with heavy loss of life.

Runa	1,575 grt, Clydesdale Shipowners Co. 12 crew and 2 gunners lost.
Lissa	1,511 grt, Clydesdale Shipowners Co. All hands, 21 crew and 5 gunners.
Rhineland	1,381 grt, James Currie & Co. All hands, 23 crew and 3 gunners.

Thirteen ships sailed from Freetown for the United Kingdom,

convoy SL87, on 14 September 1941. It was an unlucky thirteen for seven of them, all British registered, in spite of being escorted by five naval vessels, never reached their destination. Valuable foodstuffs and precious timber, much of it mahogany, were lost.

Five of those sunk were West African traders; the motorships *Edward Blyden* and *Dixcove*, owned by Elder Dempster Co Ltd; *St Clair* and *Lafian*, both operated by the United Africa Company though *St Clair* was managed on behalf of the Ministry of Supply; and the *John Holt*, built in 1938 for John Holt and Company (Liverpool) Ltd. The other two were Silver Line's *Silverbelle*, carrying sugar from Mauritius and Larrinaga's *Niceto de Larrinaga*, general produce from Lagos.

Edward Blyden (5,003 grt, commanded by Captain Exley) was carrying twelve passengers. It was *U-103* (Lieutenant Werner Winter), that torpedoed her close to midnight on 22 September. Winter was working in close co-operation with Merten (*U-68*) Müller-Stöckheim (*U-67*) and Hessler (*U-107*), trailing the convoy from 750 miles south-west of the Canary Islands to 350 miles west of Madeira.

A second torpedo struck the *Edward Blyden* just before she was abandoned though all on board got away safely and were later rescued by HMS *Bideford*. It was thirty hours later, west of Madeira that the 3,790 ton *Dixcove*, commanded by Captain Jones, was sunk. A spread of three torpedoes from *U-107* crippled *Dixcove*, *Lafian* and *John Holt* in as many minutes. On the Elder Dempster merchantman there was much devastation, No 1 lifeboat was destroyed, Captain Jones lay injured on the bridge and one of his crew was dead. Suddenly she took a heavy list to starboard yet the remaining three lifeboats were successfully launched, the survivors, including her injured master, being rescued by *Ashby* and HMS *Gorleston*.

The 15-knot Prince Line motorship *Cingalese Prince* which survived the April 1941 bombing of Piraeus harbour, was outward-bound for South America when she was lost on 20 September; she was operating the Furness Withy Rio Cape Line service. Her master, Captain Smith and 57 crew were lost. *Cingalese Prince* was the first merchant vessel torpedoed by a U-boat south of the Equator (02.00S 25.30W). Lieutenant Wilhelm Kleinschmidt, commander of *U-111*, had arrived in these waters earlier in the month sinking the Dutch *Marken*. She was followed by *U-66* and in October by *U-126* and *U-68*.

Of the 25 ships that sailed from Gibraltar on 17 September only sixteen reached their destination. The escort for HG73 was by no means weak, consisting of one destroyer, two sloops and eight

corvettes together with the 5,155 ton catapult ship *Springbank*.
There was concern that the U-boats, assisted by the Luftwaffe,
based in Western France, were increasing their hold in these waters.

On 19 and 20 September the Italian submarines *Morosini* and
Torelli, on their way to the Mediterranean, established brief contact.
They were followed by *Da Vinci* but it was *U-124* and *U-201*, fresh
from their successes against OG74, together with *U-203*, that
wrought such damage. *Empire Stream* (2,922 grt), managed by J.S.
Stranaghan on behalf of the Ministry of War Transport was the first
to be torpedoed losing four of her crew, two gunners and two
stowaways. At the time the convoy was steaming due north 800 miles
west of Cape Finisterre.

Seventeen hours later during the late evening of 25 September in
position 47.50N 24.00W, *U-203* came up from astern at periscope
depth and made a devastating attack as she drew abreast the leading
ships. Her commander, Lieutenant Rolf Mützelburg, ordered the
firing of four torpedoes and after observing one hit (the Norwegian
Varangberg) dived to avoid being detected. Only later was it known
that all four torpedoes were on target; the second struck the
commodore ship, the Yeoward Line *Avoceta* and the remaining two,
the *Cortes*, owned by MacAndrews & Co.

The 3,442 ton *Avoceta*, a cargo passenger ship routed for Liverpool,
shuddered violently as the torpedo struck the engine room. The
explosion lifted the whole ship and she then lurched and twisted in a
'corkscrew' action as if she were drunk. As the stern literally crashed
down and plunged beneath the sea the bow rose alarmingly.
Amidships, with steam screaming from abaft the funnel and with
lifeboats hanging crazily from their davits, the distress rockets,
indicating that she had been hit, roared skywards.

With way still upon her, the bows of *Avoceta* rose even higher and
as bulkheads gave way, torrents of water cascaded the length and
breadth of the ship, sweeping everything before them. Sleeping
people woke to their deaths, seamen were trapped in their quarters,
officers on watch were washed overboard. No boats could be lowered
and 43 crew, four gunners and 76 passengers perished. The convoy
commodore, Rear Admiral Sir Kenelm Creighton, reached a raft
with the master and six others and they were rescued by the corvette
Periwinkle three hours later.

Meanwhile, as the crippled *Cortes* (1,374 grt, Captain MacRae)
fell astern and was abandoned, General Steam Navigation's *Lapwing*
slowed to rescue some of her crew. Later that day, however, they lost
their lives when *Lapwing* (1,348 grt) was herself sunk losing her own

master, Captain Hyam, twenty of her crew and three gunners. Sailing in the adjoining column was her sister ship *Petrel* which was also lost; her master, Captain Klemp survived although he lost 22 of his men.

The battle was not yet over. Twenty-four hours later, close to midnight 26 September, *U-124*, which had torpedoed *Lapwing* and *Petrel* came in again, sinking a second MacAndrews vessel, the 1,810 ton *Cervantes*. The following day, in latitude 50°, some 400 miles west of Ireland, *U-201* sank three vessels including the CAM ship *Springbank* whose Fulmar fighters had driven off two attacking FW200's. It was a sad loss and one which could be ill-afforded. The remaining ships of convoy HG73 reached the coastal waters of the North Channel with great relief.

Mines continued to take their toll; five vessels were sunk in coastal waters during September 1941. The largest was Gow Harrison's 5,729 grt tanker *Vancouver* which arrived off Shell Haven with 7,500 tons of gasoline from North America. She broke in two and catching fire could not be approached for several days because of burning spirit on the water. Thirty-four of her crew of 36 and five of her six gunners were lost.

In the Mediterranean theatre Operation 'Halberd' got under way. This was a Malta supply convoy of some of Britain's finest intermediate ships – *Ajax, Breconshire, City of Lincoln, Clan Ferguson, Clan MacDonald, Dunedin Star, Imperial Star* and *Rowallan Castle*. They passed through the Straits of Gibraltar during the night of 24/25 September heavily escorted by a force of three battleships, *Nelson, Rodney* and *Prince of Wales*, the aircraft carrier *Ark Royal*, five cruisers and eighteen destroyers. Of this force, the five cruisers and nine destroyers were to form the escort for the final dash through 'the narrows' to Malta.

The convoy was sighted by the enemy 30 hours later and during the afternoon of 27 September was attacked by Italian torpedo bombers, three of the ships having narrow escapes. During a third attack, in the failing light of the evening, Blue Star Line's 12,427 ton *Imperial Star* was struck on the port side aft by a torpedo. The rudder and both propellers were blown away and she was making water slowly aft; 300 troops she was carrying were taken off by one of the escorting destroyers.

Imperial Star was taken in tow by the destroyer *Oribi* in an effort to reach Malta but she proved unmanageable and was abandoned in position 37.31N 10.46E during the early hours of the following morning. 141 people who remained on board were taken off. She was then sunk by depth charges placed below the waterline and by gunfire. As her end came, 1,000 tons of high explosive, part of her valuable cargo, blew up with a tremendous explosion.

In the days prior to 'Halberd' speculation was rife in naval circles as to the amount of resources the Axis powers were prepared to commit to the North African war. In addition to the Italian submarines it became known that German U-boats were passing eastward through the Straits. They were *U-75*, *U-79*, *U-97*, *U-331*, *U-371* and *U-559*. During 11/16 November there followed *U-81*, *U-205*, *U-433* and *U-565*.

On 27 September, the first of over 2,700 US Liberty Ships, the *Patrick Henry* (7,176 grt) was launched. Three months later she was delivered to her managers. The mass-produced Liberty ship, of simple and sturdy design, a record was set when the *Robert E. Peary* (November 1942) was completed, from laying the keel to delivery in only eight days, probably contributed as much as anything, to the defeat of the Germans in the Battle of the Atlantic.

It was October 1941 and the loss of the Cardiff-registered *Nailsea Manor* which forever imprinted upon my mind the harsh realities of the war at sea (see 'Reminiscences' Chapter 10). *Nailsea Manor*, however, was just unlucky to be sighted by the lone *U-126*, en route from Lorient, taking a southerly course towards the Equator. The battles against the wolf packs remained in the north: SC48, with nine merchantmen sunk; HG75 with five ships and the destroyer *Cossack* sunk, one merchantman damaged; SC52, with five merchantmen sunk.

Even convoy battles, however, could hardly compare with the epic stand made by a 22-year-old tanker which proudly 'died' with her Red Duster flying high. *San Florentino* of 12,842 grt, on charter to the Admiralty was an Eagle Oil steam tanker outward bound in ballast for Curaçao. She had sailed from the Clyde under the command of Captain Davis when, proceeding independently after leaving the convoy on 29 September, she was shadowed and attacked by a submarine over a period of two days. In her light state, steaming into the teeth of a westerly gale, she was difficult to manoeuvre yet from the first assault during twilight hours on 1 October until the hour she 'died', she inflicted heavy damage on her attacker.

Lieutenant Otto Ites (*U-94*) had now brought his boat further west and was in position 52.50N 34.40W when he instructed his crew to fire. The torpedo slammed into the starboard side with a deafening explosion tearing apart No 6 tank and demolishing the bulkheads between tanks Nos 4, 5, 6 and 7. Captain Davis then sighted *U-94* on his starboard quarter and brought his assailant astern, opening fire with his 4.7-inch gun. Thereafter in a hide and seek game, with *San Florentino* dropping smoke floats to conceal herself, the action continued for over two hours. The tanker's outdated gun fired a total of eighteen shells with the result that the enemy was forced to submerge repeatedly.

Two and a half hours after the first assault the tanker was again torpedoed, this time on the port side. There was widespread damage and she rapidly assumed a 20° list to port. At No 5 tank there was a vast hole the whole breadth of the ship with the seas washing right through from one side to the other.

U-94 was then seen on the port side. Again, with the sea rough and a heavy swell, she was brought astern and fired upon forcing Ites to crash dive. Within a few minutes, the submarine, with a great open wound showing on her conning tower, surfaced on the starboard beam. Simultaneously a third torpedo struck the vessel, carrying away two metal lifeboats and davits together with the main aerial and severing all communication with the engine room.

Despite this punishment Captain Davis thrust his ship through the heavy moonlit seas in an effort to escape, his engineers, as if by some magic, finding a speed of knots which had eluded them for many a year. Alas! it was to no avail. In the early hours a fourth torpedo tore into the shattered hull to deal a death blow.

With the bridge collapsed and the for'ard pumproom ablaze, with his ship beginning to break into two, Captain Davis reluctantly issued orders to abandon ship. On lowering the starboard lifeboat it was stove in against the ship's side but the men lifted it bodily and flung it into the sea where it floated on its tanks. In her the chief mate and nineteen crew took refuge, sitting up to their waists in water though nine subsequently perished through the cold and the sea water.

The gun crew successfully launched another boat whilst the third mate and an able seaman stayed at the bow end which slowly rose out of the water until it floated vertically, the after part of the tanker sinking. The two men sat astride the stem through thirteen hours of rough sea and strong wind before being rescued. They had neither food nor drink and it was twenty hours before a US destroyer found them. Captain Davis and 21 crew were lost with three brought ashore wounded. *San Florentino* fought hard but lost her battle.

The crews of two other ships sunk in these waters on 2 October told terrible tales of their survival. From *Hatasu* (3,198 grt, Moss Hutchison Line) torpedoed by *U-431* 600 miles east of Cape

Race, the survivors drifted helplessly through fourteen days of gales, high seas and low temperatures before being picked up by the escorts of an eastbound convoy. Four were suffering badly with immersion feet. *Empire Wave*, a new CAM ship of 7,463 grt, managed by Barr, Crombie & Co, was sunk by *U-562*, 500 miles east of Cape Farewell. One boatload of 30 men got safely away only to endure fifteen days of hardship with only a tarpaulin as protection against the elements. They lived on condensed milk, chocolate and a tablespoon of water per man per day.

Two died from *Empire Wave* before rescue by an Icelandic trawler. Thirty of their shipmates adrift in another boat were never seen again. Of those that survived there were ten cases of immersion feet; together with those from *Hatasu* they were moved from Reykjavik to the United Kingdom on 25 October. They were all stretcher cases. There was concern amongst the Admiralty and shipowners alike at the number of men who suffered permanent disability from injuries. Feet and hands were sometimes amputated because of exposure in northern seas.

On 17 October *U-558* operated with other U-boats against convoy SC48. She was now on her fourth war patrol, her commanding officer Lieutenant Günther Krech remaining with *U-558* until she was sunk on 20 July 1943. On this day in October 1941 she sank a Norwegian motor tanker, a Norwegian cargo vessel and the British flag tanker *W.C.|Teagle* (9,552 grt, owned by the Panama Transport Company). The convoy's position was 57.00N 25.00W.

W.C. Teagle had loaded 15,000 tons of fuel oil at Aruba and was bound for Swansea. There were only nine survivors from her crew of 40 together with one gunner; all were picked out of the sea by the destroyer *Broadwater*. All but one of these, the chief radio officer, were lost when the destroyer herself was torpedoed and sunk (by *U-101*) 24 hours later.

It was a fruitful week for Günther Krech. After being called up to attack SC48 and forging ahead at 17 knots into a heavy north-westerly swell to make his rendezvous, he encountered the independently routed 9,472 ton *Vancouver Island*. Formerly the German *Weser* she was captured by the Canadian auxiliary cruiser *Prince Robert* on 26 September 1940 soon after she had sailed from Manzanillo, Mexico. Now owned by the Canadian Government but with a British crew, she was en route from Montreal for Cardiff. All on board were lost, 65 crew, eight gunners and 32 passengers.

Silver Line's sugar carrier *Silvercedar* (4,354 grt) was the first casualty of SC48. She was torpedoed and sunk by *U-553*

(Lieutenant-Commander Karl Thurmann) in position 53.36N 29.57W two days before Günther Krech arrived on the scene. *Silvercedar* broke her back, both bow and stern sections floating briefly before plunging to the bottom; her master, Captain Keane and twenty of his crew lost their lives. Later the same evening 34 crew and nine gunners perished after they had abandoned their sinking ship, the 6,023 ton *Empire Heron*, managed by Andrew Weir and Company. At first it was the familiar story 'lost without trace', then, many hours later, a seaman was found clinging to a piece of wreckage. He was the only survivor.

A total of six tankers were lost to the U-boat in October and a further vessel, the American fleet oiler *Salinas* was seriously damaged. One of those sunk was the *Inverlee* (9,158 grt), built in Germany in 1938 for Inver Tankers. Carrying 14,000 tons of fuel oil, she had been routed independently from Trinidad to Gibraltar, there to join one of the HG convoys homewards. Torpedoed by *U-204*, subsequently herself sunk a short while afterwards, *Inverlee* was abandoned 30 miles from Cape Spartel, Morocco, on 19 October. Twenty-one of her crew of 43 died.

In mid October the Hain Steamship Company lost another of its fleet engaged on the iron ore traffic from Sierra Leone. The 5,218 ton *Treverbyn* from Pepel sailed with convoy SL89 for Cardiff and seven days later was sunk by *U-82* (Lieutenant Siegfried Rollman) which had wrought such havoc in the action against SC42. *Treverbyn* sank like a stone. None of those on board, 38 crew and ten gunners, had any chance of getting away. Ellerman Lines' *Serbino*, Mombasa for Liverpool, was sunk a few minutes earlier.

During the early hours of 24 October the log-book of *U-564* records her attack on HG75, with a spread of five torpedoes, 300 miles west of Gibraltar '. . . the first three (torpedoes) exploded with red fire columns on different ships after 21 seconds, 31 seconds and 41 seconds. The last two were heard to detonate after 3 mins 14 seconds and 3 mins 56 seconds'. These last two detonations were probably depth charges from one of the escorts as the records only confirm the loss of three ships at this time, ships and cargoes which were valuable to Britain's war effort.

Carsbreck	3,670 grt, Carslogie Steamship Company.	
Ariosto	2,176 grt, Ellerman's Wilson Line.	
Alhama	1,353 grt, Mossgiel Steamship Company.	

The slaughter of HG75 was the result of a combined U-boat and air assault. Casualties on the Gibraltar run mounted alarmingly and future convoys were suspended until a sufficiently strong escort could be assembled to get ships through. HG76 did not sail until 14 December.

During the last three months of 1941 there was great damage from Atlantic storms. Gales of force 7 or more were recorded on fifty-three days and stragglers from convoys brought many problems for the escorts. From one convoy of 46 ships, as many as 23 were stragglers, from another of 43 there were a reported 26 stragglers. From the ill-fated SC48, eleven out of 50 lost contact with their commodore. Many ships arrived in port with heavy weather damage, necessitating repair and subsequent delay. Whilst the atrocious weather curtailed somewhat the activities of the U-boats those ships that were unfortunate to be caught by the submarines, suffered heavy casualties.

One of those caught was *King Malcolm* (5,120 grt), owned by Dodd Thomson & Co. She had loaded potash in Haifa but due to the increasingly difficult situation, both in the Mediterranean and off the West African coast, she was routed through the Suez Canal, and via Cape Town to Sydney, Nova Scotia, before sailing for the United Kingdom, a seemingly unending voyage. Sailing from Sydney with SC50 for Belfast she lost touch because of storm conditions. In position 47.40N 51.50W she was torpedoed by *U-374* and sank in thirty seconds. Her crew of 34 and four gunners stood no chance in the mountainous seas and not one survived.

Few merchant ships were sunk in the Atlantic during November and December. This was due to a combination of factors; the weather, the greater number of escort vessels now protecting the convoys, increased air cover and the increase in the number of U-boats being sent to the Mediterranean. Due to their presence east of Gibraltar, November saw the loss of the aircraft carrier *Ark Royal* (*U-81*), the battleship *Barham* (*U-331*) and Cardigan Shipping Company's 4,274 ton ore carrier *Grelhead*. Torpedoed by *U-562*, two miles north of Point Negri, Morocco, she lost 35 of her crew of 37 and all six gunners.

Shuntien (3,059 grt, China Navigation Company) was engaged in the transport of prisoners of war. With between 800 and 1,000 on board during passage from Tobruk to Alexandria on 23 December, she was torpedoed and sunk by *U-559*, commanded by Lieutenant Hans Heidtmann. Her master, four officers and the chief steward were killed. Many of the Italian prisoners of war were picked up by the corvette *Salvia*, which was herself sunk shortly afterwards by *U-568*.

Five days later, Ellerman Wilson's *Volo* (1,587 grt) was also lost between Tobruk and Alexandria. Torpedoed by Helmuth Ringelman, *U-75*, 21 of her crew and three gunners were killed.

The sinking of the new 8,532 ton motorship *Nottingham*, Federal Steam Navigation Co Ltd, in the Atlantic on 7 November was nothing short of a tragedy. She was the fourteenth ship of the Federal Fleet sunk by enemy action in barely fifteen months and was on her maiden voyage independent from Glasgow for New York. Commanded by Captain Pretty formerly of *Cornwall*, she was torpedoed by *U-74* (Lieutenant Eitel-Friedrich Kentrat), in position 53.24N 31.51W.

No radio distress call was sent by *Nottingham* and it is not known whether any lifeboats were launched. There were no survivors; 61 officers and crew, including five gunners, perished. Captain Cooper of the Port Line who was proceeding to Montreal to take up an appointment in the service of the British Ministry of War Transport was among those lost.

The assault on convoy SC52 during the first week of November took place off the coast of Newfoundland; it was the furthest west the U-boats had ventured. *Everoja* was sunk within 80 miles of Belle Isle and *Rose Schiaffino* (3,349 grt, Ministry of War Transport managed by Mark Whitwill & Son) 225 miles north of St John's.

Rose Schiaffino had loaded iron ore at Wabana for Cardiff and had joined SC52 the day before. She broke up immediately the torpedo from *U-569* struck, all hands, 37 crew and four gunners were lost. Hans-Peter Hinsch, commander of *U-569* and a pre-war naval officer, had previously served as commander of *U-4* and *U-140*. On the same night of 3 November, *U-202* sank the 4,586 ton *Gretavale* (Crawford Shipping Company), bound from Baltimore to Loch Ewe for orders. Loss of life was again heavy; from her crew of 42 and five gunners, there were only five survivors.

North Sea and English Channel convoys were still much troubled by E-boat attacks, both by day and by night. In November 1941 six vessels of 12,886 grt were torpedoed and sunk by these 40 knot craft. A further vessel of 4,155 tons was seriously damaged and was under repair for four months.

Gow Harrison's 5,723 ton tanker *Virgilia*, under the command of Captain Caird was torpedoed and set on fire during a raid by three E-boats on 24 November, three miles north-east of Hearty Knoll Buoy. Twenty-three members of her crew were killed. Six days later, the Ministry of War Transport's *Empire Newcomen* (2,840 grt) managed by Martyn, Martyn & Co. and en route between London and Sunderland was sunk off Cromer. Ten of her engine room crew were killed when the torpedo exploded amidships.

On the last day of the month the enemy raider *Komet* arrived at Hamburg amid much jubilation. Disguised as the Portuguese *S Thome* she had been escorted for the last two days by *U-516* and *U-652*. Her tally was six ships of 31.005 tons sunk and two other ships totalling 21,125 tons in co-operation with *Orion*. More important to the German High Command had been her nuisance value creating much havoc in the Pacific. She had been away from her homeland for 516 days.

On Sunday, 7 December, the United States was catapulted into the war as the Japanese attacked the American fleet at Pearl Harbour. The following day Japan declared war on Britain and the British Empire, launching a heavy assault upon Hong Kong, for long an important outpost for Britain's maritime operations in the Far East. On 10 December the two capital ships *Prince of Wales* and *Repulse* were sunk off the coast of Malaya by Japanese naval aircraft followed the next day by Hitler's declaration of war on the USA. These disasters meant that within a matter of days, the Japanese virtually became masters of the China Seas and the whole of south-east Asia. Suddenly the war became a world war. Overnight Britain's merchant fleet was at risk as never before in all its history.

By 13 December British forces had been obliged to evacuate Kowloon to avoid annihilation by the Japanese 38th Infantry Division. British shipping was in disarray. The situation was chaotic. All over the region there were British crewed ships, British registered ships crewed by Chinese and Lascars, but with British masters and possibly two or three British navigating officers; there were even many British masters, who, with their wives, served on vessels of Far Eastern registry and who traded the China Seas and the river estuaries.

Some of these ships were engaged on coastal work, others, deep sea, were on charter to Far East Governments; there were others which had reached various stages of their voyages, from both east and west, those which were under repair, or refitting, such as Alfred Holt's *Tantalus* and *Ulysses* in the Taikoo dockyard at Hong Kong. All had been taken completely unawares and were ill prepared for what happened. The records of British ships lost for the month of December 1941 serve to illustrate the true extent of the disaster.

1. Seized or captured-Chinese ports or off   24 Merchantmen.
    the coast of China.
2. Seized, sunk or captured on the China   22
    Seas (including seven on charter to Japan).
3. Seized or captured at Hong Kong or in
    vicinity.   5
4. Scuttled at Hong Kong.   9
5. Seized, sunk or captured-other Far   11
    Eastern waters.
6. Bombed and sunk by aircraft – other Far   2
    Eastern waters.
7. Seriously damaged by aircraft – other Far   1
    Eastern waters.
8. Captured in Philippines.   2
9. Bombed and sunk by aircraft. Manila Bay.   3
10. Seriously damaged during air raids on   2
    Manila.
11. Seized Bangkok.   1
12. Seized North Borneo.   5

Paragraph 5 includes the 1,523 ton 40-year-old *Hareldawins* sunk on 10 December off the Luzon Islands, Philippines, by the submarine *I-124*, a new Japanese underwater craft commanded by Lieutenant Koichi Kishigami. *I-124* was sunk a month later off Manila.

A total of 94 British merchantmen were sunk and three damaged in the initial onslaught in the Far East; their British personnel either dead or captured; many were never heard of again. Shipping establishments ashore suffered a similar fate, their staff, and many had their wives and families with them, found themselves suddenly pitched into Japanese prison camps. Those that did survive suffered many hardships over two and a half years before they were released by the Americans.

In the records of Wm Thomson & Company of Leith (Ben Line Steamers) are the names of the second engineer and three able seamen of the steamer *Bennevis* who died of malnutrition whilst prisoners of war in Japanese hands. On 6 December the 8,130 ton *Bennevis* was ordered out of Hong Kong by the British naval authorities with instructions that she should tow an 800-ton lighter to Singapore. The master, Captain Wilson, informed that the instructions were highly confidential, was told to ask no questions and to sail in accordance with orders.

The 1918-built *Bennevis* was a stout old ship. She had been badly damaged during the blitz on London during September 1940 when nine of her crew were killed and after resuming her regular Far East trade had endured several convoy battles and once came close to being sighted by a surface raider.

At sunrise on 7 December, the sea calm and with a quiet cloudless sky everyone set about their normal Sunday duties. With no radio report of the opening of hostilities, Captain Wilson was not unduly suspicious about two destroyers which approached until he received a signal that on no account was he to use his radio and he was to follow the leading ship. When he queried the instruction Captain Wilson observed that both vessels had their guns trained upon him, one of which signalled 'Captured and strike colours'. *Bennevis* was then guided to Hainan Island where a Japanese party boarded and took over the vessel. The crew, apart from the four that died, remained in prison camps until released by the Allies in September 1945.

Tantalus (7,724 grt, Captain Morris) towed by the tug *Keswick*, her main engine parts which had been ashore under repair, stowed in the hold, left Hong Kong on 5 December. Her instructions were also to make for Singapore. After the Japanese declaration of war, with his ship barely able to maintain a speed of 5 knots, Captain Morris decided to put into Manila which was reached on the evening of 11 December. The city and harbour were bombed almost daily and on Boxing Day 1941, with her crew watching her fate from ashore, *Tantalus* was hit at least four times. Listing heavily she caught fire and later the same evening capsized.

Unable to leave Manila, Captain Morris and his crew were taken prisoner a few hours after the capture of the city on 3 January 1942. Subsequently, the third mate and an able seaman tried to escape but were caught and on 15 February they were executed by their captors – in flagrant violation of International Law.

Owing in no small measure to the untiring efforts of her crew in getting their ship ready for sea, *Ulysses* (Captain Russell) at 14,646 tons the biggest ship in the Holt fleet, sailed from Hong Kong on 7 December, just a few hours before the Japanese invaded. Avoiding Manila she kept on course for Singapore and, although attacked twice from the air, one stick of bombs straddled the ship, she reached her destination undamaged.

On Christmas Day the last defence capitulated at Hong Kong. In the harbour the enemy captured 26 merchantmen (52,604 tons) of British, Soviet, Panamanian and Norwegian registry; many of them were damaged. Those which were scuttled and lay on the harbour bottom were later all salvaged by the Japanese.

The declaration of war by Hitler on the United States led to an intensification of the Battle of the Atlantic to eliminate Britain from the war. After only four days, five Type IX U-boats (*U-123*, *U-130*, *U-203*, *U-552* and *U-553*) left the submarine pens at Lorient for the long voyage to the US east coast. Meanwhile it was the 32-ship 7½ knot convoy HG76 from Gibraltar which held the attention of naval warfare experts and Master Mariners alike. Was this to be a further holocaust?

The escort varied between nine and eighteen vessels together with the escort carrier *Audacity*, the whole force commanded by Commander (later Captain) Walker. It is perhaps an opportune moment to pay tribute to this gallant officer of the senior service who, through using the most aggressive and often novel tactics, was soon to become the foremost U-boat killer of the war.

As Commodore Fitzmaurice, flying his standard in Ellerman Wilson's *Spero* was to report,

> The convoy had few dull moments. The long running battle commenced in the early hours of 15 December in position 35.30N 06.17W when *Empire Barracuda* was sunk and continued for seven days, covering a wide expanse of the ocean the convoy arriving in the North Channel as late as 27 December. The ships were shadowed continuously and considering the number of times they were sighted by FW200's, and the number of U-boats which were involved, it was remarkable that the losses were not greater.

That the enemy was kept at bay was due, in part, to *Audacity*'s fighters and to the leadership of Commander Walker. Against three merchantmen lost, the destroyer *Stanley*, and in the last stages of the battle, the carrier *Audacity*, Dönitz lost four of his U-boats, including ace Engelbert Endrass.

Empire Barracuda (4,972 grt, managed by the Stanhope Steamship Company on behalf of the Ministry of War Transport) was struck by two torpedoes fired from *U-77*, Lieutenant-Commander Heinrich Schonder. She sank within ten minutes, the survivors being picked up by the corvette *Coltsfoot*. Twelve lives were lost.

In the afternoon of 16 December as five ships of the escort left to return to Gibraltar, leaving twelve still in close contact, a pack of six U-boats were taking up position, trailing the convoy throughout the following day and night. *U-108* attacked but was driven off. Two FW200's were shot down, one was damaged and on 18 December two were driven off by single seater Martlets from *Audacity*.

The following day Commander Scholtz in *U-108* closed the convoy from the port side firing a salvo of torpedoes one of which struck the

2,869 ton *Ruckinge* owned by Constants (South Wales); she had joined from Lisbon and was bound for Oban. Six of her crew were killed by the explosion, the remainder being rescued by the freighter *Finland* whose master dropped back, ignoring the many risks and by HMS *Stork*.

Ruckinge, listing badly, drifted for a while and was then boarded by a party from HMS *Samphire* who found a bag full of confidential papers lying on the upper deck. Thrown from the bridge in confusion they had not cleared the side because of the list; there was every indication that the Cardiff tramp had been hastily evacuated. Being a danger to other shipping *Samphire* shelled the wreck after which *Ruckinge* sank.

Immediately after the Norwegian registered *Annavore* was sunk by *U-567* in the darkness of the late evening of 21 December, the U-boat herself was sunk with all hands. Her commander was the experienced Lieutenant Engelbert Endrass, Knight's Cross with Oak Leaves, who, since June 1940 when he was given command of *U-46*, had been engaged in many of the Atlantic convoy battles. As HMS *Deptford* was searching for survivors, the escort carrier *Audacity*, at some distance from the convoy was sunk by *U-751*.

The year ended with two ominous events. On Christmas Eve, convoy BM9A, the first of seven relief convoys, sailed from Colombo with reinforcements for the British garrison in Singapore. The troop transports *Devonshire*, *Ethiopia*, *Rajula* and *Varsova* took part.

On Christmas Day, the German U-boat Command instructed *U-134*, *U-454* and *U-584* to the passage south of Bear Island on the convoy route to Murmansk. From the North Cape to the China Sea, the future was uncertain.

As the statistics record, 1941 was a disastrous year for Britain's Red Duster fleet.

Ships lost:	717
Tonnage:	2,824,056 grt
Personnel lost:	8,848

As Churchill said, 'We are a seafaring race and understand the call of the sea'.

> I must go down to the seas again
> For the call of the running tide
> Is a wild call and a clear call
> That may not be denied.
> *John Masefield*

CHAPTER SIX

U-Boats' Paradise
(January–July 1942)

The entry of the United States into the war in December provided the German U-boat Command with a new and welcome theatre of operation. No fewer than 260 U-boats were now available and more were coming into service at the rate of about twenty a month. In spite of the wonderful opportunity that was offered to the enemy however, the lack of operational U-boats, principally due to repairs, prolonged by a shortage of labour, and Hitler's obsession with helping the Italians in North Africa denied Dönitz the victory that would have been his had he been able to concentrate his whole force in the Western Atlantic. Hitler also insisted that twenty operational boats be held back in the defence of Norway which he thought the Allies would invade whilst his army was bogged down at the gates of Leningrad.

Nevertheless the blow fell with devastating effect. The great threat to Britain and her Allies now lay along 'the oil route' from the Caribbean. It was oil from Aruba, Curaçao and the Gulf of Venezuela and Mexico that Britain and her armed forces now relied upon for the conduct of war. No longer could Britain rely upon her empire in the Middle East and the Far East. If this vital pipeline were cut the war would virtually be won for the Axis; the Mediterranean, except for convoys which had to be fought through to beleaguered Malta, was virtually closed. Now Japan was in possession of sources of oil in Borneo and the Dutch East Indies. Additionally, surface raiders and Japanese submarines in the Indian Ocean threatened supplies from the Persian Gulf. The provision of fuel to Britain from the east in long voyages around the Cape of Good Hope was precarious in the extreme and totally insufficient for our needs.

At the end of December some twenty U-boats sailed for the American east coast. On 8 January twelve type VIIC U-boats arrived off the Newfoundland Bank and as far south as Nova Scotia. Five larger type IX 1,100 tonners arrived on 11 January. When the

Blue Funnel *Cyclops* was sunk on 12 January, it was the beginning of a holocaust of shipping such as had never been seen before. 'The happy times' began all over again.

Coastal shipping off the American east coast sailed independently; the enemy concentrated all the venom of their attacks upon such focal areas as Hampton Roads, North Carolina and Cape Hatteras. As a German Captain said, it was 'the U-boats' paradise'. Spending the days on the bottom in shallow water, the U-boats worked mainly at night, using their high surface speed to overtake and choose their targets. Their main consideration was to obtain the best possible return in tonnage for their limited armament. When torpedoes ran short ships were often gunned, and the most serious of the many disquieting features of the new campaign was the high percentage of tankers which went up in flames; in mid February the enemy was to extend his new onslaught to the Caribbean islands and the harbours where the oil was pumped aboard.

The brunt of the new holocaust was borne, firstly by the United States, then by Britain and the Netherlands. In the first eight weeks of 1942, a total of eighty ships were torpedoed and sunk (and six damaged) in the waters west of longitude 60 degrees. Of those sunk, 38 were tankers. Of those which were damaged and made port, as many as five were tankers. The Red Duster men took it all as just another extension of the war at sea. After 30 months of being 'in the front line' nothing really came as a surprise.

Coinciding with this new extension of the war against the merchant fleet was a major blunder in the 'corridors of power'. A blunder that cost the British Merchant Marine many hundreds of ships and many thousands of lives. For many months the argument had raged over very long range aircraft protection for convoys. The naval authorities put forward many arguments, backed by graphs and statistics but they fell on deaf ears. The views of 'Bomber' Harris, supported by the Prime Minister's scientific adviser Professor Lindemann, won the day. The transfer of a comparatively small number of planes was delayed.

As was seen in the years to come, the aircraft were needed to overthrow the enemy in the Atlantic and even further afield. For one who admitted in later years 'the only thing that frightened me in the war was the U-boat peril' it was a decision that Churchill came to regret. Not only were there losses which could have been avoided but unnecessary risks were taken during the invasions of North Africa and Europe which were to come.

Alfred Holt's 9,076 ton *Cyclops* (Captain Kersley) was on passage from Australia and the Far East with a general cargo when she was torpedoed in position 41.51N 63.48W. She carried a total complement of 181 which included 151 Chinese seamen which seems to indicate that, somewhere in the Far East, with the situation deteriorating daily, she had taken on board some one hundred additional seamen intent on serving again in ships of Britain's merchant fleet.

After passing through the Panama Canal, *Cyclops* steamed independently towards Halifax where she was to join an HX convoy. The night was cold and dark as Lieutenant Reinhard Hardegen, commander of *U-123*, sighted his target at close range. As the torpedo exploded abreast Nos 6 and 7 hatches, the starboard side of the ship was ripped open causing considerable damage.

Captain Kersley, known for his cool courage and efficiency, surveyed the damage and realized his ship was beyond saving. Ordering her to be abandoned he first made sure that a distress signal had been sent and an acknowledgement received from the shore station. As the lifeboats pulled away a second torpedo struck, this time on the port side abreast the bridge.

Some of the officers together with their captain remained behind to check whether all the crew had left. *Cyclops*, however, began to list badly and was likely to sink at any moment. As she began to break up those left on board jumped overboard; some were fortunate to clamber aboard a raft released by the chief mate only minutes before. Eighty-nine survivors were picked up by HMCS *Red Deer* leaving 90 souls who perished. Some had been killed aboard *Cyclops*, others had succumbed to cold and exposure.

The sinking of *Waziristan* (5,135 grt) in the first week of the new year heralded the sea war in the far north just as *Cyclops* heralded the new offensive off the American Atlantic seaboard. Owned by the Hindustan Steamship Company, *Waziristan* loaded tanks and arms at the Bush Terminal in Brooklyn, the first British ship to load military supplies in the United States destined for Russia. She arrived at Sydney, Nova Scotia, on 27 November 1941 from where she sailed with convoy SC60. Seven days later, together with two other vessels and an armed trawler escort, she dispersed for Reykjavik.

Convoy PQ7A, made up of two vessels from SC60 and five from Loch Ewe, sailed for Russian waters on Boxing Day. The destination was Murmansk. *Waziristan* was last seen at 1600 hours on New

Year's Day by the ship abeam, the Panamanian *Cold Harbor*, her position being about 300 miles north-west of Jan Mayen Island. The captain of *Cold Harbor* recorded in his log strong easterly gales and thick ice making headway difficult. He later considered it possible that *Waziristan* had straggled during the night and may have been crushed in the ice.

It was not the Arctic weather, however, but *U-134*, captained by Lieutenant Rudolf Schendel, whose torpedo sent *Waziristan* to the ocean bottom at 0648 hours the following morning. Whether lifeboats were launched was never known; certainly no one would have lived more than one minute in those northern waters that January morning. Her crew of 37 and ten gunners perished. Official sources record their grave as 74.09N 19.10E.

Convoy PQ8 which followed eighteen days later ran foul of a second U-boat; this was *U-454*, captained by Lieutenant Hackländer. *Harmatris* (5,395 grt) was torpedoed for'ard and although No 1 hold was damaged and taking water her bulkheads held and she was later successfully towed to Kola inlet. Less than four hours afterwards, *U-454* torpedoed *Matabele*, one of the escorting destroyers. It was a disaster. Staying afloat for only two minutes there were only two survivors out of a ship's company of 200. Such was the price of January in these northern latitudes.

After sinking *Cyclops*, *U-123* moved swiftly down the shipping lane towards New York. On 14 January she torpedoed and sank the Panamanian motor tanker *Norness* within sight of Nantucket lightship and on the following day, the British-registered 6,768 ton tanker *Coimbra*. She was only 100 miles east of Ambrose lightship. Owned by the Standard Transportation Company, *Coimbra* was commanded by Captain Barnard who, with 35 of his crew, perished in the explosion. Six were rescued though all were wounded and taken to hospital upon landing. Four days later *U-123* was off Cape Hatteras where she caught the unprepared American *Brazos* and then followed this up with three vessels, of 17,254 tons, in as many hours. There was much confusion in the American east coast ports and near panic by the United States naval authorities who never before had been faced with such a situation.

Further east, at 46.32N 53.00W, the 4,113-ton Cardiff tramp *Dayrose*, Claymore Shipping Co, was torpedoed by the experienced Topp (*U-552*) at the commencement of a Newfoundland cruise. Three crew and six gunners were lost. In these same waters, three vessels dispersed from convoy ON52 (fast) were caught. Two were

British, Anglo-Saxon Petroleum's *Diala* and the tanker *Toorak* which later, with a great hole in her side, made St John's, Newfoundland under her own steam.

The motor tanker *Diala*, commanded by Captain Peters was torpedoed by *U-553* in position 44.50N 46.50W on 16 January. Outward bound in ballast she was full ahead at her maximum 12 knots when she was struck. The bows of the vessel were completely blown off and there was a great deal of superstructure damage. Fifty-seven of her crew were killed; the remaining eight, led by Captain Peters, abandoned ship though *Diala* continued to float and was seen two months later on 19 March. She apparently foundered soon afterwards.

A total of 250 died when Canadian National Steamship's 7,988 ton liner *Lady Hawkins* (Captain Griffin) was lost on 19 January. She was sighted by Commander Zapp of *U-66* midway between Cape Hatteras and Bermuda and at close range he fired two torpedoes; the first exploded in No 2 hold and the second between No 3 hold and the engine room. The lifeboats were launched but only one, containing 71 persons, was ever seen again.

The lifeboat was sighted by the American *Coamo* and after their rescue the survivors told harrowing details of their ordeal in an overloaded boat in heavy weather. Designed to carry 63 the little craft had set out with 76 of whom five died from exposure. Included in those missing from *Lady Hawkins* were her Master and 88 crew members.

The American east coast losses continued at a feverish pace. There was *Empire Gem*, *Traveller* and *San Arcadio* followed by two Canadian vessels and a further six British with a tonnage totalling 66,604. American defence was slow to react and there was still no convoy system introduced despite pleas emanating from London.

The Ministry of War Transport tanker *Empire Gem* (8,139 grt), built in 1941 and managed by the British Tanker Company, was heavily laden off Cape Hatteras (35.06N 75.58W) when she was attacked. Her assailant was Commander Zapp, fresh from his triumph over *Lady Hawkins* and the American *Norvana* who, just as dusk was closing in on 24 January, saw his prey explode in a mass of flames. Her master, Captain Broad and one of his radio officers were the only survivors, 47 of her crew losing their lives.

The 3,963 ton *Traveller* (Charente Steamship Company) had sailed from Hampton Roads on the day previous and was bound for Halifax, there to join an Atlantic convoy. Commanded by Captain Fitzsimons, she was carrying a general cargo which included 600 tons of high explosives. Nothing more was heard of the Liverpool Trader or of her crew of 56 until eight months later when *Traveller* was included in a list of sunken vessels broadcast by German radio. She was torpedoed by *U-106* (Lieutenant Herman Rasch), who gave her last position as 40.00N 61.45W. Eleven days later Rasch was to sink New Zealand Shipping Company's *Opawa* (10,354 grt) with tragic loss of life; two of her engineers were killed by the explosion and three of her boats carrying 54 subsequently lost.

The 'Eagle' motor tanker *San Arcadio* (7,419 grt, Captain Flynn) was sunk by *U-107* on the last day of January. Forty-two crew including her master were killed. The commander of *U-107*, Lieutenant Harald Gelhans, surfaced his submarine after the initial strike completing the destruction of *San Arcadio* by gunfire and a second torpedo. This was Günter Hessler's old U-boat, last in action against convoy SL87 during September 1941.

Winter in the North Atlantic was never kind to good station keeping in convoy. Accompanied by poor quality bunkers it was ten times worse. Hogarth's 3,657 ton *Baron Erskine*, a 1930-built coalburner was unable to maintain her speed on New Year's Day owing to bad coal. She fell behind the main body of vessels and by dawn the following day was out of sight. Neither she, nor her master, Captain Cummings, nor her crew were ever seen again. *Baron Erskine* was sunk by *U-701* on 6 January, the first 'kill' for her commander, Lieutenant Horst Degen. Her position was given as 59.15N 18.30W.

The Royal Mail steamer *Culebra* of 3,044 tons (Captain Bonner) engaged on the Caribbean sugar trade, lost her naval escort for a different reason. Sailing from Loch Ewe, the convoy scattered on 12 January in the teeth of a force 10 gale and failed to reform. Thirteen days later *Culebra* was still struggling to reach the comparative safety of Bermuda when, in position 35.30N 53.25W, she was confronted by a surfaced U-boat. It was *U-123* which opened fire with her deck gun, the shells piercing the engine room and setting her ablaze. Before sinking 'in a mighty cloud of smoke and steam' Captain Bonner, though he stood little chance of inflicting damage on his opponent, did his utmost to defend his ship, exchanging shell for shell.

Lieutenant Hardegen, recording the action, wrote in his log,

He manned his gun and machine gun . . . he was a tough opponent. Speed was reduced and he was blowing off steam. With astonishing cold-bloodedness he fired on, although we were constantly hitting his after deck . . . I must pay the enemy every respect, they held out and did not leave their stations.

As *Culebra* sank lower in the water, *U-123* reported that survivors, using the lee side, took to the remaining boat still slung in its davits. As no survivors were rescued however it would appear that they did not survive the gale which sprang up 24 hours later. A total of 39 crew and six gunners perished.

There must be few parallels in the history of naval warfare with that of Union Castle's twin-screw 12,053 ton *Llangibby Castle* (Captain Bayer) which, after being torpedoed on 16 January, steamed 3,400 miles without rudder or stern. With 1,500 troops on board she was torpedoed by *U-402* (Lieutenant-Commander Siegfried Freiherr von Forstner) in position 46.04N 19.06W during a strong south-westerly gale accompanied by heavy seas. Twenty-six were killed and four wounded in the incident.

Steaming without escort, *Llangibby Castle*, steering by her engines alone and maintaining a speed of 9 knots, then made Horta Bay in the Azores fighting off an attack by a lone Focke-Wulf Condor during her three day ordeal. After emergency repairs she then limped to Gibraltar where she remained for 57 days whilst dockyard workers patched her stern and made her seaworthy for the voyage homewards. Still without her rudder the South African mail boat then joined a slow convoy for the Clyde keeping station far better than some of the old 'tramps' she accompanied.

Quite suddenly but not unexpectedly, underwater warfare now erupted in the Indian Ocean. Ten Japanese submarines sank a total of eighteen vessels during January. The most successful was *I-164*, commanded by Lieutenant Tsunayashi Ogawa, who sank four vessels totalling 16,244 tons. Two were operated by the British-owned Scindia Steam Navigation Company. On 30 January *Jalartarang* (2,498 grt) was lost when bound for Rangoon from Cochin. Thirty-eight of her crew of 49 died. The following day the 4,215 ton *Jalapalaka* was torpedoed taking thirteen of her crew down with her. Both vessels were shelled after the initial attack and sank some 100 miles east of Madras.

The crew of the British steamship *Kwangtung* (2,626 grt), owned by the China Navigation Company and sunk south of Java, in position 09.12S 111.10E, were the first seamen to experience the brutality of the Far Eastern aggressor on the high seas. She was carrying a crew of 96 and 35 military personnel when, on 5 January, she was intercepted and torpedoed by *I-156*. Commanded by Lieutenant K. Ohashi, the submarine surfaced and shelled the merchant vessel unmercifully. After *Kwangtung* had sunk, she then fired at the lifeboats at close range, ramming the master's boat which was smashed into several pieces. The chief mate's lifeboat, after waiting for the submarine to submerge, then went in search of survivors, picking up twelve men.

Lieutenant Ohashi then brought his submarine to the surface a second time and seeing the chief mate's boat loaded to the gunwales rammed it at a high speed cutting it into two. Both parts of the boat remained afloat with thirteen men clinging to them. In total 96 were lost, many of them Merchant Navy 'civilians' murdered whilst fighting for their lives. Thirty-five survivors including two British officers were picked up the next day by a passing steamship and landed at Sourabaya.

February 1942 was dominated by the losses in South-East Asia. The surrender of Singapore, like Dunkirk, was a military disaster but, unlike Dunkirk, there was no homecoming to fight again for those who took part. It is a story of lack of reinforcements, lack of preparedness, lack of ships and of troops and armour to fill them; a lack of aircover and naval escorts. Again, Britain's merchantmen were in the front line.

Although between 1 January and 8 February seven convoys from Bombay successfully unloaded reinforcements in Singapore it was a case of too little and too late. Many of the troops and much of the equipment was diverted from the Middle East under a panic situation. Some ships were approaching the bunkering port of Aden on their passage from the United Kingdom around 'the Cape' before instructions to divert were received. On 8 February all further inward movements were stopped. Four days later, when the Japanese had gained a secure foothold on Singapore Island the order was given to clear the harbour of all ships that could be got away.

One of the vessels which arrived with reinforcements early in January was the 27,155 ton *Dominion Monarch*, Shaw Savill and Albion Co Ltd, Captain Summers. Her owners, with little information on the advancing Japanese from the north and eager to take advantage of the facilities which the port offered, ordered her to drydock and overhaul engines.

Quickly the situation in Singapore deteriorated. Air raids intensified and the position became precarious. *Dominion Monarch* was partially dismantled and many considered her case helpless and doomed. Yet the Chief Engineer and the whole crew did a magnificent job in the face of the greatest difficulties. With her engines re-started she sailed for New Zealand about 8 February passing the still smouldering wreck of Canadian Pacific's *Empress of Asia* as she did so.

The coal burning *Empress of Asia* (16,909 grt, Captain Smith) had left Liverpool on 12 November 1941 in company with *Empress of Japan* carrying military personnel for the North African theatre. She carried 2,235 troops and a crew of 416. After bunkering at Cape Town both vessels were diverted to Bombay and arrived off Singapore in convoy on 4 February. During the following morning *Empress of Asia* was dive bombed and set on fire, the flames getting out of control in a matter of 25 minutes.

The end came swiftly for the *Empress* but miraculously only fifteen military personnel were unaccounted for and only one member of the crew died as a result of injuries sustained in the bombing. Much was due to the rescue operation mounted by the Australian sloop *Yarra* which came alongside aft and took off well over 1,000 troops and crew. Others swam to the shore close to the Sultan Shoal Lighthouse.

Many of the crew later helped in 'the small ship' evacuation of Singapore, some never to see their native land again. Those of the catering staff who volunteered for duty in the hospitals later found themselves condemned to prison camps. Forty of her crew managed to hitch a lift on the ferry boat *Ampang* to Palembang only to be confronted upon landing by the sight of over 100 Japanese aircraft dropping paratroops. Commandeering a bus, they headed south but after only short while they were stopped by the Dutch military and ordered off. They started to walk and after a few hours came to a railway siding.

The forty *Empress* survivors later clambered aboard a train which took them to the southern port of Teluk Betung. There they boarded a ship which took them to Batavia. In the port of Batavia their luck still held for on the dockside they found the steamship *Maralia*, whose crew had deserted. That same evening they sailed for Australia eventually being repatriated. It was some three months later that they arrived in the United Kingdom.

Duchess of Bedford and *Empress of Japan*, together with two other troopers stood by in Singapore during the first few days of February to evacuate women and children. Discharging military equipment and food was a slow business because of the continuous air raids which kept the native labour scurrying for shelter. Eventually the 'mercy ships' sailed carrying some 4,000 evacuees.

The 12,656 ton motorship *Empire Star* owned by the Blue Star Line (Captain Capon), was one of the last vessels to clear the port. Under aerial attack the whole time her departure was marred by much confusion in the port area. Some people missed their allotted ship, others jumped aboard the first they came upon, some tragically lost their places altogether. *Empire Star* with cabin accommodation for only sixteen passengers sailed during the hours of 12 February carrying a total of 2,154, mostly staff from the Military Hospital, Australian, Indian and British nurses.

Four hours later *Empire Star* sustained three direct hits as six dive bombers came out of the tropical dawn – fourteen were killed and seventeen badly injured. Great damage was inflicted and the ship was set on fire in three places. Although the attacks continued throughout the morning and a large number of bombs were extremely near misses, the Blue Star merchantman miraculously escaped further damage. She arrived at Batavia 40 hours later and after a short stay sailed for Fremantle.

The 1,646 ton British registered *Giang Bee*, owned by Heap Eng Moh Steamship Company, was less fortunate. Carrying 245 passengers, mostly women and children, she also cleared for Fremantle but within 24 hours, whilst steaming in Banka Strait she was bombed and sunk. The death roll was 223. Close by, the 4,433 ton *Norah Moller* was caught and four miles from Palembang Bar Light vessel, the 1,461 ton *Katong*, Straits Steamship Co. Only the captain, chief mate and three engineers survived the accurate cannonfire as the enemy aircraft came in low over the water and out of the morning sun still low on the horizon.

When the trampship *Derrymore* (4,799 grt, McCowen & Gross), was sunk north of Batavia by the submarine *I-25* (Lieutenant Commander M. Tagami), she still had the same cargo aboard; it included 2,000 tons of explosives and Spitfire aircraft in packing cases on deck, with which she left the United Kingdom five months previously.

She had voyaged 16,000 miles via Jamaica, the Panama Canal and Melbourne with reinforcements for the garrison in Singapore. She had sailed when these were peaceful waters. Now alas, it was too late; too late even to unload her cargo. Instead, she lay off Singapore taking on refugees. She served as a refuge for defeated airmen and soldiers. In the middle of an air raid on the morning of 11 February she set sail. Forty-eight hours later in the approaches to Batavia she was torpedoed.

Derrymore was a doomed vessel. She took a heavy list to starboard, the cased aircraft smashed to pieces, the accommodation amidships badly damaged. Only one lifeboat remained serviceable and although the sea was calm and the night was starlit, the crew raced against time as, led by their chief mate, they set about making rafts out of hatch covers and empty oil drums. With the after deck under water they later successfully abandoned ship; rescue was made by HMAS *Ballarat*, and miraculously only nine Australian Air Force personnel were missing.

There were casualties too among the small ships that sailed from Singapore during 'the last hours'; *Pinna, Redang, Subadar, Vyner Brooke*. They carried 3,000 evacuees. An ex P & O island boat which was taken over by the Royal Navy in 1940, *Vyner Brooke* was densely packed with over 300 hospital patients and nurses. On 14 February she was sunk off Banka Straits after being raked with gunfire and straddled with bombs. Many of her passengers, mostly women and children, were drowned.

Of the British vessels seized or scuttled in the Far Eastern theatre, Alfred Holt's 10,253 ton *Talthybius* (Captain Kent) was the largest. She was at the southern end of the Red Sea en route to Suez when she was diverted and arrived in convoy from Bombay on 25 January. She was carrying Army tanks, lorries and other equipment which were discharged at Singapore by her crew assisted by New Zealand Air Force men.

Discharge was completed on the morning of 3 February and soon afterwards she was hit by two bombs during a heavy air assault. On the dockside close by a whole salvo of near misses exploded. Fires broke out in several parts of the ship; they were brought under control by her British officers. For the rest of the day she was subjected to a terrible onslaught from the air.

Fortunately there were no more direct hits on *Talthybius* but water was now rising rapidly in the engine room and stokehold. Although pumps were located on shore some hours later and Captain Kent was successful in getting his ship moved into the Empire Dock, there was no way the vessel could be made seaworthy. Further, no assistance was available as the wharfs and godowns were now deserted. Although air raids were heavy and frequent and enemy shells were passing over the ship, attempts were still being made by her crew on 10 February to stop the leaking hull and save her. But tragically *Talthybius*, resting on the bottom, had to be abandoned.

Alfred Holt's loyal men, led by their captain, boarded HMS *Ping Wo* two days later and successfully escaped to Batavia. *Talthybius* was salved by the Japanese, renamed *Taruyasu Maru* and after the enemy was defeated she was found scuttled in Maizuru harbour on the north coast of Honshu. Later she was raised and repaired at Hong Kong, afterwards, under Ministry of Transport ownership, she was renamed *Empire Evenlode* and sailed for Swansea where she arrived 8 May 1946.

On 19 February the Japanese again struck against Britain's merchantmen. Far to the south, the north coast of Australia seemed far away from the maurauding enemy yet the air strike of 188 aircraft, just one less than the number that attacked Pearl Harbour, devastated the harbour of Darwin. Casualties aboard ships totalled 172 killed with another 320 wounded, 200 of them seriously.

In the first minutes the 5,952 ton Burns Philp motorship *Neptuna* was struck by two bombs killing her captain and fifteen of her crew. The ship, requisitioned by the Admiralty, blazed furiously; oil and debris littered the water and patches of burning oil killed and maimed many seamen. Then suddenly the 200 tons of depth charges she was carrying were detonated. The explosion rocked the town. Smoke rose to a height of 300 feet and red hot fragments of the vessel, as lethal as shrapnel, showered the harbour.

The 4,239 ton *Barossa* was then struck followed by the 6,891 ton tanker *British Motorist*. She sank by the head, her valuable oil cargo still aboard, her master, Captain Bates, lying dead upon the bridge. A second bomb then hit the tanks for'ard, fires were uncontrollable and blazing fuel oil swept across the harbour engulfing men and rescue boats.

Zealandia (6,683 grt) unloading stores from Sydney was bombed and sank at her moorings. The 9,115 ton hospital ship *Manunda* awaiting instructions to sail, since Singapore, her original destination, now lay in Japanese hands, was severely damaged from the effects of two bombs. Sixteen personnel lay dead, fires erupted throughout the vessel and water mains were severed; her radio equipment, direction finder and echo sounder were destroyed.

In spite of her 'wounds' *Manunda* remained in service. By nightfall she took on 76 stretcher cases. She then embarked 190 patients from shore hospitals and sailed late on the following day for Freemantle. Nineteen died on passage and were buried at sea.

At the end of the day in Darwin a total of seven merchant vessels of 43,429 grt together with the US destroyer *Peary* lay destroyed. Additionally, the Australian sloop *Swan*, the US aircraft tender *William B. Preston* and seven merchantmen were damaged; four small defence and harbour craft lay wrecked. It was a bombing operation of great intensity and accuracy.

There was considerable confusion amongst the military commanders in the early days of the Far East War. The story of Ellerman Lines' *City of Manchester* is just one example. She berthed at Singapore on the first day of February having brought troops and military supplies in convoy from Melbourne. Upon discharge she was ordered to Pekan where she lay for three weeks waiting to evacuate Australian troops.

Upon the evacuation of Pekan, *City of Manchester* (8,917 grt commanded by Captain Dudley) was ordered to sail without her troops. She was hardly out of the river when she was instructed to return. Under heavy fire from the advancing enemy she took on about 700 Australians sailing the same night for Batavia. Twenty-four hours later she was ordered to Tjilatjap where many of the troops were put ashore to strengthen the garrison. Although low on bunkers it was necessary that she sailed the same evening. Thirty-five miles out of Tjilatjap, in the early hours of 28 February she was torpedoed by *I-153* (Lieutenant Nakamura), one of Japan's newest and largest submarines.

The explosion ripped open the side of the ship abreast No 3 hold, bulkheads caved in and two lifeboats were carried away. *City of Manchester* lurched and listed to port. As one of the boilers burst, the night air was split asunder by the shriek of escaping steam mixed with the screams of distress. As the aggressor surfaced the ship was abandoned. It was not before time for *I-153* then commenced shelling and finally, a second torpedo sent the 1935-built *Manchester* bow first to her watery grave.

A few hours later, 100 miles to the east, British Tankers' 6,735 ton *British Judge*, bound for Tjilatjap in convoy, was struck by a torpedo fired from another of Japan's newest submarines. This was *I-158*, commanded by Lieutenant-Commander Kitamura. Fortunately *British Judge* was only damaged and was able to make port under her own steam.

Far East Naval Command was far more worried about convoy SU1, further to the north-west, than about *City of Manchester* or *British Judge*. This was a convoy of twelve ships (97,541 grt) led by the 14,204 ton *Esperance Bay* carrying 10,900 troops and military equipment from Colombo for Australia. In a panic measure they were being moved south to defend a possible attack on the Australian continent. Slowly the convoy moved out of the danger zone.

Rangoon fell to the advancing enemy on 7 March and the occupation of the Dutch East Indies was completed the following day. The number of ships lost in the region, many of them British owned, was heavy. They included the typical Far Eastern coastal craft with a Lascar crew and a British master. Trapped in the small harbours they came under heavy fire, some were captured, others were scuttled, their crews destined to spend over three long years in Japanese prison camps.

The most serious loss was British India's 4,360 ton *Chilka* employed as a troopship and commanded by Captain Bird. Sailing from Padang on 10 March she was intercepted by *I-2* (Lieutenant-Commander Hiroshi Inada) which came up from astern on the port quarter and opened fire at 2,000 yards. The fire was returned but the enemy's third shot struck the ammunition lockers, mortally wounding one of the gun crew. Fire then broke out; an Indian cadet tried to put out the fire with his bare hands and had to be forcibly removed to safety by the second and third mates who were themselves then badly burnt.

With *Chilka* steaming at her maximum 13½ knots the action continued. Nine of the fourteen lifeboats she was carrying were destroyed and there was much damage to the superstructure. Twenty-five minutes after the first shot was fired, Captain Bird, with three of his officers, three Lascar seamen and a naval gunner lying dead, decided to abandon ship to avoid further loss of life. On 16 March the survivors beached their greatly overloaded lifeboats on the shoreline of one of the Mentawei Islands. Later they walked through jungle and swamp to reach an isolated mission hospital.

When Captain Bird was informed that the Japanese invaders were approaching the islands he obtained a steel lifeboat and set sail for Ceylon, some 1,300 miles distant, accompanied by the ship's surgeon, some of the engineers and a naval gunner. On 4 May after 35 days at sea, the boat was picked up by a Greek vessel and they were landed in Karachi.

One cannot leave the Eastern theatre at this time without recording the epic Indian Ocean onslaught during the first week of April. It was the climax to the Japanese campaign against merchant ships in the region. Coupled with this was the threat to the whole Indian sub-continent. When news was received that the enemy fleet, including five aircraft carriers and four battleships was heading for Ceylon and the naval bases of Colombo and Trincomalee, Winston Churchill considered it to be one of the most dangerous moments of the whole war.

The Battle of the Bay of Bengal was to claim as many ships as the infamous Russian PQ17 convoy only thirteen weeks later. Between 4 and 9 April the Japanese squadron sank 23 ships of over 112,000 tons off the east coast of India while on the west coast, submarines added five more of 32,000 tons. In an aerial attack on Colombo on Easter Sunday, 5 April, Alfred Holt's AMC *Hector*, being decommissioned and under repair, was sunk and Wm Thomson's *Benledi* was damaged. In a second air attack four days later *Empire Moonrise* was

damaged. Also damaged was the *Anglo Canadian* lying in Vizagapatam harbour. The second radio officer of *Magician*, at Vizagapatam
on that fateful Easter Sunday, wrote in his diary

> heard of the loss of two cruisers *Dorsetshire* and *Cornwall* . . . situation
> getting worse. All ships here have orders to scuttle in the event of
> invasion which by the signs looks to be imminent.

The 7,958 ton *Sagaing* was bombed and sunk in Trincomalee
harbour on 9 April.

Shipping in the port of Calcutta was hastily sent to sea; in all, 55
merchantmen were ordered to sea from the east coast ports of India.
Twelve of British registry that sailed from Calcutta were sunk, the
first being *Harpasa* (5,082 grt), owned by the Harrison Line of
London. In the confusion of the moment, unlike some which were
formed into small convoys, though without naval escort, *Harpasa* put
to sea alone with orders for East Africa. Two days later on Easter
Sunday she was sighted by an enemy aircraft.

After circling *Harpasa* the enemy dropped a large incendiary
device which landed on the after well deck setting fire to the whole
after end. The fire spread rapidly and with the steering gear wrecked
there was no alternative for her master, Captain Atkinson, but to
abandon ship. The lifeboats were fortunately launched in good order
before the fire could reach them and the survivors were later picked
up by the 3,471 ton *Taksang*.

The steamer *Taksang*, British registered and owned by the
Indo-China Steam Navigation Co. of Hong Kong, she had a speed of
18 knots, had been despatched from a Colombo-bound convoy of
seven ships. The following morning *Taksang* herself was sunk when
the convoy was overhauled by the Japanese squadron. Heavily
shelled, with the bridge taking the brunt of the attack, her British
master, Captain Costello, was badly injured. Fifteen crew, together
with the senior radio officer from *Harpasa*, lay dead upon her deck.

Within ten minutes of the first salvo, the stricken Hong Kong
vessel rolled upon her side staying there briefly before throwing up
her stern and disappearing, accompanied by the noise of boilers
cracking and the escape of steam and air. The survivors clambered
aboard the only two serviceable lifeboats together with a raft which
floated off. Many were suffering from shrapnel wounds. Those on the
raft were rescued by a Catalina flying boat from Calcutta; those in
the boats landed upon an open sandy beach after two days and a
night.

Following the sinking of *Taksang* there was Alfred Holt's *Autolycus* (7,621 grt, Captain Neville). Four European and twelve Chinese were lost. British India's *Malda* (9,066 grt), just fitted out as a troopship, was commanded by Captain Edmonson who acted as convoy commodore. She was bombed by aircraft and shelled by cruisers and quickly became a blazing inferno. Many of the crew suffered terrible injuries; the second engineer was badly burnt, the third lost his left leg, the fourth engineer lost both feet. Men jumped overboard to escape the horror, there to float helplessly. Twenty-five of her crew perished.

British India's *Indora* (6,622 grt) Calcutta for Mauritius with 'generals' was the next to be caught. During the first six months of 1942 the British India Company lost twelve of their fleet, four of them at Eastertide. *Indora* was carrying some of the crew of *Autolycus* and *Malda* which she had plucked from the water. Other vessels lost were *Silksworth* (4,921 grt), *Shinkuang* (2,441 grt) and *Sinkiang* (2,646 grt). Six British merchantmen were sunk in rather less than 45 minutes.

Further south on the same day, in position 16.00N 82.20E, enemy warships overhauled the remnants of another convoy. The 'blue funnel' *Dardanus* (7,726 grt) was attacked by two carrier planes, two bombs exploding in the engine room. It was towed by British India's 5,281 ton *Gandara* towards Madras but both vessels were then bombed followed by shelling from Japanese cruisers which came up from astern. Although the towline was slipped, both ships were repeatedly hit; torpedoes finally sent them to the bottom. All the crew from *Dardanus* were saved but thirteen from *Gandara* were lost.

A particularly vicious attack followed on the 6,246 ton *Ganges* twenty miles off Vizagapatam. Owned by James Nourse, with Captain Vivian in command, she was repeatedly bombed and shelled resulting in fifteen of her crew being killed. The remainder jumped overboard to escape the flames which quickly engulfed the vessel from stern to stern.

Nineteen forty-two saw the renewal of raider activity in the southern hemisphere. *Thor*, commanded by Captain Günther Gumprich, sailed from Germany on 12 February and six weeks later this smallest of the ten raiders sank three British merchantmen within twelve days in the South Atlantic.

At noon on 30 March, in position 21.09S 14.06W, the Denholm steamer *Wellpark* of 4,649 tons (St John, New Brunswick, for Alexandria) passed through one of her routed positions. An hour later another ship's masts were sighted upon the horizon on a

parallel course and converging very slowly. At 1400 hours an aircraft
was heard and shortly afterwards a seaplane dived out of the clouds.
A wire was then dropped with hooks attached to tear the radio aerial
away and stop any message being transmitted. It was the familiar
pattern of surface raider attacks.

Captain Cant of *Wellpark* led his men in fighting back with the
Lewis gun and the twelve pounder but a distress signal was out of the
question. Meanwhile the raider was closing. Gumprich's second
salvo found *Wellpark*'s range, one shell penetrating No 1 hold, a
second piercing the boiler casing under the funnel and exploding
over the engine room. Salvo after salvo followed until the enemy
observed Captain Cant preparing to abandon ship. Seven of her
crew of 48 were killed.

Two days later the 4,563 ton *Willesden* was caught. Owned by
Watts Watts & Co. Ltd and commanded by Captain Griffiths, she
had sailed from New York's Bush Terminal and was also bound for
Alexandria. After the main aerial had been destroyed by the raider's
Arado seaplane, a total of 128 shells were fired at the stricken tramp.
A deck cargo of oil drums erupted in flames, the bridge was virtually
destroyed and there was much damage to the midships accommodation. The ship's bosun was killed and six others wounded, three of
them seriously.

On 10 April Ropner's *Kirkpool* (4,842 grt, Durban for Montevideo)
with coal was sunk 250 miles NNE of Tristan da Cuna. High seas
were running as *Thor* approached. Visibility was poor and the light
was fading. It was 2000 hours and as the darkness fell all around him,
and with his ship ablaze like a fiery beacon, Captain Kennington
tried to ram the raider which had to manoeuvre to avoid collision.
With their ship sinking beneath them, though still under way, the
survivors of the holocaust jumped overboard into black water. They
left behind them sixteen dead who lay upon the bridge and boat
deck.

Captain Gumprich of *Thor* remained in the vicinity for three hours
searching for survivors with his ship's searchlights. Many owed their
lives to the little red lights attached to their lifejackets. Thirty officers
and crew were plucked from the water and taken prisoner. They
included Captain Kennington who later was to die in captivity in
Japan.

After sinking several more ships over a period of four months *Thor*
proceeded to Japan for a refit and drydocking, arriving there in
September. Those taken prisoner from *Wellpark*, *Willesden* and
Kirkpool, together with the crew of the Norwegian *Aust*, were

The tankers' graveyard. January–June 1942. An all too familiar sight off the east coast of North America January–June 1942. The US tanker *Munger T. Ball* torpedoed and sunk by *U-507* on 5 May.

Convoy to Russia. A convoy of heavily laden vessels to Russia during 1942 under attack from the air showing a near miss. HMS *Eskimo* in the foreground.

But the convoy got through. The Russian convoy under attack showing a tanker exploding in flames.

(*Above*) The rescue ship *Gothland* at work. The 1,286 ton rescue ship *Gothland* (from February 1942 she escorted 40 convoys and saved 149 lives) rescues survivors. Note the seaman (*centre*) in the water. In total, the specially converted rescue ships rescued over 4,000 survivors of whom 2,296 were British and Canadian.

(*Left*) The author. New York 1942. The author given 'the Hollywood treatment' by an enterprising New York photographer who found his way aboard most British merchant vessels in Manhattan and Brooklyn. The original photograph was carried throughout those difficult days by John Slader's girlfriend whom he later married.

transferred to the supply ship *Regensburg* on 4 May 1942 and eventually arrived at Yokohama. They were then taken to the Kawasaki POW Camp where they spent three long, hard and weary years.

With all the activity in the Western Atlantic and the Eastern theatres, the Mediterranean war tended, temporarily at least, to be a forgotten one. Yet to shipping it continued to be a dangerous zone. Whilst well protected by the Royal Navy, merchantmen were often under continuous attack, from the air, from the sea and from beneath the sea.

After towing the burnt-out *Georgic*, the 7,255 ton *Clan Campbell*, commanded by Captain Vooght, returned to Suez and then to Alexandria where she loaded for Malta with aviation fuel in flimsy 4-gallon cans, ammunition and stores. She then sailed in convoy with *Clan Chattan* and *Rowallan Castle*, escorted by the anti-aircraft cruiser *Carlisle* and eight 'Hunt' class destroyers.

In passing Tobruk on 13 February the convoy was attacked by the Luftwaffe. *Clan Campbell* was hit by a bomb which went through the boat deck, the cadets' cabin, the coal bunker and then out through the ship's side in the engine room before exploding and leaving a hole about 20 feet in diameter. Damaged above the waterline she managed to limp into Tobruk harbour. The following day, 175 miles north of Benghazi, *Clan Chattan* (7,262 grt) and *Rowallan Castle* (7,798 grt) were bombed by a force of Ju88's setting both ships afire. Later, as they were carrying ammunition, they were sunk by gunfire from HMS *Carlisle* to avoid them exploding. 200 troops on board *Clan Chattan* were transferred to the naval cruiser.

Meanwhile in Tobruk harbour the ship's engineers of *Clan Campbell* managed to cut some plates from a sunken Italian warship and bolt them together to make a temporary repair. She then crept back along the coast to Alexandria entering port astern of *Ajax*, *Breconshire*, *City of Calcutta* and *Clan Ferguson* which had returned empty from Malta. They had been waiting patiently to leave the besieged island since the last convoy in September 1941.

Captain Vooght would not suffer fools gladly and when the Royal Navy told him they were going to weld plates over the hole without discharging the aviation fuel he went 'through the roof'. When the bomb exploded most of the cans had burst and the bilges were now 'swimming' with petrol. Within a few days *Clan Campbell* was discharged. Captain Vooght again protested when he saw that he now only had lifeboats to hold 105 persons when he had a crew of 150. The lifeboats on the port side had been destroyed in the bombing and the replacement boats were much smaller. To get over this difficulty he was instructed to put ashore his Indian crew and replace them with a scratch naval crew.

On 20 March, coinciding with the launching of an all out bombing offensive against Malta by the German forces in Sicily and Sardinia, convoy MW10 left Alexandria. *Clan Campbell* was making her second attempt to reach Malta accompanied by *Breconshire*, *Pampas* and *Talabot*. They were accompanied by four cruisers, the anti-aircraft cruiser *Carlisle* and ten destroyers.

After many vicious attacks, from an Italian naval force and from the air, *Clan Campbell* suffered a number of direct hits in bad weather a few miles south of Malta. She was finally struck by an aerial torpedo and abandoned. Six persons were killed, including Captain Vooght, and one was wounded. The chief mate who survived was very bitter about the way the Royal Navy had mishandled the whole business. The scratch naval crew were apparently, in his view, useless in a merchant ship.

Breconshire was also hit. She was just outside the harbour entrance and despite the efforts of tugs could not be brought in. She was beached and was then bombed again. Glen Line's 9,776 ton *Breconshire* had been in the Mediterranean since July 1940 when she was requisitioned for service as a naval auxiliary. In all she made eight trips to Malta and whilst she flew the White Ensign many of her original crew remained in her throughout her war service.

Royal Mail's *Pampas* (5,415 grt, Captain Ingram) and the Norwegian *Talabot*, though both were damaged in the action, tied up in Malta's Marsaxlokk harbour; all through 25 and 26 March they were heavily bombed. The drama continued for three days and nights and all the time efforts were made to land their valuable cargoes, both were carrying kerosene, aviation spirit and ammunition. By the evening of 26 March *Talabot* was burning fiercely and on the 28th she had to be scuttled for fear that she would explode and destroy what was left of the harbour.

With *Pampas* taking a direct hit she too lay on the harbour bottom, but it was not before 4,952 tons of stores had been unloaded from these two gallant ships, a superhuman effort achieved by stevedores, soldiers and merchant seamen working as a team.

In the Western Atlantic and the Caribbean the U-boat war waged incessantly. Along the convoy routes of the north-western approaches to Britain a small-scale offensive was still being continued by the less experienced U-boat commanders. They had little success. Counter-measures now being taken were effective and in March 1942, 450 ships reached the United Kingdom in nineteen ocean convoys without the loss of a single vessel from enemy action.

Torpedo net defences, an innovation, were now being fitted to certain medium size vessels. These were nets carried on long booms which when folded back were sometimes taller than the masts to which they were secured. They could only be used when the vessel was under way and were not always successful. The number of offensive weapons used by merchant ships increased, particularly against aircraft. The Oerlikon gun became standard equipment and there were 'pillow boxes' which fired volleys of rockets, PAC's (parachute and cable) and FAM's – floating aerial mines. Radar too began to be fitted in the larger ships.

In the Freetown area two U-boats, *U-68* and *U-505*, were operating, intent on extending defences. The most successful was *U-68* under the captaincy of Commander Karl-Friedrich Merten which left Lorient on her third war cruise on 11 February. During the 31 days of March, Merten sank seven British vessels with a total tonnage of 38,350. In addition to Alfred Holt's *Helenus* which had been plying between Britain and the Far East since the beginning of the war, there were *Allende, Baluchistan, Baron Newlands, Ile de Batz, Muncaster Castle* and the *Scottish Prince*.

Outside the Western Atlantic the enemy made the greatest effort against the convoys to Northern Russia, the protection of which soon became a major commitment for the Home Fleet. By March, heavy ships had been stationed in Norwegian bases and the submarine and air force presence had been increased.

Nineteen forty-two saw many tragedies in the northern latitudes. A half century later many of these brave seamen are forgotten. Brave like those from *Empire Ranger* and *Induna* of convoy PQ13, two of the nineteen ships which set out from Iceland for Murmansk on 20 March. Three days later, as the temperature dropped they encountered a violent storm. On 27 March, as the U-boats closed in and the Junker 88's sighted their prey they were scattered over an area of 150 miles. *Empire Ranger* had no chance to fight back as the lone bomber came over the sea at masthead height.

For six days 38 survivors from the 7,008 ton *Empire Ranger* drifted in their lifeboat through snowstorms, gales and freezing conditions. Eventually they were found by a Russian tug. Only two, the fourteen-year-old cabin boy and the ship's bosun were alive, both were badly frostbitten. In order to save the bosun's life it was necessary to amputate both his arms and legs.

The 5,086 ton *Induna*, owned by Maclay and McIntyre, was

mainly crewed by Scottish seamen. In the Barents Sea, 70.55N 37.18E, she was torpedoed by *U-376*. Of her complement of 66 only 24 survived. Many of those who lived showed great courage; several suffered from such severe frostbite that it was necessary to amputate precious limbs.

Induna never rejoined PQ13 after the storm. On the night of 28/29 March, she was towing the armed trawler *Silja*, one of the escort vessels which was running short of fuel. By daybreak they found themselves trapped in the icefield. All day they tried to free themselves and as they did so, in the fading light of day, the towline parted. At 0807 hours the following morning *Induna* was torpedoed. *U-376*, commanded by Lieutenant Karl Marks, crept away leaving the crew to continue the battle for themselves.

A battle it was. In one of the lifeboats were 32 persons instead of the maximum 25. Being overcrowded they were unable to take exercise and attempts to row were hampered. The injured lay on the bottom in freezing water whilst others constantly baled with buckets in an effort to keep the leaking boat dry. In the sub-zero temperatures even the scotch whisky, kept in metal containers beneath the seats, achieved little. At daylight seven were lying frozen and stiff; they had died during the early hours. The seamen lifted the bodies of their shipmates over the side and saw them float away.

During the second night the swirling snow and biting wind claimed a further two. With the temperature so low it was difficult to grasp the oars. The effects of frostbite were being felt. Feet and ankles were in water all the time. All were desperately thirsty as water in the containers froze solid. Even their efforts to survive were undermined.

Two more died the following night; others lost the use of their legs. The cold was intense and again the snow swirled around the lone boat, 300 miles north of the Arctic Circle. During the afternoon two slumped over their oars, then rolled into the bottom of the boat. No one moved them; no one any longer had the strength to help a fallen shipmate. They both died where they lay.

On the fourth night a further three men died. Only sixteen remained. They were about to give up all hope when from out of the mist came the eastern shore of Kolo inlet, and then Cape Sviatoi lighthouse. Later they were sighted by a Russian aircraft and then picked up by a minesweeper. The second lifeboat from *Induna* experienced a very similar voyage yet in this boat only ten survived; of these, two died in hospital in Murmansk.

The vessels of PQ13 which were able to regroup after the storm

reached Murmansk on 28 March. Almost immediately the port area
was subjected to a heavy and sustained air attack. For twenty days,
both by day and by night the aircraft returned to bomb the freighters
discharging their cargoes. The German base at Petsamo was only 50
miles away. A particularly heavy raid on 3 April sank Reardon
Smith's 4,747 ton *New Westminster City* and seriously damaged *Empire
Starlight* (6,850 grt), a unit of the Ropner fleet, and the 5,172 ton
Lancaster Castle owned by the Lancashire Shipping Company.

New Westminster City, Captain Harris, blew up when fire reached a
hold full of ammunition and later her survivors were taken aboard
Empire Starlight. She too was subject to many dive bombing attacks
and after many near misses on 6 April and 8 April she was leaking
badly. Her master, Captain Stein, leading his British officers and
Chinese crew, toiled unceasingly to plug the leaks and repair the
damage.

On the evening of 15 April a raid on the port developed and *Empire
Starlight* received a direct hit causing much damage for'ard. *Lancaster
Castle*, anchored in the roadstead, received two direct hits and three
close alongside. When the flames subsided, eleven men and her
master, Captain Sloan, lay dead. She then sank and was abandoned
as a total loss, her twenty survivors being taken aboard Ropner's
Empire Starlight.

The Hong Kong built *Empire Starlight*, now overcrowded, was
moved out of her berth to an anchorage upstream where it was
thought she would be safe. The enemy however followed. A savage
attack was launched upon her. Again and again they came in low
over the water, and again, with the Red Duster still flying, she fought
back, and her Oerlikon claimed three aircraft destroyed. On four
successive days during the third week of April, there were near
misses and then, as if to give her breathing space to lick her wounds,
the bombers left her alone. From 4 May the enemy returned; every
day for two weeks seemed to bring its attack.

On 17 May *Empire Starlight* was moved to shallower water and
again the Germans followed. Finally, on 1 June this stout old 'tramp'
settled on the bottom with decks awash at high water. Miraculously
the only casualty amongst her 77 personnel was a Chinese catering
rating killed in a shelter ashore.

Twenty-four heavily laden ships made up convoy PQ14. They
were carrying the essentials for the Russian war machine; guns,
tanks, aircraft, ammunition and trucks. They sailed on 8 April
comprising eleven British, nine American, three Russian and one

Greek, a typical breakdown of a Murmansk convoy. Six days later sixteen ships returned due to ice damage when they accidentally struck the icefield south-west of Jan Mayen Island.

The remaining eight ships led by the commodore ship, the 1941-built *Empire Howard* (6,985 grt) continued on their way. Though they were then bombed from the air intermittently but unsuccessfully for 48 hours it was the loss of their leader by submarine that struck horror into the hearts of those who pressed on. On 16 April, *Empire Howard*, managed by Raeburn and Verel and commanded by Captain Downie, was torpedoed. The enemy was *U-403* (Lieutenant Heinz-Ehlert Clausen).

The first torpedo struck *Empire Howard* in the boiler room. Five seconds later a second exploded in the engine room. All on watch below were killed instantly. After ten seconds a third torpedo struck aft between Nos 4 and 5 holds exploding the magazine. The ship was immediately doomed. Splitting in two, the upper decks disappeared and the entire cargo of army trucks spewed out of her port side. Captain Downie, wearing his lifejacket, just had time to step off the bridge into the sea as with a tremendous roar both parts of the ship disappeared. There was no sign of the convoy commodore, Captain Rees RNR. It was only 60 seconds from the time of the first torpedo to when she broke up.

There was no time to launch lifeboats. Although the temperature was well below freezing, those that survived the sinking, some 38 of them, were protected somewhat by oil which had been released from the ruptured fuel tanks. Suddenly, from out of the mist came the anti-submarine trawler *Northern Wave* firing depth charges in an effort to trap the attacker. Only those at some distance lived to tell their story. The remainder died instantly of broken necks or from internal injuries.

The survivors of this horrific event were brought aboard the trawler *Lord Middleton* barely conscious, some seriously injured. From a crew of 54 only eighteen were rescued and of these, nine died aboard the trawler. Captain Downie was one of the fortunate ones who returned to port, dutifully to submit his report on the loss of his ship.

The experiences of convoys PQ13 and PQ14 had shown already that the battle of the northern sealanes was unlike anything yet recorded in the annals of the Merchant Navy. Yet more alarming from a strategic point of view was the situation in the warm waters from which the Gulf Stream flows. The British War Cabinet was increasingly concerned about the future of oil supplies. Four large tankers a day were needed to keep the British war economy going. The U-boat fleet had now increased to 288 with 122 operational. During March 81 were at sea in the Atlantic zone. By the fifteenth of the month 110,000 tons of shipping had been sunk in the Caribbean area alone. During the month of April, 135,000 tons (23 Allied ships) were sunk in American waters.

It was during April and early May that the fifth wave of U-boats arrived off the American coast. They included *U-130*, Commander Ernst Kals, on her second war cruise in these waters. On 19 April Kals shelled oil installations at Curaçao, a follow-up to the ambitious Operation Neuland of mid-February when a carefully planned series of strikes at tankers off the Caribbean islands and at the local oil industry was mounted. On 10 March *U-161* entered the port of Castries on St Lucia and sank the Canadian *Lady Nelson* and Bullard King's 8,141 grt *Umtata*. Both were later salvaged and repaired though some four months later, on 7 July 1942, *Umtata* became the victim of Lieutenant Helmut Möhlmann's *U-571* close in shore off the south-western tip of Florida.

The Federal Steam Navigation Company lost their cargo liner *Hertford* off the American coast on 29 March. Severely damaged by a mine off Adelaide in December 1940, she had finally completed repairs before sailing. Loading 'generals' at Sydney and Brisbane she then proceeded to Wellington where she took on 175,550 carcasses of lamb and mutton, 8,250 sides of pork and 5,670 packages of beef. After passing through the Panama Canal she left Colon on 19 March for Halifax, Nova Scotia.

Zigzagging at 12 knots, the 10,923 ton *Hertford*, with Captain Tuckett aboard, her commander for seven years, was torpedoed and sunk 200 miles south of Halifax ten days later. The enemy submarine was *U-571* (Lieutenant Helmut Möhlmann). Hit abreast No 4 hold close to the engine room bulkhead, one lifeboat was destroyed and she settled rapidly by the stern; three on watch in the engine room were killed. After she had been abandoned a second torpedo struck and she sank within ten minutes.

One of *Hertford*'s lifeboats carrying 21 persons was rescued by *Glenstrae* on 1 April whilst Captain Tuckett's boat with nineteen men, landed two days later at Liverpool, Nova Scotia. They had survived five days of wet cold and windy weather. The chief steward caught pneumonia, and later died in hospital. The third boat was also at sea five days when they were picked up by the *Fort Townshend* after experiencing very low temperatures. The second engineer had to have one leg amputated due to frostbite whilst the second

refrigerating engineer lost both legs, amputated below the knees. He
spent many months in hospital at Halifax.

The 14,647 ton *Ulysses*, was also lost off the American east coast.
Commanded by Captain Russell she was on her first voyage since
escaping from Hong Kong just before the Japanese attack.
Lieutenant Georg Lassen, commander of *U-160*, a new type IX 1,120
ton 'Atlantic' boat was surfaced 45 miles south of Cape Hatteras on
11 April when he sighted her hull down on the horizon. Already he
had sunk four vessels and damaged a fifth since arriving on station
only sixteen days previously.

The first of three torpedoes struck *Ulysses* abreast No 6 hatch. She
lurched heavily to starboard, appeared to stay beam end on to the
sea for several minutes before righting herself and slowly settling.
Captain Russell quickly gave instructions to abandon ship, himself
and three deck officers remaining on board. No sooner had the
lifeboats drawn away than the second torpedo struck. It exploded
with a deafening roar deep down in the bowels of the ship – nothing
now could save her. Finally after Captain Russell and his officers had
taken to a raft, the third torpedo ripped *Ulysses* apart. She quickly
sank to her grave. The entire crew and all the passengers were
rescued by an American destroyer. Careful organisation and good
discipline had saved many lives.

During the period January–August 1942, Eagle Tankers lost
seven of their fleet; a further three had miraculous escapes. A total of
269 officers and men were lost. All but one of the incidents were in the
Caribbean or off the east coast of the United States.

The loss of the brand new motor vessel *San Victorio* (8,136 grt) in
position 11.40N 62.33W on 17 May was a disaster; of all the
catastrophes suffered by tankers of British registry this was the most
appalling. On her maiden voyage laden with a full cargo of aviation
spirit from Aruba, *San Victorio*, (Captain Perry) was struck by a
torpedo fired by *U-155* commanded by Lieutenant Adolf Piening.
The effect was volcanic. A withering flame swept the ship and almost
instantly she was blown sky-high.

All hands perished in the holocaust except a gunner of the
Maritime Regiment. He happened to be on the poop and was blown
over the stern-rail by the first concussion, far enough away from the
ship to escape the second explosion that killed everyone on board.
For sixteen hours he survived without lifejacket or any support
whatever, in warm waters infested with shark and barracuda.

San Cirilo (Captain Thomson) and *San Eliseo* (Captain Johnson) had the most remarkable escapes. The 8,012 ton *Cirilo* was

torpedoed south of Colombo when fully loaded with refined oils en route from Abadan for Melbourne. It was exactly six months and 14,246 miles later that she crawled into New York. Here she remained several months under repair.

Sighted by the Japanese submarine *I-162* (Lieutenant Takaichi Kinashi) in position 06.40N 79.40E on 21 March, *San Cirilo* was savagely attacked. Petrol shot into the air in great columns but by some miracle there was neither explosion nor fire. Assisted by a destroyer she was able to make Colombo where she managed to discharge her remaining 5,500 tons of cargo despite the Easter Sunday port bombing by the Japanese. Her complete deck bulged four feet upwards for a length of 70 feet from the midshipline to the starboard side and the near misses by high explosive bombs further damaged her hull. After temporary repairs in both Bombay and Port Elizabeth she then made the long and slow voyage from the Cape via Trinidad to the American east coast.

San Eliseo (8,042 grt) was badly holed three times in Caribbean waters on 18 May reaching the safety of Barbados 48 hours later. For Lieutenant Hartenstein (*U-156*), accredited with 105,232 tons of merchant shipping sunk (22 vessels) between February and September 1942, it was his toughest battle. Captain Johnson, after the first torpedo struck and seeing a second one spinning off course immediately took up the challenge. With speed reduced to 11 knots and with the ship still zigzagging the gun crew fired eight 4.7 inch shells at the U-boat's periscope. The last three shots were so close that the submarine was badly shaken.

After nine hours steaming Hartenstein returned to the attack seriously crippling the *Eliseo* with a third torpedo. Three hours later and now reduced to 8 knots a fourth torpedo caused more serious damage particularly to the engine room. After repairs the seemingly doomed tanker crawled along at only 5 knots. A fifth torpedo missed by inches and now *U-156* surfaced, intent on finishing off her prey with gunfire. She was clearly seen in the moonlit night by Captain Johnson who brought his ship broadside on and set on a collision course. Hartenstein was startled by the manoeuvre and put his boat into a deep dive and away to safety.

May 1942 found the Prince Lines' Mediterranean trader *Norman Prince* (1,913 grt) in the Caribbean tropics. Torpedoed and sunk on 29 May en route from Colon for St Lucia her 32 survivors were held in a 'concentration' camp on Martinique by the Vichy French authorities for four months.

During the four months and five days of captivity at Fort de

Ballata the French allowed one opportunity after another of repatriating them to pass. Many were in poor health, food was in short supply and of poor quality; there were no proper eating utensils and old tobacco and milk tins were used as cups to drink out of.

Seventeen men including Captain Harries perished when the 13 knot *Norman Prince* was sunk by Hartenstein's *U-156*. The second torpedo struck amidships on the port side and immediately the stern of the ship reared to an almost perpendicular position as she plunged under with a great roar. Captain Harries jumped from the poop deck in the last moments but was never seen again. An eerie silence amidst the gentle waves of the warm sea greeted those that jumped; they swam towards a lone raft which had floated off the deck and clambered aboard. Thirty hours later they were rescued by the Vichy steamer *Angoulême*.

American convoys along the east coast of the USA were introduced during May. There was every indication that there would be a resumption of the North Atlantic battles; the U-boats also withdrew to the Gulf of Mexico and the Caribbean. Later, in July, *U-132* penetrated the Gulf of St Lawrence sinking four ships of 14,616 tons.

Successful though the early American convoys were, they were no more than a palliative for in May, the total U-boat sinkings in all areas amounted to 125 ships of more than 600,000 tons, the highest figure for any month of the war up to date. Forty-five of these vessels were American and 44 British. The rest were mainly Canadian, Dutch, Panamanian and Greek.

During the attack on Atlantic convoy ONS92 of 41 ships (12–13 May) Lieutenant-Commander Mohr (*U-124*) and Lieutenant Ites (*U-94*) returned to their familiar hunting grounds. It was now that British seamen appreciated the real value of merchant rescue ships. The 32-year-old *Bury* (Captain Brown), falling back as the distress rockets hurtled skywards, showed great courage in plucking 45 mariners· from the sea in as many minutes. They were from the torpedoed *Llanover* owned by Evan Thomas Radcliffe & Co. Ltd. Heavily laden with Welsh steam coal for Halifax, the Cardiff tramp sank like a stone. Her position was given as 52.50N 29.04W.

Upon rejoining the convoy, *Bury* rescued 21 from the 7,065 ton *Empire Dell*, managed by Geo Nisbet & Co. on behalf of the Ministry of War Transport, and 36 from the Panamanian *Cockle*. The following day, as *U-406*, *U-509* and *U-590* tried to penetrate the escort screen, *Bury* picked up 40 from the 4,399 ton *Batna* (Cory and Strick Steamers). With 176 survivors on board in addition to her crew of

62 and with food running short she was then given permission to make for St John's Newfoundland. A fourth British ship, Elders & Fyffes' *Cristales* (5,389), was also torpedoed and sunk.

A month later, 9–12 June, during the onslaught against the 37-ship convoy ONS 100, it was the rescue ship *Gothland* (Captain Hadden) on duty. Again it was Mohr (*U-124*) and Ites (*U-94*) in the heat of the battle. On three successive days Ites torpedoed and sank *Ramsay* (4,855 grt, Bolton Steamship Co.), *Empire Clough* (6,147 grt, Larrinaga Steamship Co./Ministry of War Transport) and the 4,458 ton *Pontypridd* (Morel Ltd). On 12 June Mohr torpedoed the 4,093 ton *Dartford* owned by Watts Watts & Co Ltd. Her position was 49.19N 41.33W.

Dartford, another Welsh coal carrier, broke up immediately but *Gothland* went at once in the direction of the explosion. All who jumped clear were picked up – four were clinging to an upturned lifeboat. There were four more on a raft and seven holding on to pieces of timber, two of them without lifejackets. The last man to be rescued, the chief engineer, had been in the water for some time and he later died as a result of exposure.

In June the total of Allied ships sunk was 144, more than 700,000 tons and, even worse than May, though only 60 were of British registry. Sixty-five U-boats were now at sea in the North Atlantic alone and with new 1,700 ton 'Milch Cow' submarines now operating, they could be kept at sea a great deal longer. The first of these boats was *U-459* which, when north-east of Bermuda, victualled (fuel and torpedoes) no less than fourteen boats over a period of twelve days.

In the mid-June attack on the 23 ship convoy HG84, seven or eight U-boats were employed without loss. *U-552*, however, with Lieutenant Erich Topp in command, claimed all five sinkings. The convoy had been reported by enemy agents in Gibraltar on 9 June and two days later its position was reported by a reconnaissance FW200 which hurriedly left the scene when pursued by a Hurricane aircraft from the catapult ship *Empire Moon*. Three Flower class corvettes and the sloop *Stork* completed the escort. The rescue ship was *Copeland* accredited with picking up 172 survivors.

With the exception of the Dutch motor tanker *Slemdal*, those sunk were typical Mediterranean traders:

City of Oxford	2,759 grt, Ellermans City Line.
Etrib	1,943 grt, Moss Hutchinson Line Ltd.

Pelayo   1,346 grt, MacAndrews & Co.
Thurso   2,436 grt, Ellerman's Wilson Line.

The motor vessel *Pelayo*, with Captain Williams in command, was sunk 400 miles WNW of Corunna. She was serving as commodore ship with Commodore Hudson RNR aboard. The torpedo struck the engine room where sixteen were killed. Two more, severely wounded, were brought up on deck and carefully lowered into one of the lifeboats. Loss of life was heavy in all the stricken vessels.

The independently routed ships were still at great risk. On the first day of June, Federal Steam Navigation lost another of their fine fleet. The 8,969 ton *Westmoreland* was lost on her 42nd voyage, 240 miles north of Bermuda, position 35.55N 63.35W. In command was Captain Burton.

Westmoreland was fully laden with a precious cargo from Australia which included 3,235 tons of butter, 20,450 crates of cheese, 20,820 carcasses of lamb and mutton and 7,400 carcasses of pork; there was also 9,554 bales of wool. Clearing Panama on 22 May she was routed for Halifax and was torpedoed by *U-566*, Lieutenant Dietrich Borchert. A rough sea was running with a heavy north-west swell. Within twenty minutes she started to settle by the head and Captain Burton sounded the order to abandon ship.

Captain Burton's ship was badly blasted. With one lifeboat destroyed the deck in the port alleyway was blown away and the boat deck was partly wrecked. No 3 hatch and bunker hatch was collapsed and the force of the explosion had lifted the safety valves of the boiler so that they were blowing off with a deafening roar. Without way upon her she was rolling on her beam ends yet miraculously two lifeboats were launched.

U-566 then fired a second torpedo after which she surfaced and finished *Westmoreland* off by heavy shelling. Blazing furiously the old ship, built during the First World War, capsized and sank. Forty-five survivors were rescued by the Canadian *Cathcart* 48 hours later and the remaining boat, by the American *Henry R. Mallory* on 6 June. Only three of her crew were lost.

Three New Zealand bound vessels were lost after their convoy dispersed in the Yucatán Channel on 8 June. Unbeknown to the naval headquarters at Key West the veteran Karl-Friedrich Merton (*U-68*) was lying in wait and 48 hours later he sighted Federal's *Surrey* (8,581 grt) and the motorship *Ardenvohr* (5,025 grt, Australind Steam Shipping Co). Having torpedoed and sunk both these vessels in a matter of ten minutes of each other, Merton came across the Port

Line's 5,882 ton motorship *Port Montreal*. All three ships were proceeding independently towards the Panama Canal.

The crew of the *Port Montreal*, together with 41 survivors from the Honduran *Tela*, whom she rescued two days earlier, were picked up by the Colombian schooner *Helen* on 13 June. *Surrey*, whose master, Captain Loughheed, had been in command of *Norfolk* when she was torpedoed in June 1941, had been carrying military supplies for Australia including 2,600 tons of ammunition and other explosives. As deck cargo she carried six 6-inch guns and six medium tanks. Although hit by two torpedoes in quick succession they were both well away from the ammunition which allowed her crew to abandon ship though four of her gun crew asleep in their quarters aft were killed.

No sooner had the 63 survivors pulled away than a third torpedo struck. This time 300 tons of ammunition were detonated in No 1 hold. There was a loud explosion, a sheet of flame leapt skywards and *Surrey* disappeared. The donkeyman, floating in the water exhausted, was picked up by *U-68* which later transferred him to one of *Ardenvohr*'s lifeboats. Three vessels were engaged in the rescue operation on 13 June when survivors from both *Surrey* and *Ardenvohr* were picked up by the Colombian sailing schooner *Resolute*, the Dutch *Flora* and the American *Potomac*.

Six days later, on 16 June, the Port Line lost another of their fleet. The 8,402 ton *Port Nicholson* (Captain Jeffrey, convoy XB25, Halifax–Boston) was torpedoed by *U-87* (Lieutenant Joachim Berger). Hit by two torpedoes, she began to settle by the stern and was abandoned. The seventh engineer and a greaser were killed in the engine room. The survivors were taken on board a Canadian corvette which, as the ship remained afloat, stood by all night. At 0700 hours, Captain Jeffrey, his chief mate, and the lieutenant in command of the naval vessel, together with five seamen, boarded *Port Nicholson* to see if salvage was possible. A few minutes later, the horrified watchers on the corvette saw her begin to sink rapidly. The bow of *Port Nicholson* rose vertically and she then slid out of sight. Captain Jeffrey, his chief mate and the lieutenant were never seen again.

Little reference has so far been made to decorations for bravery at sea. There were many such decorations, and a list of them appears in the appendix, but mention must be made here of the deck officers of the steamer *Hardwicke Grange* (9,005 grt). Owned by Houlder Brothers & Co. Ltd, she was torpedoed and sunk near the Tropic of Cancer in the Western Atlantic on 13 June 1942.

Commended for brave conduct and listed in the *London Gazette* were the names of:

Captain Timothy McNamara, OBE, Master
Robert W. Wass, Chief Mate
Edward L. Warren, Second Mate
Hector D. Perry, Third Mate

Hardwicke Grange, one of the fifteen ships the company lost during the Second World War, foundered in the early hours of 13 June. One lifeboat was damaged and another fouled and jammed but the crew got safely away from the ship in the remaining four boats. *U-129* (Lieutenant-Commander Hans Witt) then surfaced and commenced shelling the stricken vessel. With three of the engine room watch left lying dead aboard, 78 survivors then set forth in an effort to save themselves, from the enemy and from the elements.

After spending nearly fourteen days adrift, Captain NcNamara's boat, with nineteen officers and men, arrived in the tiny port of Monte Cristi, Dominican Republic, on 26 June. Within the space of a few days, the survivors from the three other boats had been safely landed; the chief mate's boat was at Mole San Nicollas, Haiti; those from the second mate's boat were landed at Neuvitas, Cuba (the tanker *Athelprince* had rescued them on the eleventh day) and the third mate with his boat's crew were at Turk's Island. Fine seamanship, navigation, discipline, and brave conduct, had ensured the survival of all those who had abandoned ship in mid-ocean.

A serious mid-Atlantic loss was Shaw Savill & Albion's 12,435 ton motor ship *Waiwera* (Captain Andrews) on 29 June. Homeward-bound from Auckland on a bright and moonlit night she was torpedoed on the portside aft while zig-zagging, in position 45.49N 34.29W. The explosion smashed the port propeller and put the steering gear out of action. With the starboard engine still running and with the steering gear jammed, the ship was going round in a circle. Seeing the situation, Lieutenant Johannes Oestermann (*U-754*) slammed in a second torpedo which hit the starboard side of the engine room, stopping the remaining engine.

Waiwera now took a heavy list to starboard and began to fill rapidly. Within six minutes of the second explosion she capsized and five minutes later she went down taking her chief engineer and eight others down with her. With magnificent seamanship Captain Andrews and his chief mate nursed the two boats launched, both heavily overloaded, through four days and four nights of bad weather. Ninety-seven survivors were rescued by the Norwegian *Oregon Express*.

A week later on 6 July, some 500 miles to the south-east, in position 38.04N 22.48W, the 14,443 ton *Avila Star* (Captain Fisher) was lost, the third of nine Blue Star vessels sunk during 1942. Carrying 166 crew and 30 passengers including ten women and Captain Low and his chief mate, survivors from the *Lylepark*, *Avila Star* fell victim to the veteran Adalbert Schnee in *U-201*. Sixty-two perished in the disaster.

Homeward-bound from Buenos Aires with a refrigerated cargo of 6,050 tons, *Avila Star* was torpedoed during the night on the starboard side of the boiler room. She lurched heavily to starboard, the lights failed, the klaxons sounded 'Abandon Ship' yet there was no panic. As the lifeboats were being lowered a second torpedo struck; it exploded immediately beneath No 7 flinging all its occupants into the air. Several injured and scalded survivors were plucked from the water by No 2 boat. Within twenty minutes of the first explosion *Avila Star* sank.

Three lifeboats were picked up by the Portuguese destroyer *Lima* the following day. A fourth boat sailed for twenty days, much of the time through rough and confused seas. Of the 40 that set out ten died during the voyage, another after being rescued by the Portuguese sloop *Pedro Nunes* and two others in hospital after reaching Lisbon on 26 July. The fifth lifeboat (No 6) was never heard of again. In charge was the chief mate of the *Lylepark* (5,186 grt), a tramp steamer sunk by the raider *Michel* in the South Atlantic on 11 June. To have experienced two disasters within the space of 25 days and then to have been storm-tossed in an open boat for many a day more, probably took him beyond the limits of human endurance.

Like the *Lylepark*, the 8,006 ton *Gloucester Castle* (Captain Rose) was also blasted from the seas by the raider *Michel*. She was Union Castle Line's smallest and oldest (1911) liner which had already retired when war broke out and she was again pressed into service. Sailing from Birkenhead for Cape Town on 21 June she was carrying general cargo and mails plus twelve passengers, women and children, going to Simonstown to join relatives in the Naval Dockyard. After dispersing from the outward convoy she proceeded independently but never reached her destination and was presumed lost. The full story was not known until after the war was over.

Michel, with Captain Von Ruckteschell in command, in 1940 he had been captain of the raider *Widder*, sailed into the Gulf of Guinea on 14 July creeping up on the Union Castle liner the following night;

her estimated position was 08.00S 01.00E. Fire and terror erupted as the shells struck. The bridge and radio room were wrecked immediately; the radio operator was killed at his post. With her superstructure ablaze and her starboard lifeboats shot away she listed, first to starboard, then suddenly to port.

Within four minutes *Gloucester Castle* had sunk; only one boat got away. Men, women and children struggled in the sea in an effort to save themselves. Ninety-three perished including Captain Rose, his chief engineer, purser and surgeon and all the deck officers. Of the twelve passengers, four were saved; one woman, a girl of eighteen and two young boys. The survivors were taken on board the raider and after three weeks were transferred to the supply ship *Charlotte Schliemann*. For four weeks she lay stationary and eventually arrived in Japan on 19 October. Three distressful years in Japanese prison camps followed during which time two crew died.

June 1942 saw much Japanese submarine activity off the East African coast. With a shore base, manned by Germans, established near Porto Amélia (Mozambique) and a supply vessel cruising in the area acting as a depot ship, four submarines, *I-10*, *I-16*, *I-18* and *I-20*, accounted for 74,678 tons of shipping.

King Lud (5,224 grt, Captain Evans) owned by Dodd Thomson & Co, sailed from New York on 22 April for Bombay loaded with Government Stores together with a crew of 34 and five army and navy personnel. After bunkering in Table Bay she sailed on 31 May but subsequently was lost without trace. She was torpedoed and sunk by *I-10* (Lieutenant Commander Kayahara) on 8 June, 350 miles east of Beira.

Brocklebank's *Mahronda* (7,926 grt, Captain Hill) loaded a military cargo in New York which included 15-inch shells and depth charges in No 5 hold. Making about 12½ knots she was instructed to hug the East African coast and was therefore only a few miles off shore north of Mozambique town when dawn broke on 11 June. In her wake, slowly coming up astern was a suspicious vessel, flying no ensign and painted grey overall. Whilst she was slowly overtaking she made no attempt to actually do so.

Late that same afternoon *Mahronda* was torpedoed on the port side, No 4 hold. Both No 4 and No 5 holds, together with the engine room began to flood rapidly; this flooding probably prevented her dangerous cargo from being detonated. Five lifeboats were launched and she was abandoned. The large Japanese submarine *I-20*, she carried a midget submarine and a spotter seaplane, then surfaced taking the second mate of *Mahronda* aboard as prisoner. The same

(*Right*) Bullard King's 8,141 ton *Umtata* sinks in her watery grave. Upon seeing the *Umtata* about to sink off the coast of Florida (7 July 1942) Lieutenant Helmut Möhlmann, commander of *U-571*, prepares to leave. The survivors are left to fend for themselves.

The North African invasion convoy. The invasion of French North Africa, November 1942. The first fast convoy of twenty troopers sailed from the Clyde estuary on 26 October. At the time it was the greatest armada in history – 352 merchant ships and 169 escorts.

(*Above*) A Royal Navy cruiser defending the troopships. In the Mediterranean, anti-aircraft cruisers of the Royal Navy stoutly defended 'the cream' of Britain's merchant fleet.

(*Left*) P&O's *Strathallan* on fire and abandoned. Torpedoed by *U-562* on 21 December 1942, *Strathallan*, 23,722 grt, was the largest of the P&O fleet sunk during the war and the fourth trooper lost during the North African campaign.

evening she sank the Panamanian *Hellenic Trader* by gunfire. At 20.25 hours the 1925-built *Mahronda* sank and her lifeboats pulled towards the shore. It was later assumed that the suspicious vessel was the submarine depot ship. Within the next 24 hours Lieutenant-Commander Yamada (*I-20*) sank a further two vessels in the same neighbourhood, the 5,063-ton *Clifton Hall* and the Yugoslav *Supetar*.

Another mystery at the time was the loss of the 4,937 ton motorship *Queen Victoria*, T. Dunlop & Sons, commanded by Captain Macleod. She sailed from Table Bay on 21 June bound for Aden. Nothing more was heard of her until some months later a relative of one of the crew received a letter saying that he had been taken prisoner and was safe and well in a Japanese camp. He was the only survivor from the Glasgow trader which was sunk by *I-10* on 28 June, in position 21.15S 40.30E.

As Dönitz and his men turned their attention to the area south of the Cape Verde Islands, the waters off Freetown once again became dangerous, as ships dispersed from outward convoy OS33 found to their cost. During the four days of 12–15 July six British ships with a total tonnage of 39,692 were sent to the bottom between latitudes 32.45N and 23.48N. They were *Cortona*, *Empire Attendant*, *Port Hunter*, *Shaftesbury*, *Siris* and *Sithonia*.

The greatest loss of life in any one ship of the Port Line fleet occurred when *Port Hunter* (8,826 grt, Captain Bradley) was torpedoed by *U-582* (Lieutenant Werner Schulte). Bound for New Zealand with 85 on board including a few passengers, she was carrying a mixed cargo which included a quantity of ammunition. During the morning of 11 July, 100 miles north-west of Freetown, she left the convoy as ordered to proceed independently to her destination. Just after midnight the convoy saw a brilliant flash far to the westward. The next morning an investigating sloop found a patch of oil and three members of the crew clinging to fragments of a motor launch which the ship had carried on deck. Eighty-two persons had perished.

A short while later a few miles to the north-west, Adalbert Schnee (*U-201*) fresh from his *Avila Star* triumph brought Royal Mail's 5,242 ton *Siris* to a standstill with a torpedo that struck her amidships. Bound for Brazil and the River Plate she had been within sight of *Port Hunter* since dispersing from OS33. Her master, Captain Treweeks, had the good sense to abandon ship immediately for no sooner had the lifeboats got away than *U-201* surfaced and fired some fifty rounds to sink the steamer.

It was nine days later that the chief mate's boat was sighted by

HMS *Jonquil* but that of Captain Treweeks, an overloaded and crowded boat, which leaked badly so that pumping and baling were necessary throughout her voyage, was at sea for fifteen days. In the early hours of 27 July she sighted land and later that morning sailed into St Vincent harbour, her supply of fresh water reduced to a few cupfuls, her crew exhausted. Several were taken to hospital where the chief engineer and chief steward died three days later.

The Donaldson South American Line *Cortona* (7,093 grt) was commanded by Captain MacBrown who had been master of the *Corrientes* when she was torpedoed in September 1940. Once again he survived the ordeal though 30 of his crew were killed and another brought ashore wounded. Two torpedoes hit *Cortona* at about the same time, one from *U-116*, the other from *U-201*. Later she was sunk by a coup de grâce from *U-201*.

For *Empire Attendant* (7,524 grt, managed by Andrew Weir & Co on behalf of the Ministry of War Transport) the end came suddenly and violently. No distress call was sent. There were no survivors among her crew of 59. The only record of her loss was to be found in the log book of Lieutenant Schulte (*U-582*) 'torpedoed 0330 hours 15 July, in position 23.48N 21.51W.'

July saw the convoys to Northern Russia suspended for two months. This was due to the disaster of PQ17 which sailed from Iceland on 27 June when out of the 35 ships (22 American) which left port only eleven survived. It was a slaughter of men and ships, the subject of much controversy ever since the signal was sent by the First Sea Lord, Admiral Pound. 'Most immediate. My 9.23 of the 4th: Convoy is to scatter'. It was a fatal error.

The decision to scatter was taken as it was considered that the battleship *Tirpitz* and the heavy cruiser *Hipper* were at sea, though subsequently it was learnt that intelligence was faulty; the big ships remained at anchor in Alten Fjord awaiting Hitler's orders. As the battle progressed no enemy capital ships were seen at all; it was the numerous aircraft, credited with thirteen merchant ships and one rescue ship, the *Zaafaran*, and the U-boats (ten ships) which wrought such losses. The cost to the enemy was negligible, no U-boats lost and only six aircraft out of 202 employed (130 bombers, 43 torpedo aircraft and 29 reconnaissance).

In addition to the merchantmen, 100,000 tons of supplies, 3,350 vehicles, 430 tanks and 210 aircraft carried as deck cargo, plunged to the seabed. Over 160 trained seamen died. That such a valuable convoy could be left defenceless in the face of such powerful German forces was never understood by the 1,300 survivors who were landed at Archangel; the port of Murmansk was temporarily out of action due to dive bombing. Even half a century later the reasons behind such an order are difficult to understand. Would *Tirpitz* and *Hipper* have sunk a greater number of merchant ships or were the British and American capital ships more valuable?

The disaster of PQ17 was all the greater coming so soon after the dive bombing of PQ16, also a 35 ship convoy, only a month earlier. In addition to the commodore ship *Ocean Voice* (7,174 grt), seriously damaged (four months later she was sunk by *U-435* in these same waters), the CAM ship *Empire Lawrence* and the brand new 7,049 ton *Empire Purcell* were among the seven vessels sunk. During a single day 108 successive waves of German aircraft kept up a relentless bombing attack.

The 7,457 ton *Empire Lawrence* with her Hurricane fighter was a loss which the convoy could ill afford. Managed by Crosby and Co. on behalf of the Ministry of War Transport, her master, eleven of his crew, and three gunners, were killed. Of the sixteen rescued by the armed trawler *Lady Madeleine*, seven were badly wounded and they later died in hospital. *Empire Purcell*, managed by the Dover Navigation Company, was hit by two bombs and blew up with a deafening roar in a flash of orange flame seconds after the crew had abandoned her. Seven seamen and one gunner were killed.

The destruction of convoy PQ17, has been well documented. Of the seven British ships sunk the greatest loss was that of the commodore ship, the 5,479 ton *River Afton* commanded by Captain Charlton. Already a veteran of the Russian convoys she was owned by the Ayrshire Navigation Company and on this voyage carried Commodore Dowding RNR, DSO, RD, and his staff.

Torpedoed by *U-703* (Lieutenant Heinz Bielfeld) on 5 July (in position 75.57N 43.00E) *River Afton* was struck by three torpedoes; the first put the engine room out of action and destroyed one of the two lifeboats; the second smashed the other boat as it was being lowered. Many of its occupants were drowned. It was then that the master's dinghy being lowered from the lower bridge, collided with the smashed boat hanging in splinters from its davit. Designed to hold six persons she had twelve on board; all were thrown into the sea, the chief mate being drowned. Captain Charlton was the last to leave, going hand over hand down a rope.

River Afton was then struck by the third torpedo. This detonated the cargo of explosives and with a great roar she broke in two with the stern part sliding immediately to the seabed; fortunately her four rafts were intact and floated off. After three hours her survivors, who included Commodore Dowding, Captain Charlton and 36 crew, were rescued by the corvette *Lotus*; 23 had perished.

Many of those from PQ17 owed their lives to the three rescue ships *Rathin*, *Zamalek* and *Zaafaran*. During that fateful 5th July, when the convoy was scattering far and wide, *Zaafaran* (1,559 grt) picked up 38 survivors. Though her gunners fought off several bombing raids, one of her attackers came in low over the sea releasing a bomb which hit the hull below the waterline; two lifeboats were destroyed and she was taking water badly. All 98 persons got off in seven minutes before she sank and two hours later they climbed aboard *Zamalek*.

A further 240 owed their lives to Royal Mail's CAM ship *Empire Tide*, Captain Harvey, which plucked them from the sea. They included seven from the 5,082 ton *Hartlebury*, National Steamship Co. which was torpedoed and sunk by *U-355* (Lieutenant Günter La Baume) on 7 July. Thirty-nine of their shipmates had been left behind dead, the greatest loss of life on any of the 24 ships sunk.

During the summer of 1942 the plight of the people of Malta was desperate. With the failure of Operations 'Harpoon' and 'Vigorous' in June it was difficult to see how the island could survive. With the Afrika Korps now 45 miles from Alexandria and the loss of valuable airfields in North Africa the occupation of Malta by the enemy was a distinct possibility. Yet the enemy reckoned without the Red Duster and their white ensign escorts. Some of the most modern ships in the merchant fleet were now assembling in the Clyde estuary, rumour had it that they were about to sail for the Mediterranean. At Gibraltar, some of Britain's most powerful naval ships were gathering. August's Operation 'Pedestal' was in the making.

> The land man's troubles and hazards are only during a
> short fight – Whereas the work and labour and hazards
> are most of them constant to a seaman besides what he
> meets in a fight.
>
> *Samuel Pepys*

CHAPTER SEVEN

Business in Great Waters
(August–December 1942)

There was considerable controversy in the British War Cabinet during the summer of 1942 over the shipping situation. The first six months of the year showed a net shipping loss of over 500,000 tons and there was the great task of repairing the 2,500,000 ton backlog of damaged ships – this alone was absorbing half the total United Kingdom shipyard force.

The autumn of 1942 was an exciting period. Although losses in the Atlantic continued at a high rate, indeed there were some in high places who considered the Allies were losing the battle, it was by no means all gloom. In spite of severe losses, both in ships and personnel, we were now engaged, alongside our brothers in the armed services in discharging military hardware onto enemy beaches; it was all so different to the scenes of evacuation.

Counter-measures against the U-boats were improving steadily. Nevertheless, with our defence stretched in every direction, we still lacked the escort ships and aircraft in sufficient numbers to protect the convoys in every area in which the enemy might strike. Improved types of U-boats of longer range were completing in the German building yards and, as surface supply ships in the more distant areas were too vulnerable to our cruiser patrols, he was producing many more tanker U-boats or 'Milch Cows' as they were called. The 'paradise days' might be over but the enemy still had the initiative and he was prepared for increasing U-boat losses. His energy and resourcefulness were immense and our experience had already made it manifest that his swelling submarine fleet would be used with even greater originality and strategic skill.

Regulations as to the equipment of lifeboats and rafts on merchant ships now came to be rigidly enforced. It was not before time for already it was becoming increasingly difficult to find qualified personnel to man the new ships being built in North America. Special provisions in tabloid form and emergency stores ranging from fishing lines to apparatus for condensing sea-water were given priority. Every ship now had to carry three radio officers and at least one motor boat. All lifejackets had to have the small red lights fitted; already they had saved many lives on dark nights when the proximity of U-boats prevented the use of searchlights by the rescue ships. It became compulsory for life-boats to be equipped with manual pumps and protective clothing.

Tension in the Mediterranean had been increasing ever since the destruction of the 3,676 ton Ministry of War Transport *Ramb IV* on 10 May. A former Italian motorship captured by the British and converted for use as a hospital ship she was managed by the English Coaling Co. Bombed and set on fire by German aircraft in the Alexandria Channel she quickly became an inferno and could not be controlled. She was fully loaded with 269 wounded from Tobruk and whilst some were taken off, it afterwards became known that 150 patients died when the burning wreck was sunk by Royal Naval gunfire. *Ramb IV* was one of nine British hospital ships sunk during the Second World War.

There followed the disastrous Malta convoy (Operation Harpoon) which sailed from the Clyde on 5 June comprising five transports and one tanker. There were only two survivors, *Troilus* and *Orari*, the latter being damaged by a mine a little more than ½ mile from the harbour breakwater; the mine exploded in the same place as the torpedo fired by *U-43* in the Atlantic on 13 December 1940. Both ships were in Malta for an enforced stay of 54 days. During this time the dockyard suffered 289 air raids.

The eleven ships, convoy MW11, which sailed from Alexandria at the same time (Operation Vigorous) fared even worse. They immediately ran into trouble when German Ju87 aircraft from Crete bombed Ellerman's 8,063 ton *City of Calcutta*. She had to put into Tobruk for repairs and only escaped seven days before the port fell into enemy hands. The Norwegian *Elizabeth Bakki* was then hit necessitating her return to Alexandria. There followed more bombing attacks by aircraft based in North Africa, the Dutch *Aagtekerk* and Hain Steamship's *Bhutan* were both sunk whilst Royal Mail's *Potaro* was damaged.

Bhutan (6,104 grt, Captain Champion), carrying troops in addition to cargo, was successfully abandoned with only six lost from her complement of 180. An E-boat attack and a submarine accounted for a further merchantman and damaged another when finally, threatened with Italian capital ships, the convoy returned to Alexandria. Considerable losses were sustained by the escort forces including the cruiser *Hermione*, which sank with all hands and the destroyers *Hasty* and *Airedale*.

In the same week that *Queen Mary* arrived at the 'tail of the bank' with 15,125 American troops, the first time in history that an entire Army division voyaged in one ship, there sailed convoy WS521S, a bogus number for secrecy. Operation Pedestal was now under way, an operation designed to relieve Malta which had only three weeks to live. The situation was desperate. 'The fate of Malta was at stake and we were determined that it should not fall,' wrote Churchill.

Pedestal was an epic in naval history. It was as important as the coming battle of Alam Halfa in turning the tide in the North African campaign. It paved the way for the landings in Algeria and Morocco. As the thirteen transports and one tanker, 139,992 tons of modern construction, all heavily armed and chosen for their speed, passed through the Straits of Gibraltar during the night of 10 August, they were joined by the heaviest and most powerful naval escort of any wartime convoy.

Led by the battleships *Nelson* and *Rodney* the escort comprised the aircraft carriers *Argus*, *Eagle*, *Furious* and *Indomitable*, seven cruisers and 25 destroyers. Back-up ships included the tankers *Brown Ranger* and *Derwentdale*, four corvettes and the towing vessel *Salvonia*.

The relief of Malta is probably the best known of any action at sea. 47,000 tons of cargo were unloaded from the four merchant ships that fought through; the *Ohio*,* American registered, and one of the fastest tankers afloat, with a British crew commanded by Captain Mason, at 39 years, the youngest master of the Eagle fleet, arrived with her gunwales awash, lashed up between two destroyers. A portion of her cargo was intact and was pumped ashore though she was finally written off as a constructive loss.

During two days of action the convoy met 150 bombers and eighty torpedo aircraft supported by fighters in great strength. There were twelve submarines in pursuit as well as flotillas of E-boats; enemy minefields too lay in its path. Supplies that did get through were sufficient for Malta to survive. Without the merchantmen's timely arrival, the fortress must have fallen. When the losses were made public, there were many criticisms. Nine vessels of 91,005 tons; five sunk by aircraft, four by E-boats. 100,000 tons of stores including aviation spirit and petrol in cases and drums destroyed. 350 Merchant Navy officers and men died.

* Her Red Ensign is held by the Imperial War Museum, presented by the Eagle Oil & Shipping Co. Ltd in December 1959.

The Royal Navy suffered heavy losses too: an aircraft carrier, a cruiser, an anti-aircraft ship, a destroyer, and a second cruiser seriously damaged. If in fact Malta had fallen however, the whole course of the war, in the Mediterranean in particular, would have been far different and victory in Europe would probably have taken far longer.

In addition to the battered *Ohio*, torpedoed, lamed and set on fire, her boilers blown up, her engines damaged beyond repair, the others who broke the blockade were well known names across many oceans:

Brisbane Star	12,791 grt, Blue Star Line. Captain Riley
Melbourne Star	12,806 grt, Blue Star Line. Captain Macfarlane
Port Chalmers	8,535 grt, Port Line. Captain Pinkey
Rochester Castle	7,795 grt, Union Castle Mail Steamships. Captain Wren

What of those vessels destroyed? In addition to two American transports, *Almeria Lykes* and *Santa Elisa*, they included three of the fleet operated by Shaw Savill and Albion Ltd – the 1935-built 12,800 ton motorship *Wairangi* (Captain Gordon); the 1938-built 12,843 ton motorship *Waimarama* (Captain Pearce); and the refrigerated cargo ship *Empire Hope* (12,688 grt) built in 1941 for the Ministry of War Transport and commanded by Captain Williams.

Waimarama suffered the heaviest loss of personnel of all the merchant ships. Attacked by dive bombers which came screaming out of the sun, her cargo of petrol and ammunition blew up in a sheet of flame. She disappeared within a few seconds leaving just two of her crew alive. The third radio officer and a seventeen-year-old cadet, whose first voyage it was, were rescued by the destroyer *Ledbury*.

Torpedoed and sunk in those narrow waters between Cape Bon and the island of Malta on 12/13 August were four other fine ships of the British merchant fleet; Alfred Holt's *Deucalion* (7,515 grt, Captain Brown); Federal's 10,624 grt *Dorset* (Captain Tuckett); the 8,982 ton *Glenorchy* owned by the Glen Line (Captain Leslie), and the Clan Line's 7,347 ton *Clan Ferguson* commanded by Captain Cossar.

The only Glasgow-registered ship in the convoy, the twinscrew *Clan Ferguson*, blew up after being sunk late on 12 February, 20 miles north of Zembra Island. On watch on the bridge was the second mate who recalls that fateful day in his unpublished wartime memories.

We struggled on at full speed slowly closing on the minesweepers ahead of us, when at 2103 a German torpedo bomber dropped a torpedo aimed at us from just below the starboard beam. It was almost dark and he had approached us from the dark side. We put the wheel hard a starboard in an attempt to dodge the torpedo, without success, and were hit just forward of the after engine room bulkhead. The torpedo went through the ship's side and through the bulkhead into No 4 hold where there was a large amount of petrol stowed. The noise of the explosion and the really terrifying blaze as the petrol went up was practically simultaneous.

Before sailing, *Clan Ferguson* had taken on a Scottish crew in place of her traditional Indian crew and in addition, was carrying a naval liaison officer, a sea transport officer and a Gaumont-British News cameraman. Her total complement was 114 and her cargo included 2,000 tons of petrol in cases each containing two 4 gallon tanks plus a million pounds worth of Maltese bank notes – valueless as they still had to have a signature printed upon arrival.

Whilst loading in Glasgow the *Ferguson*, like other vessels in the convoy, had been fitted with depth charges in each side of the engine room in the bilges so that in the event of danger of being captured they could be detonated from the bridge and the ship sunk. It was the first occasion on which merchant ships had been so fitted and were in fact used in the case of the seriously damaged *Wairangi*.

Those who survived the *Clan Ferguson* holocaust managed to get away on the six rafts. It was remarkable that the loss of life was only eighteen; eleven crew, one gunner and six passengers. One of the rafts (32 persons) was sighted the following afternoon by a German three-engined Dornier flying boat from Sicily which alighted on the calm sea and took the occupants prisoner. During the evening of 15 August, Captain Cossar, his chief mate, and fourteen others, were rescued by an Italian Red Cross seaplane.

The second mate, fourth mate and fourteen seamen drifted ashore on Zambretta Island on Sunday, 16 August, where they were taken prisoner by the French and later transferred to a camp near Sfax. Here they were to join survivors from *Parracombe*, sunk 1 May 1941, *Empire Pelican*, 14 November 1941 and the 108 persons who had been landed from *Glenorchy*.

Missing from the Glen Line vessel were sixteen of her crew and her master, Captain Leslie, who, the fine sailor and gentleman that he was, chose to go down with his ship. Refusing all efforts from his loyal crew who attempted to take him with them he died in the greatest tradition of the sea. A moving event and a very sad one. Those who found themselves prisoners of war in Tunisia were reunited with their families four months later when the Orient trooper *Orontes* sailed into the Clyde from Algiers.

Of the 85 merchant ships which sailed for Malta between
February and August 1942, 24 were sunk and many others damaged.
Of the 296,000 tons of cargo shipped from Alexandria, 34 per cent
was lost. A total of 314,690 tons was consigned from the United
Kingdom of which 43 per cent was lost. Yet because of the supplies
that were delivered Malta was able to stand steadfast. It was a great
achievement.

Once more Atlantic convoy battles were gaining momentum.
Wolf packs were again on the rampage; in several cases the escorts
failed to foil their activities. SL118 of 34 ships, homewards from
Freetown lost the 7,552 ton *Hatarana* (British India Steam
Navigation) torpedoed by *U-214* later to be sunk by one of the
escorts, and the 7,452 ton *City of Manila*.

The stubborn 26-year-old *Manila* torpedoed by *U-406* (Lieutenant
Horst Dieterichs) kept under way for 24 hours until her forward
holds were completely flooded and her fo'c'sle was awash. She was
finally abandoned, in position 43.21N 18.20W, at midday on 20
August and sank two hours later. In the following convoy, SL119,
eight days later, in approximately the same position, Ellermans lost
their *City of Cardiff*. She was torpedoed by *U-566* (Lieutenant
Gerhard Remus). An engine breakdown left the 5,941 ton *Clan
MacWhirter* (Captain Masters) drifting some miles behind the main
body of ships. She was a sitting target for ace Hartenstein (*U-156*) in
position 35.45N 18.45W. There on 27 August ten men including
their captain were drowned as two lifeboats were taken down with
the ship and another boat capsized.

Convoy ON115 (41 ships) lost three vessels in mid-Atlantic, the
motor tanker *G.S. Walden* was seriously damaged. One of those lost
was Royal Mail's 9,419 ton motorship *Lochatrine* (Captain Cooper)
sunk in position 45.52N 46.44W by *U-553* (Lieutenant-Commander
Karl Thurmann). As two torpedoes exploded simultaneously during
the night of 2/3 August, four were killed in the engine room, all the
lights failed and she began to sink rapidly. She then held up with 4
feet of freeboard forward and 8 feet aft. A further five lives were lost
when she was abandoned some hours later, the survivors being
rescued by the Canadian destroyer *Hamilton* and the Canadian
corvette *Agassyz*.

SC94, a 7½ knot convoy of 36 heavily laden ships, homeward
bound from Sydney. Nova Scotia, was badly mauled. In the second
week of August ten vessels were sunk including the commodore ship,
the 4,817 ton *Trehata*, Hain Steamship Company. Her master,
Captain Lawrie, and 21 of her crew perished. Lieutenant-

Commander Reiner Dierksen (*U-176*) sent terror and near panic through the convoy as he fired three two-torpedo spreads hitting *Trehata*, *Kelso*, and the Greek *Mount Kassion* simultaneously. Immediately afterwards the 2,537 ton *Anneberg* and the American *Kaimoku* were torpedoed and sunk by *U-379* (Lieutenant Paul-Hugo Kettner). It was his one and only war action, as he was sunk by the corvette *Dianthus* a few hours later.

Few of the ships' crews had experienced such brutal warfare. Three vessels, *Empire Moonbeam*, *Empire Antelope* and *Radchurch* found themselves in the midst of the battle, their crews abandoning them in the confusion of the moment, some leaping overboard in fright. Their position was 56.30N 32.14W. It was the only instance in the long war at sea where fright and panic took the place of brave seamanship and courage. The crews of the two *Empires* eventually returned though those from *Radchurch* (3,701 grt, owned by E.R. Management Co. Ltd) refused. Drifting astern with only her captain left aboard she was subsequently sunk by *U-176*.

In the Western Atlantic, ace Adolf Piening (*U-155*), now wearing his Knight's Cross, sank nine vessels all sailing independently between 28 July and 10 August. The tonnage was 38,742. Amongst them were *Clan MacNaughton* (6,088 grt, Captain Bennett, in position 11.54N 54.25W) and the 7,045 ton *Empire Arnold*, sunk a few miles to the south-east. Managed by Sir R. Ropner & Co., three of her officers and six seamen were killed; her master, Captain Tate, and one other officer were taken prisoner.

On 9 August, the 8,071 ton motor tanker *San Emiliano* was sunk by Piening, 450 miles west of Trinidad. She was one of two *Eagle* tankers sunk during August, the other being *San Fabian* (13,031 grt, convoy TAW15, Trinidad-Key West) on 27 August. *Emiliano* was another high octaine carrier homewards from Port of Spain and like so many so loaded, was consumed with horrific flames the moment she was struck. Flames reached over a hundred feet high as those still alive threw themselves over the ship's side, some of them horribly burned and who were to die before rescue came. Her master, Captain Tozer, and 39 of his men died. Only seven survived, six of whom were taken ashore wounded.

The loss of the tanker *Tricula* (6,221 grt, owned by the Anglo Saxon Petroleum Co.) was another tragedy. On 3 August, sailing independently 250 miles north-east of Trinidad, she was shaken by a thunderous explosion as the torpedo fired by *U-108* struck her amidships. It was now all too familiar. Two other torpedoes struck forward of the bridge; she listed as much as 75 degrees to port, her back broken, her cargo, 8,000 tons of fuel oil, spewed everywhere. Swirling black smoke billowed upwards. *Tricula* heeled over, her survivors plunged into a seething emulsion of seawater and oil. In less than a minute, from the time of the first strike, she was gone. Her master, 42 of his crew, three gunners and one passenger lost their lives. Eleven crew and a further passenger were rescued by the neutral *Rio San Juan* from Argentina.

There were further losses south and west of Freetown among them the 5,728 ton *Vimeira* (Captain Caird) who was sighted by *U-109* with Heinrich Bleichrodt of *U-48* fame in command. Torpedoed on 11 August, in position 10.03N 28.55W, the Gow Harrison tanker was finally sunk by gunfire and Captain Caird taken prisoner. One lifeboat containing the second mate and sixteen men was picked up by *Sylvia de Larrinaga* (5,218 grt) who was then, three days later, sunk herself by the Italian Giovanni Bruno, commander of the submarine *Giuliani*.

Twenty-seven survivors from Larrinaga Steamships *Sylvia de Larrinaga* were picked up by the *Port Jackson* and landed at Liverpool. The unfortunate *Vimeira* survivors, alone again in the tropical Atlantic, were then adrift for 29 days during which they suffered great hardship from exposure and lack of drinking water. Captain Caird, who commanded *Virgilia* when she was torpedoed and sunk in November 1941, spent an uncomfortable 52 days on board *U-109* before reaching Lorient.

The Italian submarines, co-operating with the German U-boats were finding success in these waters during July and August. It was *Giuliani* which sank Alfred Holt's 5,444 ton *Medon* (Captain Evans) on 10 August. For nineteen years a busy trader between the United Kingdom and the Far East, *Medon* found her watery grave in position 09.26N 38.28W. In the early hours the explosion was deafening, the damage included a broken mainshaft from which the engines seized up. Then the flash of the enemy's gun could be seen. Commander Giovanni Bruno had surfaced and was intent on sinking his prey before daylight.

Despite the shelling, *Medon* made preparations to abandon ship; a distress message was sent and acknowledged. For some hours the stout vessel remained afloat though after a second torpedo struck she reared up almost to the vertical and then slipped quietly under.

The *Medon* disaster is remarkable for the voyages of its four lifeboats; every one of her crew were saved.

No 1 boat: Captain Evans with fourteen men. 8 days adrift. Voyaged 108 miles. Rescued by Panamanian *Rosemont*.

No 2 boat: Chief Mate with thirteen men. 35 days. 383 miles. Rescued by Portuguese *Luso*.

No 3 boat: Second Mate with sixteen men. 36 days. 313 miles. Rescued by Sir Robert Ropner's *Reedpool*.

No 4 boat: Third Mate with nineteen men. 7 days. 40 miles. Rescued by Norwegian *Tamerlane*.

Unhappily for the second mate and his sixteen men it was not the end of their ordeal. A week later (20 September) the 4,838 ton *Reedpool* was herself torpedoed and sunk by *U-515* (Lieutenant Werner Henke) 240 miles south-east of Trinidad. Six of her crew were lost and her master, Captain Downs, taken prisoner. The *Medon* survivors and 28 from *Reedpool* set sail in the only undamaged lifeboat; fortunately they were picked up the following day by the schooner *Millie M. Masher* and landed in Georgetown, British Guiana.

The 4,416 ton *Hamla* (Cory & Strick Ltd, Captain Shute) left Rio de Janeiro homeward-bound on 18 August for Freetown carrying a crew of 38 and four gunners. Independently routed she was never seen again and for many months she was thought to have been sunk by the raider *Michel* south of Fernando Noronha. Carrying manganese ore her end came swiftly and without warning as Lieutenant Erich Würdemann (*U-506*) torpedoed her at dusk on 23 August. Her position was given as 04.00S 24.00W.

The U-boat campaign in the tropics and in the South Atlantic was now intensified. Dönitz despatched nine additional submarines in an effort to, first of all, sever the meat lifeline from South America and secondly to create havoc amongst the many ships engaged on the Middle East supply route.

The Blue Star 6,445 ton *Viking Star* (Captain Mills) whose cargo included 4,500 tons of South American frozen meat was torpedoed and sunk on 25 August by *U-130*. Homeward bound 180 miles southward of Freetown, her master and 32 crew perished, many of them drowning when the only seaworthy boat was cast ashore in a heavy breaking sea on a lonely part of the coast of Sierra Leone.

There followed *Ocean Might* (7,173 grt) as Lieutenant Bleichrodt (*U-109*) joined in the affray and then Holt's 'Blue funnel' *Myrmidon* (6,278 grt). She was sunk by *U-506*. Another of Holt's fleet, the 7,392 ton *Agapenor* was sunk in the same waters a month later by Lieutenant Joachim Berger, commander of *U-87*. On 6 September Bleichrodt caught another refrigerated Blue Star vessel, the 11,449 ton *Tuscan Star* (Captain Rhodes) as she steamed north at 13½ knots. She too was carrying meat from Argentina, 7,300 tons for the British table; her complement was 113 including 25 passengers, women and children amongst them.

Torpedoed twice in quick succession *Tuscan Star* listed heavily to starboard and began to settle immediately by the stern; nine of her crew were killed by the explosion. The master's boat was sighted by *Otranto* on the second day and the other survivors reached safety the following day. Upon landing in Freetown however a rollcall showed that a total of 41 crew, eight gunners and three passengers were missing.

On 29 September the frozen meat carrier *Empire Ovocet* (6,015 grt, MOWT/New Zealand Shipping Co. Ltd) was sunk in position 04.05N 13.23W by Lieutenant Ulrich Folkers (*U-125*); in the same week he sent Lamport and Holt's 5.335 ton *Bruyere* and Hogarth's 3,391 ton *Baron Ogilvy* to the bottom.

Empire Ovocet was carrying beef from Rio Grande (Brazil). Immediately after the torpedo struck the port side abreast the funnel, the sea poured into the engine room. With her engines and lights failed, her communication and steering gear out of action her master, Captain Pover, wasted no time in abandoning ship. With two more torpedoes fired into her, *Ovocet*'s stern rose at a 30 degree angle and she slid under.

Captain Pover and the chief engineer of *Empire Ovocet* were taken prisoner. Two lifeboats were successfully launched from the meat carrier, the chief mate's boat being picked up by the corvette *Cowslip* on 4 October. The second boat ran ashore on Sherbro Island where the survivors led a Robinson Crusoe existence until rescued by natives who conducted them to a coastal boat which took them to Freetown.

Further east on the route to Suez and Alexandria two Japanese submarines patrolled the seas; German U-boats were presently to join them. Torpedoed by Lieutenant K. Torisu, *I-165*, 250 miles south of Ceylon on 25 August was *Harmonides* (5,237 grt, British and South American Steam Navigation Co.). She was commanded by Captain Evans who lost fourteen of his crew.

During the first part of September, Lieutenant-Commander Juichi Izu (*I-29*) torpedoed and sank four vessels: *Gazcon*, *Haresfield*, *Ocean Honour* and the American *Paul Luckenbach*. In Chapter 10 I have recalled my own experiences on board the ex-French *Gazcon* when she blew up north of Cape Guardafui on the night of 2 September.

The crew of British India's *Haresfield* (5,299 grt) sunk eight days later in the same area, spent many days in the four lifeboats under the hot sun. Having lost each other after the ship sank, one boat was fourteen days adrift, another sixteen days, the third eleven days and the remaining boat six days. All suffered extreme exposure and exhaustion.

September 1942 saw the controversial *Laconia* affair, a subject raised at the Nuremberg War Trials. 500 miles south of Cape Palmas (Liberia), *Laconia* (19,695 grt, a Cunard White Star liner commanded by Captain Sharp) homeward-bound from Suez with a crew of 692, 766 passengers and 1,793 Italian prisoners of war was sighted by Lieutenant-Commander Hartenstein in *U-156*.

Closing in on the surface after sunset on 12 September Hartenstein placed his torpedo dead amidships; the liner's engines failed and listing heavily to starboard she began to sink. As the lifeboats pulled away from the crippled ship Hartenstein cruised amongst them; there were also many swimmers who had jumped overboard. It was then that he heard cries for help in Italian. He immediately started to haul some of them aboard and discovered to his dismay that they were Italians taken prisoner by the British Army in North Africa. He immediately summoned other U-boats in the area to the rescue.

Informed of the situation, Dönitz sent orders for other U-boats to go to the scene and arranged for the Vichy French to send surface vessels from Dakar. By dawn the next day *U-156* had picked up 250 Italians; *U-506* then arrived rescuing some 132 and on 15 September *U-507* was in the area followed by the Italian submarine *Cappellini*. The rescue operation however was abruptly terminated the next day when an American aircraft from Ascension attempted to bomb the cluster of rescuing craft and ships' boats.

German U-boat Headquarters reacted violently to the news but Dönitz insisted on seeing the operation through despite what he considered Allied brutality. Subsequently he issued his 'Laconia order' which forbade rescue of survivors except to take prisoners of war. Observers interpreted it as a 'kill survivors' order though U-boat commanders continued, in many cases, to assist those from sunken merchant ships. From this day however, men torpedoed on the high seas were no longer classed strictly as civilians by the enemy.

Loss of life on Cunard's *Laconia* was heavy; only 975 were rescued. Many reached Casablanca in the Vichy French cruiser *Gloire* but from two lifeboats which each made four week voyages only twenty out of 119 survived to tell their story. Captain Sharp who went down with his ship was master of *Lancastria* when she was sunk in June 1940. A total of 5,109 lives were lost in the two vessels under his command.

The familiar pattern of wolf pack forays on the Atlantic convoys continued. The 36 vessels of ON122 were attacked for several days by seven U-boats; four vessels were lost. Seven merchantmen were sunk and four were damaged as ON127 (32 ships) sailed westward during a three day battle against thirteen U-boats. In the Western Atlantic on 6 September six enemy U-boats, *U-135*, *U-176*, *U-373*, *U-432*, *U-569* and *U-755*, having refuelled from tanker *U-462*, formed a new patrol line in an effort to trap the merchantmen; it was all a curtain-raiser to the bloody winter of '43.

Among the four vessels lost from ON122 was the 5,017 ton *Sheaf Mount* (Captain de Gruchy) owned by the small Newcastle company, Sheaf Steamship. Of the 51 officers and men who formed the crew, 31, including her master, were lost. Five torpedoes were fired simultaneously by *U-605*, Lieutenant Herbert Viktor Schütze, from which both *Sheaf Mount* and the 3,163 ton *Katvaldis* were sunk.

Convoy SC100 homeward bound between longitude 38 degrees and 32 degrees west lost her commodore ship the 8,882 ton motor tanker *Athelsultan* (United Molasses Co.). Commanded by Captain Donovan, 37 crew, seven DEMS gunners, the convoy commodore and five of his staff lost their lives. The attacker, *U-617* (Commander Albrecht Brandi), one of the more successful of the newer submarines coming into service, was responsible for three of the five vessels sunk. In the case of Common Bros' 2,342 ton *Tennessee*, sunk on 23 September, ten of her crew and five gunners were posted as missing. She was on charter from the MOWT and loaded with Canadian wheat.

Casualties were again mounting in the 'black hole'. Three Canadian vessels, taken over by the MOWT and managed by Coast Lines Ltd, together with others being transhipped for the planned invasion of Europe, were torpedoed and sunk, convoy RBI. There were no survivors from the *New York* (4,989 grt, Captain Mayers); only two were saved from *Boston* (Captain Young, of the same tonnage). Although the master, Captain Boylan, was saved from *Yorktown* (1,547 grt) sixteen of his crew and two gunners died; 44 were brought ashore wounded.

U-96 and *U-216* erroneously reported the Great Lakes steamers *New York* and *Boston* as passenger liners of the *Viceroy of India*- and *Reina del Pacifico*-type because of their high passenger superstructure and two funnels. This subsequently led to exaggerated claims when the 'destruction' of convoy RBI was reported on German radio.

Heavy storms in mid-Atlantic during October played havoc with ships and escorts. Convoy ONS136, 36 vessels, UK – New York, lost

(*Above*) Submarine Type VII-C. A type VII-C U-boat outward bound 1942. On her foredeck is one 88 mm gun with 20 mm anti-aircraft gun on the 'winter garden'.

(*Right*) The Victors. June 1942. *U-124*, Lt-Commander Johann Mohr, returns triumphantly to base after her June 1942 patrol.

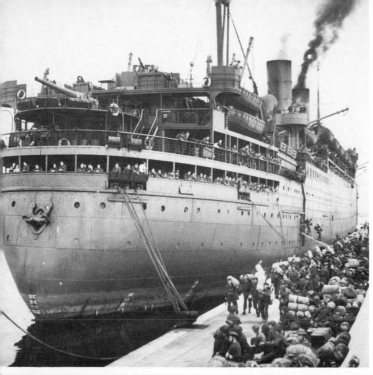

(*Left*) *Duchess of Richmond* at Algiers. The twin screw 20,022 grt *Duchess of Richmond*, built in 1928 for Canadian Pacific Steamships Ltd disembarks troops and baggage at Algiers, 14 November 1942. A sister ship to the *Duchess of Atholl* on which the author was torpedoed, she survived the war.

Another of Ellerman's *'City'* fleet is lost. Ellerman's *City of Baroda*, 7,129 grt, her back broken, after being torpedoed by *U-509*, 2 April 1943. She was beached at Lüderitz Bay and became a total loss.

four including Graig Shipping Co.'s 4,212 ton *Newton Pine*. She lost contact and was never seen again. Her destruction was claimed by *U-704* (Lieutenant Horst Kesler). *Empire Turnstone* (6,113 grt, MOWT/Kaye Son & Co, Captain Collins) was another straggler. Caught by *U-621*, Lieutenant Horst Schunemann, she went down with all hands, her master and 45 crew.

In the same area was homeward-bound SC104. Seven vessels totalling 43,970 tons were sunk. They included:

Ashworth	5,227 grt. Owner R.S. Dalgliesh. Captain Mourat. 41 crew and 7 gunners lost.
Southern Empress	12,398 grt. Chr. Salvesen & Co. (Captain Hansen). 24 crew, 4 gunners and 20 passengers lost.
Empire Mersey	5,791 grt. MOWT/Larrinaga Steamship Co. Captain Bastarrechea with 15 of his crew killed. 2 wounded.

Captain Bastarrechea was in command of *Empire Clough* when she was sunk on 10 June 1942 in the very same area. His new ship, formerly the *Ramon de Larrinaga*, capsized in the Delaware River on 9 February 1941 with the loss of two lives. She was salvaged, reconditioned and taken over by the MOWT. She was then renamed and handed back to the Larrinaga Company to manage.

It was Captain Haddon of the rescue ship *Gothland* whose vivid description of the SC104 battle lives with us to this day: 'The white combers of the breaking waves, the red distress rockets soaring into the air from the stricken ships, the brilliant light of the snowflake rockets fired by the escort vessels, searching for the surfaced enemy ships and the thunder of exploding depth charges'.

Although Captain Haddon and his crew found it virtually impossible to lower a boat due to the heavy sea and swell they rescued 41 men from two foreign ships and 39 from *Empire Mersey*. They then spent 24 hours searching for survivors from *Southern Empress* but without success.

In the Indian Ocean and off the coast of South Africa, October saw 25 vessels sunk of which sixteen were British. Only six of these were destroyed by the Japanese, the rest by German U-boats which by this date, had established a victualling base at Penang (Malaya). They included the new 1,600 ton *U-178* which sailed from Kiel on her first war cruise on 8 September 1942 and did not return to Europe for fourteen months.

In the 1920s and 1930s British merchant ships were often away from their home port for long periods of time. So it was with *Clan MacTavish* (7,631 grt, Captain Arthur) which had been trading in the Middle East and Indian Ocean for twelve months. Homeward bound and sailing alone, she picked up 35 survivors from the ex Danish 5,821 ton *Boringia*, now flying the red ensign. Nine hours later (8 October) 100 miles off the Cape of Good Hope, the Clan Line steamer herself was torpedoed, crippled by *U-159*, the same submarine. *Clan MacTavish* sank quickly. Fifty-four person including Captain Arthur and seven survivors from *Boringia* perished.

The 5,970 ton *Empire Chaucer* (Captain Jennings, managed by W.J. Tatem Ltd), homeward bound from Calcutta with tea was sunk in position 40.20S 18.30E on 17 October. *U-504* (Commander Fitz Poske) was surfaced 450 miles south of Cape Town when the *Chaucer* was sighted. Taking his submarine to periscope depth, Poske fired two torpedoes before resurfacing. He found the sea littered with hundreds of tea chests.

There were several casualties from the two explosions. Captain Jennings was thrown from the bridge into No 2 hold by the force of the second explosion. As the ship went down he was tossed up by the pressure of water rushing in which carried him over the side of the ship into the sea. Battered and half drowned he crawled onto a tea chest. Then commenced fine examples of feats of endurance and discipline, combined with skills of navigation and seamanship.

No 1 boat: Captain and 17 men. Rescued by Stag Line steamer on third day.

No 2 boat: Third Mate and 20 men. Bad weather conditions yet on the fourteenth day they arrived at Simonstown having sailed over 400 miles.

No 3 boat: Senior Radio Officer, Ship's Carpenter and 13 men. Gales for three days and after fourteen days food was exhausted.

There followed one of the few instances where flesh from a shark has kept seamen alive. The fifteen survivors in boat No 3, in spite of their weakness, managed to tempt a shark aboard by trailing their arms in the water. After a long struggle they killed it with a 4 foot axe. Without the shark it is probable they would have perished. A further nine days were to pass before they were sighted – rescued by the Royal Mail *Nebraska*, 23 days after being torpedoed. They had sailed nearly 1,000 miles and were near Walvis Bay when picked up.

In the days following the destruction of *Empire Chaucer*, *U-504* torpedoed and sank *City of Johannesburg* (5,669 grt), *Empire Guidon* (7,041 grt) and the 5,113 ton *Reynolds* around which there remained a mystery. Sunk without trace, the Bolton Steamship tramp with 40 crew and seven gunners was assumed for many years to have met her fate at the hands of the surface raider *Michel*.

October 1942 was the month of the great troopship losses, in Royal Navy parlance, auxiliary transports. *Duchess of Atholl, Orcades* and *Oronsay*, 18/21 knot vessels, the three were homeward-bound on the busy route from the Middle East and North Africa. 63,618 tons of valuable shipping. In addition there were *Abosso, President Doumer*, an ex-French vessel sunk in convoy and the 16 knot *Andalucia Star*, a 14,943 ton vessel heavily laden with meat from Buenos Aires and carrying 83 passengers.

My own experience in the *Duchess* disaster is told in Chapter 10. On that same day, 10 October, the 23,456 ton liner *Orcades* (Captain Fox), the newest and largest of the Orient Steam Navigation fleet, was sunk WSW of Cape Town, in position 35.51S 14.40E.

Carrying 711 passengers, some were survivors of sunken ships, the 21-knot *Orcades* was torpedoed in the port quarter, the port propeller and her steering gear were seriously damaged. *U-172*, with the already successful Lieutenant Carl Emmermann in command, then fired a second torpedo. Now badly holed, Captain Fox gave the order to abandon ship though with a moderate gale blowing and with a heavy swell, some difficulty was experienced in launching the lifeboats. Thirty-eight lives were lost when one of the boats was upset while being lowered.

Although Captain Fox and 52 volunteer crew stayed aboard in case she could be saved, they had to abandon her only twenty minutes later when a third torpedo ripped into the liner and she started to break up. Sinking bow first with her Red Duster still flying at the gaff, she went under amidst a muffled explosion as the boilers exploded.

Answering the distress call the Polish *Narvik* (Captain Zawarda) had to search for many hours in deteriorating weather. The rescue of 1,021 survivors lasting twelve hours, with the possibility that Emmermann was still in the vicinity, ranks among the finest rescue operations.

During these same hours 266 survivors from *Oronsay* were being landed in Freetown, a few in one of the lifeboats were rescued by the Vichy French sloop *Dumant d'Urville* and taken to Dakar where they were interned. The 18 knot 20,043 ton *Oronsay* with Captain Savage in command, was torpedoed by the Italian submarine *Archimede* (Lieutenant Guido Saccardo) before daylight and in drizzling rain. Her position was 04.29N 20.52W.

The explosion wrecked the engine and boiler rooms and brought the ship to a standstill. As the lifeboats were being lowered, Saccardo fired a second torpedo which destroyed one of the boats, drowning five persons. Captain Savage was previously in command of the Orient liner *Orford*, a sister ship, bombed and sunk off Southern France in June 1940.

A serious loss to Elder Dempster Ltd was that of their 11,330 ton twin screw motorship *Abosso* on 29 October. Commanded by Captain Tate she was their largest ship and flagship of the fleet. Neither Captain Tate nor any of his officers survived.

Requisitioned by the Government and serving as an HM Transport, *Abosso* was sailing unescorted at 15 knots. On passage from Cape Town for Liverpool she was carrying 182 crew and 100 passengers. As dusk closed in, her position 48.30N 28.50W, she was torpedoed by *U-575* (Lieutenant Heydemann) whose last battle was with *San Gaspar* in the Caribbean on 18 July. Here, north of the Azores, *Abosso* was mortally wounded. Listing to port with her main engines stopped and lights extinguished she was abandoned with great difficulty. It was then that the second torpedo struck and five minutes later her stern rose nearly vertical and she sank bow first.

The following day the weather deteriorated badly and on the second day those in No 5 lifeboat were rescued by HMS *Bideford*. No further news was heard of the other boats. 251 perished including 168 crew.

With Freetown bursting at the seams again with survivors there sailed the ill-fated convoy SL125 of 37 ships of which only 25 reached their United Kingdom destination. On 16 October they nosed their way out of the Sierra Leone river with only six corvettes as ocean escort, two of which left before the U-boat attack commenced.

On board the 17-knot *President Doumer* was Commodore Reyne and his staff together with a large number of servicemen. Sailing on a broad front of eleven columns west of Morocco and Gibraltar the convoy, heavily laden with fuel oil and foodstuffs, sugar and tea, timber, manganese and iron ore, steamed right across a patrol line of eight U-boats: *U-103*, *U-203*, *U-409*, *U-440*, *U-509*, *U-510*, *U-604* and *U-659*.

The first casualty was the tanker *Anglo Maersk* (7,705 grt, Captain Valsberg), managed by Houlder Brothers and Co. Ltd. A straggler, she had been stopped for 27 hours for repairs but was now on passage at full speed to catch up and resume her position. Alas! on the afternoon of 26 October, she cut across the path of *U-509* (Lieutenant Werner Witte). Considerably damaged she managed to limp along at 7 knots only to be torpedoed and sunk by *U-604* (Lieutenant Horst

Höltring) some 25 hours later. All 37 crew members reached Ferro Island, Canary Islands, in two lifeboats.

The battle then continued for five days. Eleven British ships were destroyed and the Norwegian *Alaska* seriously damaged. In addition to 260 persons lost aboard the 11,898 ton *President Doumer* (Bibby Line, Managers), 166 were posted as missing from the other vessels. Lost on board Alfred Holt's 6,148 ton *Stentor* were her master, Captain Williams, and Captain Garstin, vice-commodore. The death toll was nineteen aboard Peninsular and Oriental's 5,283 ton *Nagpore* including her master, Captain Tonkin and yet another master perished as the tanker *Bullmouth* (7,519 grt) blew up in a sheet of flame. Owned by the Anglo Saxon Petroleum Co. Ltd she was commanded by Captain Brougham; 47 of his crew also perished.

Other casualties of SL125 were *Baron Vernon* (3,642 grt, Kelvin Shipping); *Brittany* (4,772 grt, Royal Mail Line); *Corinaldo* (7,131 grt, Donaldson Line); *Hopecastle* (5,178 grt, Novocastria Shipping); *Pacific Star* (7,951 grt, Blue Star Line); *Silverwillow* (6,373 grt, Silver Line Ltd) and the 6,405 ton *Tasmania* owned by the Ministry of War Transport and managed by Thomas and Juno Brocklebank Ltd.

The heavy loss of life in the sinking of *President Doumer* was principally due to panic as the torpedo struck amidships. It was dark, the lights failed and she started to settle by the stern almost immediately. Many lifeboats fell from the davits into the sea full of survivors – they were never seen again. Some boats crashed empty 50 feet – they too were lost. The sea was covered with struggling people, many crying frantically for help.

The *Alaska* rescued 48 survivors from the water, many were badly injured, two died, crushed against the side of their rescue ship as they were hauled aboard. Then *Alaska* herself was wounded though not mortally (she eventually made Lisbon). Then occurred something which rarely happens in war at sea, and happened in spite of Dönitz's *Laconia* order.

With the convoy in confusion, Captain Cameron, master of the *Baron Elgin*, who had picked up the distress signal from *Alaska*, turned his ship around and started to rescue survivors from several ships. One of the U-boats who witnessed the rescue operation circled *Baron Elgin* on the surface. Captain Cameron with his gunners at the ready held his fire and after some minutes the enemy withdrew allowing Hogarth's *Elgin* to proceed alone to Madeira. She arrived fourteen hours later where she landed the rescued seamen.

The escort screen was so ineffective that the enemy were within the convoy columns. In five separate sinkings more than one submarine was involved. *Corinaldo* was first struck at 2216 hours (*U-509*) on 29 October. The second torpedo, fired by *U-659*, exploded after midnight at 0207 hours. The final torpedo which was to sink her and which was fired by *U-203*, came two hours later.

As the crew of Donaldson's *Corinaldo* were struggling to save their stricken vessel north of the Canary Isles another Glasgow registered ship was loading troops 'for an unknown destination' in the King George V Dock, upriver from the 'tail of the bank'. Here the Anchor Line *Circassia*, Captain Bone, built to carry 300 passengers embarked 2,700 troops and took on board her 300 crew. At anchor off Gourock she was joined by other vessels; a similar operation was being carried out in many other ports along the west coast of the British Isles. Operation Torch was under way. The First Army Information Bulletin pinned to *Circassia*'s notice board as she set sail that first day of November read, 'Our object is to clear the Axis Forces out of North Africa'.

The convoy of 1 November was the third to leave the Western Approaches for North Africa; on 22 October the slow cargo ships, on 26 October the first fast convoy, twenty British and Allied troopships, among them five ships of the P & O Company – *Cathay*, *Ettrick*, *Mooltan*, *Strathnaver* and *Viceroy of India*. From the Union Castle fleet there was *Durban Castle*, *Llangibby Castle*, *Winchester Castle* and *Warwick Castle*. The greatest armada in history was converging on North Africa. 240 merchant ships and 94 naval escorts from the United Kingdom. 112 merchant ships and 75 naval escorts from the United States.

Only months later did those engaged in the battle of convoy SL125 come to learn that ships and men had been 'sacrificed' so that landings in North Africa went ahead without interruption. The poorly defended merchantmen had, unknowingly, drawn the U-boats away from Torch. In Volume Four of *The Second World War* Winston Churchill refers to the episode.

> By the end of October about forty German and Italian U-boats were stationed to the south and east of the Azores. They were successful in severely mauling a large convoy homeward bound from Sierra Leone and sank thirteen ships. In the circumstances this could be borne.

Operation Torch was the dress rehearsal for the invasion of Europe; victory in war depends upon several factors but without good supplies and good transport, it is impossible.

The Merchant Navy were in the front line – at Oran, Algiers,

Bougie, Philippeville and Bône. A heavy price was paid. The 15,225 ton *Cathay* (Captain Stuart) lying off Bougie disembarking troops was a fine target. Diving out of the clouds the Ju88's, flown by resolute and experienced pilots, attacked for many hours on 11 November. At 1700 hours the ship was shaken violently by the explosion of three bombs dropping close to and abaft the engine room. Immediately she listed to port with the engine room wrecked, the boiler room a mass of fuel oil. The order was given to abandon ship.

Five hours later *Cathay* was torn apart when a delayed action bomb exploded with a great roar. She took fire amidships and burned all night. At daybreak, as the depth charges she was carrying exploded in the intense heat, the stern blew up and she disappeared. Miraculously only one person, a naval gunner, was killed.

A few hours later *Strathnaver* arrived amidst a scorching air raid. No sooner had she anchored outside the breakwater than British India's 9,890 ton *Karanja* was hit by seven bombs. Flying the white ensign and serving as a landing ship infantry, *Karanja* blazed furiously. There was great loss of life among her engine room crew and she had to be abandoned. The remainder of her personnel, together with those from *Cathay*, were then taken aboard *Strathnaver*.

The 23-knot turbine engined *Awatea* (13,482 grt, Captain Morgan) also foundered. Owned by the Union Steamship Co. of New Zealand she was crewed mainly by New Zealanders. Soon after sailing from Bougie for Gibraltar on 11 November she became a target for six bombers which came out of the sun in the west. Badly damaged by aerial torpedoes and bombs, she shot down two of her attackers before being abandoned.

The turbo electric *Viceroy of India* (19,627 grt, Captain French) was torpedoed and sunk that same night not far from Cape de Gata (Spain). Bound for Gibraltar and the United Kingdom after disembarking her commandos at Algiers she was torpedoed by *U-407* (Lieutenant Ernst-Ulrich Brüller). She had only 22 passengers on board and everyone got away except those killed in the explosion; they were rescued by HMS *Boadicea*.

The great and loved *Viceroy* turned over and her funnels disappeared. She kept her bows up for a moment and then went down into the sea. For Brüller (*U-407*), it was his first wartime action and the only vessel he was credited with sinking.

One of the biggest explosions heard off the coast was when the 5,332 ton *Browning*, Lamport & Holt Line, blew up for'ard on 12 November. Torpedoed by *U-595*, Lieutenant Jürgen Quaet-Faslem, she was loaded with TNT and several crew members were blown overboard by the blast and lost. The remainder, in spite of the dark night with all lights extinguished, evacuated the ship before she disintegrated. Close by, on the following day, in position 36.27N 00.55W, Lieutenant Friedrich Guggenberger, commander of *U-81*, sank Alfred Holt's *Maron* (6,487 grt, Captain Hey). Having discharged her cargo, she had left Algiers Bay after dark the previous evening in a small convoy of four ships.

The Union Castle motorship *Warwick Castle* (20,107 grt), under the command of Captain Shaw, sailed homewards, convoy MKFI, from Gibraltar on 12 November but was caught 36 hours later by *U-413* (Lieutenant Gustav Poel) in heavy seas. The largest of the Union Castle fleet to be lost it is a story of bravery and devotion to duty. Torpedoed in position 38.44N 13.00W, she broke up very quickly, sinking bow first with her screws still rotating. Launching the lifeboats and rafts proved a hazadous operation.

The destroyer *Vansittart* sighted a raft with Captain Shaw, his chief mate and two men, clinging for their lives. As the naval vessel approached the chief mate was swept away and not seen again. Captain Shaw, lying the full width of the raft, refused help when a line was thrown to him, so that the other two could be hauled aboard first; when eventually he was rescued he was in a very poor condition. After an hour's fight for life he was pronounced dead by the destroyer's doctor. After a brief service he was buried at sea. Sixty-three officers and men lost their lives.

Back at Bougie that same day, P & O's *Narkunda*, the commodore ship of the Second Assault convoy, was preparing to sail for Algiers. As the 16,632 ton liner, commanded by Captain Parfitt, passed seaward of the breakwater, she was dive bombed by enemy aircraft. A stick of bombs burst close alongside causing considerable damage; 31 were killed outright. After a further bomb attack she began sinking by the stern and orders were given to abandon ship.

The following day, 15 November, another P & O auxiliary transport was sunk. This was the liner *Ettrick* (11,279 grt, homewards from the Mediterranean, convoy MK1). Commanded by Captain Legg, she was west of Gibraltar, in position 36.13N 07.54W when she was torpedoed. The crew were already safely away when *Ettrick* sank vertically, stern first, in 700 fathoms. The enemy this time was the successful *U-155* which also sank the escort carrier *Avenger* and seriously damaged the American *Almaak* with the same four-torpedo spread. *U-155* was last seen in the Caribbean during August when she sank *San Emiliano*.

A heavy price was paid wherever the Red Duster was routed. November 1942 has for long been remembered as the month when sinkings reached their peak; 76 vessels with a tonnage of 474,606. To economise on escorts, homeward-bound merchant vessels were now routed from the Cape of Good Hope westward to the Caribbean. OS convoys outwards for Freetown were suspended; ships bound for West Africa and beyond joined ON (New York) convoys and dispersed in mid Atlantic. The enemy became well aware of these changes.

Losses on the Cape–Caribbean crossing mounted daily. In the five weeks commencing 6 November they included five of Ellermans' *City* fleet; *City of Cairo*, *City of Ripon*, *City of Corinth*, *City of Bath* and *City of Bombay*. Their tonnage was 31,939; some 200 persons perished. The elegant 8,034 ton *Cairo* built during the First World War, was sunk by *U-68* on 6 November in position 23.30S 05.30W. For Commander Karl Friedrich Merten it was his last kill. For those cast adrift, loss of life was heavy: 82 crew and 22 passengers. In her holds was silver bullion now estimated to be worth £20,000,000.

Three boatloads including the ship's master, Captain Rogerson, were rescued by *Clan Alpine*. Adrift for thirteen days there were eleven children, the youngest only thirteen months old; all suffered from thirst, hunger and sunburn and were very weak. The fourth boat containing Lascar seamen, five women and eight children was sighted by *Bendoran*, also after thirteen days. They were in a poor state and had been badly burned by the sun.

The third mate and one other survivor were rescued from a raft by the Brazilian minesweeper *Caravelas* and landed at Pernambuco. Subsequently repatriated by *City of Pretoria* (8,049 grt), they were killed when this vessel was lost with all hands in the North Atlantic on 3 March 1943.

From lifeboat No 1 with 54 aboard only two survived, the chief quartermaster and the ship's steward. Their experience is one that has few equals. Day by day they saw their colleagues die, shipmates and passengers alike. They died from overcrowding, from wounds, thirst and hunger. They alone, together with a young woman passenger, were rescued; rescued on the 36th day by a German blockade runner, the *Rhakotis*. The woman died soon after her rescue and they were then bombed by the RAF and shelled by a British cruiser. Abandoning ship with their German captors, the quarter-master in the port lifeboat was rescued by a U-boat which on 4 January landed him in St Nazaire. Subsequently he was taken as a prisoner to the Milag Nord Camp near Bremen. The steward found

himself in the starboard boat which eventually reached a Spanish
port from where he later got a passage home.

Discipline is probably the one quality which is paramount in
saving life. This is particularly illustrated by the day by day diary
kept by the 22-year-old second mate of John Cory's *Start Point* (5,293
grt) sunk on 10 November, in position 13.12N 27.27W (*U-128*,
Lieutenant-Commander Ulrich Heyse). The most senior officer to
survive, the captain, and chief engineer had been taken prisoner, he
took charge of the two lifeboats, ensuring that they kept together,
navigating, attending the wounded and 'burying' the dead. They
were adrift for thirteen days.

The rescue of a Chinese steward after 133 days on a raft is one of
the most remarkable in the records of survival after shipwreck. He
was the only survivor from Ben Line's *Benlomond* (6,630 grt, Captain
Maul), another casualty on the westward route from Cape Town.
Torpedoed by *U-172* on 23 November, 24 British and 22 Chinese
crew were taken down with their ship. The steward lived partly on
provisions stowed on the raft and partly on fish and seagulls which he
occasionally caught. Picked up by a Brazilian fisherman he was
taken to hospital in Belem.

The feat of the *Benlomond* steward is in fact surpassed by two
survivors from the 7,128 ton *Fort Longueuil* (James Chambers & Co.,
Captain Edwards). Torpedoed and sunk by *U-532* south of Chagos
Island (Indian Ocean) on 19 September 1943, their raft landed them
on a beach in Sumatra, 134 days later. They were taken prisoner by
the Japanese.

Wintry gales in December 1942 in the North East Trades brought
heavy casualties. *Ceramic*, *Henry Stanley* and *Peter Maersk* are just three
ships whose names head a long list of personnel on the Merchant
Navy War Memorial at Tower Hill in London. Sunk within four
hours of each other during the night of 6/7 December, they were
following their independently routed course west of the Azores.

Because of the storm which blew up the following morning, all
those who got away in the lifeboats from *Henry Stanley* and *Peter
Maersk* were lost, their frail craft overwhelmed by the high seas and
force 10 wind. Rescue ships at St Michaels were unable to put to sea
because of the weather. From the 272 crew and 378 passengers on
board the much loved *Ceramic* (18,713 grt) there was only one
survivor.

Ceramic was carrying bombs and ammunition in two of her holds
and was bound for the Middle East. The survivor, a sapper of the
Royal Engineers, was taken prisoner aboard *U-515* (Lieutenant

Werner Henke). Captain Jones, master of Elder Dempster's 5,025 ton *Henry Stanley* – he had been master of his company's *Dixcove* (see page 162) – was also taken prisoner. On 31 December he was landed at Lorient from *U-103* (Lieutenant Gustav-Adolf Janssen), from where he was taken to Milag Nord.

The passage of two Atlantic convoys proved disastrous; SC107, 43 ships which sailed from Halifax on 27 October, and ONS154, 45 merchantmen which sailed from Loch Ewe on 18 December. ONS154 crossed the path of nineteen U-boats; thirteen vessels were lost of which ten were British registered: *Baron Cochrane, Empire Shackleton, Empire Union, Empire Wagtail, King Edward, Lynton Grange, Melmore Head, Melrose Abbey, Ville de Rouen* and *Zarian.* 150 British seamen died. Without the presence of the rescue vessel *Toward*, the loss of life would have been far greater. The Vichy French *Ville de Rouen*, taken as prize by the Royal Navy, was now managed by Alfred Holt & Co.

Eight U-boats trapped convoy SC107 500 miles east of Belle Isle Strait when ten British ships were sunk. It was the familiar pattern of convoy wolf pack warfare. Sighted by Lieutenant-Commander Siegfried V. Forstner (*U-402*) on 1 November, he was also first in at the kill sinking *Dalcroy, Empire Antelope, Empire Leopard* and the Greek *Rinos* between midnight and 0600 hours. He also torpedoed *Empire Sunrise* but she held up for some three hours before being sunk by a coup de grâce from *U-84*. Without the rescue ship *Stockport* there would have been heavy loss of life; falling back astern she saved 149 British seamen and 26 survivors from *Rinos*.

The 5,676 ton *Empire Leopard*, MOWT/Maritime Shipping and Trading Co, which had loaded munitions in Botwood (Newfoundland) for Avonmouth blew up with a devastating roar, illuminating the whole convoy. There were only four survivors, one of whom subsequently died from his injuries. On board ship, 37 crew and seven DEMS gunners lost their lives.

The night of terror continued with J & C. Harrison's 5,496 ton *Hartington*, Halifax for Belfast (24 lives lost) and *Maritima* (5,801 grt) owned by Neill & Pandelis, which had loaded in New York for Glasgow. Thirty of her crew were killed. *Jeypore* (5,318 grt, Peninsular & Oriental Steam Navigation Co. Ltd, torpedoed the following day by *U-89* (Lieutenant-Commander Dietrich Lohmann) burst into flame immediately she was hit and became a furnace from bridge to fo'c'sle; nine of her crew were burnt to death. She started to sink rapidly and twenty minutes later she was abandoned. With her propeller boss out of the water she then sank bow first, the flames being extinguished by the seawater and casting a great cloud of steam over the whole convoy.

As 1942 drew to a close *Queen Mary* forged her way through mountainous seas in mid Atlantic on one of the greatest voyages of her career. Creeping from her Clyde anchorage on Christmas Eve she set out on a 38,000 mile voyage by way of Freetown, Cape Town, the Middle East, Australia and back to Scotland. During her four month voyage she carried 28,990 troops. Together with *Queen Elizabeth* she played no small part in the new Allied offensive. 250,860 United States troops were brought to the United Kingdom in 1942, 153,379 of whom were carried in British troopships. Of these, 129,000 were re-embarked for the invasion of North Africa.

The 'slaughter of '42' sent 646 British vessels to the ocean floor; 3,559,923 tons of shipping. In trained merchant seamen, nearly 8,000 lives. With some 250 U-boats operational and 150 doing trials and training crews, the decisive battles were still to come. In addition, the western ocean raged with all its ferocity. Captain Bone of *Circassia* wrote 'The winter of '42 will long be remembered by sailors for bitter weather in the North Atlantic, the like of which has not been experienced for many years. It was a season of continuous heavy gales which set up the most terrific seas ever seen, even by the most aged of active mariners'.

> Stooping, stumbling, swearing, dull-eyed men
> Slouch in long lines across the slippery deck
> Emerging slowly from their smelly pen–
> Look out there or you'll break your blasted neck! –
> And shamble to a blocked companion-way
> Where drovers wait to urge them up and on,
> While others, from the top, hold them at bay
> Until a thousand more have safely gone.
>
> *H.H. Tilley*

CHAPTER EIGHT

The Storm Abates

(January–December 1943)

At the height of 'the storm' came the crises. With the atrocious weather of January 1943 U-boat operations were reduced. Then came the crises weeks when escorts in greater numbers fought an increasing fleet of enemy underwater craft. At last, in March and April, came the very long range Liberator aircraft. It meant the closure of the mid Atlantic gap some 600 miles south-east of Greenland which, since early 1941 had been 'the graveyard', both of ships and of men.

With the Liberators and more planes operating from escort carriers, the U-boats faced an increasingly difficult task. By May the Germans had lost their grip on the situation, a situation which virtually resulted from the Casablanca Conference in January which laid down that the defeat of the U-boats should be the first charge on the combined Allied resources. At the Atlantic Convoy Conference which followed in Washington a closer understanding of the air problem and a redistribution of available aircraft was brought about.

Speaking on 11 February Winston Churchill said:

> It is, however, a horrible thing to plan ahead in cold blood on the basis of losing thousands of tons a month, even if you can show a favourable balance at the end of a year. The waste of precious cargoes, the destruction of so many noble ships, the loss of heroic crews, all combine to constitute a repulsive and sombre panorama. We cannot possibly rest content with losses on this scale, even though they are outweighed by new building, even if they are for that reason not mortal in their character. . . . A ship not sunk is better than a ship built.

Over Christmas and the New Year there was alarm at the mounting losses off the coast of North Africa. With the sinking of Peninsular & Oriental's *Strathallan* and Hall Bros' *Bretwalda* three days prior to Christmas, sixteen vessels had been lost with a tonnage of 143,346.

In addition ten ships of 81,539 tons had been damaged and withdrawn from service. These were *Cameronia*, *Empire Centaur*, *Forest*, *Glenfinlas*, *Harmattan*, *Hindustan*, *Lalande*, *Ocean Vanquisher*, *Ousel* and *Scythia*.

The 23,722 ton *Strathallan* (Captain Biggs) was commodore ship of convoy KRS5 from the Clyde. Her complement was 5,122 which included 4,000 British and American troops and 250 Queen Alexandra nurses. Breaking the escort screen in the early hours, the sea, flat calm, an unclouded sky with a brilliant moon, was *U-562* (Lieutenant Horst Hamm). The torpedo exploded on the port side of the engine room killing four crew members on watch; immediately *Strathallan* listed to port. First reports seemed to suggest she was not badly damaged and she was taken in tow by HMS *Laforey*; 3,000 troops remained on board as the other personnel were taken off by HMS *Verity*.

At midday *Strathallan* was lower in the water and fire was spreading rapidly. She was then abandoned with a skeleton crew left aboard; *Laforey* and *Panther* attended to the disembarkation. HMS *Restive* then took up the tow ropes and later that afternoon took off Captain Biggs, his chief engineer and a cadet. At 1700 hours, 22 December, *Strathallan* turned over and sank; she was twelve miles from Oran, the fourth P & O liner lost in the six weeks of the North African campaign.

On New Year's Day the Naval Commander, Expeditionary Force, Admiral Sir Andrew Cunningham (Later Admiral of the Fleet, Viscount Cunningham of Hyndhope) sent a message to the officers and men of the Allied merchant vessels. In giving his good wishes he said that when victory came it would be due in no small measure to the courage and tenacity with which the merchant vessels of the Allied nations had kept the sea in face of continued and savage attack. 'Many examples have been brought to my notice of bravery, devotion and skill which has only added to the admiration I already have for the work you have performed.' He added: 'Navy, Army and Air Force alike know how much they depend on your efforts. May success prosper those efforts in the coming years.'

Bône, the main supply base for the First Army since 12 November, was virtually in the front line. Since 27 November 86,053 tons of military cargo had been discharged there. 31,085 personnel and 4,491 vehicles including guns and tanks had been landed from merchant ships. In January there was carnage. On New Year's Day *Novelist* and the *Harpalyce* were both damaged during a bombing raid and on the following day *St Merriel* (4,980 grt, South American Saint

Line Ltd) and the tanker *Empire Metal* (8,201 grt) were destroyed.

St Merriel, under the command of Captain Owens, was discharging 2,500 tons of Welsh coal and 50 tons of coke when she was struck by two bombs. Six crew were killed outright. Blazing furiously, she was of considerable danger to *Dalhanna* and *Melampus* lying alongside; both were severely damaged. On board British Tankers' *Empire Metal*, her master, Captain Shaw, and five of his crew lay dead. Due to temporary enemy air supremacy the port was under attack 24 hours a day, port facilities were heavily damaged necessitating ships having to discharge cargo with their own lifting gear. Crews abandoned ship in the evenings and slept ashore on the jetty and even in the harbour lighthouse.

Coastal convoys carrying military supplies between Algiers and Bône became a constant target for enemy aircraft. Sunk were *Benalbanach* and *Hampton Lodge*; among those damaged were the 7,178 ton *Ocean Rider* and the 7,135 ton *Fort Babine*. The Ben Line steamer *Benalbanach* (7,153 grt, Captain Macgregor) had already performed valiant service forming part of the North African invasion fleet. She was the first ship in the Oran section to land troops and equipment on the beaches. Now on her second voyage to the war zone she was cruelly attacked by a lone bomber during the evening of 7 January.

Carrying a crew of 74, *Benalbanach* was loaded with explosives, ammunition, petrol and stores, motor vehicles and tanks. She also had on board three naval signallers, six army officers, nine staff sergeants and 357 other ranks. In position 37.07N 04.38E two aerial torpedoes pierced her hull with devastating effect. There were heavy explosions, the air was black with fumes, dust and debris.

Benalbanach began to sink rapidly by the stern. With the seas breaking over her deck amidships, with her bow rising out of the water forward, it was impossible to launch the lifeboats. With a great hissing of air and the terrible noise of crashing vehicles in her holds, she disappeared in less than two minutes. There were only 40 survivors. Captain Macgregor was not among them.

Far out into the Atlantic, convoy TMI, comprised mostly of tankers, was proceeding from Trinidad, eastwards towards North Africa. The armed forces depended upon its arrival; U-boat Command realizing its importance pursued it over nine days from as far west as longitude 45 to within 850 miles of Gibraltar. Eight U-boats were employed; fourteen vessels were sunk, all tankers apart from three American freighters. Three of the tankers lost were owned by British Tankers Ltd.

 3 January *British Vigilance* 8,093 grt. (Captain Evans) 27 crew killed.
 8 January *Oltenia 11* 6,394 grt. Captain Ladle and 16 crew killed.
11 January *British Dominion* 6,983 grt. (Captain Millar) 38
                        crew killed.

Also torpedoed and sunk was the tanker *Empire Lytton* (9,807 grt, MOWT, managed by Messrs Harris & Dixon). She was carrying 12,500 tons of benzine from Curaçao and lost thirteen of her crew and one gunner.

The weather during this terrible winter has already been mentioned. The overwhelming of the commodore ship of convoy ONS160 on 24 January is just one example of its ferocity. In the northern latitudes, with freezing spray endangering the stability of many of the labouring merchantmen, the 6,276 grt *Ville de Tamatave* (Captain Dault) sank with all hands with little or no warning. An ex-French vessel she was managed by Alfred Holt & Co Ltd. Among those drowned was Admiral Sir H.J. Studholme Brownrigg, KBE, CB, DSO, the most senior officer on either side to be killed on active service. He was one of 21 convoy commodores who died during the war.

Position 24.59N 43.37W is just about as far away from land as it is possible to get in the North Atlantic, 1,200 miles in fact. It was here on 3 February 1943 that the 7,957 ton *Rhexenor* (Alfred Holt & Co. Ltd, Captain Eccles (Freetown for St John, New Brunswick) was torpedoed by *U-217*. Her loss is another lifeboat saga; the seamanship and strength of her officers and senior ratings enabled every one of her crew to reach friendly shores. Every one, that is, except the fourth mate. He was taken prisoner by Lieutenant Kurt Reichenbach-Klinke who was on his way home from the Caribbean.

The four boats which had been successfully launched set sail west-south-west for the West Indies. On the second day of the third week the second steward, who was in No 3 boat with sixteen shipmates, wrote in his diary, 'getting dizzy spells now, especially when moving about after rest'. The following day he adds:

> Boys getting more argumentative, less conversation, on watch, off watch; sleep except mealtimes, majority sleeping fifteen hours daily. Second Mate says we have 390 miles to go, not allowing for being off course. Must be doing sixty miles a day. All hoping for a ship this weekend. Had 8 ozs of water for breakfast, 2 ozs for lunch, hunger not bothering me, although wasting away like everyone else, the vitamin foods just about keep one going, no fat left now to live off. Making 2 knots.

(*Left*) 'He's the type the Merchant Navy needs'. Apprentice John M. Slader. *The Daily Mirror*. Wednesday 27 October 1943. (*Right*) The Eyes of the Convoy. Without air cover the merchant ships were doomed. It was this, more than anything else, that finally defeated the U-boats.

New York. February 1944. Identity Cards were necessary for all merchant seamen who wished to go ashore in New York.

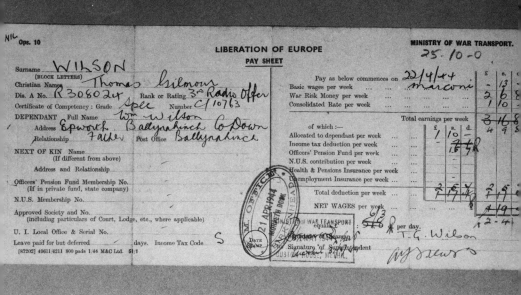

(*Above*) Liberation of Europe 1944. The first week's pay of the Third Radio Officer, SS *Fort Gibraltar*, commenced on 22 April 1944. This was over six weeks before D Day.

(*Left*) 'Heaving the Lead'. Young merchant seamen under training at the Royal Navy's shore establishment, HMS *Gordon*. Here in the school motor launch the seamen undergo practice in steering and taking soundings.

February 19 Passed a fair night, suffering from nightmares and bad dreams, mental state now very disturbed. Long shower this morning, all had good drink, made us notice our hunger. Head rather muzzy and thick, feel very weak.

February 20 Fair breeze, one shower this morning not enought to collect any water since all the rain I drank yesterday my hunger has not been appeased, am now hungry and thirsty, 250 miles to go. How dirty I feel, my underwear is almost black. . . my teeth and mouth indescribable.

They were not sighted until 24 February. Picked up by the American *Conqueror* they were landed in St Thomas, Virgin Islands. It was an epic 21 days. 1,236 miles in an open boat; a remarkable sailing time.

What of the other boats? No 1 with Captain Eccles and nineteen men landed in Guadeloupe after eighteen days. No 4 with the chief mate in charge and whose complement was seventeen was towed into St John's Antigua after nineteen days. The fourth boat (No 5) with the third mate and seventeen crewmen anchored off Jost van Dyke island in the Tobago Group having taken twenty days.

Worth noting is another astonishing story of 'men alone against the sea'. Of the fourteen crew who survived the sinking of the *Lulworth Hill* (7,628 grt, Counties Ship Management Co Ltd) in the South Atlantic on 19 March 1943, only two, a carpenter and an AB, lived to tell their story. Yet they survived on a raft for fifty days before they were sighted 400 miles south of Liberia by the destroyer *Rapid*. On the 29th day their families had been informed that the *Lulworth Hill* must be presumed lost with all hands.

On the day that the Germans were turned back at Stalingrad (2 February) the 64 ships and twelve escorts of convoy SC118 passed north of latitude 50 on its passage homewards from New York. There was a heavy sea running and because of this the convoy occupied an area of some 52 square miles which greatly increased the work of the escort vessels. The weather also restricted the use of the VLR Liberator aircraft based in Iceland although incredible feats of navigation enabled planes from Northern Ireland to give daylight air escort.

By 8 February however the convoy was in a sorry state. Sighted and reported by *U-187*, in position 53.00N 33.00W, sixteen U-boats were called to the attack by U-boat headquarters from a reported sixty in the area. Eleven merchantmen were sunk, Siegfried Von Forstner (*U-402*) being awarded the Knight's Cross for raising his total score to over 100,000 tons. The enemy however did not have it all their own way and Dönitz recorded it as the hardest convoy battle of the whole war.

During the night of 6/7 February Von Forstner slipped into the convoy's ranks sinking two ships in quick succession, one of them the 1,571 ton rescue vessel *Toward* (Clyde Shipping Company). Her master, Captain Hudson, 57 crew, eleven gunners, a naval surgeon and sick bay attendant, together with a signalman and two men transferred from other ships, all perished.

An hour later *U-402* torpedoed and sank the Norwegian *Daghild* carrying LCT No 2335 (Landing Craft Tank) as deck cargo. The 143 ton landing craft, of which many crossed the Atlantic as deck cargo, was one of the most difficult feats of cargo handling. At dawn Von Forstner sank East Asiatic Company's *Afrika* (8,597 grt) sailing under the British flag and then followed this up with the American trooper *Henry R. Mallory* and the Greek *Kalliopi*. Gowland Steamship's 5,730 ton *Harmala*, homeward on the long haul from Rio de Janeiro, was also sunk (by *U-614*) during the same night. Forty of her complement of 64 were lost. On the following day it was the turn of C. Strubin & Company's *Newton Ash* (4,625 grt). Loaded with grain, St John, New Brunswick for Hull, she also was sunk by *U-402*. There were only four survivors from a crew of 38 and five gunners.

Even on arrival off British coasts, merchant ship crews were still unable to relax. E-boats were particularly troublesome in November and December 1942; during a coastwise convoy attack on 12 December off Lowestoft, *Avonwood*, *Glen Tilt*, *Knitsley* and *Lindisfarne* were sunk. Now, on 27 February, fourteen miles east of Berry Head in the English Channel, the 4,858 ton motorship *Modavia* was torpedoed and sunk together with an LCT and two escort vessels, the trawler *Lord Hailsham* and the whaler *Harstad*.

There was another rescue ship tragedy towards the end of the month. Rescue ships, by their size and build were easily identified although they were not marked as such. But this was war and the enemy was becoming desperate for a kill. Outward convoy ON166 was only making 4 knots as its 63 ships with a large escort ploughed through heavy seas on 22 February, there were many stragglers. Fourteen vessels, more than 85,000 tons, were lost during a five day battle. They included *Empire Trader*, *Empire Redshank*, *Eulima*, *Manchester Merchant*, and the rescue vessel *Stockport*.

Torpedoed by *U-604* (Lieutenant Horst Höltring) the 1,683 ton *Stockport*, built in 1911 for the London and North Eastern Railway Co., fell behind to rescue survivors from *Empire Trader*. All hands were lost, her crew of 51, nine gunners, four naval personnel and 91 survivors she had on board.

Following the suspension of sailings to Northern Russia after the despatch of convoy JW53 (15 February) more valuable escort vessels were released for the mid-Atlantic battles. Primarily this suspension was due to the onset of summer daylight and the presence of German capital ships in Norway though the lack of merchant ships and the continuing wintry weather were additional reasons. Sailings were not resumed until November 1943 though imports were secretly being delivered via Persian Gulf ports. It was through Iran that military equipment was supplied during 1942 and which helped to defeat the German Army at Stalingrad.

During March 1943 there were 116 U-boats at sea. The United Kingdom was now consuming 750,000 tons more goods than imported and this could not be allowed to continue. It was not so much food but oil and military supplies. The invasion of Europe's 'underbelly' was at stake; the landings on the beaches of Normandy had secretly already reached an advanced planning stage. It was in 1943 that General Eisenhower was appointed supreme commander.

Now came a whole series of great convoy battles. SC121 (61 ships) sailed from New York on 23 February. Thirty-four U-boats lay in wait north-east of Newfoundland, later a further six were called up. For five days commencing during the night of 6/7 March the battle raged; from longitude 38 West to longitude 21 West. It was fought in extraordinary bad weather, a force 10 storm, blinding snow blizzards, hail and rain. Twelve ships were sunk of which eight were British; *Egyptian*, *Empire Impala*, *Empire Lakeland*, *Fort Lamy*, *Guido*, *Leadgate*, *Nailsea Court*, and the tanker *Rosewood*. The 3,670 ton *Coulmore* was seriously damaged but was able to make port under her own steam. The commodore ship, the Norwegian *Bonneville*, was lost with all hands, including Commodore Captain Burnie, DSO, RD, RNR.

Bonneville was carrying a 143 ton tank landing craft on deck as was John Cory's *Fort Lamy* (5,242 grt), which had recently been delivered from her Canadian builders. Also carrying TNT in the forward holds she blew up and there were only three survivors. *Empire Impala* (6,116 grt, managed by the Sun Shipping Company) fell back from the convoy to rescue survivors from the stricken 2,868 ton *Egyptian*, only to be torpedoed herself. Only three escaped alive. The 7,015 ton *Empire Lakeland*, Blue Star Line, staggered from the convoy during the evening of 8 March and was never seen again. Waiting astern was Lieutenant Max Wintermeyer (*U-190*) who claimed her destruction in 58.00N 15.00W. Other vessels in which all hands perished were Consett Iron Company's 2,125 ton *Leadgate* and the 5,989 ton *Rosewood*, owned by Oil & Molasses Tankers.

In the middle watch action of 10 March against *Coulmore* and *Nailsea Court*, *U-229* (Lieutenant J.G. Robert Schetelig) surfaced and fired at point blank range. Nailsea Shipping Company's 4,946 ton flagship exploded amidships killing her master, Captain Lee, the company chairman's nephew, articled as an apprentice, and 42 others. There were only three survivors.

Probably more merchant seamen were lost during the SC121 action than from any other convoy assault during the whole war. Even some of the survivors did not reach port. Fifty seamen rescued by HMS *Harvester* lost their lives when the destroyer herself was torpedoed. At the time *Harvester* had been called to escort HX228 which had also come under attack.

During March, convoys were resumed to and from Freetown. Eager to take advantage of the better weather that the north-east trade winds offered, the enemy struck against OS44. Gelhaus in *U-107* achieved remarkable success in torpedoing and sinking four vessels with a five-torpedo spread though *Clan Alpine* had subsequently to be sunk by one of the escort vessels.

Position 42.45N 13.31W became the graveyard of *Clan Alpine*, *Oporto*, the Dutch *Sembilangau* and the 4,592 ton *Marcella*, Kaye Transport Co., whose master, Captain Downie and her entire crew of 34 together with nine gunners perished. Cayzer Irvine & Co's 5,442 ton *Clan Alpine* (Captain Crellin) lost 26 of her crew, the remainder were picked up by the sloop *Scarborough*.

The following convoy, OS45, sailed from the Clyde on 20 March. It was escorted by HMS *Black Swan* and seven corvettes. Thirteen days later, in position 41.02N 15.39W, after a long detour into mid-Atlantic, the 5,190 ton *Gogra* and the Henderson Line *Katha* (4,357 grt), following astern, were both sunk in the blackness of the night. It was a surprise attack by Lieutenant-Commander Mohr, Knight's Cross with Oak Leaves (*U-124*), who shortly after was depth-charged and sunk by *Black Swan*. For Mohr it was the end of an illustrious naval career.

The British India Company's *Gogra* (Captain Drummond) illuminated by a tremendous white flash which extended in an arc from bow to stern and was as high as the mast, started to break up immediately. Some fifteen men struggled in the water shouting for help and blowing their lifejacket whistles but the convoy passed on; some died within the hour. Only *Katha*, in similar circumstances and with her stern well down, crippled and sinking, was in the immediate vicinity. Several hours later *Black Swan* plucked 38 from the water. They were holding on to pieces of debris.

The homeward-bound 9-knot convoy SL126 of forty ships sailed from Freetown on 17 March; it was the first direct convoy from Sierra Leone since the near destruction of SL125, five months before. Twelve days later, 425 miles north-west of Cape Finisterre, four merchantmen, all flying the red ensign, were lost – Royal Mail's *Nagara*, British India's *Umaria*, *Empire Whale* and *Empire Bowman*.

Nagara (8,791 grt, Captain Cooper, ex *Lochkatrine* (see page 218), was carrying a full cargo of Argentinian beef. Torpedoed by *U-404* (Lieutenant-Commander Otto von Bülow), she was later taken in tow but was so badly damaged that she sank on 5 April. Another Royal Mail meat carrier, the *Nariva* (8,714 grt, Captain Dodds) routed via New York was sunk by *U-90* during the wolf pack assault on convoy HX229, 17 March. These were serious losses for the traditional Sunday dinner table.

The 6,852 ton *Umaria* (sunk by *U-662*, Lieutenant Heinz Eberhard Müller) which left her builder's yard on Boxing Day 1941 was loaded with manganese ore, coir products, tea and rubber from Ceylon. She listed instantly the torpedo struck. By the time SL126 had been summoned to an emergency 90 degree turn to port, *Umaria* was well down by the head. She continued under way however until a second torpedo put her bows under with her propeller almost out of the water. She ploughed under as her crew took to the boats. Rescue was made by HMS *Wear*.

The period 16–20 March saw the largest battle of all. In the atrocious weather of the northern latitudes three homeward convoys sailed in close proximity to one another. They were SC122, HX229 and HX229A. In their path lay 44 U-boats. Twenty-three merchant ships of 146,000 tons were sunk; ten of them were British.

The three convoys totalling 129 ships sailed from New York over a period of four days. Following the great circle track north-east of Nova Scotia, SC122 was buffeted by force 11 storms, sub zero temperatures, snowstorms and 40-foot waves. Several ships were damaged by ice and the 14,795 ton tanker, *Svend Foyn*, plunged to the bottom after striking an iceberg. Even today mystery surrounds the fate of Evan Thomas Radcliffe's 28-year-old *Clarissa Radcliffe* (5,754 grt). She was heavily laden with iron ore, a crew of 41 with ten gunners and one sick British seaman being repatriated. Drifting out of sight she was never seen again. Was she sunk by *U-663* on 18 March or did she break up, overwhelmed by the storm?

From 34 West to 32 West lie the remains of *Canadian Star*, *Coracero*, *Fort Cedar Lake*, *King Gruffydd*, *Kingsbury*, *Nariva*, *Port Auckland*, *Southern Princess* and *Zouave*. Lieutenant Manfred Kinzel, commander of *U-338*, on his first war patrol, was the most successful of the attacking force. Breaking through the escort screen of SC122, (16/17 March) position 51.55N 32.41W, he torpedoed four vessels simultaneously, three of them sinking within minutes.

Captain Griffiths of King Line's *King Gruffydd* (5,072 grt) was killed on his bridge; 23 were subsequently posted as missing. The survivors together with those from Alexander Shipping Co's *Kingsbury* (4,898 grt), *Fort Cedar Lake* and the Dutch *Alderamin*, 134 in total, were picked up by the rescue vessel *Zamalek*; three died as they were brought aboard.

Later the same night, in convoy HX229, the whale oil refinery ship *Southern Princess* (12,156 grt, Captain Nillsen) was sunk by *U-600* (Lieutenant Bernhard Zurmühlen). Carrying 10,053 tons of heavy fuel oil, all but two of her crew and two passengers abandoned ship. Later the survivors were rescued by New Zealand Shipping Co.'s *Tekoa* which, at great risk to herself, fell back from the convoy.

Captain Millar of Blue Star's motorship *Canadian Star* (8,293 grt) lost his life when she was torpedoed during the afternoon of 18 March. Carrying a crew of 69 and 22 passengers, a refrigerated and general cargo in her holds, she was being tossed about by a full north-westerly gale. Fresh from his triumph against convoy HX228, Lieutenant Hans Trojer (*U-221*) fired two torpedoes which wrecked *Canadian Star* amidships. She settled rapidly by the stern with great seas breaking overall.

Two boats and a raft got away but *Canadian Star* sank within fifteen minutes. Twenty-four crew and nine passengers were missing. Captain Millar, when last seen, was concerned only with the safety and welfare of his crew and passengers. In the words of Winston Churchill this was a war 'of groping and drowning, of ambuscade and stratagem, of science and seamanship.'

Nearly two-thirds of the ships sunk during March 1943 were in convoy. For a time this seriously shook the Admiralty's faith in the whole convoy system. Even at this date it was by no means certain that the Allies were on the point of winning the battle.

With the battle of the supply lines at its peak, both in the Atlantic and the Mediterranean, the Indian Ocean was a forgotten theatre. During March and April a total of eighteen ships of 116,102 tons were sunk. Eleven of them were British.

It was on 18 April, 500 miles due east of Port Elizabeth that the Anglo-Saxon motor tanker *Corbis* (8,132 grt, commanded by Captain Appleton) was sunk by *U-180*. It was still dark, 0400 hours, as Commander Werner Musenberg fired two torpedoes, in quick succession. Some ten minutes later a third torpedo struck; the high octane cargo was set alight in a flash. Captain Appleton and many of his crew jumped overboard there to be covered in oil and surrounded by the blazing sea. They were never seen again.

One lifeboat got away after a near disaster when the falls jammed upon lowering; an attempt was made to chop them through simultaneously but one was released before the other and the boat nose-dived to the water, throwing its occupants out. Fortunately the boat was afterwards righted and 32, including the chief engineer and the second mate, clambered aboard. *Corbis* was now on her beam ends, the sea, for two square miles around, was ablaze. Flames reached high into the sky. It had not been possible to send any distress message. A second lifeboat engulfed in the flames blazed furiously; there was no escape for those aboard.

As the sun rose above the horizon the 32 survivors for ever superstitious in the seafaring tradition, noticed a white albatross dead in the sea. She was one of a pair which had been following the vessel for three days and had evidently been killed by the explosions. The brown male bird, whom the crew named 'Captain Brown', remained with the boat through calm and storm until rescue came. A strong bond of friendship has always existed between the albatross and the mariner.

After ten days of deteriorating weather the boat met disaster. Four times during 24 hours the boat overturned. Each time men were lost until there were only fourteen. Each time 'Captain Brown' swam in the sea with them and seemed pleased when the boat was righted. Two days later only eight survivors remained. All the oars had been lost as had most of the rations – a few Horlicks tablets, some beef extract and a little water was all that was left. On the thirteenth day land was seen on the horizon and 24 hours later they were sighted by an aircraft. A rescue launch which put out from the coast brought them to safety.

The Atlantic battle now moved in favour of the Allies. Convoy HX231 of 61 vessels sailed from New York on 25 March led by Commodore Admiral Sir Charles Ramsey flying his flag in the 'Blue Funnel' steamer *Tyndareus*. It was a typical convoy of the 1943 period: 36 British, fourteen American, six Norwegian, three Dutch, one Swede and one Panamanian. Of these vessels, 22 were tankers. Of the 600,000 tons of cargo, 523,000 tons arrived safely. Sighted by

Lieutenant Kurt Lange, *U-530*, on the eighth day, twenty submarines were called up. The attack raged for 48 hours; six vessels were sunk.

The battle which was fought under difficult conditions was opened by Lieutenant J.G. Heinz Eckelmann (*U-635*) when he torpedoed Peninsular & Oriental's 5,529 grt cargo ship *Shillong* during the night of 3/4 April. Ninety minutes later, British India's *Waroonga* (9,365 grt), commanded by Captain Taylor and carrying 11,000 tons of New Zealand butter and cheese was struck; her chief mate and thirteen men were drowned after their lifeboat overturned in the high seas. The enemy was *U-630* (Lieutenant J.G. Werner Winkler) which, together with *U-635*, was on its first war cruise. Both were depth-charged and sunk later in the day.

Lashed by the heavy storm, *Shillong* (Captain Hollow) loaded with over 4,000 tons of zinc and some 3,000 tons of wheat, had only just rejoined the convoy. For a time, after the mainmast snapped above the cross-trees, she had been hove to. Her two port lifeboats were iced up, the davits bending under the weight of ice and rendered useless; two rafts had carried away. All hands turned out to effect repairs and to secure hatches.

There was still half a gale blowing when the torpedo hit the port side, just forward of the boiler room. The chart room and part of the bridge was demolished; by the time No 3 lifeboat was launched she was well down by the head. *Shillong* then shipped 30 foot waves overall, some of her crew were swept overboard, whilst others, jumping towards a raft which had been released, were overwhelmed by the mountainous seas.

After the 1939-built motorship had disappeared those that were still alive huddled together on the raft in the bitter cold. Many, including Captain Hollow, died that night during the remaining hours of darkness. Though they were sighted by one of the escorts, the hunt for the enemy was more important; the convoy went on ahead, they were alone in the wild sea. Struggling aboard a lifeboat which was found empty, the survivors were adrift seven days before being sighted by a Catalina flying boat. Later, they were picked up by the rescue ship *Zamalek*.

Of *Shillong*'s complement of 78 only seven survived. But the immersion in the water had blackened their limbs and made them useless. Three of the seven lost both their legs, the feet of another were amputated, the fifth lost most of his fingers. Only three left hospital with their limbs intact; one of these three had already survived the loss of *Trecarrell*, torpedoed on 4 June 1941 and *Bhutan* sunk by bombing on 14 June 1942.

Two vessels with famous war records were sunk at this time, *Empress of Canada*, the Canadian Pacific liner, and Blue Star Line's *Melbourne Star*. Together with *Canadian Star*, *California Star*, *Celtic Star* and *Empire Lakeland*, a standard wartime-built managed vessel, the Blue Star loss totalled 41,989 tons within four weeks.

Sailing independently homewards via the Cape, the 21,516 ton *Empress of Canada*, in service as a troopship and carrying a crew of 362, was torpedoed by the Italian submarine *Leonardi da Vinci*, Lieutenant-Commander Gianfranco Gazzana-Priaroggia, on 14 March. Her position was 01.13S 09.57W. The 1,528 passengers included many Allied military personnel and 500 Italian prisoners of war. Total loss of life was 392 of which 45 were members of the crew. Rescue was made by HMS *Corinthian*.

Melbourne Star, famous for her successful berthing in Malta after Operation Pedestal was now commanded by Captain Hall, a survivor from *Andalucia Star*. Bound for Sydney via the Panama Canal she carried a crew of 86 and 31 passengers. In her holds were stowed torpedoes, shells, small arms ammunition and a variety of other war cargo.

Buffeted by heavy seas in position 28.05N 57.30W, some 500 miles south-east of Bermuda was *U-129* under the captaincy of Lieutenant-Commander Hans Witt. He was on his way to the American east coast, waters which he knew well. At about 0300 hours on 2 April *Melbourne Star* was struck by two torpedoes simultaneously; her dangerous cargo was detonated and a tremendous white flash shot skywards. Three-quarters of the vessel was destroyed, many were killed asleep in their bunks. There was no distress signal, no lifeboats launched.

What remained of the 12,806 ton *Melbourne Star* disappeared within two minutes. When dawn broke, eleven people were alive on two rafts which had floated off. One of these was never seen again but the second raft drifted for 38 days; the four seamen aboard, augmented their meagre rations with fish which they caught and ate raw. On 9 May they were sighted by an American flying boat which landed on the water and taxied alongside. Within 2½ hours they were landed at Bermuda. The loss of life was 113.

Those who sailed with convoy ONS5 and reached their destination safely, witnessed the last of the great convoy battles. Forty-five vessels flying the flags of nine nations sailed westward through the North Channel on 22 April. Six days later the convoy was sighted and a group of U-boats closed in. Again, the conditions were appalling; heavy seas, snowstorms and poor visibility. By 2 May a full gale was blowing and during the night the ships became scattered over an area of some 30 miles. Some vessels were hove to, others found themselves having to dodge small icebergs and pack-ice. (ONS Convoys were renumbered from March 1943.)

One of the ships which fell behind was *Lorient* (4,737 grt), an ex-French vessel managed by the British Continental Coal and Investments and in ballast for Halifax. Manned by a British crew she was under the command of Captain Manley.

On 6 May the US coastguard cutter *Manhassetts* came across a derelict merchant ship in position 54.04N 44.18W. Nearby were empty lifeboats and fragments of wreckage. The ship's name, as was the custom, had been painted out and the cutter was unable to identify her. This undoubtedly was *Lorient* which *U-125*, Lieutenant Ulrich Folkers, reported torpedoed and sunk in the same position on 4 May. It would appear the lifeboats had been successfully launched but what happened to her 46 crew? No bodies were seen floating in the water. There was no sign of life on board. *Manhassetts* lost sight of the derelict during the night and no trace of her could be found the following day. She was presumed to have sunk.

As the convoy reformed, the 4,635 ton *North Britain*, North Shipping Company, was still six miles astern. It was an opportunity which Lieutenant j.g. Günter Gretschel commanding *U-707*, new from the builder's yard, could not afford to miss. His torpedo virtually broke the Tynesider in two, only eleven of her 42 crew survived. As the armed trawler *Northern Spray* dropped back to the rescue, the main assault developed. Within five hours, five merchantmen were torpedoed – *Harbury*, *Harperley*, *Bristol City*, *Wentworth* and the American *West Maximus*.

National Steamship's *Harbury* (5,081 grt, Captain Cook) loaded with 6,820 tons of Welsh anthracite for St John, New Brunswick was torpedoed by *U-628* (Lieutenant Heinrich Hasenschar). In the grey misty dawn of 5 May, 500 miles south of Cape Farewell, *Northern Spray* again turned to the rescue; seven crew were never accounted for. For the third mate of *Harbury*, this was his fourth loss through enemy action, a 'distinction' reserved for a certain few. After serving in *Hardingham*, mined off the Thames Estuary, 8 June 1940, he joined *Harpasa* and was with her when she was sunk in the Indian Ocean (see page 190). He was again a survivor when *Taksang*, which came to the rescue, was herself sunk.

Harbury's sister ship, the 4,586 ton *Harperley* (Captain Turgoose) with coal and mails for Buenos Aires now 'fell' to two torpedoes fired simultaneously by *U-264* (Lieutenant Hartwig Looks). It was Looks who gave the death blow to *Harbury* some four hours later when she persisted in staying afloat. *Harperley* listed heavily with a gaping hole in the port side through which the water flooded. Lying dead in the wrecked engine-room lay three of her engineers, trapped when the explosion occurred. Captain Turgoose, whose first command it was, had no alternative but to abandon his ship. Altogether eleven of his crew lost their lives.

U-358 (Lieutenant Rolf Manke) now on the surface, raced from astern on the port side; at 18 knots he quickly overhauled *Bristol City* and *Temple Arch*, the remaining ships in the first column. Captain Webb's 1919-built *Bristol City*, a sturdy 2,864 ton 'western ocean' boat built in the British City Line of Steamships own shipyard, had taken the storm in her stride. Carrying China Clay from Fowey with 'generals' in the 'tween decks, she carried a crew of 38, four DEMS and three Marine Regiment gunners.

In position 54.00N 43.55W, *Bristol City* was hit at almost the same time by two torpedoes, one piercing the shell in way of No 2 hold, the other in No 4. The main topmast collapsed, the engine room was immediately flooded. Though she sank in under nine minutes, two serviceable boats got away in good time. Fifteen men lost their lives, some of these being killed by the explosions.

Six minutes later *U-358* struck at *Wentworth* (Captain Phillips) owned by the Dalgleish Steamshipping Company. Though she held up for some twelve hours, eventually she was sunk by *U-628*, with considerable damage. A hole could be seen amidships on the port side some 12 feet across and the funnel lay across the boat deck; the main deck was split amidships the whole width of her beam. The radio room was a shambles whilst the main and emergency aerials were destroyed.

The survivors from the 5,212 ton *Wentworth* (five men were killed) and those from *Bristol City* were picked up by the corvette *Loosestrife*; on her way to St John's Newfoundland was *Northern Spray*, loaded to the gunwales with another 143 survivors. But the battle was far from over. ONS5 lost a total of twelve merchant ships, three of them American and nine British. They included *Dolius*, *Gharinda* and *Selvistan*.

A work of this nature allows little space for relating the experiences of the submarines as they were hounded by the escorts, hunted by the new 10-centimetre radar, depth-charged and rammed, bombed and depth-charged by the increasing numbers of the VLR 4-engined Liberator aircraft. As each week passed, as the defence forces slowly gained the upper hand, more and more U-boats were sunk; the total was 41 during May 1943; the death toll amongst Dönitz's submariners mounted alarmingly.

It was at this point that Dönitz temporarily withdrew his boats. As Admiral Dönitz wrote in his Memoirs:

> Wolf-pack operations against convoys in the North Atlantic, the main theatre of operations, were no longer possible. They could only be resumed if we succeeded in radically increasing the fighting power of the U-boats. This was the logical conclusion to which I came, and I accordingly withdrew the boats from the North Atlantic – we had lost the Battle of the Atlantic.

The defeat of the enemy at this stage meant that the campaign in the Mediterranean and above all, the Normandy landings in 1944, could be conducted without serious interference. It also coincided with the surrender of Axis forces in North Africa on 12 May which in turn led to the opening up of the Mediterranean to through convoys. Seven days later the first convoy to reach Malta unopposed arrived in Valetta harbour. By 7 June minesweepers had cleared a passage through to Alexandria, so shortening the distance between the United Kingdom and Egypt by about 6,000 miles.

Through their work behind the front line, the Merchant Navy now became known as 'the fourth service'. On 1 March 1943 Lord Leathers, Ministry of War Transport said:

> The volume of shipping engaged on military operations has increased and is increasing and we are now more seriously short of shipping than at any previous stage of the war. Merchant ships, carrying troops and equipment actually sail into the battle line. Merchant shipping has become a fourth service so far as major combined operations are concerned.

The battle of the supply routes was the one upon which all other battles depended.

The operation of 'the service' in the North African landings was unparalled. Eleven million tons of Allied merchant shipping entered the ports of North Africa and Casablanca. In the period December 1942–May 1943 over 1,000 ships sailed from the United Kingdom alone; liners, tankers, tramps, colliers and coasters. Amongst other stores, they carried 394 aircraft, 63,784 vehicles, 901 tanks, 3,677 guns, six heavy locomotives and tenders. Cased petrol, 239,796 tons, bulk oil, 67,188 tons, coal 345,713 tons. There was also 450 million cigarettes, 9 million bars of chocolate, 500,000 lbs of soap, 7,000 tons of barbed wire and 71,000 bags of mail. Only 2.16 per cent of the total tonnage of escorted ships was lost during the campaign.

The Mediterranean in early spring however was not without its risks. U-boats and enemy aircraft made renewed efforts; the names of sunken ships are still remembered in these waters: *City of Guildford, City of Perth, Dafila, Empire Banner, Empire Standard, Empire Webster, Fort à la Corne, Hadleigh, Kaying, Merchant Prince, Ocean Seaman* and *Windsor Castle*. There were those sunk on the supply route from the United Kingdom – *Baltonia, Empire Mordred, Empire Tower, Fidra, Fort Battle River, Ger-y-Bryn* and *Mary Slessor*.

The 19,141 ton *Windsor Castle*, Captain Brown, was hit by a torpedo from a German aircraft on 23 March, 110 miles north-west of Algiers. The Union Castle liner was in convoy with more than 2,000 troops on board when at 0230 hours, with a calm sea and a bright moon, she was struck. After twenty minutes, Captain Brown abandoned ship but he, together with 35 officers remained in the hope that she could be taken in tow by two destroyers. After twelve hours all hope was given up and at 1720 hours her bow nosed up, slowly she slid stern first beneath the sea. The only casualty was one member of the crew killed.

At this time, from the other side of the world, some 12,000 miles distant, came news that Alfred Holt's 3,222 ton motorship *Centaur*, Captain Murray, had been sunk by the Japanese Navy off the east coast of Australia. A dastardly crime, *Centaur*, serving as a hospital ship was fully illuminated with her Red Cross lights when she was wantonly attacked during the night of 14 May. The submarine was *I-177* (Lieutenant Commander H. Nakagawa). The ship sank in less than three minutes, no distress signal could be sent, no boats could be launched; only rafts and some hatch boards gave the necessary buoyancy to save life. Of the 335 persons on board, including crew, nursing staff and military personnel, only one nurse and 63 men were saved.

Yet Winston Churchill had every confidence. Addressing the US Congress the following week he said:

> While I rate the U-boat danger as still the greatest we have to face, I have a good and sober confidence that it will not only be met and contained, but overcome. The increase of shipping tonnage over sinkings provides, after the movement of vital supplies of food and munitions has been arranged, that margin which is the main measure of our joint war effort.

Four months later, in September 1943, he praised those mariners who, in his view, were making such a great contribution towards the successful conclusion of the war.

> I cannot pass from this subject (the U-boat warfare) without paying tribute once more to the officers and men of the Merchant Navy whose losses have been greater in proportion than those even of the Royal Navy. We never call upon them in vain and we are confident that they will continue to play their part in carrying our men and their munitions to any place that may be required and under whatever conditions may exist at the time.

On 10 July the Allies invaded Sicily. Code-named Operation Husky it was the greatest seaborne force ever embarked at that time. A miracle of combined operations, 160,000 men, their equipment and stores were brought ashore; 155 British and 66 American troopers and freighters were employed. There were 14,000 vehicles, 600 tanks, 1,800 guns. Some 2,500 self-propelled landing craft took part. Air cover was provided by over 3,000 aircraft. Convoys sailed from the United Kingdom and the USA, from Alexandria and from Algiers, Bizerta, Oran and Tripoli. On the forenoon of 9 July they merged south of Malta to spearhead the operation.

The invasion was led by some of the great names of the British merchant fleet; *Almanzora, Ascania, Circassia, Derbyshire, Duchess of Bedford, Dunera, Durban Castle, Llangibby Castle, Monarch of Bermuda, Otranto, Orontes, Reina del Pacifico, Strathnaver, Winchester Castle.* There were those ships taken over by the Royal Navy though many of their crew were Red Duster men; *Glengyle, Keren, Princess Beatrix, Queen Emma, Royal Scotsman, Royal Ulsterman.* There were four hospital ships from British India's Company's fleet; *Amra, Tairea, Vita* and *Talambra*; the latter were bombed and sunk off the beaches on 10 July.

In a letter addressed to masters of Allied merchant ships Rear Admiral Sir Philip Vian said 'a great part of its success [of Operation Husky] is entrusted to the well-proved steadfastness and seamanlike skill of the Merchant Navies of the Allies whom I am proud to have under my command in this momentous task'.

Sicily showed, as did the Battle of the Atlantic, the convoys to Malta and Northern Russia and every other maritime operation in which the two sea services were engaged that in war, the navies and merchant navies were interdependent and indivisible. The merchant seamen were not mere transporters of men and material but fighting seamen giving the same service as, and often enduring greater risks and hardships than, those in many of the warships. Without the crushing weight of sea power built up in merchantmen of all types as well as warships, the Axis powers could never have been driven from North Africa and Sicily could not have been invaded.

Convoy KMS18B of nineteen ships sailed under sealed orders from the Clyde on 24 June. After entering the Mediterranean three vessels were lost, *St Essylt* and *City of Venice* to *U-375* on 4 July and the commodore ship, Lamport & Holt's *Devis* (6,054 grt, Captain Denson) to *U-593* the following day.

Ellerman's 8,762 ton *City of Venice* (Captain Wyper) was well known in the battle area. In November 1942 she was at Philippeville; in December and again in January at Algiers. In February she returned to Algiers for the third time. Now, loaded with military vehicles, stores and equipment for the 'underbelly' of Europe, she fell victim to the enemy. Ten miles north of Cape Tenez (Algeria) Lieutenant Jürgen Köenkamp gave his command. The torpedo ripped through the starboard side of No 2 hold hurling beams and hatches aloft; the fore part of the bridge structure was badly damaged, No 1 lifeboat was destroyed.

Immediately *City of Venice* began to settle by the head, first listing to starboard and then righting herself. 26 feet of water was reported in No 3 hold and a fierce fire quickly got out of control in No 2 and No 2 'tween decks. Heat and smoke were intense; there were frequent explosions from petrol and ammunition in No 1. Nothing could be done to save her.

The 302 military personnel which the City Line vessel carried plus her crew of 180 abandoned ship in an orderly fashion; boats and rafts were lowered without panic. Then came disaster. In the failing light of the evening, with a moderate sea running, the frigate *Teviot* came to the rescue but in doing so she fouled and capsized No 8 boat, throwing the occupants into the water. Twenty-two persons including Captain Wyper, ten members of his crew and the major in charge of the troops were never seen again. It was over eight hours later that *City of Venice*, on fire fore and aft, sank beneath the sea. The 460 survivors were picked up by the corvettes *Honeysuckle* and *Rhodedendron* and HM Tug *Restive*.

During 20 to 27 July the Luftwaffe counter-attacked with heavy raids on shipping at Augusta and Syracuse. On the night of 20/21 July at Augusta the Heinkel 111's together with some 3-engined SM79 Italian heavy bombers came in low from the sea creating great havoc in the dock area. *Fort Pelly* (7,131 grt, MOWT managed by Sir

R. Ropner & Co.), discharging ammunition alongside the quay, received several direct hits. She blew up leaving four of her officers and 34 crew dead; many were injured. *Empire Florizel* (7,056 grt, J. & C. Harrison Ltd), which arrived in convoy from Bizerta the previous day, was hit by two bombs and exploded amidst a sheet of flame. She burned for several hours. *Ocean Vulture* (7,174 grt) lying at anchor received a near miss and was severely damaged.

Lying close to *Empire Florizel* was *Empire Moon* (7,472 grt, Captain Thomas) managed by Haldin & Phillipps Ltd. The sound of four-gallon cans of petrol exploding as they floated in the harbour is still an abiding memory for those young seamen who stood by and watched helplessly. The following day the merchant ships from Bizerta retreated; *Empire Moon* received instructions to divert to Malta.

Alas! *Empire Moon* was torpedoed by *U-81*, only hours after weighing anchor. Lieutenant j.g. Johann Otto Krieg, active in the Mediterranean for over six months, was lying in wait off Cape Passero, the south-eastern tip of Sicily. Listing heavily to port, *Empire Moon* was abandoned, the crew being rescued by a corvette which stood by. After two hours she was reboarded and with the assistance of a tug brought into Syracuse Harbour. There she settled on the bottom to become a total loss but not before her coal cargo was discharged, to be used as bunkers for the coal-burning minesweepers. The Yorkshire coal, loaded at Immingham, had been on board eight weeks, most of the time in North African ports awaiting instructions.

Syracuse suffered the most savage bombing raid of the Sicilian campaign on the night of 27 July. The Ju88's and FW190's came in two waves doing much damage in the port area. The 4,950 ton motorship *Fishpool* (Captain Cole, Pool Shipping Co), carrying 4,000 tons of munitions and 1,000 tons of aviation spirit in drums was set on fire. Within ten minutes she blew up and sank leaving her captain, 27 crew and several soldiers dead; many were wounded. *Fishpool* was an unlucky ship; she was bombed off Scotland on 14 November 1940 while on her maiden voyage. After some five months under repair on the Clyde she was bombed again (9 May 1941) whilst loading at Barrow and still on her maiden voyage.

The Luftwaffe were active in other areas. There were many casualties as the 4-engined FW200, the 'scourge of the Atlantic' as Churchill called it, returned to waters west of Portugal, longitude 12 West to 16 West. Anchor Line's *California* (16,792 grt) and Canadian Pacific's *Duchess of York* were both sunk during the passage of convoy

(*Above*) Support from the Navy's big guns, Normandy. Sword Beach, Normandy, 6 June 1944. The merchant ships disembark troops and equipment whilst the 15-inch guns of the battleship *Ramillies* give support.

(*Right*) Liberation of Europe. Account of Wages. Over a period of seventeen weeks the third radio officer of SS *Fort Gibraltar* earned a total of £77.12.7.

OPS. 16

Form approved by the Minister of War Transport under paragraphs 6 and 7 of Regulation 47ADA of the Defence (General) Regulations, 1939.

LIBERATION OF EUROPE.
ACCOUNT OF WAGES.

Surname and initials of Seaman .... WILSON   T. G.
(*In Block Letters*)
Dis. A. Number ..... R 308024 ..... Rank or Rating ..... 3rd Radio Off

EARNINGS.	£	s.	d.
Basic wages at £ ... 13/- ... per week			
from 22/4/44 to 19/8/44 (... 17 weeks ... 1 days)	11	2	11
War Risk Money and Consolidated Rate for ... 17 weeks ... 1 days	65	14	4
Increase of Wages on promotion by £ ... s. ... d. per week			
for ... weeks ... days			
War Leave due ... 8 ... days at ... 1/11d ... per day ...		15	4
Subsistence Allowance ... days at ... per day ...			
TOTAL ...	77	12	7

DEDUCTIONS.			
Payments to relative ...	25	10	·
Total Advances ...	35	15	·
Income Tax (Code S) 17 weeks 1 days at 15/7 per week	13	7	1
Fines and forfeitures ...			
Health and Pensions Insurance for ... weeks ...			
Unemployment Insurance for ... weeks ...			
Officers' Pension Fund : Number ... (at 9d. in the £ on basic wages)			
N.U.S. Contribution ...			
TOTAL DEDUCTIONS ...	74	12	1
FINAL BALANCE ...	3	·	6

RELEASE.

I, the undersigned, having been during the above-mentioned period a member of the crew of one or more ships to which Regulation 47ADA of the Defence (General) Regulations, 1939, was applied or of the Merchant Navy Reserve Pool whilst kept for employment on such ships, do hereby release all such ships and the masters and owners thereof as well as the Minister of War Transport and the Shipping Federation Limited from all claims and demands accruing during that period in respect of any voyage, engagement or employment, except as regards the claims or demands which are set out on the back hereof.

Date ..... 19/8/44 ..... Signature ..... I. G. Wilson

And I, a Mercantile Marine Superintendent, do hereby release the said ..... T. G. Wilson from all claims and demands accruing during the said period in respect of any voyage, engagement or employment.

Date ..... 19/8/44 ..... Signature .....

The Cardiff registered *Nailsea Moor* at Dubrovnik. March 1945. SS *Nailsea Moor* was among the first vessels to deliver military supplies to Marshal Tito. Just four weeks previously Winston Churchill had written to the Marshal: 'This alone will enable tanks and anti-tank guns and other heavy munitions, together with other necessary supplies, to be brought in in the quantities which your armies require.'

OS51 on 11 July. Fifteen days later, on convoy OS52, there was Houlder's motor vessel *El Argentino* (9,501 grt) and Cayzer Irvine's 5,298 ton *Halizones* whose master, Captain Crellin, suffered his third loss in command. Many vessels were damaged; *Fort Fairy*, *Empire Brutus*, *Empire Darwin* and *Empire Highway* were among them.

Under the threat of attacks from the air, the merchant fleet provided the back-up for the first landings in Italy, at Reggio on 2 September and at Salerno, seven days later. Assault convoys sailed from Bizerta, Tripoli, Oran and Palermo. At Salerno the Germans used a new and potent weapon, the radio controlled bomb, a menace to ships operating off the coast. Among the shipping in support were the ubiquitous tankers of the Shell fleet, some equipped with spar decks for the conveyance of aircraft in addition to their normal cargo.

Three merchant ships and the hospital ship *Newfoundland* were destroyed at Salerno. *Newfoundland* (6,791 grt, owned by Furness Withy Co Ltd, Captain Wilson) was fully illuminated as laid down by the Geneva Convention. The sanctity of the Red Cross meant nothing to a desperate enemy and on 13 September she was struck by two aerial torpedoes. There were no wounded personnel aboard but 23 perished including all the medical staff and many of the ship's officers. The hospital ships *Leinster* and *Somersetshire*, at anchor close by, took off survivors which included 103 nurses attached to the American Fifth Army. After burning for two days, *Newfoundland* was sunk by gunfire.

During the remaining months of 1943 a large amount of military equipment and stores were transported to Southern Italy, to the ports of Bari, Barletta, Brindisi, Naples and Taranto. The gross tonnage of merchant shipping passing eastward through the Sicilian Channel, from 12 May to 8 November, was 2,419,322 tons. The greater part of this tonnage arrived at its destination safely though there were still sporadic attacks, one of which sank the new Canadian-built *Fort Fitzgerald* upon which I was serving. The details of this assault are related in Chapter 10.

In another attack the 8,602 ton *Rohna* (Captain Murphy), built for the British India Steam Navigation Company in 1926 to carry 60 passengers, was sunk. She was the first success accredited to the radio controlled guided missile and on this occasion, her total complement was nearly 2,000 including 1,770 American troops.

Sailing from Oran on 25 November she joined eastbound convoy KMF26 of fifteen merchant ships under Commodore H.D. Wakeman Colville who had his standard raised in *Ranchi*. At 1630 hours the following day (wind force 4, sea rough) when in position

36.56N 05.20E and escorted by ten naval vessels including the anti-aircraft cruiser *Colombo*, the convoy was attacked from the air. Thirty He177 twin engine monoplanes, escorted by Ju88's, followed by nine torpedo-carrying aircraft dived from the direction of the sun three-quarters of an hour before sunset. An estimated 60 glider bombs were released, one of which hit the *Rohna*; there were a number of near misses.

The bomb hit the port side of *Rohna* abaft the funnel at the after end of the engine room and in the vicinity of one of the troop decks. The ship was immediately out of control with no steering gear or engines, no means of pumping water to fight the fire which had broken out, a ten degree list and no means of internal communication except by word of mouth and messengers. There was near panic as she quickly became a vast fireball. Liferafts were thrown overboard but the crew experienced great difficulty in lowering the few undamaged lifeboats.

Some 1,015 United States infantrymen died in the *Rohna* disaster. The survivors, 830 in total, were rescued by the new 9,545 ton *Clan Campbell*, HMS *Atherstone* and USS *Pioneer* assisted by the naval tug *Mindful*. Rescue work went on all night, some men were lost as they scrambled up nets on to the decks of the rescue vessels, many had fractured arms and legs. The survivors were landed at Philippeville and Bougie during the early hours of the following day. From her crew of 195, five British officers and 115 Asiatic ratings were lost.

A much greater disaster was the heavy air raid on the port of Bari on 2 December, a raid shrouded in secrecy for many years. In a concentrated sneak assault they came in from the sea, as low as 150 feet, a total of 105 Ju88 aircraft, from bases in Northern Italy and Yugoslavia. For twenty minutes the British-controlled port area was pounded with high explosives; seventeen ships were destroyed, eight others were badly damaged; 38,000 tons of cargo were sunk, over 1,000 Allied military personnel and seamen, together with some Italian civilians, died. Flames reached over a hundred feet as ammunition ships blew up and aviation fuel was ignited.

The harbour was congested with Allied shipping, some 40 merchant ships in total; sixteen had just arrived in convoy from Augusta (Sicily). Being close to the front line, ships were being worked around the clock; cranes and wharves were blasted. Acknowledged by the military as a 'bombers' paradise', defence of the port against aerial attack was largely up to the ships themselves.

From the *John Harvey* there were no survivors. The secret of her cargo died with her for the American Liberty ship, amongst her shells and ammunition, was carrying 100 tons of mustard gas in containers. It was the only major poison gas incident of the Second World War. As the *John Harvey* exploded in a sheet of flame, the crew of the 5,083 ton *Testbank* were preparing to abandon ship. The Bank Line vessel was lying close by and surrounded by burning ships and warehouses.

Testbank was herself ripped apart by the explosion. Seventy of her crew, all those on board, were killed. Her only survivors were five seamen ashore in the town at the time. Anchored near the East Jetty lay J. & C. Harrison's *Defender*, herself undamaged; her crew looked on helplessly.

Moored stern on to the jetty was *Devon Coast* (646 grt); alongside lay the Norwegian *Lom*. Both were straddled with bombs, fire raged all around them. With a bright green flash, *Lom* blew up. Fortunately the crew of the Coast Line's vessel had already jumped overboard and though most were suffering from burns, they were not caused by fire but from coming into contact with mustard gas in the water. One member of *Devon Coast*'s crew was killed on board.

The American *Joseph Wheeler* loaded with 8,000 tons of munitions took a direct hit. She immediately blew up killing all on board. Anchored close by was *Fort Athabaska* (7,132 grt, MOWT/J. & C. Harrison. Loaded with 'generals' and mail for North Africa she also carried two captured 1,000 lb German rocket bombs in No 2 'tween deck. When the 'Wheeler' exploded, *Fort Athabaska* caught fire; in a matter of minutes the rocket bombs were detonated by the extreme heat and flames. She was reduced to a shattered hulk. From a crew of 56, there were only ten survivors.

The 1,807 ton British registered *Lars Kruse* (Lambert Bros) and the Polish *Lwow*, managed by Ellermans, were also sunk. Severely damaged were *Brittany Coast*, *Crista* and *Fort Lajoie*. For many years there were those who suffered from the 'fall-out' of Bari. Few realized that deadly mustard gas was the cause.

In the sixteen months from the time that I witnessed the war in the Indian Ocean at first hand (*Gazcon* 2 September 1942) 151 merchant ships were sunk by Axis submarines in the region, 71 of them British. Here the Red Duster men often had a different enemy to contend with. There was always the fear of Japanese brutality as they were cast adrift in open boats.

In June 1943 the unlucky Captain Waite of the Eagle tanker fleet had to give the order 'abandon ship' for the third time. In December 1939 it was *San Alberto*; in November 1940, *San Demetrio*; now, on 16

June as master of *San Ernesto* (8,078 grt), in ballast from Sydney for Bahrain, he was torpedoed by the Japanese *I-37* (Lieutenant-Commander K. Otani). The second mate's boat with eight men was adrift for 28 days during which time they suffered great thirst and terrible sunburn. They landed their boat on Fanhandu Island in the Maldives. As for *San Ernesto* herself, the derelict drifted 2,000 miles before running aground on Pulua Nias Island, where it was dismantled by the Japanese.

On 11 August Commander Wolfgang Lüth had already turned *U-181* homewards when, in position 23.00S 51.11E he sighted *Clan MacArthur* (Captain Matthews) the largest and fastest of the Clan Line fleet. Zigzagging at 17 knots in the middle watch, a dark night, alone, and on passage to India, two torpedoes immediately crippled the 10,528 ton vessel.

One of the torpedoes struck *Clan MacArthur* on the port side aft, lights were extinguished and both propellers were blown off. Many of her native crew were trapped in their quarters. The fore deck was fractured across her beam and the complete ship was covered in black cordite fumes. As the remaining boats were being lowered, three had been destroyed, a third torpedo struck, this time forward of the bridge. Suddenly the foredeck and the bridge dipped, her stern came up at an acute angle and amidst a terrifying noise of crushing bulkheads and steam she went under. From a complement of 151, 99 survivors were picked up the next day by a French sloop.

The German *U-181*, her supply of torpedoes exhausted, continued her passage without further incident, arriving in Bordeaux on 13 October. Commander Lüth, Knight's Cross, the last of the aces, was promoted commanding officer of the 22nd Submarine Flotilla.

The survivors from Brocklebank's *Sambridge* (7,219 grt, Captain Bain, ex *Makalla* [see page 63] sunk on 18 November on her maiden voyage) were fortunate to escape the savagery of the Japanese.

> We were ordered to cast off [reported the master] and as we were pulling away [from the submarine] I heard a burst of machine gun fire. Everyone crouched down in the lifeboat, then a second burst was heard, which I was afterwards told went over the rafts, one bullet actually hit the raft on which the chief officer was lying. . . . I consider it was an act of deliberate terrorism.

The second mate of *Sambridge* was taken prisoner aboard the 2,000 ton *I-27* (Lieutenant Toshiaki Fukumura). On 22 February 1944, her sister submarine, *I-37* (Lieutenant Commander H. Nakagawa), was responsible for machine gunning, and killing thirteen of the crew from British Tankers' *British Chivalry* (7,118 grt). Seven crew were killed on board by the explosion and as their master, Captain Hill, was ordered aboard the submarine, he was taken prisoner, the remaining 38, fearing no one would survive, crouched low in their boats. Nakagawa, the same commander who in *I-177* destroyed *Centaur* (see page 253), then left them to the scorching sun and the shark-infested sea. They were adrift 37 days before they were sighted. Forty-three of British Tankers' pre-war fleet were sunk during 1939–45.

Ten days prior to Christmas 1943, Lieutenant Kazuro Ebato (submarine *RO-110*) was responsible for killing 55 of the 69 crew members and two passengers from the 4,087 ton *Daisy Moller* (Captain Weeks). As the Moller Line lifeboats and rafts endeavoured to clear their sinking vessel, Ebato rammed and strafed the frail craft with machine gun bullets.

To return to the Atlantic, the autumn of '43 saw the U-boats armed with the new acoustic torpedo, a weapon also under development by the Allies which homed on the noise of a ship's screws. Convoys ONS18, ON202 and SC143 were attacked, six merchantmen and three escorts were lost together with one escort severely damaged. In reply three U-boats were sunk and three damaged. It was a temporary success for the enemy however and the combined efforts of surface and air escorts prevented the U-boats from making a comeback. In November and December, 2,218 Allied merchantmen sailed the North Atlantic in 72 convoys without loss.

As the year drew to a close the Christmas message of King George VI came across the airwaves:

Without your devoted service, there could be no victory for our armies. From the master in command, to the boy on his first voyage, you have worked together with the steady discipline of free men who know what is at stake. Your reward is the consciousness of duty done and the affection and respect of all your countrymen.

Unrecognized, you put us in your debt;
Unthanked, you enter, or escape, the grave;
Whether your land remember or forget
You saved the land, or died to try to save.
John Masefield

CHAPTER NINE

The Calm Returns
(*January 1944–May 1945*)

The year 1944 opened with renewed activity on the Italian Front. Without the merchant fleet, Operation Shingle, launched at Anzio, would not have been possible. The troops contained in the narrow bridgehead had to be reinforced and supplied by sea for more than four months by a regular shuttle of landing ships and craft from Naples as well as by larger merchantmen with ammunition and other stores. During the early morning of 22 January the three large Landing Ships Infantry, *Ascania*, *Circassia* and *Winchester Castle* were lying off at anchor. They had been placed at the orders of the American Admiral Force P and disembarked troops from Naples.

On 24 January the Germans deliberately attacked three hospital ships lying some distance seaward and fully illuminated in accordance with the terms of the Geneva Convention. *St David* (2,702 grt) was sunk by enemy dive bombers, the 4,303 ton motorship *Leinster* and the 2,702 ton *St Andrew* were set on fire though both were saved by the gallant action of their crews. Captain Owen and 56 others were killed aboard the packet *St David* owned by the Fishguard and Rosslare Railways and Harbour Co.

Eastward in the Indian Ocean some two weeks later (12 February) the Royal Naval destroyers *Petard* and *Paladin* took revenge on the maurauding Japanese based in Penang. The submarine *I-27* having left *Sambridge*'s second mate to languish in a Malaysian camp – subsequently he ended up in a camp outside Nagasaki – was destroyed along with the notorious Fukumura and his crew. Sadly it was at enormous cost for a few hours earlier *I-27* had blasted *Khedive Ismail* from the ocean with the loss of 1,383 lives including 137 of her 183 crew.

Khedive Ismail (7,513 grt) owned by the British India Steam Navigation Company was one of five troopships comprising convoy KR8 which sailed from Kilindini on 5 February for Colombo. Seven days later, during the afternoon watch, position 00.57N 72.16E, *Khedive Ismail*, acting as commodore ship, was struck amidships by two torpedoes. Breaking in two, she immediately disappeared in a cloud of yellow smoke. Most of those aboard, including 84 nurses and Wrens, were below decks watching a concert at the time.

The periscope of *I-27* was so close to *Varsova* that her gun crew were unable to depress the Bofors gun on the starboard quarter sufficiently. Within seconds the torpedoes struck. To everyone's horror the British India trooper crumbled like an eggshell. To port steamed *City of Paris*, helpless to assist. Immediately astern was *Ekma* which had to alter course to avoid the wreckage which included two upturned lifeboats. Speeding away from the scene at full speed, she had to ignore the cries of 'Help' from some 50 survivors as they struggled in the water. It was a scene of horror which seafarers, powerless to help, never forget.

The holocaust of Bombay on the afternoon of 14 April, though not of enemy origin as was that of Bari, (though enemy saboteurs were at the time suspected) was one of immense devastation. Fifteen merchantmen and two warships of the Royal Indian Navy either sunk or damaged beyond repair. Warehouses over a wide area were burned and shattered. 336 people were killed and over 1,000 injured. So great was the destruction of foodstuffs in the port area that risk of famine was brought to the region. The disaster, though not so great in extent resembled the blowing up of the ammunition ship *Mont Blanc* in Halifax harbour during the First World War.

The 7,134 ton *Fort Stikine* (MOWT/Port Line Ltd), carrying cotton and 1,400 tons of munitions, took fire soon after arriving from Baltimore. So sudden was the outbreak and so quickly did it spread that little could be done to keep the flames from the ammunition. The ship, which was lying in a crowded dock, blew up at 1606 hours with terrible consequences to all around her. Bales of blazing cotton were hurled over a wide area, starting other fires where they fell. Many of the fires on shore continued for two days and nights.

British India's *Baroda*, lying close to *Fort Stikine*, was blown across the end of the next berth, slewed around and dropped with her forepart on the quay thereby breaking her back. She was ablaze from stem to stern. Whilst Royal Mail's *Empire Confidence* was towed away to safety by a tug, the Norwegian *Graciosa* caught fire. She too exploded and the wreck was still burning eight days later. The whole dock area became an inferno.

'Britain will fight on, if necessary for years, if necessary alone. We shall go back.'

And so it was that on 6 June 1944, backed by the greatest armada ever to sail from the shores of the United Kingdom, Churchill's words came true. There was perhaps a hint of what was to come in

the radio broadcast which he made three months earlier when again
he made reference to the dangers at sea which the nation had faced.

> When I look back upon the fifty-five months of this hard and obstinate
> war, which makes even more exciting demands upon the life-springs of
> energy and contrivance, I still rate, highest among the dangers we have
> overcome, the U-boat attacks upon our shipping, without which we
> cannot live or even receive the help which our Dominions and our grand
> and generous American ally have sent us.

The execution of Neptune, the maritime side of the whole Overlord
undertaking, was highly complex. Plans for a return to the beaches
were made in 1942. During the following year a shipbuilding
contract was placed with the Consolidated Steel Corporation of
Wilmington, Los Angeles, for the supply of thirteen Infantry
Landing Ships Large. A much more positive sign was the million
troops carried across the North Atlantic, mainly in British troopers.

Queen Mary made six crossings from New York during January to
June 1944; she carried over 72,000 military personnel. *Queen
Elizabeth*, on passage to the Clyde during a heavy storm in February
was so heavily laden – she carried 12,000 infantrymen – that there
were fears for her stability. Zigzagging was abandoned for a time
after she listed 37 degrees to port. She had also drifted 90 degrees off
course.

The Infantry Landing Ships were built at San Pedro, California,
amid great secrecy. Built to the order of the British Government they
were delivered under Lease-Lend agreement and were managed by
the large liner companies with British crews. They had troopdecks to
take about 1,500 men and were ballasted with concrete for they were
not intended to carry cargo. Equipped with eighteen LCA's
(Landing Craft Assault), nine on each side with two tiers, they were
well armed – 4.7-inch guns forward and aft, one Bofors gun,
numerous Oerlikons and a smoke-making apparatus.

Based upon the American C3 Victory ships, they were powered by
turbine engines (Westinghouse and General Electric) of approximately 12,000 hp with two Babcock 'Sinosoidal' boilers. With a top
speed of 18 knots, 16 knots cruising, they were probably one of the
best kept secrets of the war. One by one the 7,177 ton 'weapon' class
sailed from the West Coast for lochs in the remoter parts of Scotland:
*Empire Anvil, Empire Arquebus, Empire Battleaxe, Empire Broadsword,
Empire Crossbow, Empire Cutlass, Empire Gauntlet, Empire Halberd,
Empire Javelin, Empire Lance, Empire Mace, Empire Rapier, Empire
Spearhead.*

Crews led by experienced masters were sent, first to New York, then overland to San Francisco. Captain Patchett of Cunard White Star Ltd and Captain McLean of Blue Star Ltd arrived in San Francisco together with their chief mates and chief engineers in August 1943. The remainder of their crews followed a month later.

After a wait of some three months, during which time many crew members found themselves jobs, Cunard White Star took over *Empire Broadsword* and Blue Star, *Empire Javelin*. Before crossing to Scotland, *Broadsword* embarked 800 troops in New York and *Javelin*, 1,500 in *Newport News*.

The crews of the 'Weapon' class signed COMNO articles (Central Office Merchant Navy Organisation) on arrival in the Clyde and then commenced intensive training. COMNO was responsible for manning all the ships in the invasion and ensuring that they were kept manned. It had draconian powers; crews could be transferred, if need be, from one ship to another, they could be instructed to any job aboard ship, no matter in what department they were employed. At the same time, every seaman participating was a volunteer, hence it became known as the 'V' scheme.

February 1944 saw the Cunarder in the Cromarty Firth for a period of training with the White Ensign LSI *Glenearn* and *Glenroy*. They had recently returned from service in the Mediterranean. Later when they were joined by a sister Cunarder, *Empire Battleaxe*, Royal Mail's *Empire Spearhead*, and Canadian Pacific's *Empire Cutlass* and *Empire Lance*, the Army was brought in and combined exercises at brigade strength took place. Blue Star's *Javelin* meanwhile was allocated to the American forces with her training based on Loch Long. In the ensuing landings she served Omaha on three sailings weekly. Torpedoed by *U-772* (Lieutenant Ewald Rademacher) in December 1944, she was carrying 1,448 United States infantry from Southampton for Le Havre. Only seven lives were lost.

On 23 May General Eisenhower, the Supreme Allied Commander, provisionally fixed D Day for 5 June. Two days later, Admiral Sir Bertram Ramsay, the Allied Naval Commander, ordered all holders of the operation orders for Neptune to open them. On 29 May briefing of ships took place at Cowes. Some 400 naval commanders and Merchant Navy masters were present.

Empire Bittern (ex-*Iowa*, ex-*Bohemia*, ex-*Artemis*) was another vessel brought over from the United States. Built in Belfast in 1902 as an emigrant and cattle ship she was taken over by the MOWT in the summer of 1941 and prior to D-Day had lain in one of the Scottish lochs. Familiarly known as the 'Five and Ten' because of her five masts and ten holds she ended her days filled with concrete as one of the 75 blockships, 28 of them British, sunk to form the initial breakwaters at Arromanches, Courseulles, Ouistreham, St Laurent and Villerville.

For'ard of *Empire Bittern* at Courseulles lay Evan Thomas Radcliffe's 5,587 ton *Vera Radcliffe*, requisitioned on 30 March 1944 for £75,000. Astern lay Ben Line's 1910-built 8,550 ton *Bendoran*. She had given fine service during two great wars. The blockships, code name 'Gooseberry', were just a small part of 'Mulberry', a convenient code word used to embrace all the details of the great scheme of the prefabricated ports during the days of the greatest secrecy. The American sector was known as 'Mulberry A' and the British as 'Mulberry B'.

Later, concrete caissons together with the blockships screened the moorings inside the harbours for ships drawing up to 27 feet to lie at all states of the tide. The concrete caissons, the floating breakwaters and the Spud pierheads which completed the harbours were assembled after what was undoubtedly the biggest towing operation in history (132 tugs were employed). Coasters and medium sized craft drawing up to 18 feet could discharge their cargoes at the pierheads.

Some eighty troop-carrying vessels took part in the initial assault. Amongst them was Union Castle's *Llangibby Castle* (11,951 grt, Captain McAllen) which was also fitted out with eighteen assault craft. With a crew of 200 she carried about 1,700 Canadian troops. She was attached to J. Force (Juno) which consisted of sixteen vessels.

Upon sailing during the night of 5/6 June, Captain McAllen broadcast to his officers and men:

> The show is now on. I assure you it will be the greatest show ever with tremendous air cover; I repeat, tremendous air cover, which cannot be too much emphasised. I require you all to be on your toes and carry out your duties to the very best of your abilities. Remember, it is our privilege to take part in this the greatest operation in history.
>
> We have all waited long for this opportunity. By your determination and resource we shall again prove to the world the great spirit of Britain which will inspire the world. May Almighty God speed us in this great enterprise. Good luck to you all.

At 0630 hours 6 June *Llangibby Castle* anchored off the beach near Courseulles. Over the next six months she crossed the Channel more than 60 times and ferried more than 100,000 troops. By mid-November she was using the port of Le Havre. Anchored close to *Llangibby Castle* at Courseulles was Clan Line's twinscrew 7,250 ton *Clan Lamont* (Captain Campbell). In the first assault she carried 1,400 officers and men of the Canadian Army. In five Channel crossings she transported 8,218 to Normandy.

Without fuel the Allied forces would have ground to a halt. PLUTO (Pipeline under the Ocean) from the Isle of Wight to Cherbourg was not laid until mid-July. Prior to this a fleet of tankers were engaged in transporting the essential supplies; they were led by the motor tanker *Empire Russell* (Captain Fiddler), managed by Bulk Oil Steamship Co. Ltd, and Anglo Saxon Petroleum's *Empire Settler*. Some 50 others, each around 900 gross tons, were the back-up force. Many of these vessels continued to serve the Normandy beachheads and ports until Le Havre was occupied on 12 September.

Empire Russell, at 8,028 tons the largest tanker in the invasion force, carried a million gallons on each crossing. She was the first Allied merchant ship to enter Cherbourg after the port fell on 27 June, the first Red Duster ship to enter a Northern European port for over four years.

The total fleet of tankers, known as the Hamble Circus, loaded fuel at the Hamble Jetty in the Solent. The two large tankers could come within two miles of the beach at Port-en-Bessin where they would drop anchor and tie up to two large buoys. Their tanks were then connected to the shore by a 6-inch flexible hose.

Several of the Shell tanker fleet, including *Goldmouth*, *Goldshell*, *Juliana* and *Opalia* were equipped with filters and other special means to enable them to transport and supply fresh water in addition to their task of bunkering landing craft. *Dolabella* left Southampton on D-Day plus One and continued in the role of water-carrier for three months.

Many of the ships requisitioned were the small passenger ships well known on the various cross-channel services including those operating on the Irish Sea. Two of them became casualties, Southern Railway's 2,386 ton *Maid of Orleans* (Captain Masters) sunk by *U-988* on 28 June (five killed) and the 4,220 ton *Amsterdam* which struck a mine on 7 August. The 1930-built *Amsterdam*, owned by the London and North Eastern Railway Company (Captain Pickering) was serving as a hospital carrier. She sank in the Baie de la Seine with the loss of 33 lives. Twenty-six were brought ashore injured.

The rendezvous point off the southern point of the Isle of Wight became known as 'Piccadilly Circus'. The great procession of ships came from the waterways of the Thames and the Bristol Channel, the Clyde and the Mersey, from the Scottish lochs and the north-east coast. 'Overlord' was the most complicated military operation ever faced in history. The weather, however, is the one thing that cannot be controlled by man; so it was that the opening of the operation had to be postponed for 24 hours. The sea in fact played greater havoc than the enemy. The violent storm which blew up on 19 June lasted for three days. Unloading came to a virtual standstill and hundreds of smaller craft were driven ashore.

The landing area was 50 miles wide. From the Orne on the port side to the Vire estuary to starboard there stretched five main assault beaches; the British areas, Gold, Juno and Sword for which the assembly points were Solent (west), Solent (north) and Spithead, and the American sectors, Utah and Omaha, assembly points, Tor Bay and Portland. From the assault ships, several miles out to sea were launched the tiny craft which took in the first troops. With these columns went the support craft and flak craft for laying a curtain of fire in front of them as they landed on the beaches. Also with this wave went the craft carrying naval beach commandos.

The second wave brought such things as mobile kitchens, food, more ammunition and, of course, more and more men and guns and tanks. At the head of the invasion fleet steamed the minesweepers, sweeping a channel through the minefields, repeating the job they did in the landings on the Libyan coast, at Sicily, Salerno and Anzio.

The first supply convoy of twelve vessels sailed from the Thames estuary in the early hours of 6 June. They were 7,219 ton Liberty ships specially ballasted with tops trimmed level and dunnaged to take heavy vehicles. The 'tween decks were fitted for the carriage of troops. They included *Sampep*, managed by Houlder Bros, *Samsip* (New Zealand Shipping Co.), later to be mined and sunk in the Scheldt Estuary (7 December 1944), Royal Mail Steamships *Samphill* and *Samzona*, and 'Paddy' Henderson's *Sambut*.

Carrying 580 troops together with army vehicles, *Sambut* was caught by heavy shelling from the French coast as the convoy was passing Dover. Catching fire and covered in a dense cloud of smoke, her ammunition cargo in No 2 hold exploded. The starboard side of the ship blew outwards and she sank in position 51.08 01.33E. Eighty lives were lost.

'The most dramatic and exhilarating voyage of my life,' wrote the *Daily Telegraph*'s special correspondent with the Merchant Navy. He sailed aboard *Sampep* whose master was Captain Smail of *Imperial Transport* fame.

I have been given an insight into the comradeship, courage and unfailing humour of this civilian brotherhood of the sea. I shared with them the hazards of war. As for grit – well, every one of the 50,000 men now ferrying a thousand merchant navy ships with war supplies to France, is doing the job of his own free will, as a volunteer under 'V' articles he signed months ago.

Men of the merchant ships are a tough breed, determined now to avenge their comrades who have died at sea in this war. Britain's Merchant Navy is living to-day its proudest hour. At last the chance has come for the men of the merchant ships to hit back.

The statistics of 'the Armada' speak for themselves:
4,126   Landing Ships and crafts
 736   Auxiliary Ships and crafts.
 864   Merchant Ships.

The wartime standard ships, in particular the *Sams*, the *Forts* and the 7,000 grt *Empire* class constructed in British shipyards, were a great advantage in as much that tonnages, dimensions, drafts and equipment etc were identical in each class. The whole question of ballasting, fuelling and loading was therefore simplified. Without this standardisation, the organisation of supplies would have been a great deal more difficult.

In the first seventeen hours of assault 130,000 Allied soldiers were put ashore. In the first 36 hours 307 ships sailed from the Port of London. They carried some 50,000 men, nearly 80,000 tons of stores and about 9,000 vehicles. In the first fourteen days, 638,045 troops were landed, 97,668 vehicles and 224,636 tons of equipment and supplies. By D-Day plus 3 no less than 47 convoys had crossed to Normandy.

By 8 July, five weeks after D-Day, 1,754,200 troops were transported to France, 373,400 vehicles (including tanks) and more than 2,000,000 tons of supplies had been shipped. Sailings across the Channel during the week ending 8 July averaged 10,000 men, 3,200 vehicles and 15,600 tons of supplies daily.

Samphill and *Samzona* continued their voyages between London and Normandy until September when the ports of Le Havre, Brest, Boulogne and Calais were liberated. Captain Mason, in command of *Samphill*, made fifteen trips (carrying 4,500 troops and 3,500 vehicles in total). Captain Anderson of *Samzona* made thirteen trips and when the flying bomb attacks on the London area began on 13 June, both vessels were under fire at all stages of their journeys.

Cunard's *Empire Broadsword* became a casualty on 2 July with the loss of seven lives. Together with *Empire Battleaxe* she weighed anchor at about 1600 hours to return to the Solent. As soon as she was underway she was blown up by a mine. Her back was broken in way of No 4 hatch and the engine room rapidly filled with water. She sank in less than twenty minutes. The survivors, many of them injured, were transferred to the *Battleaxe* which then continued her cross-channel voyage. *Empire Broadsword* was the only LSI ship, sunk off the beaches although *Empire Halberd* was mined four miles north of the Longships Lighthouse on 6 July and *Empire Cutlass* was lost off Digue Nord Lighthouse, Le Havre, on 21 November. She was torpedoed by *U-978* commanded by Lieutenant Günther Pülst. The smaller LSI *Prince Leopold* (2,938 grt) was sunk in mid-channel by *U-621* on 29 July.

It was *U-621* (Lieutenant J.G. Hermann Struckmann) which torpedoed and damaged Alfred Holt's *Ascanius* on the following day. Having served as a troopship based in Bombay *Ascanius* was now depot ship for the British Naval Task Force and also acted as barge headquarters ship. She was commanded by Captain Whitehouse and was in convoy between Southampton and Arromanches. Two torpedoes struck the 10,048 ton vessel forward of the bridge killing many of the barge crews who were sitting atop No 2 hatch enjoying the sunshine. The stout old *Ascanius*, built in 1910, limped to port and was eventually drydocked at Birkenhead. She was out of service until April 1945.

In May 1944 the German Schnorkel apparatus had come into widespread use. In essence a breathing tube, *U-621* was so equipped and it enabled her to remain submerged for much longer than hitherto thus evading radar detection.

Further east between Eastbourne and Dungeness, on the supply route from the Thames and the Humber, E-boats were active. The last of the big E-boat battles took place on 27/30 July. *Samwake* was torpedoed and sunk and six vessels of 42,916 tons, *Empire Beatrice*, *Fort Dearborn*, *Fort Kaskaskea*, *Fort Perrot*, *Ocean Courier* and *Ocean Volga*, were severely damaged.

Fort Gibraltar (C.T. Bowring Co., Captain Hubbard) made a total of seven round trips between London and the beaches. On each voyage she survived, not only U-boat and E-boat attacks but 'human torpedoes' and midget submarines, flying bombs and shelling from the French coast, aerial bombardments and mines. Lying off from the beaches on 24 June she was too close for comfort as *Fort Norfolk* set off a mine 200 yards away. With her back broken, her crew pouring over the side as naval craft rushed to the scene, her bow and stern came up and *Fort Norfolk* slid under. Managed by Sir

William Reardon Smith & Sons Ltd, *Fort Norfolk* lost eight of her crew.

On 28 June *Fort Gibraltar* was proceeding up the Thames under pilot's orders with tugs fore and aft when the distinctive flying bomb engine was heard. As the deadly weapon cruised over Rotherhithe the engine cut out, men flattened themselves and waited with bated breath. Then came the explosion. *Fort Gibraltar* was showered with shrapnel. Astern, the 87 ton tug *Toro* was a mangled wreck; all her crew lay dead. A short while later, in another flying bomb incident, the 1,957 ton *Viking* and the tug *Jacob* were damaged.

On 23 June, and again on 12 July, *Empire Tristram* was damaged in the Surrey Commercial Docks. On 26 July *Fort McPherson* was hit in the Victoria Dock, on 18 August *Samdel* in the West India Dock. There were many near misses and extensive damage to dock installations and warehouses.

The supply of live ammunition and bombs to the invasion forces presented many problems to the masters of the small coasters engaged in this work; many of these vessels were colliers. After making six trips to the British sector, the 600 ton *Southport* (Captain Campbell) was assigned to the Americans and visited among other ports the small tidal harbours of Balfeur, St Vaast and Isigny.

Whilst on this run, *Southport* loaded 450 tons of live bombs, each of 1,000 to 2,000 lbs, from a United States Liberty ship at Southampton. They all had to be carefully handled, specially stowed and blocked off, employing a squad of carpenters for this operation. At Isigny Captain Campbell found that this particular type of bomb was no longer required and he was instructed to return. After threats of U-boat and E-boat attacks during her return voyage, *Southport* arrived safely in the Solent only to lie at anchor for a week. Surviving an air raid she was at last instructed alongside to discharge. For over fourteen days she had held her deadly cargo.

The support invasion of the beaches between Nice and Marseilles, Operation Dragoon is now virtually forgotten. Yet here, along the French Riviera, between 15 and 31 August 1944, there were landed 184,900 troops, 39,390 vehicles and 191,230 tons of supplies. 103 merchant ships were employed in the initial landings, the main object of which was to capture the coastal towns of St Raphael, Ste Maxime, St Tropez, Toulon and Marseilles.

A large proportion of the merchant tonnage involved was British. The main task force and supporting convoys sailed from Italy and Sicily, from Egypt, Algeria and Corsica. Vice Commodore of the initial invasion fleet emanating from Taranto was Captain Bone of

Circassia. Astern lay Bibby Line's *Derbyshire* and *Staffordshire*, and the Polish *Batory*, now at the end of her spectacular wartime career which commenced when she escaped from Danzig in August 1939.

Just after sunset on 15 August Heinkel aircraft attacked the Gulf of St Tropez from seaward; shipping of almost every conceivable size and shape lay at anchor. Before a smoke screen could be laid, the floating jetty on which the troops had been landed earlier in the day was destroyed. Two American Liberty ships were sunk and a third was beached after her hull was damaged.

Anchor Line's *Circassia*, based at Algiers, returned to her headquarters next morning. In normal circumstances, a merchant transport's radio installation is sealed when in port but with *Circassia*, the navy's all-hearing network, built into what had once been a swimming pool, provided almost hourly bulletins relating to the Army's advance in France towards the Rhine. Everywhere the tide appeared to be running in favour of the Allies.

Much larger Atlantic convoys were now sailing, the majority crossing without loss. In July, HX(S) 300 of 187 ships, the largest fleet of vessels ever to sail in convoy; a fast section of fourteen left in mid ocean and 88 ships for Loch Ewe and Oban were detached at 21 degrees West. In August, HX 303 (S) of 167 merchantmen sailed from New York which included nine bound for Northern Russia. The 158 ships for the United Kingdom carried over a million tons of cargo including 207,874 tons of petroleum products. 216,676 tons of foodstuffs and more than 10,000 vehicles.

Of the merchant ships which crossed the Atlantic, September–December 1944, only fourteen were lost, against 55 U-boats sunk. Of the 159 vessels despatched to Northern Russia during the autumn of 1944, not one was lost. During the five years of war a total of 85,775 merchant ships were escorted across the Atlantic to and from the United Kingdom in 2,889 ocean trade convoys.

In his Christmas 1944 message, King George VI acknowledged the debt which Britain owed to its merchant service.

> Never was I more proud of the title 'Master of the Merchant Navy and Fishing Fleets' than at the time of the Normandy landings, when thousands of merchant seamen, in hundreds of ships, took across the Channel on that great adventure, our armies and their equipment.
> Never was pride better justified. This was the greatest combined operation the world had ever seen – perhaps the greatest it will ever see. The three fighting services and the Merchant Navy worked as one vast, complex, but perfectly constructed machine, and won a resounding victory.

(*Above*) Dubrovnik. March 1945. The author, third mate of the *Nailsea Moor*, is on the left. The third 'sparks' to the right.

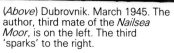

(*Left*) The last of the *Nailsea* ships. 1945. Beneath her proud 'red duster' sits her 4.7-inch armament. It was never fired in anger.

A group of Merchant Navy Officers. The deck officers of the steamship *Empire Kangaroo*, Donaldson Bros & Black Ltd. *From left to right*: G. Howison, second mate; J. Stevenson, chief mate; Captain G. W. Cockburn and J. Field, third mate. Captain Cockburn of Aberdeen had been at sea 32 years.

The first peacetime Christmas for six years. SS *Fort Tadoussac*, Ellerman & Bucknell Steamship Co. The author is in the middle row, second from right.

In a New Year message the Rt Hon A.V. Alexander, First Lord of the Admiralty, said, 'The Royal Navy and the Merchant Navy are equal partners in a gigantic task which is now on the way to a triumphant conclusion. The fight is now going to us, it is now a winning battle, but we shall never forget the ordeals of the Merchant Navy which have made these huge successes possible and Britain must never forget either.'

Yet the war was not yet won. In late January 1945 Hitler ordered the U-boat war to be strengthened by every means. The Schnorkel fleet now had 50 boats and 80 of the new Type XXI were delivered. Dönitz boasted 185 operational boats and the first of the new type XXI were on trials. They were of 1,600 tons with a range of 15,000 miles, and a submerged speed of 17 knots capable of being held for one hour. Yet it was all too late. For one who had declared, 'I will show that the U-boat alone can win this war,' Grand-Admiral Dönitz had to admit defeat.

In the months of February, March and April 1945 only 23 British vessels were sunk by German U-boats. On 7 May, when the fighting in Europe had already ended, a convoy was assembled for the north-east voyage up through the Pentland Firth, but this was a convoy with a difference. On ship and on shore the lights were blazing, and at 2030 hours the little group of five ships set out in an atmosphere of thanksgiving that at last it was all over. Rockets and flares were ignited, messages of goodwill exchanged between merchantmen and ships of the Royal Navy, impromptu parties, and prayers, were shared by the men and women remaining on shore to celebrate the return of peace.

At 2300 hours, two massive explosions were heard rolling in from the sea, and by midnight the ladies of the Methil Mission were once again at their appointed posts, on the pierhead, in the kitchen, waiting for the survivors who had been picked up by other vessels in the Firth. There were 54 of them, from the 2,878 ton *Avondale Park* and the Norwegian *Sneland 1* but they had left eleven shipmates behind, two British and nine Norwegian and another was to die before the night was out. Many more were injured.

Germany's U-boat force had ended the war in Europe as it had begun it, with an unprovoked, unresisted, totally indefensible attack upon people with whom they had no war. *U-2336* (Lieutenant Emil Klusmeier), a new 230 ton coastal class type XXIII, sped away into the night and to surrender.

From the first day to the very last, Britain's Red Duster fleet was at war.

Eternal Father, strong to save,
Whose arm hath bound the restless wave,
Who bidd'st the mighty ocean deep
Its own appointed limits keep;
O hear us when we cry to Thee
For those in peril on the sea.

W. Whiting

CHAPTER TEN

Reminiscences

The west of England and Wales, separated by the Bristol Channel and buffeted by the Atlantic have always had a close association with the sea. With my west country origin and education it was with a certain amount of pride that, having signed my Indentures and been kitted out, I left the Manse in the Welsh Valleys early in 1941 and sailed from Newport aboard the Cardiff-registered *Nailsea Manor*. Built by Bartram & Sons of Sunderland four years earlier for E.R. Management Co. Ltd, an Evans and Reid Company, she was a typical trampship of the period.

After loading anthracite at Swansea for Boston, the 4,926 ton *Nailsea Manor* (Captain Hewitt) together with 32 other vessels joined convoy OB289 and headed north through the Minches. With my life as a deck apprentice under way and with my ambition to travel about to be fulfilled, the war and the terrors which the North Atlantic held could not have been further from my mind. Off Cape Wrath, speed and course was set at 8 knots, 320 degrees and on the night of 23/24 February we were positioned some 140 miles west of the Faeroe Islands. It was crisp and cold, a moderate sea with good visibility, the wind Force 5, and a brilliant display of the Northern Lights.

A little after midnight came the sound of depth charges from the outer edge of the convoy. There then followed a cascade of 'snowflakes' casting an eerie light on the steel grey vessels as they steamed in line ahead; as *Nailsea Manor* shuddered violently we knew we were at war. The surfaced *U-97* (Lieutenant-Commander Udo Heilmann) dived as her deadly torpedoes devastated two ships almost simultaneously and distress rockets hurtled skywards. Without thought for ourselves we gathered at the ship's rail and wondered at the fate of others.

On board the 4,973 ton *Jonathon Holt* (owned by John Holt and Co. Ltd of Liverpool, Captain Stephenson) 38 crew, two gunners and eleven passengers perished. Blazing furiously she dropped astern, her engine room and bridge destroyed. Still with way upon her she disappeared in a vast cloud of smoke and steam. There were only three survivors. Signalling a 60 degree emergency turn, the commodore ignored the fact that the *Thomas Holt*, another of John Holt's West African traders, had fallen out of line. She had stopped to rescue seventeen survivors from the other casualty, Ropner's *Mansepool* (4,894 grt). It was a brave but dangerous action for *U-97* was still in the vicinity.

Four hours later in the early light of dawn Heilmann struck again. British Tankers' *British Gunner* (6,894 grt) was destroyed and the Norwegian *G.C. Brovig* extensively damaged; later she was able to make port under her own steam. As the enemy withdrew the depleted convoy was left to continue on its way. During those days the horizon was the limit of one's knowledge of the war; in total however 47 merchant ships were sunk by submarines in the North Atlantic that February. Possibly it was due to this lack of knowledge that few at sea took the war seriously; most approached it in a jocular manner. It was part of the job and rarely did anyone live in fear.

Arriving in Boston, *Nailsea Manor*, painted in her wartime grey but still at this time, proudly displaying her owner's house-flag on the funnel, the yellow Prince of Wales feathers on a blue band, discharged her cargo and after hosing down, loaded bulk grain for Manchester. To visit cosmpolitan Boston with the USA still at peace with the world, with the stores crammed full of merchandise, the streets and houses brightly lit, life sorely contrasted with that which we had left behind. It seemed quite natural to be entertained by one's enemies, the Germans and the Italians. When ashore in a neutral territory we rarely differentiated between friend and foe.

The arrival in a congested Mersey at the end of April coincided with the heavy German raids on the region. At Salford, at the head of the Manchester Ship Canal, I was given the task, together with a shore watchman, of defending the ship against the might of the Luftwaffe. Whilst the bombs fell and the searchlights lit the sky, others were either on leave, or were 'bedded down' ashore; the men of whom John Pudney wrote:

> Those humble men who drown,
> Dreaming of narrow streets, of alleys snug
> In lamplight, love in a furrowed bed,
> Pints in some Rose and Crown.

Time charted to HM Government, as were all merchant ships the

Nailsea Manor, then traded to Philadelphia. After loading military supplies at Philadelphia we joined convoy HX133 of 27 ships sailing from Halifax on 16 June. Across the treacherous 'banks' of Newfoundland we ploughed ahead in thick fog and rough seas with wind Force 9–10, unusual weather for the time of the year. Communication was by sounding convoy numbers at intervals on the ship's whistles with those in line astern also trailing the fog buoys of the vessels ahead. *Nailsea Manor* was No 41, the leader of the fourth column, supposedly a safe position but this was no ordinary fog; the blackness during the hours of darkness added considerably to our difficulties.

Certainly this was the worst weather I experienced in convoy throughout the whole war. We seldom sighted another vessel; three 'look-outs' were posted, on the fo'c'sle head, the poopdeck and on the monkey island. Captain Hewitt was on duty on the bridge virtually the whole time.

At dusk on the third day with the storm at its height and the fog at its thickest, there was sudden chaos. As always in such conditions there was a tendency to close up but being one of the column leaders we were taken completely unawares when from out of the gloom a vessel was sighted ahead only yards from our port bow. On watch on the monkey island (atop the bridge) clad in oilskins and sou-wester, with torrential rain now adding to the hazards, I was the first to sight her large cruiser stern. Taken by the seas and the heavy pitching our bow literally fell upon her stern. The sound of crushing bulkheads could be heard even above the storm. We had collided with No 32 *Dolabella* who was completely off station.

It was a night of nights in the annals of convoy work. Altogether eight ships were involved, a rare occurrence even in the North Atlantic. *Nailsea Manor* quickly fell astern and 24 hours later we arrived in St John's where we stayed thirteen days whilst they poured concrete into our damaged bow.

In addition to *Dolabella* three other ships returned to port – *Skeldersgate* 74, *City of Oxford* 77 and *Primero* 95. A further three were damaged but continued their passage; they were *Treworlas* 71, *Kongsgaard* 81 and *Tricula* 52. To illustrate how disorganised the convoy had become it is believed that four of the vessels concerned had drifted to starboard. Thus *Dolabella* had drifted ahead of *Nailsea Manor*, *Tricula* had crossed two columns to collide with *Treworlas*, *Skeldersgate* had strayed into the adjoining column to collide with *Kongsgaard* and *City of Oxford* had strayed two columns to steer a collision course with *Primero*. Naval records indicate that confusion arose over a change of course that had been ordered due to reports of the enemy south-east of Cape Farewell.

HX133, having lost the fog on 20 June, when ships from Bermuda and Sydney, Cape Breton, joined, then met up with a pack of U-boats. Before reaching the North Channel, six vessels, including *Brockly Hill*, *Grayburn* and *Malaya II* were torpedoed and sunk. Another two were damaged but were able to make port.

In September 1941, having completed our collision repairs at drydock in Cardiff, we loaded 6,000 tons of military stores at Newport for the Middle East. They included 4,500 tons of ammunition and mail for the troops; mail bags were carried in a wide variety of vessels. Sailing coastwise in convoy for Belfast we then took on board a Landing Craft Tank Mark 11, in four sections with a total weight of 250 grt; two sections over hatches on the fore-deck, they were as high as the bridge, and two sections on the after hatches.

Now at long last fully armed with a 4 inch gun, a 12-pounder, two Hotchkiss, four Lewis guns and two PAC rockets, *Nailsea Manor* joined convoy OS7 (Outward Sierra Leone) of 34 merchantmen. Our crew numbered 42 including three DEMS gunners, two Maritime Regiment gunners and one Royal Navy Petty Officer in charge of the Landing Craft.

Nine days later (1 October) west of Cape Blanco, as we encountered bad weather, we ran into trouble. With a strong wind from the south-west and a heavy swell, it was necessary for us to drop astern and hove to, together with *Ger-y-Bryn* and *Hazelside*, which were similarly loaded, in order that deck cargoes, which had started to move, could be secured. In company with HMS *Violet* we later proceeded on our voyage and as the weather moderated we increased speed with the intention of catching up with OS7. On 9 October, making 10 knots, course 165 degrees, sea rough with a north-east wind, force 5/6, the weather was fine and clear. The night was dark and humid, the 'white horses' glittering with phosphorescence.

At 0245 hours the following morning, visibility good with a half moon, the torpedo struck. Our position was 18.45N 21.18W. It was not a particularly loud explosion but by the time I had vacated my cabin, *Nailsea Manor* was listing to starboard and as I passed the forepart of No 4 hatch, I noticed the deck cargo was hanging over the port side. Beneath, a mass of flame could be seen in the shelter deck where the mail had been stowed. In No 4 hold below, between where lorries and trucks had been secured lay some 1,000 tons of ammunition.

U-126, about 500 yards off on the port side, crash-dived as her commander, Lieutenant Ernst Bauer, caught sight of our escort coming up fast from astern. Making good his escape Bauer went on to be decorated with the Iron Cross, his total tally being 24 ships of 115,876 grt sunk and four ships of 29,997 grt damaged.

Captain Hewitt recorded in his report to the Admiralty:

> I rang the telegraph for the engines to stop and at the same time fired two rockets. The telegraphs were broken so I sent the First Mate down to the engine room and the Engineer on watch stated that the main injection was broken and he was unable to do anything. As I did not know whether the ship would capsize with the weight of the deck cargo, or the ammunition explode, I gave six blasts (on the ship's whistle) and ordered the lifeboats away.

Before doing so, a roll call was taken and we were all present.

As we drifted astern, there was still a certain amount of way on the ship, we could see a large jagged hole from below the waterline to the shelter deck and inside was just like a ball of fire. At 0325 hours we were picked up by the corvette *Violet* and some forty minutes later we witnessed the death of the *Nailsea Manor* as she dived beneath the sea in a cloud of smoke and sparks. Later that day we caught up with convoy OS7 and were transferred to Ellerman's *City of Hong Kong*. Neither *Ger-y-Bryn* nor *Hazelside* survived the war, the latter being sunk by *U-68* in the South Atlantic only eighteen days later.

We arrived in Freetown on 14 October; convoy WS12 had arrived the day before, there being few occasions when the Sierra Leone River and the town were so congested. From *City of Hong Kong* we taken ashore to what could only be described as a doss-house. Some 300 Distressed British Seamen (DBS), a nauseous term when applied to seamen sunk by the enemy and rescued from the deep, were quartered there. Running water was scarce, it was far from clean and the donkey's breakfast (bedding) far from wholesome. We later discovered it was a requisitioned school.

Three days later Captain Hewitt was asked to take an ex-Vichy French ship (the *Gazcon*), which had been intercepted by HMS *Albatross*, home to the United Kingdom. All the crew, that is all the crew apart from the Apprentices, worked 'the Frenchman' home to the Clyde. Young deck apprentices of 50 years ago were often a means of cheap labour yet there were some enlightened shipowners always anxious for their welfare and their well being. One of these was Lieutenant-Commander Charles Evans, RNVR, founder and owner of the Evans and Reid Company. Hence it was thought necessary that we should fully recover from our ordeal; for some three weeks, before we boarded Cunard's *Samaria* for the voyage home, we lived as members of a coloured civil servant's family in a small wooden bungalow on the outskirts of Freetown. It was an education in itself, a memory which has always remained.

On my eighteenth birthday I caught up with the ex-French *Gazcon*, now under Evans & Reid management. She was built in 1932 for Cie de Nav. d'Orbigny of La Rochelle and of 4,224 grt. I boarded her, together with her new master, Captain Jones, at the shipyard of H. Stephen & Sons, her builders on the Clyde where she had been undergoing a refit.

Captain Thomas Jones born in New Quay on the West Wales coast, came from a long line of seafarers. His father, a master mariner in sail, together with his mother, were lost in a storm-tossed Pacific (1898) on passage from Hong Kong to Vancouver. He had himself rounded Cape Horn in sail before the turn of the century, been master of Western Counties Shipping's *Southina* when she was sunk by the Germans in July 1917, been 'running' to Spain as master of E.R. Management's *Alex* during the Civil War and now, at 63 years of age, had come out of retirement because of the shortage of experienced master mariners. No one could have been schooled by a greater seafarer.

We voyaged to North America to bring home food and munitions, to West Africa for timber and iron ore and in July 1942 we loaded 6,500 tons of military supplies, including high explosive shells, in New York for the Middle East. With a crew of 49 including three DEMS gunners and two Maritime Regiment gunners we sailed independently for the Cape of Good Hope. Possibly the most vivid memory of New York is that of Tommy Dorsey and his band at the Paramount with an unknown Frank Sinatra singing, 'I'll be seeing you'.

The voyage was long and lonely. Somehow we escaped the attention of *U-506* and *U-507* then operating along our route. Amazingly we avoided meeting up with the raider *Michel* which was crisscrossing the South Atlantic at this time; on 18 August she sank *Arabistan* on our instructed course, position 11.30S 26.00W. Only an albatross, shot down in full flight by an over-zealous young cabin boy on his first trip to sea, cast gloom overall. It was an ill omen.

From Durban, where we took on bunkers, we crept up the East

African coast towards the Mediterranean war theatre. With reports of submarines operating only well to the south of Beira we ceased zigzagging as instructed on reaching latitude 10 degrees North and rounded Cape Guardafui at midday on 1 September; that evening, course 267 degrees with a half moon, a slight sea with moderate swell, wind south-south-west, Force 2, all was peaceful. With the temperature into the eighties it was too hot for sleeping attire. What set out to be a restful night however was soon to be interrupted.

At 0230 hours, sailing at 8 knots, position 13.01N 50.30E, an explosion and shock wave reverberated through the steel bulkheads. One immediately knew what had happened. The cabin and alleyway reeked of cordite. The deck rose alarmingly, as *Gazcon* apparently already started to plough under. Running aft to the port side I passed the Bosun who said to jump, the sea was already past the 'midships accommodation. After less than three minutes she was rapidly sinking. The torpedo had struck forward of the bridge on the port side; Nos 1 and 2 holds flooded immediately.

It was dark on the water. Where a sturdy ship had sailed there was only a confused sea. For an hour I swam amidst a mass of wreckage. Then I heard voices and silhouetted against the moon was the outline of a submarine, a large grey monster, much larger than any underwater craft I had seen. As I sighted a dark object and began to swim towards it, a voice rang out above the throb of the diesel engines. It was unmistakably Japanese; 'Please, name of ship please.' It was the voice of Lieutenant-Commander Juichi Izu, captain of *I-29*.

The dark object proved to be a raft and together with some other members of the crew, I clambered aboard; for the first time in my seagoing career I felt an element of fear. I was clad only in shorts, hastily pulled on amidst the confusion of the moment. In the darkness there had been no time to search for my lifejacket. Yet it was not the sea, or fear of drowning or being attacked by sharks, of thirst or of being burnt to a cinder by the mid-day sun of which I was afraid but the cruelty of man. The cruelty of the Eastern enemy was already known in these waters. And the enemy knew no distress signal had been radioed. They alone knew of our plight.

At daylight we discovered there were 37 of us huddled together on three rafts. Fortunately there was no sign of *I-29* of the Japanese Navy. As we rigged the canvas screens for protection we discovered that twelve of our crew were missing. They included Captain Jones, the second mate, second and fourth engineers, the second radio officer and one of the naval gunners. The water was warm and as the sun rose a number of sharks circled us; we were thankful we were no longer in the sea.

The chief mate's report to the Admiralty on the loss of the steamship *Gazcon* records our rescue.

At mid-day on 2 September we sighted a ship and the Chief Engineer climbed on to the Carpenter's shoulders and waved a yellow flag. The ship sheered 20° away from her course on account of the large amount of wreckage in the vicinity. A few minutes later she saw our flag and altered course and came towards us. We paddled as fast as we could towards her and she came alongside and by 1415 we were all aboard this ship, the ss *Grainton*.

Two days later we arrived in Aden aboard Chapman's *Grainton* and after a week 'recuperating' at the Marina Hotel, Steamer Point, we awoke early on 11 September to find *Oronsay* at anchor in the harbour. By noon we sailed aboard the Orient trooper for the United Kingdom only to be transferred, along with survivors from Canadian Pacific's *Princess Marguerite* (sunk in the Mediterranean on 17 August), to *Duchess of Atholl* at Durban.

Little did we think more action was to come so soon. *Duchess of Atholl*, *Oronsay* and also *Orcades*, sailed homewards from Durban at intervals of 24 hours. Security was sadly lacking at this time in South Africa and we later learnt that these three, together with *Laconia* (sunk 12 September), lost within four weeks of one another, were all sailing at over 17 knots. They were the only fast unescorted vessels to be sunk by U-boats during 1942.

Calling at Cape Town, *Duchess of Atholl*, commanded by Captain Moore and with a crew of 296 embarked 529 passengers including 58 women and 34 children. Sailing on 3 October 1942, the 'Drunken Duchess' was six days later some 200 miles west of Ascension Isle. Canadian Pacific's trans-Atlantic Duchess class were familiarly known as 'Drunkards' for their ability to roll heavily.

Waking early on the following morning (10 October) I had every intention of celebrating the first anniversary of being torpedoed in *Nailsea Manor*. Little did I know that at that very moment we were being shadowed by a 1,600 ton U-cruiser. *U-178*, (Captain Hans Ibbeken – see Appendix XII) outward bound for the Indian Ocean; she had sailed from Kiel on 8 September, it was her first war cruise and she had yet to make a kill.

At 0629, ship's time, came the now familiar shudder from deep down in the bowels of the ship followed immediately by the explosion which resounded through every rivet of the 1927-built liner. Within ten seconds of the strike came the alarm bells. Ten minutes later came a second torpedo which struck in almost the same spot, on the port side in the centre of the engine room killing four engineers on duty. Whilst a distress call had been transmitted, the receiving set had been put out of action by the first explosion and no confirmation could be obtained that the signal had been heard.

At 0721, a third torpedo exploded on the starboard side, forward of the bridge. Although four lifeboats were unserviceable 888 survivors then abandoned ship within twenty minutes, a feat of discipline and skilled leadership from Captain Moore. At 0925 hours, the stately *Duchess of Atholl* (20,119 grt, registered at London) turned briefly on her port side and slid gently under by the stern; her position was 07.03S 11.12W. All were aghast at the spectacle, we forgot all about our own apparently hopeless situation. To witness the death of an ocean liner is something which, even to a seafarer, is unreal. A good servant of Britain, she had steamed 159,600 miles during her three years of war service.

With *U-178* now cruising amongst us a degree of uncertainty set in. We were alone in a smooth tropical sea, twenty lifeboats full of shocked humans who never thought it could happen to them. Yet we were led by professional British seamen, a great many of them with long years of service. For 24 hours we waited.

The next morning smoke was seen on the horizon. Rescue was at hand. HMS *Corinthian* took all the survivors aboard by 1330 hours and on 14 October we arrived at the King Tom anchorage in Freetown. This time we were fortunate in being transferred directly to Union Castle Mail Steamship's 20,122 ton *Caernarvon Castle* which sailed for the Clyde 24 hours later. Also on board were 266 survivors from *Oronsay*, the crew from *Agapenor* (see page 221) together with 38 survivors from *Glendene* who had been rescued by the 'Blue Funnel' vessel only hours before she herself was torpedoed.

On New Year's Day 1943 I again reported for duty. On this day I boarded the Royal Mail flagship *Andes* of 25,676 tons bound for Halifax, Nova Scotia. Built in 1939 she was designed to carry 606 passengers but her trooping capacity was now 4,500. I was one of a ship's crew led by Captain Brown and signed on in Cardiff which had instructions to proceed to Canada. After an uneventful crossing we traversed the snow-covered railroad track running parallel to a frozen St Lawrence which brought us to the Ford Hotel in Montreal.

Here Ministry officials appeared uncertain as to where they should send us but then suddenly one morning we were aboard Canadian National's transcontinental express for Vancouver.

In Golden Arrow-like opulence we travelled for five days and five nights, across the Prairies and through the Rockies. It was a train journey that time can never dim, as far away from life at sea as one could get. And as the Pacific Ocean, gleaming in the cold January sunlight came into view, it was like descending into another world.

Another world it was. For six weeks we enjoyed life at the Woodstock Hotel. We were wined and dined by British Columbians in their homes, we were escorted by their daughters, more than one romance blossomed; we were entertained by the local radio station, given free theatre tickets. Everywhere we were made welcome.

Two ships of the 'North Sands' type sailed from the yard of West Coast Shipbuilders as we waited. The *Fort Rampart*, delivered 23 January was sunk by *U-628* (convoy HX233) only twelve weeks later. *Fort Stager* was delivered mid February and on 9 March E.R. Management Co Ltd. took over *Fort Fitzgerald* on behalf of HM Government. She was the last but one of the 90 Canadian-built *Fort* vessels which were purchased by the American Government and transferred to Britain (bareboat charter) on Lease-Lend terms.

Merchant vessels were now sailing with greatly increased armament and *Fort Fitzgerald* was equipped in addition to a 4-inch gun, with five Oerlikon guns, two Pig Troughs, one Pillar Box, two FAMS and four PAC Rockets. In addition a balloon was carried, for inflation in the case of air attack. We carried six Naval and four Army gunners and a crew of 46.

After loading lumber at New Westminster and foodstuffs at Tacoma, the 7,133 ton *Fort Fitzgerald* topped up with cased machine parts at the port of Los Angeles. Here I am reminded of Sir Walter Runciman, an eminent shipping magnate of the twenties who went to sea himself in his youth. 'Life at sea is often hazardous', he said, 'but life without hazard is an empty thing; mostly it is a glorious life that is of itself the chief reward.'

In Los Angeles we certainly sampled 'the glorious life'. These were the 'Golden Era' days when Hollywood was the centre of the world and just prior to our visit, the Hollywood Canteen on Cahuenga Boulevard, just south of Sunset Boulevard, founded by Bette Davis and John Garfield, opened its doors to servicemen. We were met and entertained by Hedy Lemarr and John Loder, Ava Gardner, Sir Cedric Hardwicke and John Carradine, plus a host of starlets, some of whom could offer additional 'entertainment' though they were strictly forbidden to do so. All the way homewards, through the Panama Canal, at Newport News (for bunkers) to Halifax and Atlantic convoy HX235 – the crisis days were now over, and finally to Manchester, we dreamt of those halcyon days in California.

There were not many days in 1943 one could call halcyon. The heat of a Mediterranean June found the *Fort Fitzgerald* discharging a military cargo in Bône, the region bustling with invasion activity. On the day that Operation Husky (the invasion of Sicily) was launched we were on passage for Mers-el-Kebir, near Oran with over 1,000 Italian prisoners of war packed into the 'tween decks.

We were one of a number of vessels engaged in this traffic; some were given the unsavoury title of 'floating latrines'. Suitable shipping was available at Oran to take the Italians to camps in the USA but *Fort* vessels were by no means adequate. By the time we had passed Algiers we were short of water, by daybreak the stench was overpowering. Only the setting sun on the starboard bow with the light of Cape Caxine winking at us to port, heralded the discharge of these humans.

That August we again loaded in New York; 6,500 tons of military stores including 1,400 tons of ammunition for the Eastern Mediterranean, packing cases were clearly stencilled 'Alexandria'. The Atlantic crossing was uneventful, the Straits of Gibraltar were peaceful and it was already dusk as the 90 ships of convoy UGS18 (from Norfolk, Virginia) altered course abreast Cape Tenez, 100 miles west of Algiers. It was the nineteenth day at sea and we were anxious to reach our destination. No one thought of enemy action in such apparently tranquil waters yet we were less than 500 miles from enemy airfields in Sardinia. Suddenly from out of the northern sky at over 200 mph came a formation of twenty Do217s, equipped with the new German glider bombs, and 25 Heinkel 111H-6's each carrying two 1,686 lb torpedoes.

I was reading alone in my cabin when everything seemed to collapse around me. The explosion was deafening. I experienced a crushing sensation; all the lights went out, machinery stopped, there was escaping steam which burnt my throat and nostrils. The steel bulkheads on either side collapsed, all the surrounding accommodation fell in. Momentarily I was knocked unconscious. It was all of five minutes before I could crawl out from beneath the debris.

Later I found myself collapsed in the outside alleyway. My shirt was soaked in blood. I was violently sick and in a state of shock. From the porthole through which I had just clambered black smoke was pouring and further aft, flames flickered. Someone led me forward where Captain Brown, himself injured, was already about to lower the port bridge boat, both those amidships and the starboard bridge boat had been destroyed. As the enemy attack continued the anti aircraft barrage put up by the escort vessels and the merchant ships was ear-splitting.

The chief steward bandaged my head and we then orderly abandoned ship, using the bridge boat and four rafts. Just as we did so, fire suddenly roared through the wrecked accommodation which minutes before I had vacated. There was no one more welcome than the senior service in the presence of HM corvette *Lotus* which picked us up at 1930 hours.

The chief mate who was on the bridge timed the attack at 1855. We were steering 90°, convoy speed 8 knots, the torpedo was released from one of the Heinkels at only 30 feet striking us abreast the boiler room, apparently only detonating after it had pierced the ship's side. This was borne out, by the large amount of damage with the funnel being thrown forward onto the navigation bridge.

Captain Brown concluded his report of the sinking with the following:

> The corvette returned to the ship about 0100 (5 October) by which time she was burning fiercely, the fire having spread to No 4 hold. As No 4 'tween deck was full of high explosives and the corvette had 200 depth charges on board, the Commander decided it was much to risky to remain alongside. He sent a party on board who reported that the deck around No 4 hatch was red hot. We left the scene about 0200 and the last I saw of my ship she was heavily on fire, listing to starboard, and well down by the stern, with little hope of her staying afloat much longer.

We later learnt that the burning wreck had been sunk by gunfire from one of the destroyers. The second engineer, one greaser and three firemen were missing, presumed dead. Three other vessels had been hit including the American *Hiram S. Maxim* and Alfred Holt's *Samite*, both being damaged by glider bombs though both were able to make the Algiers anchorage.

HMS *Lotus* landed us in Algiers at 0830 hours the same morning and we were taken to the Merchant Navy Club in the Rue de la Liberté where we were fitted out with clothes. Later that day I was admitted to Number 99, British General Hospital at St Eugène where I spent five days under the care of the Army Medical Corps and Queen Alexandra's nurses. Before boarding Cunard White Star's *Franconia* for the voyage home to the United Kingdom I was to 'enjoy' sixteen days in the idyllic surroundings of Number 9

Convalescent Wing at Tipaza overlooking the blue Mediterranean 38 miles west of Algiers. I could not speak too highly of the attention which I had been given.

To have been sunk by enemy action four times over such a short period of time was by no means an enviable reputation. Three times I had been routed to Egypt but never reached my destination. Inevitably the name 'Jonah' stuck but notwithstanding this, after a Christmas at home, I was ready to return. On the second day of 1944, with a crew of 45 led by Captain Lambert I was bound for the United States where E.R. Management Co. Ltd was to take delivery of one of the new 7,176 ton Liberty ships. By daybreak we were abreast Ailsa Craig aboard Cunard Steamship's 81,237 ton *Queen Mary*, voyage WW31W. With Captain Illingsworth in command and with a crew of 1,087, her passengers on this west-bound crossing numbered 2,847.

Six days later we tied up at a snowswept Pier 90 on Manhattan's waterfront, a short distance from the Belvedere Hotel on 48th Street which was to be our home for some four weeks. The most memorable event during this time was the exquisite performance of the beautiful Norwegian Sonja Henjie with her Ice Show at Madison Square Garden. Entraining at Penn Station we proceeded to Baltimore (Southern Hotel) where at the fitting out basin of Bethlehem-Fairfield, lay hull No 2332. There was no christening ceremony but named *Samnethy* (all vessels built for the British Government took their prefix from 'Uncle Sam') she had been built on the same slipway as the first Liberty ship, No 2001, *Patrick Henry*.

The United States shipyards were at the peak of their production. In this month of March 1944, ten other ships were delivered by Bethlehem-Fairfield, seven of them to British managers. They were *Samgaudie* (No 2328), *Samaffric* (2330), *Samconnon* (2331), *Sameden* (2334), *Samcolne* (2336), *Samlea* (2337) and *Samshee* (2338).

My service aboard *Samnethy* was shortlived for upon arrival at New Jersey to load for the Mediterranean I was granted compassionate leave and returned to the United Kingdom as a DBS aboard Ellerman's *City of Agra*. Compassionate leave was extended to include eight weeks at the Cardiff Nautical College, a period which included the Normandy landings and it was not until early September that I resumed my seagoing career.

As third mate of the 4,926 ton *Nailsea Moor*, Captain Caldcleugh, the only surviving *Nailsea* ship, my service took me to Montreal, to Naples and supplying the Armed Forces in the Adriatic – Ancona, Brindisi and Dubrovnik. Although I was spared from being torpedoed a fifth time, I was uncomfortably close to *Blackheath* (4,637 grt, Watts Watts & Co. Ltd), torpedoed in convoy on the approach to Gibraltar, 10 January 1945. Lieutenant-Commander Ernst Hechler (*U-870*) had been operating in the area for several days.

May 1945 saw *Nailsea Moor* in West Africa loading homewards and where, in Lagos, as peace was declared in Europe, we celebrated. For five years and eight months the war had lasted at sea. Although hostilities continued in the Far East for a further three months no further British merchant ships were lost. Peace once more came to the seas the world over.

> I must go forth again to-morrow,
> With the sunset I must be,
> Hull down on the trail of rapture,
> In the wonder of the sea.
>   *Richard Hovey*

APPENDICES

APPENDIX ONE

Losses – Ships and Tonnage (British Registry)

Chapter I September 1939–May 1940

Month	Ships	Tonnage	Month	Ships	Tonnage
September	30	153,634 grt	February	21	110,372 grt
October	21	104,712	March	13	39,302
November	22	57,173	April	9	74,838
December	23	103,496	May	31	82,429
January	24	101,869			

Chapter II June–October 1940

Month	Ships	Tonnage	Month	Ships	Tonnage
June	61	282,560 grt	September	62	324,030 grt
July	64	271,056	October	63	301,892
August	56	278,323			

Chapter III November 1940–February 1941

Month	Ships	Tonnage	Month	Ships	Tonnage
November	73	303,682 grt	January	41	208,567 grt
December	61	265,314	February	75	315,304

Chapter IV March–June 1941

Month	Ships	Tonnage	Month	Ships	Tonnage
March	83	364,575	May	92	386,953 grt
April	75	361,578	June	60	268,548

Chapter V July–December 1941

Month	Ships	Tonnage	Month	Ships	Tonnage
July	30	94,310 grt	October	32	151,777 grt
August	26	96,196	November	26	90,711
September	57	214,664	December	120	270,873

Chapter VI January–July 1942

Month	Ships	Tonnage	Month	Ships	Tonnage
January	37	147,716 grt	May	56	258,245 grt
February	59	314,028	June	48	233,492
March	67	250,679	July	41	232,454
April	52	292,882			

Chapter VII August–December 1942

Month	Ships	Tonnage	Month	Ships	Tonnage
August	56	344,311 grt	November	76	474,606 grt
September	50	274,952	December	45	232,152
October	59	404,406			

Chapter VIII January–December 1943

Month	Ships	Tonnage	Month	Ships	Tonnage
January	18	91,056 grt	July	30	187,759 grt
February	29	166,947	August	14	62,900
March	61	384,898	September	11	60,323
April	32	194,247	October	11	57,565
May	31	146,496	November	15	61,593
June	11	44,826	December	10	55,611

Chapter IX January 1944–May 1945

January	13	66,588 grt	October	1	1,155 grt
February	11	63,180	November	4	11,254
March	10	49,637	December	10	46,715
April	3	21,439	January	9	45,691
May	5	27,297	February	12	43,449
June	16	54,611	March	12	45,862
July	9	40,167	April	9	52,131
August	17	80,590	May	1	2,878
September	4	26,407			

TOTAL   2,426   11,331,933 grt

APPENDIX TWO

Troopships – Lost from all causes

	Grt
3 September 1939–31 May 1940	25,739
Fall of France–31 December 1940	143,066
January–December 1941	42,643
January–December 1942	290,527
January–June 1943	55,893

APPENDIX THREE

Casualties – Largest loss of life

	Lost	Rescued	Total on board
Lancastria	2,833	2,477	5,310
Laconia	2,276	975	3,251
Khedive Ismail	1,383	207	1,590
Rohna	1,135	830	1,965
Arandora Star	805	868	1,673
Ceramic	649	1	650

Notes: Of the 805 lost on *Arandora Star* 613 were German/Italian internees. The one saved from *Ceramic* was taken prisoner.

APPENDIX FOUR

Troopships

Tonnage employed and capacity (including tonnage under repair) 1 October 1941–27 March 1944

	W.S. CONVOYS		OTHERS + INDEPENDENT		TOTAL IN SERVICE	
	Gross tonnage '000 tons	Personnel Capacity	Gross tonnage '000 tons	Personnel Capacity	Gross tonnage '000tons	Personnel Capacity
1 October 1941	1,240	155,512	848	104,752	2,088	260,264
23 March 1942	1,341	168,883	834	108,415	2,175	277,298
20 October 1942	1,451	256,712	829	125,959	2,280	382,661
14 July 1943	1,270	227,007	701	113,433	1,971	340,440
1 December 1943	1,280	232,454	697	117,344	1,977	349,798
14 January 1944	1,291	234,551	685	115,540	1,976	350,091
27 March 1944	1,328	244,036	669	113,997	1,997	358,033

APPENDIX FIVE

W.S. Convoys

Total personnel embarked from the United Kingdom including civilians and ships' crews. August 1941–October 1942

Convoy number	Sailing Date	Number of Ships	Gross tonnage troopships	Personnel embarked
WS 10	2 August 1941	18	252,500	30,452
WS 10X	16 August	6	96,300	10,004
WS 11	30 August	18	159,400	24,430
WS 12	30 September	20	248,700	32,673
WS 12X	12 November	15	204,500	27,787
WS 14	8 December	27	279,800	38,148
WS 15	11 January 1942	22	282,800	37,841
WS 16	16 January	19	234,000	45,114
WS 17	23 March	30	351,700	59,231
WS 18	15 April	20	274,600	44,953
WS 19	10 May	16	235,100	41,491
WS 19W	22 May	1	81,200(QM)	9,502
WS 19P	31 May	23	317,200	60,295
WS 19Y	17 June	1	83,700(QE)	10,718
WS 20	21 June	20	297,000	54,386
WS 21P	17 July	5	105,200	19,284
WS 21	29 July	12	155,600	28,290
WS 22	28 August	18	302,700	50,770
WS 23	4 October	4	72,100	11,771
WS 24	29 October	7	118,300	18,213

Notes: WS 12X sailed from Halifax and comprised six foreign vessels.
WS 19 includes two United States troopships of 14,000 grt carrying 3,041 troops.
WS 19P includes five United States troopships of 36,500 grt carrying 9,196 troops.
In convoys WS 17, 18, and 19P, 1,902 personnel were carried in HM Ships.

APPENDIX SIX

Sailings to North Russia (British Registry)
August 1941–June 1945 excluding rescue ships and one ice-breaker

Date		Dry-cargo	Tankers	Total
August–September	1941	11	1	12
October–December		26	3	29
January–March	1942	27	4	31
April–June		27	2	29
July–September		10	1	11
October–December		9	4	13
January–March	1943	15	2	17
April–June		—	—	—
July–September		—	—	—
October–December		30	4	34
January–March	1944	20	7	27
April–June		—	—	—
July–September		14	6	20
October–December		15	10	25
January–March	1945	8	6	14
April–June		4	5	9
Total 1941–45		216	55	271

APPENDIX SEVEN

Convoys to North Russia
Total number of Allied merchant ships and casualties

	1941	1942	1943	1944	1945	Total
Number of Convoys	8	13	6	9	4	40
Number of Ships	64	256	112	284	95	811
Total ships sunk by enemy action (Outward and Homeward convoys)	1	63	4	7	6	81

Notes: There were 19 additional casualties as follows:-

Sunk after arrival North Russia	5
Sunk – British minefield	5
Sunk – Ships independent	6
Foundered (gale)	1
Sunk – Rescue ship	1
Sunk – Fleet Tanker	1

APPENDIX EIGHT

War Equipment & Supplies
Sent to North Russia in merchant ships of British Registry

7,400 aircraft, including 3,000 from USA.
5,200 tanks, including 1,390 from Canada.
5,000 anti-tank guns. 4,000 rifles and machine guns.
1,800 sets radar equipment. 4,000 sets radio equipment.
2,000 telephone sets. 472,000,000 projectiles 4 submarines.
9 motor torpedo boats. 14 minesweepers.
Foodstuffs. Machinery. Industrial plant. Medical supplies and hospital equipment.

TOTAL VALUE – £428 million

APPENDIX NINE

Sailings: United Kingdom to North Africa
Ships of British Registry. August 1942–June 1943

Date	Number of Ships	Gross Tonnage	Deadweight Tonnage
August 1942 (Gibraltar)	5	27,936	42,015
September (Gibraltar)	5	12,811	23,047
October	128	573,649	794,952
November	131	693,335	1,057,080
December	73	474,078	707,842
January 1943	91	534,696	804,342
February	92	505,717	780,845
March	75	435,962	649,187
April	38	206,147	310,950
May	80	409,465	603,528
June	66	287,705	458,499
TOTALS	784	4,161,501	6,232,287

Notes: No British ships sailed to North Africa from North America until June 1943.
The increase in sailings in May and June is accounted for by the build-up for 'Husky' (the invasion of Sicily).

Normandy Invasion.
Vessels taking part 6–19 June 1944

Aard	Ben Robinson	Catherine
Ability	Benguela	Caverock
Activity	Benjamin Sherburn	Cedarwood
Alacrity	Biarritz (LSI)	Cefn-y-Bryn
Albert C. Field	Bidassoa	Channel Fisher
Algol	Bilton	Channel Queen
Ainwick	Birker Force	Charles H. Salter
Amsterdam (LSI)	Blacktoft	Charles Treadwell
Andoni	Blackwater	Chelwood
Anglo Indian	Bonawe	Cheshire
Anthony Enright	Boston Trader	Circe 11
Anticosti	Brackenfield	Citrine
Antrim Coast	Bradford City	City of Canterbury
Antiquity	Bramhill	City of Charleroy
Apricity	Briarfield	City of Malines
Arbroath	Brigadier (LSI)	Clan Lamont (LSI)
Argantock	British Engineer	Clara Monks
Ardgyyfe	British Faith	Claudius Magnin
Aridity	British Princess	Clement T. Jayne
Ary Lenson	British Renown	Clermiston
Asa Eldridge	British Scout	Colwith Force
Ascanius	British Statesman	Coombe Hill
Aseity	Brockley Coombe	Coral
Ashanti	Broomfield	Coral Queen
Ashbel Hubbard	Broomlands	Corbridge
Ashmun J. Clough	Brynhild	Cordale
Assiduity	Bucklaw	Corglen
Asteria	Busiris	Corminster
Atlantic Coast	Cairngorm	Corsea
Avance	Calshot	Corundum
Avanville	Calvin Coggin	Coxwold
Bailey Foster	Cameo	Cragside
Balteako	Canterbury (LSI)	Crewhill
Baron Ruthven	Cape Sable	Cromwell
Baronscourt	Capitol	Cushendun
Beal	Caradale	Cyrus Sears
Beechfield	Carnalea	Dagenham
Beeston	Carrick Coast	Dalewood
Belford	Cassard	Dallas City
Ben-My-Chree (LSI)	Castle Combe	Darst Creek

Dawlish
Dearne
Deemount
Demerterton
Denbigh Coast
Derry Cunihy
Devonshire
Dicky
Dinard
Dolabella
Dona Flora
Donaghmore
Dorrien Rose
Downleaze
Downshire
Drake
Duke of Argyll (LSI)
Duke of Lancaster
Duke of Rothesay
Duke of Sparta
Duke of Wellington (LSI)
Dungrange
Dunkeld
Dunvegan Head
Durward
East Coaster
Eastwood
Eaglescliffe Hall
Ebbrix
Edenside
Edina
Edith
Egee
Eildon
Eilian Hill
Elkanah Crowell
Emerald Queen
Empire Alderney
Empire Anvil (LSI)
Empire Arquebus (LSI)
Empire Atoll
Empire Audrey
Empire Bank
Empire Barrie
Empire Battleaxe (LSI)
Empire Bond
Empire Boswell
Empire Broadsword (LSI)
Empire Brutus
Empire Cadet
Empire Call
Empire Canyon

Empire Cape
Empire Capulet
Empire Celia
Empire Cliff
Empire Coast
Empire Creek
Empire Cricketer
Empire Crossbow (LSI)
Empire Cutlass (LSI)
Empire Daring
Empire Deed
Empire Dombey
Empire Duke
Empire Dweller
Empire Earl
Empire Estuary
Empire Falstaff
Empire Farmer
Empire Flaminian
Empire Flint
Empire Foreland
Empire Gauntlet (LSI)
Empire General
Empire Gipsy
Empire Gladstone
Empire Grey
Empire Halberd (LSI)
Empire Hearth
Empire Heywood
Empire Homestead
Empire Javelin (LSI)
Empire Jet
Empire Jonquil
Empire Kingsley
Empire Lagoon
Empire Lance (LSI)
Empire Lankester
Empire Lough
Empire Mace (LSI)
Empire Mandarin
Empire Mariner
Empire Mull
Empire Ness
Empire Newton
Empire Nutfield
Empire Ortolan
Empire Osborne
Empire Patriot
Empire Perdita
Empire Pickwick
Empire Pitt
Empire Ploughman

Empire Plover
Empire Portia
Empire Pym
Empire Rapier (LSI)
Empire Resistance
Empire Rhodes
Empire Rider
Empire Russell
Empire Rosebery
Empire Scout
Empire Seaman
Empire Sedge
Empire Settler
Empire Shoal
Empire Snowdrop
Empire Spearhead (LSI)
Empire Strait
Empire Stuart
Empire Symbol
Empire Traveller
Empire Tapley
Empire Trotwood
Empire Wrestler
Enid Mary
Erica
Errol
Eskwood
Fane
Felspar
Fendris
Fenja
Fire Queen
Flathouse
Florence Cooke
Fluour
Folda
Foreland
Formigny
Fort Alexandria
Fort Assiniboine
Fort Augustus
Fort Bedford
Fort Biloxi
Fort Brule
Fort Brunswick
Fort Charnisy
Fort Chipewyan
Fort Covington
Fort Crevecoeur
Fort Dearborn
Fort Esperance
Fort Finlay

Fort Fork	Gudrun Maersk	Kylecastle
Fort Gibraltar	Guedel	Kylegorm
Fort Henley	Guernsey Queen	Kylequeen
Fort Island	Gurden Gates	Kyloe
Fort Kaskaskai	Gwenthills	Laban Howes
Fort Lacla Ronge	Haarlem	Lady Connaught
Fort Lajoie	Halo	Lady of Mann (LSI)
Fort Livingstone	Harpagus	Lairds Isle (LSI)
Fort McMurray	Harptree Coombe	Lambrook
Fort McPherson	Hastings	Lambtonian
Fort Norfolk	Hawarden Bridge	Lancashire
Fort Perrot	Helder	Langlecrag
Fort Pic	Helmond	Lapland
Fort Poplar	Herbert W. Walker	Larchfield
Fort Romaine	Hetton	Leoville
Fort Rae	Heyser	Lilian I
Fort Reliance	Highwear	Lilleaa
Fort St Croix	Holburn Head	Llangibby Castle (LSI)
Fort Stave	Houston City	Lloydcrest
Fort Steele	Hove	Loanda
Fort Tinconderoga	Imperial Valley	Loma Novia
Fort Tremblant	Indian City	Lottie R
Fort Wallace	Invicta (LSI)	Lowestoft Trader
Fort Wrigley	Ipswich Trader	Luling
Fort Yale	Isac	Macville
Fort Yukon	Isle of Guernsey (LSI)	Maid of Orleans (LSI)
Freeman Hatch	Isle of Jersey	Majorca
Fylla	Isle of Thanet (LSI)	Malayan Prince
Galacum	J.F.V.	Maplefield
Garesfield	Jade	Marlanne II
Gateshead	Jargoon	Marsden
Gem	Jellicoe Rose	Marsworth
Gladonia	Jesse G. Cotting	Marwarri
Glamis	Jim	Marx
Glanton	Joffre Rose	Maurice Rose
Glen	Josewyn	Mecklenburg (LSI)
Glenearn (LSI)	Josiah P. Cressey	Melissa
Glen Gairn	Justin Doane	Melito
Glengarriff	Justine C. Allen	Merstone
Glenroy (LSI)	Juta	Methilhill
Goldfinch	Kaida	Moelfre Rose
Goldshell	Kalev	Monkleigh
Golden Meadow	Kaolack	Monkstone
Goldmouth	Karabagh	Monksville
Granby	Kenrix	Monowai (LSI)
Grangetoft	Kentish Coast	Moorlands
Graslin	Kimball Harlow	Moses Gay
Greenwich	King Edgar	Mr Therm
Grenaa	King William	Maushon
Greta Force	Knowlton	Naviedale
Greyfriars	Kylebank	Nephrite
Gryfevale	Kylebute	Neuralia

New Bedford	Rembrandt	Sandhill
New Royal Lady	Reuben Snow	Sarnia
Newlands	Ribblebank	Sax T
Nivernais	Richard Bearse	Scheldt
Normandy Coast	Richmond Hill	Scottish Cooperator
Northgate	Rio Bravo	Seaville
Nugget	Rockleaze	Sedulity
Obsidian	Rockville	Serenity
Ocean Angel	Rodney Baxter	Seven Sisters
Ocean Coast	Rodsley	Shanklin
Ocean Courier	Roebuck	Sherbrooke
Ocean Strength	Romney	Sherwood
Ocean Vagrant	Ronan	Signality
Ocean Vengeance	Rondo	Sincerity
Ocean Vigil	Rose	Sir Walter Venning
Ocean Vigour	Rouseville	Skelwith Force
Ocean Vision	Rowanfield	Slemish
Ocean Vista	Royal Ulsterman	Soborg
Ocean Volga	Runnelstone	Sodality
Olev	S.N.A.8	Sojourner
Opalia	S.N.A.10	Southport
Oriole	St Angus	Sphene
Orminster	St Bedan	Spirality
Ortolan	St Enogat	Staley Bridge
Palacio	St Helier (LSI)	Stanley Force
Parknasilla	St Julian	Stanridge
Parkwood	St Rule	Stanville
Pass of Ballater	Salt Flat	Stuart Queen
Paul Emile Javary	Samakron	Sulphur Bluff
Pebble	Samark	Summity
Penstone	Samarovsk	Swift
Polgen	Sambre	Teeswood
Polly M	Sambut	Temple Yard
Porthrepta	Samdauntless	Thames Coast
Portia	Samdel	The Baron
Prague	Samholt	The Duke
Prase	Saminver	The Earl
Prince Baudouin (LSI)	Samlong	The President
Prince Charles (LSI)	Sammont	The Viceroy
Prince David (LSI)	Samneagh	Thornaby
Prince Henry (LSI)	Samnesse	Thyra III
Prince Leopold (LSI)	Samneva	Tolsta Head
Princess Astrid (LSI)	Samolka	Tomsk
Princess Margaret (LSI)	Samos	Topaz
Princess Maud (LSI)	Sampep	Torquay
Prins Albert (LSI)	Samphill	Transoil
Prinses Josephine Charlotte(LSI)	Samsip	Trevelyan
Procris	Samuel Very	Trevider
Queen Emma (LSI)	Samvern	Tudor Queen
Quentin	Samyork	Tully Crosby
Redcar	Samzona	Ulster Hero
Regfos	San Ubaldo	Ulster Monarch (LSI)

Valborg	*Welsh Trader*	*Winona*
Vancouver City	*Westburn*	*Wooler*
Vestra	*West Dale*	*Worcestershire*
Victoria (LSI)	*Weston*	*Yarmouth Trader*
Vilk	*Westown*	*Yew-Glen*
Waldo Hill	*Wheatcrop*	*Yewmount*
Wallace Rose	*Wild Rose*	*Yewpark*
Walnut Bend	*William Bursley*	*Yewtree*
Watergate	*William Homan*	*Yokefleet*
Watson Ferris	*William Howland*	*Zelo*

Notes: LSIs – Infantry Landing Ships
        Royal Ulsterman – Landing Ship Headquarters

APPENDIX ELEVEN

Normandy Invasion.
Vessels of British Registry sunk as blockships

Alynbank	*Empire Waterhen*
Beecheville	*Flowergate*
Bendoran	*Forbin*
Bosworth	*Ingman*
Dover Hill	*Innerton*
Elswick Park	*Manchester Spinner*
Empire Bittern	*Mariposa*
Empire Bunting	*Maycrest*
Empire Defiance	*Saltersgate*
Empire Flamingo	*Stanwell*
Empire Moorhen	*Vera Radcliffe*
Empire Tamar	*Vinlake*
Empire Tana	*Winha*

APPENDIX TWELVE

Duchess of Atholl. 20,119 grt. Canadian Pacific Limited.

Sunk 10 October 1942. Position 07.03S 11.12W. Translation from log book of U-178, Captain Hans Ibbeken.

Date and Time	Indication of place, wind, weather, state of sea, lighting, visibility	EVENTS
10.10.1942.		
0400 *h*	Mar. square FM 3428, SE 2–3, sea 2, cloudy, low-lying cloud cover, bad visibility, 1016 mb.	
0756 *h*	Mar. square FM 3734, SE 2–3, sea 2, cloudy, low-lying cloud cover, visibility changing between 2,000 and 10,000 m, 1016 mb.	0756 *h* comes into 210° at dawn, shadows in sight. Turned to heading 60°. Both engines good headway. It quickly becomes bright; boat lies before the bright horizon. 0803 *h* Crash dive. Distance about 60 hm. Position 60°, bow left. Steamer is made out as type in Duchess class. 0815 *h* Enemy's change of course to 340° ascertained. Shortly after steamer zig-zags back so that rear tubes are ready to fire.

0829 h Double, 1 hit behind mast. Ship runs on, turns to port.

0837 h Double from tubes I and II. One hit heard but not observed for periscope cuts under. After the shot the steamer shows list to starboard, but soon rights herself again.

By 0915 h no changes ascertained. Lowered boats approach ship again.

0918 h Single shot from tube II. Miss, because too much seaway estimated (5 nm).

0921 h Single shot from tube IV. Hit below front mast. Disengaged and observed.

1100 h Ship suddenly has strong list to port and 1125 h steamer heels over and sinks via the stern post.

1200 h	*Day's run* 152 nm Mar. square FM 3490

Name subsequently confirmed from life-boats as 'Duchess of Atholl' (20119 Br. T.). Cruise from Kapstadt to England.

Headed deception course 0°.

1425 h	Alarm!

Aircraft visible on port beam. Dived.

1600 h	Mar. square FM 3739

Underwater cruise used to reload and check torpedoes.

2000 h	Mar. square FM 3871 SE 3–4, sea 3, cloudy, medium visibility.

Source: Hergestellt im Bundesarchiv Militararchiv – Bestand

Sailing List
Convoy KMF 33 UK Mediterranean Fast, 18 July 1944

Liverpool Ships:

13	*Sibajak* (Du.)	12226	15	Gibraltar and West Africa
22	*Volendan* (Du.)	15434	14	Naples
54	*Mooltan* (Br.)	20952	15	India
44	*City of Capetown* (Br.)	8046	16	India

Belfast Ships:

43	*Clan Cameron* (Br.)	7243	14½	India

Clyde Ships:

12	*Sterling Castle* (Br.)	25550	18	Gibraltar and Oran
61	*Empress of Australia*	21833	17	Algiers
21	*Queen of Bermuda* (Br.)	22575	18½	Naples
51	*Capetown Castle* (Br.)	27000	18	Egypt
62	*Ruys* (Du.)	14165	17	Egypt
52	*Reina del Pacifico* (Br.)	17702	18	Egypt
31	*Strathaird* (Br.)	22281	18	India
42	*Clan Campbell* (Br.)	9545	16	India
32	*HMS Wolfe* (Br.)		14	Ceylon
53	*Eastern Prince* (Br.)	10926	15	?
63	*Worcestershire* (Br.)	11402	14	?
23	*Cameronia* (Br.)	16297	16	?
34	*HMS Largs* (Br.)		15	?
33	*HMS Eastways* (Br.)		15	?
41	*Strathnaver*	22283	18	India

Convoy will be joined off Gibraltar by following ships.

To assist Commodore on vessels joining up, the following is for information:

Signal Letters		
GYVM	*Dunnottar Castle* (Br.)	?
GCT Y	*Highland Chieftain* (Br.)	?
B M S W	*Indrapoera* (Du.)	?
B M N C	*Johan Van Oldenbarnvelt* (Du.)	?
G S M T	*Moreton Bay* (Br.)	?

Note: Figures quoted above represent Convoy position number, gross registered tonnage and maximum speed in knots.

Merchant Navy and Fishing Fleet.
Honours and Awards

George Cross	5
Empire Gallantry Medal	1
Knighthood	10
Commander of the British Empire	50
Officer of the British Empire	1,077
Member of the British Empire	1,291
Distinguished Service Order	18
Distinguished Service Cross	213
Albert Medal	11
George Medal	49
Distinguished Service Medal	421
Sea Gallantry Medal	24
British Empire Medal	1,717
Mentioned in Despatches	994
Commendations	2,568
Total	8,449

APPENDIX FIFTEEN

Awards of Lloyd's War Medal

Aagtekerk	Captain A. Romeijn, Hon. OBE
Abukir	Captain R.M. Woolfenden, MBE
	V.P. Wills-Rust, Second Officer
Accrington	C. Draper, MBE, Third Officer
Adams Beck	B.C. Covill, Gunner
Afric Star	A.E. Fry, Sailor
Alacrity	D.N. Bond, MBE, Second Engineer
Alaska	Captain B. Movatne
Alexander Kennedy	Captain J.W. Johnson
Alexia	Captain H.J.A. Peters, OBE
	E. Kelly, OBE, Chief Engineer
Alhamo	G.E. Mayne, Chief Officer
	R.A. Barrance, Gunner
Alipore	R. Chard, MBE, Second Engineer
Alpera	Captain W. Reid, OBE
	A. Frisken, OBE, Chief Engineer
Amerika	Captain C. Nielsen
	J.J. Andersen, Second Engineer
Amsterdam	R.H. Wright, Second Officer
	D. MacNeil, Quartermaster
Anchises	D.J. O'Brien, BEM, Able Seaman
Anglo-Canadian	Captain D.J. Williams, OBE
	B. Beavis, MBE, Chief Officer
	E. Bergstrom, BEM, Carpenter
Arandora Star	Captain E.W. Moulton, deceased
	R.B. Brown, Chief Officer
	S. Ransom, Second Officer, deceased
	R. Liddle, Fourth Officer, deceased
Ascot	H.M. Fortune, BEM, Apprentice
Asphalion	H.S. Clarke, DSC, MBE, Chief Officer
Assyrian	Captain R.S. Kearon, OBE
Athelcrown	D.S. Pinnington, OBE, Chief Engineer
Athelduke	H. Speed, Engineer
Athelknight	D.J. Davis, OBE, Chief Officer
Athelsultan	Captain J.D. Donovan, OBE
	H.C. Ham, BEM, Cadet

Atheltemplar	V.T.B. Godfrey, MBE, Chief Engineer
	J.A. Reeves, Albert Medal, Chief Officer
Athenia	B.M. Copeland, OBE, Chief Officer
	W. Harvey, BEM, Boatswain
Auris	M. Hennerty, Radio Officer, deceased
Avila Star	E.R. Pearce, OBE, Chief Officer
	Miss M.E. Ferguson, BEM, Passenger
Avonwood	W. Hutchinson, Steward, deceased
Awatea	Captain G.B. Morgan, DSC
Aymeric	W.N. Moffatt, BEM, Boatswain
Balfron	W. Murray, Mate
Baron Cochrane	C.S. Marshall, Chief Radio Officer
Baron Elgin	Captain J.S. Cameron, OBE
Baron Nairn	Captain J. Kerr, OBE
Bassano	C.G.O'Keefe, Radio Officer, deceased
Benledi	E.F.P. Pointon, MBE, Third Officer
Bennevis	Captain J.N. Shipton
	C.H. Olivant, Able Seaman
Ben Screel	Skipper D.T. McRuvie, MBE
	W.C. Jarman, BEM, Deck Hand
Benvorlich	A. Dalziel, BEM, Seaman
Benvrackie	Captain W.E.R. Eyton-Jones, OBE
Benwyvis	J.A. Ross, BEM, Apprentice
Bhima	D.B.J. Morris, MBE, Engineer
Bhutan	Captain S.F. Champion, OBE
Birtley	Captain C.V. Catling, OBE
	P.G. Ludlow, MBE, Chief Engineer
Black Osprey	J. Patterson, Able Seaman
Blairathol	Captain D.S. MacDonald, GM
Bolton Castle	Captain J. Pascoe, OBE
	W.M. Keating, MBE, Chief Officer
Bonita	Miss V.A. Drummond, MBE
Botavon	Captain J.H. Reardon Smith, OBE
Britannia	Dr Adeline N. Miller, MBE, Ship's Surgeon
British Colony	A.C. Reynolds, MBE, Second Engineer
	C. Beckett, BEM, Donkeyman
	J. O'Sullivan, Mess-room Steward
British Dominion	E. Hawkins, Gunlayer
British Endeavour	W.M. Youngson, MBE, Third Engineer
British Fortitude	T.H. McCuaig, OBE, Chief Engineer
British Judge	Captain T. Gaffney, OBE
British Merit	C. Craggs, Chief Engineer
British Premier	E.O. Griffiths, BEM, Seaman
British Resource	F.R. Clark, Chief Radio Officer
	N.M. Coleman, MBE, Radio Officer
British Viscount	H.R. Knight, BEM, Apprentice
Brittany	L.A. Cook, MBE, Third Officer
Broomdale	A. Ballantyne, OBE, Chief Engineer

	W.J. Littledale, MBE, Second Engineer
	W.V. Davis, MBE, Engineer
Broompark	Captain O. Paulson, OBE
Browning	B. Preston, Deck Boy
Bury	H. Lyne, Third Officer
Calcium	Captain J.R. Atkinson, GM
	T.E. Bramley, GM, Chief Engineer
California	E.J. Stormont, MBE, Chief Officer
	D.M. Moir, MBE, Engineer
	J. McKechnie, MBE, Engineer
California Star	E.O. Pedersen, Ship's Surgeon, deceased
	R. Stewart, Chief Radio Officer, deceased
Canadian Star	Captain R.D. Miller, deceased
Cardita	Captain R.L. Bruce
	H.C. Thurston, BEM, Apprentice
Carlton	G.W. Robinson, OBE, Chief Officer
Catford	E.H. Elstob, Messroom Boy
Celtic Star	J. Nuttall, MBE, Third Engineer
Cerne	H.A. Gibbons, BEM, Able Seaman
Chandos	C.G. Rawlins, Fireman
Chevychase	W. Copeland, Fireman
Chilka	Captain B. Bird, OBE
	Kawsi Sayed Shahabuddinn, BEM, Cadet
City of Bath	J.W.E. Hay, Chief Radio Officer, deceased
City of Lancaster	A.J. Chafer, OBE, Chief Engineer
City of Shanghai	D.C. Gilchrist, Third Officer
Clan Campbell	Captain J.F. Vooght, OBE, deceased
Clan Ferguson	Captain F.S. Lofthouse, OBE, DSC
Clan MacArthur	R.F. Cole, MBE, Chief Radio Officer
	A. Mair, Third Officer
	C.S. Currie, Chief Engineer, deceased
	R.Y. Taylor, Purser, deceased
	J.M. Ruthven, Chief Refrigeration Engineer
	E. Ungr, Ship's Surgeon, deceased
Clan MacBean	Captain E. Coultas, OBE
	R.W.C. Bainbridge, MBE, Second Engineer
Compaganus	J. Swanney, Deck Hand, deceased
Congella	I.A. Clark, BEM, Apprentice
Copeland	Captain W.J. Hartley, DSC
Corabella	S. Byatt, MBE, Radio Officer
	G.R. Newton, BEM, Steward
Corbis	T.E. Simpson, OBE, Chief Engineer
	J.M. Heap, MBW, Engineer
	J. Frost, MBE, Engineer
	J.S. Mitchell, Second Officer, deceased
Corinaldo	R.H. Henderson, Cadet, deceased
	S. Strang, Cadet, deceased
Cormount	N.E. Longthorpe, BEM, Able Seaman

	H.H. Reed, George Cross, Gunner, deceased
	C.W. Davies, MBE, Chief Officer
	E. Chalker, BEM, Steward
Cornish City	N.R. Bradley, Engineer, deceased
Crista	R.W.A. Cliff, MBE, Second Officer
Cyclops	D.H. Stewart, Midshipman
Dagmar	Captain M.H. Bantz
	O.A. Winslow, Chief Officer
	K.N. Vogn, Second Officer
Dalegarth Force	Captain W.J. Thomas, MBE
	T. Hart, MBE, Second Engineer
Darlington Court	R. Cameron, MBE, Gunner
Dapper (Salvage Ship)	D.J. Thomas, Chief Engineer
Denpark	H. Sturdy, Radio Officer, deceased
	H. Wilson, Fourth Engineer, deceased
Derrymore	D.G. Purdie, OBE, Chief Engineer
	E.J. Fenn, OBE, Chief Officer
Devon Coast	Captain A.T. Mastin, MBE
	T.H. Fairhurst, MBE, Chief Officer
Deucalion(M.V)	Captain R. Brown, DSC
	J.S. Gregson, Albert Medal, Apprentice
Deucalion(S.S.)	Captain P.J. Pycroft, OBE, DSC
Domala	B.J. Duval, Cadet
Doric Star	Captain W. Stubbs
	W. Comber, Radio Officer
Dorset	Captain J.C. Tuckett, DSC
	J. Trotter, DSC, Chief Officer
	T. Spence, DSC, Chief Engineer
	P.A.T. Gordon, DSM, Apprentice
	W.R. Anderson, DSM, Gunner
Dover Hill	Captain W.G. Perrin, OBE
Duchess of York	R.V. Burns, Chief Officer
	S.W. Keay, OBE, Chief Officer
	E.E. Vick, OBE, Chief Engineer
Duffield	H. Thompson, MBE, Chief Engineer
Dunstan	H. Shaw, Steward
Earlston	D.M.L. Evans, MBE, Second Officer
	A.V. Watt, BEM, Able Seaman
Empire Avocet	I.B. Rose, MBE, Second Officer
	A.E. Kale, BEM, Fireman
Empire Baffin	E. Wardman, OBE, Chief Engineer
	T.J.L. Renwick, MBE, Third Engineer
Empire Bard	Captain H.R. Sealmans, OBE
	W. Hedley, Able Seaman
Empire Bowman	G.L. Bastian, MBE, Albert Medal
Empire Byron	Captain J. Wharton, DSC
	R. Phillips, Radio Officer, deceased
Empire Chaucer	T.W. Chapman, Carpenter

	S. Young, Chief Officer, deceased
Empire Cromwell	E.R. Lupton, Second Officer, deceased
Empire Crusader	J.E. Cowper, MBE, Chief Engineer
	W. Robson, Able Seaman
Empire Endurance	D.S. Davies, MBE, Chief Officer
Empire Eve	C.F. Birmingham, BEM, Cook
Empire Glade	Captain G.M. Duff, GM
Empire Guidon	G.S. Decker, BEM, Cadet
Empire Light	R. Renney, Third Officer, deceased
Empire Lightning	S.O. James, BEM, Seaman
Empire Metal	G.C. Watson, DSC, Chief Engineer
	N. Leybourne, DSC, Second Officer
Empire Purcell	W.H. Thomson, GM, Able Seaman
Empire Rowan	A. MacDonald, MBE, Refrigeration Engineer
Empire Selwyn	Captain J.T. Hair, CBE
Empire Starlight	Captain W.H. Stein, OBE
	B. Morgan, OBE, Chief Engineer
Empire Strait	H.M. Caroline, BEM, Able Seaman
	J. Dowie, BEM, Seaman
	S. Carroll, BEM, Seaman
Empire Tide	Captain F.W. Harvey, DSO
	A.H. Hughes, DSC, Chief Engineer
	W.I. Griffiths, DSC, Second Engineer
	H.J. Carswell, DSM, Chief Steward
Empire Toucan	M.R. Gerard, Radio Officer, deceased
	E.R. Campbell, Radio Officer, deceased
Empire Wave	J. Cameron, Chief Officer
Empire Webster	H. Phillips, BEM, Apprentice
Empire Zeal	S.D. Haines, MBE, Chief Radio Officer
Ena de Larranaga	Captain R.S. Craston
Eskwood	Captain A. Wright, deceased
Eumaeus	Captain J.E. Watson, OBE
Eurylochus	Captain A.M. Caird, OBE
	D. Hay, Albert Medal, Cadet
Eurymedon	Captain J.F. Webster
Everleigh	Captain C.A. Gentles, OBE
Ferryhill	J.M. Ovenston, MBE, Chief Officer
Fort Buckingham	E.H. Greenway, OBE, Chief Engineer
Fort Louisbourg	J. Gallagher, Engineer
Fort Qu'Appelle	J. Gair, MBE, Chief Officer
Fowberry Tower	Captain C.E.W. Hersee
Franche Comte	Captain L.C. Church
Frontenac	Captain W. Thorsen
	S. Arngsen, Chief Officer
	E. Larsen, Pumpman
Gairsoppa	R.H. Ayres, MBE, Second Officer
Ganges	J. Hartridge, Gunner
Gasfire	T.A. Umpleby, Donkeyman

Goodwood	R.A. Black, Second Officer
	T. Broderick, Able Seaman
	W. Gill, Able Seaman
	R.H. Percival, Able Seaman
Gowrie	Captain A.F. Cargill, OBE
Gwynwood	T. Collier, Chief Officer
Harberton	E.S. Anholm, MBE, Second Officer
Harmatris	Captain R.W. Brundle, OBE
Harpagon	R.D. Creser, GM, Chief Officer
Harpagus	W.J. Lawton, Boatswain
Hatasu	W. Manning, Carpenter
Haxby	G.W. Hackston, OBE, Chief Radio Officer
Hazelside	Captain C.K. Evans, OBE
	J.S. Miller, MBE, Chief Officer
Helena Margareta	Captain O.T. Jones
Holmpark	Captain A. Cromarty, OBE
Induna	E. Rowlands, MBE, Second Officer
Inishtrahull	F. Hobson, Able Seaman, deceased
Jamaica Producer	J.C. Myers, Radio Officer
Jean Jadot	P.J. Damiens, Third Officer
Jura	G.D.M. Reid, Chief Officer, deceased
Kelmscott	B. Shaw, BEM, Seaman
Kenordoc	D. Kerr, OBE, Chief Officer
	G.T. Barker, Radio Officer, deceased
Kentucky	Captain C.R.J. Roberts, OBE
Keynes	C.A. Coleman, OBE, Radio Officer
	S.L. Brown, BEM, Gunner
Kingfisher	W. Pybus, BEM, Second Engineer
King John	Captain G. Smith, OBE
Kohinur	S.L. Smith, Chief Officer
Kyle Castle	A. Ross, MBE, Second Officer
Lady Brassey (Tug)	V.D. Brockman, BEM, Seaman
Lady Connaught	A. Mackay, MBE
Lady Hawkins	P.A. Kelly, Chief Officer
Lady Olga	Captain L.B. Anderson, MBE
Lapwing	J.B. Woodhouse, MBE, Chief Officer
Laurieston	D.N. Harvey, Seaman
	A. Gott, Seaman
Leinster	Captain J. Wilson, OBE
Leto	Captain E.H. Venderveen
	J. Breet, Chief Officer, deceased
Lieut. Robert Mory	B. Bateman, Chief Engineer
Llangibby Castle	Captain R.F. Bayer, CBE
	J.A.F. Ferguson, OBE, Chief Officer
	J. Mills, OBE, Chief Engineer
Lochkatrine	H.E. Gibson, Third Engineer
Loch Ranza	Captain A. Mackinley, OBE
	J. Inglis, GM, Second Officer

	J.J. Dalziel, BEM, Carpenter
Lubrafol	J. Michaelsens, Chief Officer
	R.F. Van Dorst, Third Officer
Lulworth Hill	K. Cooke, GM, Carpenter
	C.H. Armitage, GM, Able Seaman
Maclaren	Captain T.G. Smith, OBE
Macumba	G. Dew, Donkeyman, deceased
Maja	S.G. Moffitt, OBE, Chief Engineer
	Chen Chou, Pumpman
Manaar	J.G.M. Turner, BEM, Radio Officer
Mandasor	Captain A. Hill
Marina	Captain R.T. Payne, GM
Melrose Abbey	W.J. Kerrison, BEM, Able Seaman
Menelaus	Captain J.H. Blyth, OBE, DSC
Michael E.	N. Macleod, Able Seaman, deceased
Mijdrecht	Captain J. Swart
Mizpah	Skipper J.C. Locke, BEM
Moorwood	S. Bell, Chief Engineer
Mostyn	E.J. Butler, GM, Gunlayer
Muncaster Castle	Captain H.W. Harper, OBE
Narkunda	Captain L. Parfitt, DSC
	J.B. Lakin, Engineer
	J.I. Allister, DSC, Engineer
	H. Bailey, DSC, Carpenter
Narvik	Captain C. Zawarda
Nephrite	J. Gibson, MBE, Chief Officer
Neptuna	Dr J. Hyde, Ship's Surgeon
Newminster	Captain A.A. Lawrence, MBE
	E.A. Small, MBE, Chief Officer
	R. Sibbald, Steward
	C. Coates, Donkeyman
	W.A. Peter, Able Seaman
New Westminster City	Captain W.J. Harris, OBE
Noreen Mary	J. MacAllister, BEM, Deck Hand
Norman Monarch	D. Macphee, Able Seaman
Nyholt	H. Hansen, Chief Officer
Ocean Courier	T. Pearson, MBE, Second Officer
Ocean Faith	Captain C. Patton, OBE
	W.N.D. Smith, MBE, Chief Officer
	C. Quinn, BEM, Fireman
Ocean Freedom	Captain W. Walker, DSO
Ocean Vagabond	J.F. Wilson, Radio Officer, deceased
Ocean Viceroy	Captain N. Macfadyen
	N. Kennedy, Chief Engineer
	P. Lochtie, Second Engineer
	E. McCutcheon, Third Engineer
Ocean Voyager	G.P. Stronach, Chief Officer
	H. Hotham, Second Engineer

	E.A. Gardner, Boatswain
Ohio	Captain D.W. Mason, George Cross
Omega	H. Foulkes, OBE, Chief Engineer
Onward	W. Mussell, BEM, Engineman
Orari	Captain N. Rice, CBE
Orcades	Captain C. Fox, CBE
Orminster	J.K. Lowrie, MBE, Second Engineer
Oud Beijerland	K. Cavanaugh, deceased
Pacific Grove	N. Watson, GM, Third Officer
	S. McEashran, MBE, Chief Cook
	L. Jensen, Boatswain
Palma	A. Macquarrie, MBE, Third Engineer
Pampas	Captain E.B. Ingram, OBE
Patella	F. Andrews, MBE, Chief Radio Officer
	W. Kirby, MBE, Second Engineer
Pauletta	R.E.N. Davey, Able Seaman
Perth	D.A. Low, BEM, Carpenter
Peterton	G.D. Howes, Second Officer
	T.C. Gorman, Chief Engineer
Petrel	Captain J.W. Klemp, OBE
Pinna	Captain W.P. Thomas, OBE
	T. Simkins, MBE, Radio Officer
	R.W. Armstrong, BEM, Apprentice
Pitwines	O.F.H. Gilbert, Second Engineer, deceased
Port Auckland	P.J. Shirley, BEM, Donkeyman
Port Brisbane	E.W. Dingle, MBE, Second Officer
	J.H. Magee, Chief Radio Officer, deceased
Port Fairey	A.J. Knell, DSC, Chief Officer
	J.K. Swales, MBE, Chief Electrician
	F.C.P. Styles, MBE, Purser
	T.T. Morgan, BEM, Carpenter
	C. Reed, BEM, Boatswain
	J.A. Phipps, BEM, Lamp-trimmer
Port Gisborne	Captain T. Kippins, OBE, DSC
	S.H. Light, GM, Able Seaman
Port Nicholson	T.W. Blundell, Fireman
Port of London	Dock Pilot A. H. Coe
Port Victor	R. Matthews, MBE, Apprentice
Rangitane	Mrs E. Plumb, BEM, Stewardess
	W. Francis, BEM, Cook
	J.R. Walker, BEM, Mechanic
Rathlin	Captain A. Banning, DSO
Regent Lion	W.J. Dryden, BEM, Able Seaman
Retriever(Cable Ship)	Captain C.A. Foy, deceased
Rigoletto	T. MacArthur, BEM, Third Hand
Ringen	J. Hauje, Second Officer
Rio Azul	H.A. Wyatt, Boatswain, deceased
Rio Bravo	Captain M.W. Thomas, MBE

	J.O'Regan, BEM, Able Seaman
River Afton	E. Miller, OBE, Chief Engineer
	G. Garstin, MBE, Radio Officer
	P. Grey, GM, Chief Steward
	A. Waller, Cook, deceased
Robert W. Pomeroy	J. Butler, Gunner
Rosenberg	G.E. Cusworth, MBE, Chief Engineer
	W.E. Gibbon, MBE, Second Engineer
	N.J. Bacon, MBE, Radio Officer
Ross	C. Hayes, BEM, Able Seaman
Royal Sovereign	Captain T.J. Aldis, DSC
	A.J. Webster, BEM
	J. Thomas, BEM
Royal Star	Captain T.F. MacDonald, OBE
Rushpool	W. Walker, MBE, Engineer
St David	Captain E.W. Owen, deceased
St Essylt	Captain S. Diggins, OBE
	W.L. Marrs, OBE, Chief Engineer
St Patrick	N.W. Campbell, MBE, Radio Officer
	F.J. Purcell, MBE, Second Engineer
	Miss E.M. Owen, GM, Stewardess
Saltwick	M.W.K. Barrett, Chief Radio Officer
Sambridge	H. Scutt, MBE, Second Officer
Sampa	J. Allerton, MBE, Chief Officer
San Alberto	M. Pirie, Able Seaman
	J. Young, Seaman
San Alvaro	Captain G.A.H. Knott, OBE
	G. Blackhall, MBE, Third Officer
	H.W.H. Norcliffe, MBE, Chief Radio Officer
San Acadio	J.R. Stephen, MBE
San Casimiro	J. Flett, Radio Officer
San Cipriano	Captain G.W. Highley, OBE
	C. Fookes, GM, Apprentice
San Demetrio	Captain C. Vicot, OBE
	G.W. Jennings, MBE, Radio Officer
	C. Pollard, OBE, Chief Engineer
	J.L. Jones, BEM, Apprentice
San Eliseo	Captain P. Johnstone, OBE
	G. Brodie, MBE, Third Engineer
	E.G. Booth, MBE, Engineer
San Emiliano	T. Finch, GM, Chief Officer
	D.O. Clarke, GC, Apprentice, deceased
	D.W. Dennis, GM, Chief Radio Officer
	C.D. Bennell, Chief Steward, deceased
San Fabian	F. Hughes, Able Seaman
San Forentino	S. Miller, OBE, Chief Officer
	G. Taylor, GM, Second Officer
	L.V. Grinstead, MBE, Third Engineer

	S. Freeman, BEM, Gunner
	P.W. Needham, BEM, Able Seaman
	T. Carters, deceased
Sanfry	Captain H. Lawson, MBE
	L. Depledge, Steward
	J. Lawson, Deck Hand
	W.E. Jewell, Gunner
San Gaspar	Captain D.K. Blyth, OBE
San Gerardo	K. Olin, BEM, Boatswain
Satellite	J.E.A. Symons, Gunner
	R.F. Edwards, Able Seaman
Scalaria	F.A. Armitage, MBE
Scotia	I. Claesson, Greaser
	F.O. Granstrom, Fireman
Scottish Heather	D. Crook, GM, Second Officer
	S.G. Allen, MBE, Engineer
	D.A. Bryne, BEM, Greaser
Scottish Standard	E.R. Clark, Chief Officer
	A.L. Tamlin, Boatswain
	D. Johnston, Able Seaman
	R. Radley, Sailor
Segundo	A.O. Torgensen, Chief Officer
Severn Leigh	Captain R.G. Hammett, OBE
	E.L. Barnes, GM, Second Officer
Shahristan	R.E. Gardiner, MBE, Chief Officer
	B.H. Smith, MBE, Radio Officer
Shakespear	P.D. Jones, Third Officer
	S. Anderson, Seaman, deceased
Sheaf Field	Captain T.O. Wright, OBE
Silvercedar	R.S. Adamson, Chief Engineer
	R.J. Stewart, Second Engineer
	J.N. Senst, Third Mate
	G.F. Chivers, Chief Officer
Silvermaple	G.F. Wiggin, MBE, Electrician
Sire	J.H. Burnett, Chief Radio Officer
Southgate	Captain H. Austin, OBE
Staffordshire	R.E. Stankley, OBE, Chief Engineer
Starling	Captain C.T. Stone
	P.K. Hope, deceased
Starstone	Captain W.R. Thomas
Start Point	V.G.A. Upton, Second Officer
Statira	N. Rose, Gunner
Stentor	W. Chisholm, MB, ChB, Albert Medal, Ship's Surgeon
Strathallen	Captain J.H. Biggs, CBE
	G.J. MacLennan, OBE, Chief Engineer
	J. Simpson, MBE, Fourth Engineer
	C.H. Goodall, BEM, Steward
Sultan Star	P.G. Windsor, MBE, Radio Officer

Sussex	F. Trundley, Assistant Steward
	P.P. Croxford, Seaman
Sutlej	A.S. Bennett, MBE, Third Engineer
	Fazle H.K. Manglee, BEM, General Servant
Svend Foyn	A.N. Bekken, Chief Engineer
Swedru	R.C. Ellis, MBE, Third Officer
Sydney Star	Captain T.S. Horn, OBE
	G. Haig, OBE, Chief Engineer
	J.H.A. Mackie, MBE, Chief Officer
Tai Koo (Tug)	L. Fook, Seaman
Taksang	N.A. Nair, MBE, Radio Officer
Talabot	Captain A. Toft
Tanda	W. Harris, Chief Radio Officer, deceased
	B.C. Humphrey, Second Radio Officer, deceased
	C. St K. Begdon, Third Radio Officer, deceased
Teesbank	J.A. Milton, MBE, Third Officer
Terlings	T. Ludlow, MBE, Chief Officer
	W.C. Prescott, Gunner
Tewkesbury	G.L. Turner, GM, Second Engineer
	B.P. de Neumann, GM, Second Officer
Thelma	H.T. Stamp, BEM, Able Seaman
Thistlegorm	A. Mcleay, GM, Seaman
Thorold	J.B. Bell, MBE, Second Engineer
	N. Kiely, BEM, Able Seaman
Thursobank	E. Johnson, Third Officer
Tilawa	E.B. Duncan, Chief Radio Officer, deceased
Titan	Captain W.F. Dark
Togston	Captain L. Laurenson
Toorak	N. Makepiece, MBE, Second Engineer
Torinia	F.S. Grant, MBE, Second Engineer
Trevanion	Captain J.N. Edwards
Treverbyn	T.H. Eagles, BEM, Apprentice
Troilus	Captain W.G. Harrison, CBE
Tucurinca	E. Andrews, BEM, Fireman
Tulagi	J.R.T. Ward, Chief Engineer
Turakina	J.R. Mallett, Third Officer
	S.K. Jones, Chief Radio Officer, deceased
	L. McGowan, Able Seaman
Twickenham	Captain W.D. Wilson, OBE
	J.L. Coates, OBE, Chief Engineer
Umona	E.G. Elliott, Gunner
Victo	Captain G. Jakobsen
Ville de Strasbourg	G.N. Ellioo, MBE, Fourth Officer
	G.C. Granger, BEM, Able Seaman
Vulcain	Captain J.R. Lewis
W.B. Walker	A.H. Johnson, GM, Chief Engineer
Waimarama	F.W. Treves, Cadet
Waiwera	Captain C.M. Andrews, OBE

	E.A. Hickling, OBE, Chief Officer
Walmer Castle	Captain G.L. Clarke, deceased
	A. Lawson, MBE, Chief Officer
	F.W.T. McGowan, GM, Radio Officer
	A.C. Davis, BEM, Boatswain
	H.V. Hill, Cook, deceased
Warfield	W.J. Callegari, Gunner
William Wilberforce	J.V. Watson, Chief Radio Officer, deceased
Windsor	E. Cole, Chief Engineer
Yewarch	W. Donn, Boatswain
Yorkwood	E. Langan, MBE, Second Engineer
Zaafaran	Captain C.K. MacGowan, DSC
Zamalek	Captain O.C. Morris, DSO

Awards of Lloyd's Meritorious Medal

Ah Kwang	Captain T.A. Lupton
	W.R. Thomas, Second Officer
	T. Choi, Boatswain
	K. Tai, Sailor
	Y.M. Yau, Sailor
Belray/Fort Stikine	S.A.R. Hayward, Able Seaman
Benedict	A.S. Richardson, Chief Officer
B.P. Newton	Captain J.W. Calvert
	Captain B.E. Ragnvald
Capsa/Fort Stikine	C.D. Michael, Chief Officer
Craster	R. Tinmouth, Second Officer
Empire Hawk	W.R. Howell, Chief Officer
	R.O'Neill, Able Seaman
Fort Confidence	L. Fillikes, Sailor
	R.H. Hansen, Greaser
Fort Stikine	N.H. Harris, Second Officer
Harpenden	Captain C. Parry
	J.J. Simmons, Chief Engineer
Hororata	Captain F.S. Hamilton
Hudson (Tug)	Captain B.C. Weltevreden
Iran/Fort Stikine	A. Hartmark, Chief Officer
Leeds City	Captain A.E. Ward
Lidvard	Captain N.F. Lindtner, OBE
Lind	Captain J.R. Nicol
	Captain H.A. Trovik
Loch Ranza	Captain A. Mackinlay, OBE
Norton	J.M. Sibbald, Chief Officer
Port Chalmers	S.G.L. Bentley, Chief Engineer
	W.B. Craig, Chief Officer
	H. Murray, Chief Electrician
	R. Stewart, Carpenter
Rajahstan	G.R. Charlton, Chief Engineer
St Merriel	Captain S. Diggins

E. McKay, Chief Engineer
G.T. Rees, Chief Officer
A.H. Holmes, Second Engineer
G. Emmerson, Third Engineer
W.C. Morris, Junior Second Engineer

Awards of Lloyd's Silver Medal for Saving Life at Sea

Baron Ruthven	M. McCarthy, Boatswain
Dundee	J. Murphy, Fireman
Empire Gladstone	G.S. Bird, BEM, Fireman
Empire Knight	H.V. Nielsen, Third Officer
Greystoke Castle/	
Cheldale	R. English, Apprentice
Oxshott	R.S. Brown, Second Mate
Paul (Tug)	T.H. Ghanim, Fireman
Pelican	Captain R. Carrick
Soborg	K.K.J. Duurhuus, Second Officer
Spondilus	L.E. Clayton, Chief Officer
Steelopolis (Tug)/	
Danegarth (Tug)	B.H. Bradley, Mate

Bibliography

Attard, Joseph, *The Battle of Malta*, William Kimber, 1980

Attiwill, Kenneth, *The Singapore Story*, Frederick Muller, 1960

Barker, A.J., *Dunkirk. The Great Escape*, Dent, 1977

Barker, Ralph, *Goodnight, Sorry for Sinking you*, (City of Cairo), Collins, 1984

Behrens, C.B.A., *Merchant Shipping & the Demands of War*, HMSO, 1955

Belfield, E & Essame, H, *The Battle of Normandy*, Batsford, 1965

Ben Line, *The Story of a Merchant Fleet at War 1939–1945*, Thomas Nelson, 1946

Bond, Geoffrey, *Lancastria*, Oldbourne, 1959

Bone, Captain Sir D.W., *Merchantmen Rearmed*, Chatto & Windus, 1949

Bowen, Frank C, *The Flag of the Southern Cross 1939–1945*, Published by Shaw Savill & Albion, 1947

Brennecke, H.J., *Ghost Cruiser HK 33*, William Kimber, 1954

Broome, Captain J., *Convoy is to Scatter*, (PQ17), William Kimber, 1972

Brown, Maurice, *We sailed in Convoy*, Hutchinson, n.d. 1942?

Bushell, T.A., *Eight Bells, History of the Royal Mail Lines*, Trade & Travel Publications, 1950

Campbell, Commander A.B., *Salute the Red Duster*, Christopher Johnson, 1952

Caulfield, Max, *A Night of Terror. The Story of the Athenia Affair*, Frederick Muller, 1958

Churchill, Winston S., *The Second World War*, Cassell, 1948–52

Cooke, Kenneth, *What Cares the Sea* (Lulworth Hill), Hutchinson, 1960

Costello, John, and Hughes, Terry, *The Battle of the Atlantic*, Collins, 1977

Cowden, James E., *The Price of Peace. Elder Dempster 1939–1945*, Jocast, 1981

Creighton, Rear Admiral Sir K., *Convoy Commodore*, Futura, 1976

Dickens, Captain Peter, *Narvik, Battles in the Fjords*, Ian Allan, 1974

Dönitz, Admiral, *Ten Years & Twenty Days*, Weidenfeld & Nicholson, 1959

Dorling, Captain Taprell, (Taffrail), *Blue Star Line at War 1939–1945*, Foulsham, 1973

Dorling, Captain Taprell, (Taffrail), *Western Mediterranean 1942–1945*, Hodder & Stoughton, 1947

Edwards, Commander Kenneth, *Operation Neptune*, Collins, 1946

Edwards, Captain Bernard, *They sank the Red Dragon*, CPC Books, 1987

Falk, Stanley L., *Seventy days to Singapore*, Robert Hale, 1975

Gibson, J.F., *Brocklebanks 1770–1950*, Henry Young, 1953

Gilchrist, Derek C., *Blue Hell, (City of Shanghai)*, Heath Cranton, 1943

Gretton, Vice Admiral Sir Peter, *Convoy Escort Commander*, Cassell, 1964

Gretton, Vice Admiral Sir Peter, *Crisis Convoy. The Story of HX 231*, Peter Davies, 1974

Harding, Steve, *Gray Ghost. RMS Queen Mary at War*, Pictorial Histories, (USA), 1982

Harris, John, *Dunkirk. The Storms of War*, David & Charles, 1980

Hay, Doddy, *War under the Red Ensign*, Jane's, 1982

Heaton, P.M., *Reardon Smith Line*, Published by the Author, 1984

Heaton, P.M., *The South American Saint Line*, Published by the Author, 1985

Hill, John C.G., *Shipshape & Bristol Fashion* (Bristol City Line of Steamships) Journal of Commerce & Shipping Telegraph. Liverpool n.d. 1950?

HMSO, *British Vessels lost at Sea 1939–45*, Reprinted Patrick Stephens (2nd Edition), 1983

Hocking, Charles, *Dictionary of Disasters at Sea during the age of Steam 1824–1962*, (2 Vols), Lloyds Register of Shipping, 1969

Holman, Gordon, *In Danger's Hour* (Clan Line), Hodder & Stoughton, 1948

Hope, W.E. Stanton, *Tanker Fleet. The War Story of the Shell Tankers and the men who manned them*, Published by The Anglo Saxon Petroleum Co. Ltd, 1948

Houlder Bros, *Sea Hazard (1939–1945)*, Published by Houlder Brothers & Co. Ltd, 1947

Howe, Leslie, *The Merchant Service of to-day*, Oxford University Press, 1941

Huxley, Elspeth, *Atlantic Ordeal. The Story of Mary Cornish, (City of Benares)*, Chatto & Windus, 1941

Infield, Glenn B., *Disaster at Bari*, Robert Hale, 1974

Jackson, W.G.F., *The North African Campaign 1940–43*, Batsford, 1975

Jones, Geoffrey, *Autumn of the U-boats*, William Kimber, 1984

Jones, Geoffrey, *Defeat of the Wolf Packs*, William Kimber, 1986

Jones, Geoffrey, *The Month of the Lost U-Boats*, William Kimber, 1977

Jones, Geoffrey, *Under Three Flags; the story of Nordmark & the armoured supply ships of the German Navy*, William Kimber, 1973

Kerr, Geo. F., *Business in Great Waters; The War History of the P & O 1939–45*, Faber, 1951

Kerr, J. Lennox, (Edited by) *Touching the Adventures of Merchantmen in the Second World War*, Harrap, 1953

Kerslake, S.A., *Coxswain in the Northern Convoys*, William Kimber, 1984

Konings, Chris, *Queen Elizabeth at War*, Patrick Stephens, 1985

Lucas, W.E., *Eagle Fleet*, Weidenfeld & Nicolson, 1955

Lund, Paul, & Ludlam, Henry, *Night of the U-Boats* (convoy SC7), Foulsham, 1973

Macintyre, Captain Donald, *The Battle of the Atlantic*, Batsford, 1961

McAughtry, Sam, *The Sinking of the Kenbane Head*, Blackstaff Press, 1977

McKee, Alexander, *The Coal-Scuttle Brigade*, Souvenir Press, 1957

Manderstam, Major L.H. (with Roy Heron), *From the Red Army to SOE*, William Kimber 1985

Masters, David, *In Peril on the Sea; War exploits of Allied Seamen*, Cresset Press, 1960

Middlebrook, Martin, *Convoy. The Battle of Convoys SC122 & HX229*, Allen Lane, 1976

Milner, Marc, *North Atlantic Run*, University of Toronto Press, 1985

Ministry of Information, *Merchantmen at War*, HMSO, 1944

Ministry of Information, *The Battle of the Atlantic*, HMSO, 1946

Muggenthaler, Karl August, *German Raiders of World War II*, Robert Hale, 1978

Murray, Marischal, *Union Castle Chronicle 1853–1953*, Longmans Green, 1953

Musk, George, *Canadian Pacific*, David & Charles, 1981

Pack, S.W.C., *The Allied Invasion of Sicily*, David & Charles, 1977

Pack, S.W.C., *The Battle for Crete*, Ian Allan, 1973

Pearce, Frank, *Last Call for HMS Edinburgh*, Collins, 1982

Poolman, Kenneth, *The Catafighters and Merchant Aircraft Carriers*, William Kimber, 1970

Poolman, Kenneth, *Escort Carrier 1941–45*, Ian Allan, 1972

Poolman Kenneth, *Focke-Wulf Condor, Scourge of the Atlantic*, Macdonald and Janes, 1978

Poolman, Kenneth, *The Giant Killers (Cam Ships)*, William Kimber, 1960

Porten, Edward P. Von der, *The German Navy in World War II*, Arthur Barker, 1970

Port Line, *Wartime Experiences 1939–1945*, Published by Port Line Ltd, 1947

Revely, Henry, *The Convoy that nearly died* (The Story of ONS 154), William Kimber, 1979

Robertson, Terrence, *The Golden Horseshoe*, (Otto Kretschmer), White Lion Publishers, 1975

Rohwer, Jürgen, *Axis Submarine Successes 1939–1945*, Patrick Stephens, 1983

Rohwer, Jürgen, *The Critical Convoy Battles of March 1943*, Ian Allan, 1977

Rohwer, J. & Hummelchen, G., *Chronology of the War at Sea 1939–1945* (2 Vols), Ian Allan, 1972

Roskill, Captain S.W., *A Merchant Fleet in War 1939–45*, (Alfred Holt & Co.), Collins, 1962

Roskill, Captain S.W., *The Secret Capture*, Collins, 1959

Roskill, Captain S.W., *The War at Sea*, (2 Vols), HMSO, 1959

Saunders, Hilary St George, *Valiant Voyaging: a short history of the British India Steam Navigation Company in the Second World War 1939–1945*, Faber, 1948

Schofield, B.B., & Martyn, L.F., *The Rescue Ships*, Blackwood, 1968

Schofield, B.B., *The Russian Convoys*, Batsford, 1964

Seth, Ronald, *The Fiercest Battle*, (The Story of Convoy ONS5), Hutchinson, 1961

Shankland, Peter, & Hunter, Anthony, *Malta Convoy*, Collins, 1961

Smith, Peter C., *Arctic Victory: The Story of Convoy PQ18*, William Kimber, 1975

Smith, Peter C., *Hold the Narrow Sea* (Naval Warfare in the English Channel 1939–45), Moorland Publishing, 1984

Smith, Peter C., *Pedestal. The Malta Convoy of August 1942*, William Kimber, 1970, (2nd Edition 1987)

Taylor, John P., (Editor) *The Prefabricated Port of Arromanches*, Shipbuilding and Shipping Record, February–May 1945

Taylor, Lt Cdr J.E., *The Last Passage*, Allen & Unwin, 1946

Thomas, David A., *Japan's War at Sea*, Andre Deutsch, 1978

Tute, Warren; Costello, John & Hughes, Terry, *D.Day*, Sidgwick & Jackson, 1974

Warner, Philip, *The D Day Landings*, William Kimber, 1980

Waters, S.O., *Ordeal by Sea. The New Zealand Shipping Company in the Second World War 1939–1945*, Published by N.Z. Shipping Co., 1949

West, Frank, *Lifeboat Number Seven (Britannia)*, William Kimber, 1960

Winton, John, *The Defence of Sea Trade. 1890–1990*, Michael Joseph, 1983

Index of Ships

A general index follows on page 337

General Index

A separate index of ships starts on page 323

Edwards, (capt, *Fort Longueuil*), 234
Egypt, 65, 107, 117, 118, 252, 271, 287
Eisenhower, Gen, 243, 265
El Alamain, 109
Elder Dempster Ltd, 58, 60, 90, 91, 102, 122, 144, 145, 162, 228, 235
Elders & Fyffes Ltd, 78, 79, 83, 88, 203
Eleuthera Island, 64
Ellerman Lines, 27, 56, 66, 68, 70, 76, 85, 102, 108, 110, 130, 132–134, 141, 168, 170, 174, 187, 203, 204, 214, 218, 233, 255, 259, 279, 287
Embleton, (capt, *Westbury*), 115
Emirau Island, 97
Emmenes, 41
Emmermann, Carl, 227
Empire Transport Co, 35
Endrass, Engelbert, 51, 126, 174, 175
English Coaling Co, 214
E.R. Management Co Ltd, 146, 219, 275, 280, 284, 287
Evan Thomas Radcliffe & Co, 202, 245, 266
Evans, (capt, *Aeneas*), 55
Evans, (capt, *British Vigilance*), 240
Evans, (capt, *Glenartney*), 136
Evans, (capt, *Harmonides*), 222
Evans, (capt, *King Lud*), 208
Evans, (capt, *Medon*), 220
Evans, (capt, *North Cornwall*), 40, 41
Evans, (capt, *Piako*), 140
Evans, (Lt Cdr, RNVR), 280
Evans & Reid Co Ltd, 275, 280
Ewan, (capt, *Automedon*), 94
Exley, (capt, *Edward Blyden*), 162

Falmouth, 23, 32, 49, 51, 53, 55
Fanhandu Island, 260
Faeroe Islands, 19, 29, 89, 275
Federal Steam Navigation Co, 29, 62, 104, 112, 147, 153, 170, 199, 204, 216
Fegen, Captain E.S.F, RN, 83–85, 87
Fernando Noronha, 221
Ferracuti, Carlo, 104
Fiddler, (capt, *Empire Russell*), 267
Fisher, (capt, *Avila Star*), 207
Fishguard & Rosslare Rly & Harbour Co, 262
Fitt, (capt, *Domala*), 38
Fitzgerald, Rear Adm, 99
Fitzmaurice, Cdre, 174
Fitzsimons, (capt, *Traveller*), 180
Florida, 199
Flowerdew, (capt, *Empire Ability*), 145
Flynn, (capt, *San Arcadio*), 181
Folkers, Ulrich, 222, 250
Forstner, Siegfried Frhr V, 182, 235, 241, 242
Fort de Ballata, 291
Fowey, 59, 251
Fox, (capt, *Orcades*), 227
France, 21, 22, 29, 46, 47, 51, 58, 72, 80, 95, 109, 119, 154, 160, 163, 228, 269, 272
Francis Harbour, 74, 77
Frauenheim, Fritz, 53
Freetown, 26, 30, 53, 58, 62, 91–94, 103, 105, 111, 114, 115, 124, 125, 139, 140–147,

151, 154, 156, 157, 161, 195, 209, 218, 220–222, 227, 228, 233, 236, 240, 244, 245, 279, 280, 283
Fremantle, 185, 187
French, (capt, *Viceroy of India*), 231
Friend, (capt, *Beacon Grange*), 129, 130
Fukumura, Toshiaki, 260, 262
Fuller, (capt, *Robert L. Holt*), 49
Funchal, 115
Furness Withy Co Ltd, 40, 162, 257

Galway, 111
Gardner, Ava, 284
Garfield, John, 284
Garlick, (capt, *Toronto City*), 151
Garstin, Vice Cdre SL125, 229
Garston, 79, 83
Gaulle, Gen de, 72
Gazzana-Priaroggia, Gianfrance, 249
Gelhaar, Alexander, 26
Gelhaus, Harald, 181, 244
General Steam Navigation Co, 43, 44, 163
George VI HM King, 137, 261, 272
Georgetown, 221
Germany, 19, 20, 21, 24, 25, 37, 56, 57, 80, 88, 95, 137, 148, 154, 168, 191, 273
Gibraltar, 20, 22, 27, 37, 52, 80, 95, 102, 110, 118, 119, 142, 152, 153, 156, 160, 162, 164, 168, 169, 174, 182, 203, 212, 215, 228, 231, 232, 239, 285, 288
Gibson, (capt, *Scottish Maiden*), 92
Gibson, George & Co, 40
Giles, (capt, *Clan Fraser*), 133
Gironde, River, 51, 154
Glasgow, 16, 66, 77, 80, 101, 122, 130, 138, 144, 147, 170, 209, 217, 230, 235
Glen & Co, 156
Glen Line, 73, 136, 194, 216, 217
Glover Bros, 104
Goble, (capt, *Navosota*), 31
Goffey, (capt, *Clytoneus*), 103
Gordon, (capt, *Wairangi*), 216
Goring, (capt, *City of Shanghai*), 141
Gough, (capt, *Clan Ogilvy*), 123
Gourock, 65, 230
Gowan Shipping Co, 78
Gow Harrison & Co Ltd, 164, 170, 220
Gowland Steamship Co, 139, 242
Graig Shipping Co Ltd, 225
Granwell, (capt, *Clan MacPhee*), 62
Greece, 109, 117, 131, 132
Greenall, (capt, *Matheran*), 78
Greenland, 19, 37, 84, 156, 158, 237
Greenock, 95, 114
Greger, Eberhard, 158
Gretschel, Günter, 250
Griffin, (capt, *Lady Hawkins*), 180
Griffiths, (capt, *King Gruffydd*), 246
Griffiths, (capt, *Willesden*), 192
Grosse, Harald, 25, 35
Guadeloupe, 241
Guggenberger, Friedrich, 158, 232
Gumprich, Günther, 191, 192
Gysae, Robert, 140